Rhetorics and Politics in Afghan Traditional Storytelling

Publications of the American Folklore Society
New Series

General Editor, Patrick Mullen

Volume 12 in the Persian Studies Series

General Editor, Ehsan Yarshater

This book has been awarded a grant in aid of
publication by the Persian Heritage Foundation.

Rhetorics and Politics in Afghan Traditional Storytelling

Margaret A. Mills

υρρ

University of Pennsylvania Press

Philadelphia

Library of Congress Cataloging-in-Publication Data

Mills, Margaret Ann.
  Rhetorics and politics in Afghan traditional storytelling / Margaret A. Mills.
      p.   cm. — (Publications of the American Folklore Society. New series)
  ISBN 0-8122-8199-3
  1. Tales—Afghanistan—Herāt (Province) 2. Storytelling—Afghanistan. 3. Folklore—
Political aspects—Afghanistan. I. Title. II. Series: Publications of the American Folklore
Society. New series (Unnumbered)
GR302.7.H47M54   1991
398'.09581—dc20   90-22019
                                                                                        CIP

IN MEMORIAM
to the many martyrs to Afghanistan's future
and especially

'Abdul Ahad
Gholām Nabī "Bīnawā"
Sayd Bahauddine Majrooh

Chūnk vā gashtam zi paykār-i-bīrūn,
rūī āvardam bih paykār-i darūn.
Qad raja'nā min jihād al-asghar-īm
bā nabī andar jihād-i akbar-īm.

When I turned back from the outer battle,
    I set my face toward the inner battle.
We have returned from the lesser Jihad,
    we are with the Prophet in the greater Jihad.

—Jalāl ud-Dīn Rūmī, *Mathnavī-e Ma'anavī* I:1386–87

Contents

Preface

THIS STUDY has been more than eight years in the making, retarded by the difficulties of finding advisors familiar with Herati Persian and continuing my study of that language, after my involuntary separation from the community that inspired my work. In 1980, when this project was conceived, and the full import of the Soviet invasion of Afghanistan was making itself clear, it became extremely painful just to listen to the tapes from which the voices of friends and teachers, their whereabouts and condition now unknown to me, issued forth in humor, safety, wisdom, and calm. I do not now know the whereabouts of the Ākhond and Khalīfah Karīm, the two master storytellers whose words are presented here. Both were elders in 1975. The area of Herat province where they lived was an early center of local resistance to the Marxist government. I now thank them, wherever they may be, for the artistry and humor they brought to a performance event which was probably a nuisance to themselves but of fundamental— ultimately transformative—educative, and aesthetic value to me.

This study focuses on one series of stories, performed in sequence over an evening and part of the next morning in January of 1975, by two storytellers, friends of one another. They brought to the performance different educational and professional backgrounds, personal histories, and relationships to the sponsor of the event, who was the central government official responsible for administration of the district in which they had grown up and raised their families and then resided. The traces of these different backgrounds and relationships, as well as the play of words, themes, and ideas detectable in the storytellers' choice and sequential arrangement of the stories, are explored in my commentary on their stories. Their performance was a product of their traditionally acquired verbal artistry and expectations for storytelling. It was also conditioned by the anomalous presence of a stranger, an unveiled foreign woman, with a modest array of recording and photographic equipment. Their traditional rhetorical resources and strategies were also drawn upon to handle a relatively new ideological juxtaposition: that between the two performers, both devout Muslims, and their host, a Marxist and avowed atheist.

An understanding of the complexities of this series of narrations has come to me slowly in a process of translation, interpretation, reinterpretation, and retranslation, which could not have gone forward without the patient help and encouragement of a number of other people. During the two years of my research in Afghanistan, and by some correspondence thereafter, the folklorist Dr. Hafizullah Baghban, his brother, Aminollah Azhar, who acted as my research associate during many recording visits in and around Herat (though not in this early visit), and their parents and other relatives gave me the most generous and patient guidance and help. Mohammad Mokhtār Moslem, who accompanied me in the first days of my research, including the visit here discussed, and introduced me to his friend, the Woləswāl Abdul Matīn, also has my thanks, as does Matīn himself for his hospitality. The transcription and interpretation of these stories, which I completed in the United States, was made possible by the unstinting generosity of time and linguistic and local knowledge offered by M. Kazim Alami, formerly of Herat, now a refugee in California. Other friends and teachers who by conversations and correspondence have since contributed to this work in general and specific ways include Roger Abrahams, Sekandar Amanollahi, Jon Anderson, Whitney Azoy, John Baily, Charles Briggs, Pack Carnes, Hamid Dabashi, Veronica Doubleday, Dr. Ravan Farhadi, Elizabeth Fernea, Michael M. J. Fischer, Hamid and Hanifah Ghazanfar and their family, Dr. Ahmed Jawaid, Martin Kumorek, Nasratullah Laheeb, the late Dr. Syed Bahauddine Majrooh, Michael Meeker, Patrick Mullen, Annemarie Schimmel, Nazif Shahrani, Brian Street, Wheeler Thackston, and Sabra Webber. Special thanks are due to Virginia Hymes, who spent hours in close communion with a tape recorder spewing forth the sounds of a—to her—totally unfamiliar language, in order to work through with me the protocols for ethnopoetic arrangement of narratives used in this study. I am also especially grateful for Roxanne Haag-Higuchi's generosity in providing photocopies from an unpublished manuscript relevant to chapter 6. All these friends and colleagues have my gratitude for their many insights, advice, and aid. The final forms of translations and interpretations offered here, together with their remaining misconstructions and misunderstandings, are my own responsibility.

Virginia and Dell Hymes are prominent among the many colleagues and students who have made the University of Pennsylvania a supportive environment for this work. To name a few is to slight others, but special mention must also be made of Roger Abrahams, Dan Ben-Amos, Kenneth Goldstein, Teresa Pyott, and John Roberts, and the members of the Mellon Seminar on the Diversity of Language and the Structures of Power, especially Linda Brodkey, Joanne Mulcahy, Phyllis Rackin, and Carroll Smith-Rosenberg. Kate Wilson helped with forays into the tale type and motif indices and the organization of the glossary. Others whose ideas, in published form, were important to me are mentioned in the bibliography.

Financial support over the years has contributed to my continuing education and to this project in particular. The original recording was supported by the United States Fulbright Foundation, Harvard University's Sheldon Traveling Fellowships, and the NSF Program for the Improvement of Social Science Research. Subsequent translation and analysis were supported by a translation grant from the National Endowment for the Humanities and research grants from Pomona College and the University of Pennsylvania Research Foundation. The Persian Heritage Foundation and the University of Pennsylvania School of Arts and Sciences (Dean Hugo Sonnenschein) have my gratitude for help with publication costs. The copyeditor, David Prout, was patient and painstaking throughout. The University of Pennsylvania Press staff, especially Patricia Smith and Alison Anderson, were unfailingly gracious and meticulous in guiding this book through to publication.

A Note on Transliteration

THE TRANSLITERATION SYSTEM used here corresponds in consonant values to the Persian transliteration system of the *International Journal of Middle Eastern Studies* (IJMES). Vowel values differ somewhat between literary Persian, for which the IJMES system is here employed, and spoken Herati, of which certain phrases appear in the notes to the translations. In particular, *o* (as in English "mote") and short *u* (as in English "foot") are nonphonemic differences in Persian, and I have transcribed the sound as *o*, which seems to me to correspond to the more frequent Herati formation of that vowel. Likewise short *i* (as in English "pin") and *e* (as in English "pen") are not phonemically distinct and have been transcribed as *e*. The schwa or neutral vowel (ə) occurs only in Pashto, not in Persian, and thus in the Pashto title, *woləswāl*, "subgovernor."

Place names for which there are already established English spellings are spelled accordingly, without diacritics. Personal names of published authors or others whose preferred spellings in English are known to me are also spelled without diacritics, according to the individual's preference.

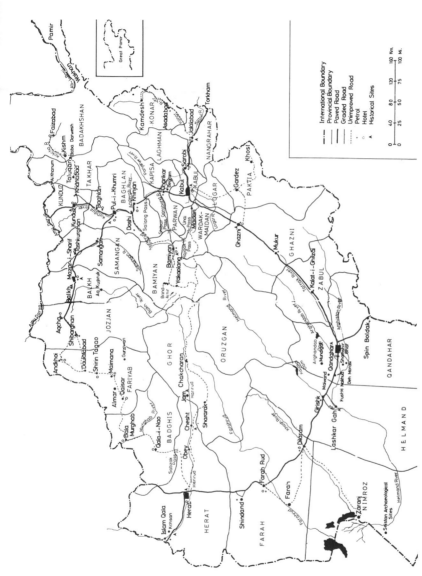

1. Afghanistan (adapted from Nancy Hatch Dupree, *An Historical Guide to Afghanistan*, Afghan Tourist Organization, 1970).

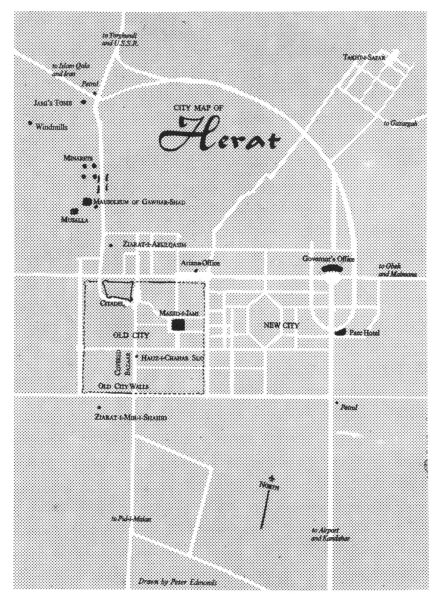

2. Herat City (from Nancy Hatch Wolfe, *Herat: A Pictorial Guide*, Afghan Tourist Organization, 1966).

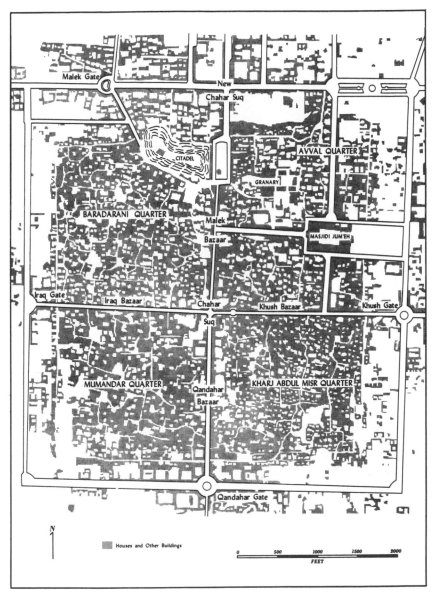

3. The Old City, Herat (from Paul English, "The Traditional City of Herat, Afghanistan," in L. Carl Brown, ed., *From Medina to Metropolis: Heritage and Change in the Near Eastern City*, Princeton, N.J.: Darwin Press, 1973).

1. Where We Were

İn sukhan shīr ast dar pistān-i jān
  Bī kashandah khūsh namigardad ravān.
This discourse is milk in the teat of the soul
  It will not flow well without someone to suck.

—Jalāl ud-Dīn Rūmī, *Mathnavī* I:2378

THIS IS A STORY ABOUT SOME STORIES, my own dialogue with some conversations. The two storytellers who traded the stories here discussed constructed a dialogue with each other through those stories as well as a more general conversation within which the stories were told. They constructed, in addition, an implicit dialogue through the stories with their audience, who were largely silent partners in these narrative performances but whose known and presumed understandings, beliefs, and values are factors in any able storyteller's choices in performance. As a member of that audience, and with my visit as the immediate reason for the performance, I here assume the interpretive responsibilities of audience membership, but with some reservations. Edward Bruner (1984:4) reminds us, "The meanings of a story are the constructions placed on it in a particular telling by socially positioned persons at given historical moments." My position at the time and in the social milieu of the performance was anomalous and quite uninformed, and the construction I have here placed on the event has been concluded at a very different moment in my own life and the life of that Afghan community than that in which the story performance unfolded. In analyzing such stories, one must strike a balance between general rhetorical processes and individual strategic moves, for while "it is individuals, not social institutions, who make and act on cultural meanings" (K. Basso 1984:49), yet "For the analyst to appreciate the constructedness of the 'individual' requires attention to the ideological devices operating in the cultural order" (Chock 1986:200). The storytellers constructed their narrative dialogue quickly and deftly in the flow of conversation and performance.

My dialogue with their words has been constructed with open-ended leisure to ponder and review their recorded voices; their word choices; the
nuances of their intonation, pauses, and laughter as well as the patterns of
events and other representations within and among their stories. In the
silence of distance, it would be fair to read all my remarks on their words
as interrogatives, "Did you mean this? Did you mean that?"—questions
now beyond the reach of answers.

Yet the absent and distant also figured crucially in the event itself: "For
all the physical presence of any given speaker, the meaning[s] of her words
are as much dependent on other words (unspoken, absent) as the words of
any text" (Krupat 1987:115). My interpretive responsibility extends to the
words I have substituted for their own in translation, through which their
artistry is mediated to a new, English-speaking audience. In the words of
Alton Becker (1984:135), "All language use is . . . translation to some degree, and translation from one language to another is only the extreme
case." The extremities involved will be described in more detail in the next
chapter, in a discussion of the principles of translation and formats for presentation here employed. In any case, my story about these stories remains
just one of many possible, privileged to reach a new audience which cannot
go to my interlocutors for their independent opinions, but that reading
audience in turn has the responsibility and opportunity of interpretation,
extrapolation, and evaluation.

My story is this: In the autumn of 1974, I arrived in Afghanistan to
undertake dissertation research on traditional oral narrative performance,
with an eye to its relation to literary tradition. I had studied literary Persian
in the United States after acquisition of some conversational Persian in
Tehran years earlier. I chose the city of Herat, in the northwest of the country, as my center of operations because of its lengthy and important history
as a center of traditional Persian-language arts and learning[1] and its com-

---

1. "The city, located at 34° 22′ N., 62° 9′ E., is mentioned in the Old Persian inscriptions
([as] Haraiva), in the Avesta, and in Greek as Aria or Areia. Alexander the Great built a city
here called Alexandria in Aria." (Frye 1954:177). The city, situated in the fertile and well-
watered Hari Rud (river) valley, supported a large agricultural population and was an important trading center on the overland route from the West to India and China according to the
earliest historical records. The surviving square plan of the old walled city (see map no. 3)
dates from the Hellenistic period. The city came under Arab Muslim domination together
with the rest of the Khorassan region in about 652 C.E. (A.H. 30), and at various times served
as capital city to different Islamic dynasties, notably the Ghurids in the sixth century A.H.
(twelfth century C.E.), who constructed the oldest surviving parts of the Great Mosque, and
the Kurts of the seventh century (thirteenth century C.E.), also great builders and patrons of
the arts. It was devastated by the Mongols in 618/1221, and again in 619/1222, remaining in

parative lack of mass-media exposure. One government newspaper was produced in Herat itself with a nominal circulation of 1,150 (Government of Afghanistan 1972:125); only a few copies of Kabul dailies made their way there. In 1978, the Marxist regime estimated the literacy rate at 5 percent for males, 1 percent for females nationwide (*Kabul Times* July 18, 1978). The World Bank estimated a somewhat higher overall rate of 8 to 10 percent of adults "able to read and write" (*Wall Steet Journal* Jan. 16, 1979). There was no television in Afghanistan at the time of my visit. While there was radio, and cassette recordings of music and sermons circulated both commercially and informally, there was no rural electrification, and electricity in the residential neighborhoods of Herat City was available only from dusk to the late evening hours. A set of four batteries for a portable radio-cassette player cost the equivalent of a day's wages for an ordinary laborer in Herat's small cash economy. Radio-cassette machines were a popular possession, especially for young men who had been guest workers in Iran and saved their wages to buy one, but many homes had none. Thus, radio programs and cassette recordings were listened to sporadically, some individuals having relatively free access to them, many others little or none. There was one movie house in Herat City, and two operating theaters mounted live performances of plays and music in a vaudeville-like format, attended by a limited, almost exclusively male, clientele.

Arriving in Kabul, the capital city, in September, I spent several weeks negotiating final clearance to base my research in Herat, and during that time I took intensive instruction in the Kabul dialect of Persian, but on

---

ruins until about 634/1236. The Kurt dynasty was founded in 642/1244 by a local prince appointed to rule by the Mongol governor of Khorassan. Timur (Tamerlane) captured the city in 782/1380, ending the Kurt dynasty but ushering in the period of Herat's greatest cultural flowering, that of his descendants, the Timurids of the eighth to tenth centuries A.H. (fourteenth to sixteenth centuries C.E.) whose massive achievements in arts, letters, and architecture still survive in monuments and documents. Major destruction of Timurid buildings occurred during the joint British-Afghan defense of the city against a threatened invasion by an Iranian force in the mid-nineteenth century, and again in the last ten years, in the Afghan-Soviet war. Frye's article in the *Encyclopedia of Islam* supplies references indicating the extensive historical documentation of Herat, by both Muslim and western scholars, and more details of its history. English (1973) has an informative general essay on the city's history and organization with an interpretation of its political conditions at the time. In 1972, the population of Herat was variously estimated: the province at 706,100, and the city itself 73,700 (Government of Afghanistan 1972:3, 4) or of the Herat urban area, 110,000 (Kerr 1977:67). The city, equipped with an airport with daily flights to the capital, paving on major city streets, some electrification, and a piped water supply, was the center of provincial administration and trade, and a major stop on the overland route from Iran to India, the first city on the Afghan side of the border, with a steady flow of young overland travelers from the West in the 1960s and 1970s.

arrival in Herat in mid-December, I found myself in a very alien dialect environment. Accent, morphology, and lexicon differed significantly from the Persian of either Kabul or Tehran with which I was acquainted. Accompanied at the prudent behest of the Ministry of Culture by Mohammad Mokhtār Moslem, a native of Herat City then on winter vacation from his job as English-language supervisor and teacher at a boys' high school in Kabul, I made the rounds of the governor's office and other officials who needed to be informed of my arrival and approve my plans. Much bemused by my language problem, I then set about investigating what sorts of narrative performers and performances were to be found in Herat and its surrounding villages. The governor's office referred us to two provincial subgovernors, representatives of the central government who served under the governor as peacekeepers and civil administrators of provincial districts adjacent to the city. They in turn introduced us to village headmen present in their offices on business, several of whom invited us to visit them and record men who were known for their storytelling ability in their respective villages.

With Mokhtār's help I also met a third subgovernor (*woləswāl*), a friend he had known in college, who was stationed in a more remote district, Pashtūn Zarghūn (or Posht-e Zirghān, in the older, Persian form of the name) three to four hours from the city by public transportation (trucks serving as both freight haulers and buses). The Woləswāl's wife had found the district center too isolated and had returned with their children to their native Jalalabad, in the Pashto-speaking southeast of the country, to live with family and wait out his three-year posting in hopes that the next one would be less lonely. Mokhtār contacted his friend by telephone, and we were invited with a promise of introductions to storytellers.

Thus, in the second week of my eighteen months of research in and around Herat, feeling very tongue-tied and understanding perhaps 20 percent of the speech around me, I found my way to the village of Gīm, district center for Pashtūn Zarghūn. Mokhtār expressed the hope that our visit would divert the Woləswāl, who was lonely in the absence of his family. He also explained, as we traveled, that Matīn was a Parchamī Marxist and generally a very forward-looking man. I learned later that the prime minister, Mohammed Daud, having had the backing of the Parchamī and Khalqī Marxist factions, together with others, in the bloodless coup of 1973 in which he had deposed and exiled his cousin, the king Zaher Shah, had soon become uneasy about their further consolidation into effective political parties. By 1974, he had undertaken a policy designed to reduce the influence of the Marxist factions by removing young, activist Marxists from Kabul, giving them provincial government postings at a distance from the capital and its political activities and away from their home areas where they might have or develop more traditional personal power bases (cf. Dupree 1984:59; Keiser 1984:124–25; Fischer 1984:177). In the latter strategy of posting bureaucrats away from their home areas and rotating their postings every two or three years, Daud continued an older practice designed to prevent the development of special relationships between central government officials and local factions, originally intended to keep the loyalties of the representatives of the central government firmly focused on the center. All this information about current politics came to me after this visit in conversations in Kabul and elsewhere, however. At the time of our visit, I hoped to hear what a dedicated modernist thought of rural life and what his goals were for the governance of his district.

Gīm proved to be an agricultural village along the one-lane dirt road which was a main arterial through the district, with one tea house and a few small shops selling cigarettes, matches, batteries, and a mixture of other supplies and dry goods not produced in the community, as well as a small array of seasonal produce. Village lands in the area were watered by irrigation canals drawing from the Hari Rud and its tributaries. The major difference between Gīm and other roadside villages was the presence of the district office, a building of cement-plastered mud brick and glazed windows, with the Woləswāl's office and office space for his half-dozen aides and clerks, plus some buildings housing the small contingent of militia attached to the district for policing purposes.

We left some of my luggage, a backpack, and a sleeping bag, which seemed to cause Mokhtār some (to me) unaccountable embarrassment, at the tea house, and made our way to the Woləswāl's office, where he was at work. (I learned about a week later, from joking conversations with another of our hosts, that the backpack connected me with the hashish-smoking overland travelers who had become a common sight in Herat. As a semi-official visitor, I was expected to stay not in tea houses but as a guest in people's homes, which made my sleeping bag superfluous if not insulting.) The Woləswāl, though busy receiving local people with administrative business, greeted us cordially and led us from the office to his home, passing in the outer office, but not introducing, two elderly, traditionally dressed men who later proved to be the storytellers he had lined up for the evening. We were lodged in a guest room in his house, a conventional

Afghan home with rooms opening onto a small open courtyard surrounded by mud walls seven or eight feet high.

We ate with our host in one room, then were ushered into another,
about ten by twelve feet, with a standard type of wood-fired heating stove
of galvanized steel, shaped like an upended oil drum, in the corner near the
door. We found several adult and adolescent males together with the two
elderly storytellers already seated in the room, on the sort of cotton-stuffed
mattresses and flat-weave carpets which are common furnishings in Afghan
homes. We were seated in the area for the most important guests, at the
end of the room opposite the door. The Woləswāl and Mokhtār sat against
the wall, still dressed in western-style straight-cut pants, less comfortable
for floor-sitting than the traditional long shirts and loose trousers worn
by the rest of the audience. I, likewise wearing western dress (navy wool
trousers and a sweater), glasses, and a scarf covering my hair, moved forward slightly so as to position my tape recorder's microphone closer to the
storytellers, seated side by side about halfway along the right-hand wall
perpendicular to us. I had lost the use of my primary tape recorder the day
before, in the first of what proved to be a series of breakdowns, and was
using as backup a small cassette recorder with rather poor tape and sound
gauge visibility. The room was lighted by one kerosene lantern, so I
wanted to be near the machine and the microphone in order to monitor
the sound level and adjust the microphone position when necessary. The
result was that I was sitting somewhat in front of Mokhtār and, awk-
wardly, entirely in front of our host, with my back mostly to him. My field
of vision was divided between the storytellers, seated about four feet from
me (in a medial position as far as the prestige expressed in seating arrangements is concerned), and the tape recorder, whose recording capacities in
such a room I did not know. This awkwardness over placement of the machine and myself, and my anxious attention to a machine whose capacities
I was unsure of, added to the awkwardness of my inarticulateness and
spotty comprehension of Herati Persian. Though I was trying to speak
only Persian in this setting, however clumsily, Mokhtār and I would also
occasionally resort to English in speaking to one another, when I could not
express an idea in Persian or we wished to give each other directions discreetly. No one else present spoke or understood English, to my knowledge.

I detail all these awkward qualities of the evening because they are
germane to the way the storytelling session unfolded. Everyone in the
room (adolescent and adult males of various ages, numbering around ten

or twelve as a few people came and went during the evening) was soon aware of my inarticulateness in Persian, though they were probably less aware that I could understand somewhat more than I could express, the usual case for language learners. Mokhtār had the task of carrying the conversation with the storytellers forward, running through, in what we planned would be a conversational tone, a rough list of questions which would cover basic biographical information I wanted to assemble for each storyteller. The full awkwardness of this interview-style exchange is translated and discussed in chapter 3 (cf. Briggs 1986 passim; Stoller 1986:51–53). Besides setting a rather stiff and peculiar conversational tone between us and the storytellers, it also established Mokhtār as the main interlocutor, with the result that both storytellers addressed most of their words, gestures, and eye contact to him. The Woləswāl stayed in the background, essentially silent during all the narrative performances. During the stories, Mokhtār responded to the storytellers' words with murmurs of comprehension and occasional questions or comments, which are translated as they occurred, and he engaged in more extended conversational exchanges between the stories. Others in the room also murmured, laughed, and occasionally commented and questioned, and I have translated their remarks to the extent that the small microphone was able to capture them.

It was evident to me that my foreign presence added interest to the night's event for this audience of rural, traditional Afghan men, who had no opportunity for close scrutiny of any woman other than their own family members. But the many awkwardnesses of recording and our attempt at interviewing interrupted the natural flow of conversation and may have inhibited more active conversational participation by others in the room.

The rowdy, sexually explicit humor which appeared with Karīm's second story and carried over into more than half of the rest of the stories was one aspect of the performance which surprised and even shocked Mokhtār as well as other native Persian-speakers who later audited the tapes and commented on them for me. After Karīm had completed that story and I was scribbling a few notes, Mokhtār warned me (in English) to mark the tape in some way so that it could be set aside and omitted from any inspection the Ministry of Culture might require of my recordings. Later auditors expressed surprise at so much sexual frankness in the presence of a woman and/or a government official like the Woləswāl, whose presence they felt should have had a formalizing effect on the proceedings (cf. Başgöz 1975). By the testimony of Mokhtār and culturally informed auditors of the tapes, something odd was going on in this performance. The strange mix of conversational stiffness and rowdy sexual humor in this series of performances, which did come to seem anomalous to me in light of my later recording experiences, brought my puzzled attention back to several of the stories and ultimately figured in my interpretation of the social tenor of the whole event.

One of my overall goals in recording was to develop sufficient rapport with storytellers and others present at such gatherings that it would be possible to leave the tape recorder running continuously, capturing the flow of conversation in which stories were embedded as well as the stories themselves, on the assumption that information about mnemonic associations and audience interpretation of stories would emerge from such conversations. My recording sessions in male groups rarely reached a level of informality where such recording was possible. In domestic settings with family audiences, women and children along with one or more adult men, informality eventually did prevail to a great extent, but it was only after some weeks of work and friendly visiting that I could regularly record myself in extended conversation with one such family who became some of my principal informants, of whom the main storyteller was a woman who became my best friend in Afghanistan. It was her narrative art that ultimately formed the subject of my dissertation (Mills 1978 [1990]), not just because of her energy and creativity as a storyteller, but also because of the richness of the information which her conversations conveyed and my trust in the freedom of our exchanges as our friendship grew.

But for the time I spent at the Woləswāl's, no such spontaneity was possible. In these early visits in general, there was no possibility of continuous recording, because of the expectations of the Afghan participants that I was after stories, and that stories, with clearly marked beginnings and endings, were performances and therefore appropriate for recording like songs or other music might be, but that conversation, rambling and not intensely, consciously artful (even if not particularly consequential or confidential), did not belong on tape. There was, in any case, little possibility of normal conversation in these male groups, given my anomalous presence—female and foreign.

But in the case of the Woləswāl's invitation, there was yet another kind of distance, which I only learned of from Mokhtār as we made our way back to Herat. We were discussing how the visit had gone, and I expressed my feelings of extreme unease over what I perceived to be the Woləswāl's lack of respect for the storytellers and his religiously disrespectful behavior during a visit to a small local shrine we had made together the day after the storytelling (see chapter 16). I was glad to have recorded a number of stories, some of them long and complex, but was not in much of a position to know what they were like, given my language problems. Despite my communicative limits, though, I had taken away a distinct feeling of unease which made me reluctant to seek out the Woləswāl or the two storytellers we had met for follow-up contacts, which I assumed would be the real body of my research.

Mokhtār explained that the unease I felt had some more specific causes besides my own limitations, that the Woləswāl knew himself to be much disliked in the district. He said he was not accepted because he refused to take bribes in an effort to convince his charges of the moral superiority of Marxist ideology and the possibilities for secularly based government reform (cf. Keiser 1984:125). Furthermore, according to Mokhtār's report, he had tried to bring some of the more influential members of the community into compliance with national law over such matters as property taxes and had, a few months earlier, locked up the Ākhond, the more senior and articulate of the two storytellers, for a few days over nonpayment of some governmental levy. The Ākhond, as his title indicates, was a mulla (Islamic clergyman) and a teacher in his village's religious school, and thus had fundamental ideological differences with the Marxist Woləswāl.

All this painted a rather problematical picture both of our visit with the Woləswāl and the elderly Ākhond and of the political effectiveness of idealistic Marxists in rural Afghanistan in the middle 1970s. I was already uncomfortable with my manifest ties to the central government, necessary in these early days of fieldwork but to be shed, I hoped, as soon as they could be replaced with more personal and informal sorts of contacts through a more diversified social network which I hoped to develop. Nongovernmental Afghans I met before arriving in Herat advised that people would be inhibited by any obvious government presence. The relations between the central government and local populations, whether elite or ordinary citizens, have been described as traditionally distant (Shahrani 1984:39; 1986 passim). I was interested in traditional pedagogy and the values and expressive patterns promulgated through it. I did not think that sponsorship by someone visibly inimical to traditional views, like the Woləswāl, would be helpful in that regard. Despite my correlate interest in social change and thus in his modernist views and how they were played out in his daily work, I wanted to keep my distance from him and other aggressively modernizing officials.

Government officials, for their part, were initially protective of me, understandably dubious about how I would get on (and perhaps what mischief I might get into) as an unaccompanied female in a society in which women did not go about without male supervision and protection. In Herat City all adult women wore the full *chāderī* veil on the street if they went out at all and, by my count, there were only about half a dozen women my age, exclusive of girls' school teachers, working outside the home. (The three I knew were all daughters of a modernizing elite family and worked as clerks in one of the banks.) With the help of prior personal contacts, the few other foreigners already resident in Herat and some generous souls I met during my early official contacts, I did develop an informal network and was able to visit acquaintances freely in the city of Herat, but my visits to outlying areas were always accompanied by male friends, members or friends of those families I visited.

Under those circumstances, unwilling to accept the Woləswāl's sponsorship, and afraid that if I proceeded without it while in his district I would give trouble to those I tried to contact, including the Ākhond and Karīm, I never returned to Pashtūn Zarghūn or recontacted those two men. Close study of their joint performance occurred to me as a special project after the Marxist coup of 1978 and the beginning of the resultant civil war, which threw into high relief the hostility of provincial communities to the new ideology and new leadership at the center, superimposed on the older center-periphery tensions.

It seemed clear from my experience and the observations of others (Shahrani and Canfield 1984 passim) that the tinder for that violent popular rejection of Marxist leadership had been laid during the period that Daud had exiled people such as the Woləswāl to the provinces, and that it was readily volatilized because of the historical hostility to the Soviets dating from the Czarist Russian expansion into Central Asia in the nineteenth century. All across northern Afghanistan were villages and communities with living members who were refugees from Russian expansion (cf. Shalinsky 1979a, b; 1983; Shahrani 1979, 1984:50). Afghan Muslim hostility to Christian Czarist expansion had been replaced by an even more pointed ideological hostility to the Soviets for their avowed atheism as well as their expansionist activities.

The Marxist regime which came to power in April 1978 governed by decree in the first years while it was preparing a new constitution. Several of the early decrees created considerable turmoil and dissatisfaction outside the capital, as well as in it among non-Marxists. Early attempts at land reform and redistribution were hampered by undercapitalization and ideological uncertainties. One decree attempted to dismantle the traditional credit system, founded on *gerau*, a form of non-interest-bearing lending whereby one individual signs over use of some real property to another for a period of seven years in return for a certain amount of cash. At the end of seven years, if the money is returned, the property reverts to the original owner; if not, it becomes the property of the money-lender. Under this system small farmers could easily lose their land to larger and better capitalized landowners when they put land in *gerau* to a lender during periodic droughts in order to meet living expenses. But it was not just economically marginal families that participated in *gerau* contracts, for they were the main form of secured borrowing in the country. The Marxists attempted to cancel by decree existing, unrepayable *gerau* contracts undertaken by small landowners (Decree No. 6; *Kabul Times* July 17, 1978), but had no adequate system of rural credit to replace them. That, coupled with Muslim views on the sanctity of private property, made the decree unpopular even with many of its intended beneficiaries.

Probably the most inflammatory decree, however, Decree No. 7 (published in part in the *Kabul Times*, October 18, 1978), was aimed at family law reform. Prior to 1978, the money paid by a prospective groom's family to that of his intended bride could be substantial, $1,000 to $2,000 and up in a society with a per capita annual income of under $200 ($78 in 1969, according to the Government of Afghanistan 1972:169; probably a low estimate in a report aimed at aid providers), and his family would incur other expenses in the wedding itself. The Marxists, in what they perceived to be the interests of the younger generation, among other attempted reforms abolished marriage payments beyond a token sum of about $7 and tried to impose a minimum age for engagement in order to limit parents' ability to choose their children's spouses. I heard the repercussions of the decree just days after its promulgation, on a brief visit back to Herat in November of 1978. My young women friends, whom I had first met at their bank workplace, were very hopeful for the new regime, whom they called *roshanfekrān*, "enlightened ones." But other male friends, who worked at the UN-sponsored livestock and meat-processing project, reported with disgust how one young male coworker, hearing of the decree, had said to three unmarried female clerks, "This is great—I've got enough money, I could have you today, and you tomorrow, and you the day after," highlighting the traditional understanding of high marital payments as a deterrent to unsuitable or lightly undertaken marriages. Even among the miniscule young professional class of Herat, the implications of the marriage decree were not all attractive. Yet as the storytelling here described reveals, the regulation of sexuality is also part of traditional visions of social order and good governance.

The Kabul-based Marxist coalition government, composed mainly of members of an urban, secularly educated elite, remained ignorant and contemptuous of more traditional worldviews in and out of the capital and were naively optimistic about the radical potential of the rural poor (cf. Ghani 1988 and Fischer 1984 on the historical and geographical distribution of such modern urban elite misconceptions, certainly not peculiar to Marxists, in the Persian-speaking world). Marxist ideologues early in the period of conflict wrote and spoke as if the good intentions and effects of their legislation would be transparently obvious to uneducated, poor rural Afghans. They seemed to expect that Marxism would fill an ideological void, overwhelming what they took to be a mechanical, stagnant, and simplistic allegiance to Islam (*Kabul New Times*, passim). In retrospect, one quality of the traditionally educated worldviews which seemed to emerge from the storytelling of the Ākhond and Karīm as well as many others, educated and uneducated, who later recorded stories for me, was the intricacy and coherence with which values relating to religion, governance, personal ethics, and sexuality were intertwined. Traditional thinking was not intellectually weak, but powerfully integrated, nor were traditional people unreflective, though analytic and evaluative statements were often enmeshed in the, to western-educated ears, anecdotal fabric of narrative, personal or fictional.

Ideologically predisposed to no great respect for the persons or views of the two traditionally educated, devoutly Muslim storytellers he had brought to us, the Woləswāl could listen to their slightly unseemly performance from an insulated position, perhaps chalking up their more outrageous statements to ignorant country manners. Even if he was familiar enough with traditional storytelling to detect rhetorical strategy in their choice of material and expressions, which may not have been the case given his modern-style urban education, a traditional dynamic of socially situated performances would also militate against his interference with the trend of their narrating. For him to try to interfere with their expressive choices would have undercut any strategy of his to treat them as socially insignificant, as mere entertainers, and might have implied that he had seen some uncomfortable reflection of himself in their narratives.

Paid performers—musicians, dancers, and actors—were of very low status and manipulated that low status to convey critical and satirical messages to and about their audiences (Baghban 1977, 1:144). Though neither of these two elderly men were professional performers (the Ākhond at least certainly had ample independent means and a respected position as a local teacher), they had been summoned to entertain strangers, the Woləswāl's guests. Reputed excellence as raconteurs, which both men had, was not necessarily an enhancement to prestige in their own community, where storytelling as a pastime was relegated to periods of agricultural inactivity, preferably dark evenings in winter when little work of a productive nature could be done, and amateur excellence in other performative modes, such as music, was only very circumspectly displayed (Sakata 1983).

In other Middle Eastern entertainment traditions, like that of the professional actors described by Baghban (1977), the comparatively low and somewhat ambiguous status of the professional performer vis-à-vis the patron enables the artist to veil insults and criticism within his discourse (cf. Slyomovics 1988 on Egyptian Bani Hilal epic performance). Raconteurship may have provided the Ākhond and Karīm with some similar cover for veiled criticism of the Woləswāl and his taste in guests. But there is another aspect of traditional Afghan narrative discourse which also provides for an integration of the ludic, including the obscene, with the deeply serious, and that is the highly metaphorized and highly narrative-dependent dimension of mystical language. Both the Ākhond and Karīm, in conversation and narrative, revealed a familiarity and respect for certain aspects of Sufi thought and discourse, which works its transformative power on everyday experience by a complex and often funny process of ironization and inversion. Thus, apparent uncouthness of language or subjects becomes a test of the listener's ability to recognize a higher decorum. The inappropriateness of the storytellers' speech may have been not country manners but risky business, ideological and political challenge.

The unintentional inappropriateness of our own conversational strategies, the stiffness of the interview, the hesitancies, the times when Mokhtār momentarily lost his place in the question list, the distractions of tape recorder manipulation in the midst of conversations and stories, all belied our lack of control despite the directive quality of our questioning and may have encouraged the storytellers (especially the Ākhond, as it appears in his interview in chapter 5), to play with us and turn us into foils for humor. My own inarticulateness and marginality to the conversations as they unfolded were paradoxically appropriate to my sex, from a traditional male viewpoint, despite my highly anomalous presence, appearance, and behavior otherwise. My incomprehension enabled the storytellers to speak over my head about "country matters" to Mokhtār and through him, by implication, to our silent host. My language problems prevented me not only from taking offense, had I been so inclined, but also from verbally asserting a presence which might have distracted the storytellers from the oblique representation of preexisting relationships which so enriched this storytelling session. If I could have distanced myself from the peremptory, systematically antitraditionalist Woləswāl, I would have tried to do so and thus perhaps not have heard the rich but focused discourse addressed to him through Mokhtār and me as his guests. Even as the session unfolded, my dialect comprehension increased and I began to respond a little more articulately. One aspect of my presence to which the Ākhond and Karīm began to respond systematically was my desire to note down titles and subject matter for the stories. As they observed me doing this, they began to encourage, even direct me to do so, seconding the clear implication that their words were worthy of written representation. Eventually, the Ākhond tendered a polite request to the Woləswāl that I be allowed to visit his home and meet his family, an invitation that was brushed aside by the Woləswāl and Mokhtār.

For the Ākhond and Karīm, the storytelling session I recorded was an anomalous opportunity to display gifts of articulateness honed in more traditional settings. My presence became an opening for certain kinds of risks and liberties, but all playing off a central system of values and skills of which the elderly storytellers were avowed masters.

2. What Gets Said

Ma'anī andar shi'r juz bā khabt nīst,
    chūn falāsang ast, andar żabṭ nīst.
The meaning in poetry is nothing but blunders,
    like a stone-sling, it is out of control.

—Jalāl ud-Dīn Rūmī, *Mathnavī* I:1528

IT IS NECESSARY TO TURN BRIEFLY from the central dialogue of this study, that with the recorded words of the Ākhond and Karīm, to locate this project in the presently highly self-reflective discourse of cultural interpretation.[1] While this study is meant to be about Afghan expressive culture and politics, it is also, unavoidably, about how *we* think about narrative. So active is ethnographers' present need to articulate what it is we are doing when we explain what someone else has said, that this chapter could as well be constructed completely out of snappy quotations from other people's reflections on the last decade of collision between postmodern interpretation and ethnographic observation. So entranced are we by the metaphorical nature of representation that we are in danger of thinking ourselves poets just because we deal in descriptions. The social situatedness and interpretive openness we presently emphasize in approaching expressive constructions—which were known in a more innocent age as "texts," oral or written—seem a welcome antidote to the more arid forms of positivism or structuralism, admitting as a breath of fresh air the notions of

---

1. Earlier versions of chapters of this book were presented as delivered papers at various American Folklore Society and Middle East Studies Association annual meetings, and benefited from audience commentary. The main thesis of the book, that political commentary of direct relevance to current events could be articulated by Afghan storytellers through the deployment of traditional narratives, was rejected for presentation by the American Anthropological Association's annual program committee in 1980. The reason, as communicated to me through the panel organizers, was that the topic was "not anthropology." I am glad to say that anthropological perspectives are ever widening, and this early rejection served the useful purpose of annoying me into arguing my case at somewhat greater than twenty-minute length. Individual anthropologists were supportive of the project then and thereafter, and are thanked in the Preface.

choice, creativity, and improvization to our explanatory schemata and, more cogently, to the cultural goings-on they trace. The snake in this new Eden of lushly emancipatory verbiage is a new kind of authoritarianism, the situational kind, which, once admitting that all history is interpretation, in its logical extension gives carte blanche to revisionist history.

One strong theme in postmodern interpretation is the idea that all representation (analysis, interpretation) is dialogic, not only with our chosen audience (to be heard from, in our case, in reviews and letters columns, refutations, and sequels), but also with those whose representations inspired our own, the "informants" of the pre-postmodern ethnographic age. The second wing of this double dialogic relationship tended to escape our notice for some time because, ultimately favoring different discourses (and not incidentally, different power structures) than our informants, we privileged the set of interlocutors who shared our preferred discourse, that is, our colleagues and our own society. Now, however, "It is intrinsic to the breakup of monological authority that ethnographers no longer address a single general type of reader" (Clifford 1988:52). Furthermore, having recognized the dialogic dimension both of propositions and of whole discourses, postmodern ethnographers mount urgent pleas that we find some mechanism to let those other voices, the other halves of our information-gathering conversations, be heard:

> We need to describe others as people and give them a voice in our discourse. We need to write ethnographies as multilayered texts that communicate to a number of audiences. We need to acknowledge in the text the presence of an ethnographer who engages in dialogue with his or her subjects. (Stoller 1989:140)

But if there is "liberation, too, in recognizing that no one can write about others any longer as if they were discrete objects or texts" (Clifford 1986:25), yet some recognize that "giving a voice" itself is highly problematical, hardly empowering; "plural authorship" remains a "utopia," and the "authoritative stance of 'giving voice' to the other is not totally transcended" (Clifford 1988:51). One cannot stand clear out of the way while the other speaks, because one *is* the "way," the conduit through which more or less alien ideas and forms, crafted sometimes in a thoroughly alien language, are transmitted to an interested audience of strangers. This being a process of translation, the subjects of our descriptions are rarely likely to find our representations of them as elegant or accurate as their own. Yet there is redemption, we hope, in our own current reading style, which detects and rejects monologically authoritative interpretations even when they are attempted (Crapanzano 1986), a can opener theoretically capable of opening up any "text" falsely contained by our representations of its meanings.

Even so, some "texts"—as mediated by our representations—are more open than others, and the goal of "giving voice," though utopian, motivates one to look for mechanisms by which to render texts more, rather than less, open. One way is to let the other finish a sentence, or better yet, a whole series of sentences. "If accorded an autonomous textual space, transcribed at sufficient length, indigenous statements make sense in terms different from those of the arranging ethnographer [and also, I would add, of the eliciting fieldworker, a different persona in flesh or spirit—*M.M.*]. Ethnography is invaded by heteroglossia" (Clifford 1988:51). With all due respect to what I think is a very healthy trend in anthropological representation, folklorists have, unlike anthropologists, tended historically to be respectful of the verbal integrity and semiotic self-sufficiency of texts, i.e., of continuous speech, to the extent that pre–tape-recorder technologies permitted. In the eyes of the previous generation of anthropologists, they were perhaps fetishistically so, to the point of impoverished theory and underanalysis. My intention in this volume is to provide that "sufficient length" (in Clifford's words) in a translation format which is an earnest attempt at giving the storytellers' words "autonomous textual space," not a particularly radical thing to do from the viewpoint of folklore studies, and then to include, in separate intervening chapters, reflections and extrapolations about things I think were going on around and beyond the words, both implicitly within the texts and in the largely undiscussed social configuration within which the words were constructed. (Cf. Bourdieu 1977:167, "*What is essential goes without saying because it comes without saying*: the tradition is silent, not least about itself as a tradition.")

Readers who want to draw their own first impressions of the coherency or incoherency of the whole tale series can read all the texts in sequence first, then return to the analytic chapters as they see fit. The interpretive dimension is the one that folklorists have tended to regard as secondary to the "texts" which were its object, even in recent decades when we have engaged in it more intensively. Older comparative folklore studies (those prior to or independent of the "performance-based" study of folklore which began in the 1960s; cf. Bauman 1977) were inspired either by literary or comparative typological concerns. Though they have dealt more consistently with "whole texts" than have the ethnographies of the same period, they have tended to ignore the individuals and particular circumstances behind the texts' production just as ethnographers did. It is time folklorists too owned up to the politics of our choices and procedures: there is no such thing as disinterested representation, even in a type index (cf. Kodish 1987). The performance studies field itself is still striving to realize its goal of full engagement with the particulars of expressive interaction in the performance events which are its focus (cf., e.g., Kirshenblatt-Gimblett 1972; Hoppál 1980; Wiget 1987; Briggs 1988).

And how can one gauge success in "opening" a text? Surely, the many general and specific choices entailed by translation, even lengthy "total" translation, to use Tedlock's (1972a,b) term, compromise the original storyteller's voice in myriad ways. Becker's words on the inevitability of translation (chapter 1) are cold comfort. The one gauge we have of the "other's" autonomy, by no means a sure one, is the document's openness to reinterpretation. Clifford holds up Malinowski's texts as an example of openness because of his inclusion of "material that did not directly support his own all-too-clear interpretive slant. In the many dictated myths and spells that fill his books, he published much data that he admittedly did not understand. The result was an open text subject to multiple interpretations" (Clifford 1988:46). Other examples are Alois Musil's (1928) Arabian ethnography, recently provocatively reinterpreted by Michael Meeker (1979), and the Northwest Coast texts collected by Boas, Sapir, and Jacobs which have inspired Dell Hymes's ongoing work (e.g., 1981, 1985). But Krupat (1987:119) argues that the magnitude of *omissions* from these Northwest Coast texts is precisely what makes them "stable enough for perpetual analysis." Textual ellipsis imposed from without also apparently provides varieties of interpretive openness.

It seems to me that, while openness may be achieved in different ways, not all of which are empowering to the "native" voice, current attempts at a fuller rendering on the page of the auditory and visually expressive qualities of oral texts (pioneered by Tedlock in *Finding the Center* [1972]) and our efforts to provide and arrange more information about the social settings of performance in all their ramifications do not ultimately serve to disambiguate performances, and thus to "close" texts, but ideally only to move our sense of the ambiguities and multiplicities of meaning closer to those of informed audience members. The recordings discussed here, made in a pre-video age, are analyzed "blind" and correspondingly lack dimensions that a record of gesture, eye contact, etc., might have provided, but it must also be acknowledged that working extensively with either still or video photography in a group of virtual strangers, as this group was, is likely to affect their patterns of gaze and gesture in massive and unpredictable ways. The small cassette tape recorder, an already familiar object, was less intrusive, though not totally so.

Bruce Jackson (1988:282), quoting Henri Korn, describes a congruence he finds between natural and humanistic science: "To be scientific is not to present facts. It is to extract what is meaningful from what is not." But following Clifford, I see the openness of texts as fostered by the compiler's willingness to present things which may *not* be immediately meaningful to him- or herself. One must resist, to an extent, what Kermode characterized as our preference for enigma over muddle, our tendency to avoid interpretations asserting that a text is defective or confusing (1979, quoted in Josipovici 1988:233; cf. Kermode 1980:96). To be scientific may be to extract what is meaningful from what is not (to us), but to be honest (cf. Tyler 1986), we must also find ways to include the muddle, that midden of our representations through which later analysts will sift for the objects we could not interpret or did not recognize as artifacts. Doing so will present a fundamental challenge to the paradoxical politics of academic discourse, which celebrates and rewards, even as it denies the possibility of, the definitive word.

Textual openness in our representations is a mere reflection of textual unboundedness in action. Alton Becker (1984:136) provides a sixfold schema of dimensions of context in need of consideration when elucidating meaning in a proverb (or any verbal form):

1. structural relations (of parts to wholes)
2. generic relations (of text to prior text)
3. medial relations (of text to medium)
4. interpersonal relations (of text to participants in the text act)
5. referential relations (of text to nature, the world one believes lies beyond language)
6. silential relations (of text to the unsaid and unsayable).

(Cf. Jacobson 1960, Hymes 1964, 1972, and Briggs 1986 for developments in a multiphasic model of the communication event which stresses the copresence of all these factors.) While these categories help us clarify and distinguish the kinds of observations and connections one makes when deciphering a text, they *are*, as Becker points out, categorical, and therefore, their "improvisational quality is weak." Some of these relations, especially interpersonal and referential, were suggested in chapter 1 with reference to

the stories translated here. Other aspects (structural, generic, and silential)
are manifested in the translations and discussed in the analytic portions.
The medial relations are probably the most weakly represented here because of the visual and kinetic aspects of the performance that were not
available for scrutiny in the translation process, and the comparative weakness of writing to convey the multiple expressive dimensions of spoken
language.

Silential relations, the relations of the said to the unsaid and the unsayable, are probably the most problematical and the most intriguing for
this collection of stories and figure a good deal in the analysis (cf. Tyler
1978). Observations about particular silences are by their nature more obviously speculative even than other aspects of interpretation. The unsaid in
stories comes in a number of forms, including the obvious or consensual
unsaid, the things any competent member of the social group is expected
to know (but the ethnographer may not; see Bourdieu 1977:167); the unsaid of privileged or private knowledge (cf. Price 1983), including intentional puzzles which test or winnow out the audience; the unsaid which is
omitted because it is not central to the speaker's goals in this particular
performance but could be present and foregrounded in other performances
of "the same story"; the unsaid which is repressed, unsayable because un-
thinkable in the sense of inhibition, for personal and/or cultural reasons;
and the unsaid which is culturally irrelevant, essentially absent from the
cultural and personal repertoire of the speaker but possibly imported by
the ethnographer or other listener who brings it to the performance in his
or her own cultural baggage (Betteridge 1985). Radner and Lanser (1987)
address the problem of intentionality in coding and decoding narratives
(though with a narrower definition of coding than a linguist's). They acknowledge the possibility of meanings which may be covert even to the
author, and offer a caveat, "because ambiguity is a necessary feature of
every coded act, any instance of coding risks reinforcing the very ideology
it is designed to critique" (p. 417). In any case, the above varieties of silence
are not closed categories, nor can consciousness or implicature be treated
as either/or, yes/no propositions. The textual openness created by tactically
oblique or elliptical expression (Radner and Lanser's "coding") is also subject to misinterpretive ricochet, to direct inversion in interpretation. An
example is the Ākhond's good-humored description of himself as a raconteur who could, by his talk, "turn a funeral into a wedding" (see chapter 5)
and the interpretations which the Woləswāl or other nonstoryteller listeners might put on that boast. (An unsympathetic listener might, for in-

stance, see it as an admission of a lack of dignity or decorum.) Cultural ambivalence toward raconteurs, both traditional and in the eyes of the new elite like the Woləswāl, hinges on the raconteur's power to redefine circumstances through narrative and the social uses to which she or he is thought to put that power.

If silential relations suggest the most obvious enigmas, other contextual dimensions also have their complexities. In this study, structural or part-whole relations are considered not only internally to individual stories but intertextually among stories as parts of the storytelling sequence conceived as a joint act, an improvisational duet. Though the combination of stories is treated as emergent on this particular occasion, there is also the possibility, untestable without prolonged research with the same storytellers in multiple performances, that some of these stories were already linked or clustered in the storytellers' repertorial memory before this event. They may have been linked either as formally similar or as functionally complementary, according to the dichotomy constructed by Tyler: "Things are stored in memory analogically, according to their character, as in a rebus, or relatively, according to the work they signify; according, in other words, to what will best evoke them when needed for speech and thought" (1986:29). Both types of connection are suggested for individual stories in this series. But in fact, we know virtually nothing about actual repertoire mnemonics in practice. Tyler's elegant abstract configurations of mental and intellectual functions (1978:58; 1986) have yet to find their application in ethnographic method on the ground.

Intertextuality of the kind explored here (cf. Chock 1986) is not quite captured by either Becker's structural relations or his generic relations, but it is central to figuring out what a story might be about in any given performance. Hence, the linkages among these stories are traced with an eye to what, formally or propositionally, is picked up, retained, and reconsidered from various angles in *this* series of stories, and the currently operative meanings are thus foregrounded from the multiplicity of potential meanings the stories have. Part of the aesthetic of Afghan traditional storytelling, it will be argued, is that stories of differing genres, scales of complexity and construction, as well as other kinds of discourse (proverbs, conversational remarks) are juxtaposed and caused to reflect on one another in a full-blown oral performance of varying verbal texture. This cluster of tales includes, in part or whole, examples of most of the categories into which Stith Thompson's Tale Type Index divided traditional narratives plus some, such as personal experience narrative, not represented there and a number of other, nonnarrative elements, such as proverbs and idiomatic expressions which have ready cultural associations for the audience.

Implicit in the consideration of emergent intertextuality in performance is the recognition (following Bruner and Gorfain 1984) that a story can also be dialogic with itself, simultaneously conveying mixed or opposed messages, and thus be open-ended, ambiguous, and paradoxical. Bruner and Gorfain, in identifying three levels of the dialogic ("stories responsive to and interactive with themselves, with communities and their histories, and with the self," p. 73) do not go into how stories can be made to interact with *each other* in order to expose more clearly aspects of their self-dialogues and accomplish the other two kinds of interaction. One problem of the older ethnographic *and* folkloristic formats was the tendency to isolate individual texts (whole or hacked up) and then juxtapose them in extrinsically derived comparative-analytic schemata. Now our problem is to decide how to carve up an essentially unbounded phenomenon, how large and how detailed a chunk of text-context must be to ground a responsible interpretation of "integral" texts.

Becker's interpersonal dimension also deserves a special word with regard to these stories. Baghban (1977) identifies as part of a general Herati repertoire of humorous topics most of the targets for the humor presented in these stories. He also argues persuasively that social criticism which appears to be of a general kind in the humor of folk plays is always available for more specific readings by the audience. The players make their critical statements general and their praise specific, but this does not prevent the audience from seeing more personal dimensions to their critical observations. The stories here discussed are similarly generic-sounding, and the storytellers did not analogize between the content of the stories and local events in conversation.[2] I argue, however, that the operating principle of socially situated didactic storytelling is, "If the shoe fits, wear it." Obliqueness which renders the interpersonal dimension of such performances deniable is a basic element of this traditional rhetoric.

The generic quality of the content of oral tradition and the regularity of its styles of expression, together with our own preference for broad cultural generalizations and totalizing theories, have tended to direct the eth-

---

2. On one occasion, much later and in another village, when an elderly listener began to connect a fictional story about premarital sex with actual events in the village, naming names, my then research associate vigorously signaled me to turn off the tape recorder, which I did out of respect for the community's sense of discretion.

nographer's and folklorist's attention away from the specific social uses to which utterance is being put on a given occasion. Thus, Ellen Basso says (1985:12), "the various and often changing ends to which a narrator addresses listeners can be understood with considerable subtlety through attention to narrative patterning," but it becomes clear from her remarks that what she is interested in at this point is what is *Kalapalo* about these narrative "ends," not the more particular qualities I set out to isolate in the Ākhond's and Karīm's performances, even to the point of being able to distinguish *between* the preoccupations of the two cooperating performers. This difference of directions, hers and mine, perhaps illustrates a more general, lingering difference in the otherwise convergent efforts of folklorists and anthropologists regarding the analysis of socially contexted narrative.

Recognizing the multiplicity and unboundedness of context and the potential specificity and obliqueness of narrators' goals, we must also confront the fact that our interpretive procedures will remain far different from those indigenous to the social habitat of the stories. We decode by exhaustive, reiterative examination of a finite set of texts. Poring over a set of stories reveals symmetries and asymmetries probably not immediately evident even to a native listener in a single performance, raising the question of how much the culturally informed listener is expected to "get" from a single performance. But there are other reiterative mechanisms in oral tradition, not repetitive scrutiny of one utterance like ours, but repetitive, socially situated acts of interpretation directed to an open-ended series of utterances. An oral tradition's aesthetic is one of familiarity: the jokes, the narrative tensions and crises, the admonitions all take forms and positions more or less familiar from other performances in the same modes, but the intertextual dimension within a conversational narrative sequence also provides variety, creativity, and unpredictability of *juxtaposition*—story to story, story to self, and story to community.

Hernadi and Kermode (both 1981) address the problem of the differences between ordinary and critical reading methods in our own culture which are likely to yield different meanings. Kermode's "overreading" presents a particular problem with regard to ethnographic interpretation, if the goal is to come at an indigenous understanding of *how* things are meant. Among other things, such close reading as we employ potentially breeds a failure to reflect on relations between realized and latent meanings in a performance. For me, the present project is a remedial reading, since while attending the performance I was largely incompetent to decipher it, but at best, this rereading can only be an exploration of the possibilities of signification. What was realized by others at the time remains unclear. Nor was what they thought at the time necessarily all they "got." Oral audiences also engage in mulling over and reviewing, the latter partly in sequential performances of "the same" stories in different contexts, to which they as audience thus bring prior and posterior understandings. Native criticism may routinely take place at a time and place other than that of the performance under consideration (Baghban 1977:193). Keenly aware that our interpretation is not an indigenous procedure, one can only acknowledge, at a different level, the responsibilities of the translator.

On Translation and Reading These Texts

A few words are in order about the form these stories take on the page, and the specific choices made in their textual representation. One overall goal was to reflect lexical, syntactic, and aural *patterns* of the original spoken Persian as faithfully as possible in written English. In word choice, every effort was made to translate the same word or phrase in Persian with the same word or phrase in English, wherever they occurred, so that patterns of lexical repetition would not be obscured by a translator's word choice. In a few instances, such consistency could not be achieved, the semantic domains of the English and Persian words being divergent. Syntactical consistency was aided somewhat by the fact that Persian is an Indo-European language, like English, and so word order is used in some similar ways, though Persian sentence order is generally verb-final (subject + predicate + verb, as in German). This caused alterations of effect when repetitive patterns were carried by words in different positions in Persian and English sentences. I also tried to represent as closely as possible such things as narrative tense shifts (from simple past to historical present and back), but occasionally, the shifts could not be placed on exactly the same verbs where they occurred in Persian and still produce an idiomatic effect in English, so the switch was slightly repositioned. Such adjustments are noted in footnotes. As in all translation, there is a tension between verbatim accuracy and equivalency of effect. What is not an awkward expression in Persian should not be translated with an awkward expression in English, or an inaccurate impression of the original will result. On the other hand, where the storytellers did grope for words, stumble, or make corrections, those effects have been carried over in translation. I can sometimes suggest a reason for those moments of faltering fluency, while others remain to be explained.

I have tried to note every place where my own translation was speculative, usually because a word or phrase cannot yet be translated. Sometimes the problem was audibility, sometimes an utterance was perfectly audible but neither I, my dictionaries, nor my Persian-speaking collaborators could supply a translation for it. The first story, which is an extended dialect joke, presented special problems in this regard, since a good deal of its humor rested on verbal obscurity even by local standards. Thanks to my collaborators, apart from that first story in chapter 3, very few speculative bits remain, and readers may be able to suggest further corrections. Access to tapes and transcripts of the stories can be arranged for readers interested in particulars of translation. Barre Toelken (1976; Toelken and Scott 1981) has courageously demonstrated that later self-correction of translation errors and reinterpretation in print is not only possible, but an intellectually valuable route to interpretive openness.

The aural qualities of spoken narratives—variations in pitch, volume, voice quality, and the arrangement of pauses—are more elusive to capture in print than lexical patterns, and the discriminative choices involved less easy to describe. Aural qualities are nonetheless essential in the organization of speech, conveying to the listener a sense of the relative importance of propositions and their connections with each other, which are essential aspects of meaning (cf. Becker 1984:149, "and rhythm is probably the most basic and powerful cohesive force in language"). The features I have singled out for representation in the layout of these texts, especially pitch, volume, and pause, are not all such aural effects but those most reliably accessible to me, given the quality of my recordings. I have taken them into account in only a rather simple way compared to others' current efforts in this line (e.g., Wiget 1987). William Bright (1982) and Virginia Hymes (personal communication, unpublished lectures) have done important work on integrating the work of Dell Hymes on lexical and syntactic patterning in the segmentation of transcribed oral texts, and Dennis Tedlock's work on aural effects in segmentation. I have attempted this integrative technique in laying out the translated words in patterns on the page which are meant to integrate auditory, syntactic, and topical arrangements of the spoken words.

In these translations line breaks, indentations, and a few special symbols represent audible patterns of intonation and pause, while conventional punctuation is also used to some extent. A period indicates a full-stop intonation, which is usually but not always followed by an audible pause. That pause, if it occurs, is represented by a line break and a return to the left-hand margin for the next line. There is also at least one semi-stop intonation characteristic of each speaker (their intonation patterns being "signatures" with characteristic individual contours) represented by a comma, which is often but not always followed by a pause of a shorter length than the full stop. Where such a pause occurs, the comma is followed by a line break and an indentation of the beginning of the next line. Both full- and semi-stop intonations sometimes are sounded without following pauses, and such configurations are represented by a period or comma without a line break or, where the print must run over to another line, by a no-pause symbol at the end of the first line of print, thus: ». Sometimes there is a particularly extended pause, after either a full stop or a semi-stop, which is indicated by ‹› on a line by itself at the left-hand margin. Often these lengthier pauses occasioned a prompt, a murmur, or grunt of comprehension and/or assent from the audience. Such prompts, of which Mokhtār's were the most audible, both in the performance (for he was the main addressee) and on tape, are included in the translation, on their own lines when they occurred during a pause by the storyteller. Becker (1984:149–50) points out the importance of the counterpoint such prompts establish:

> When two people speak comfortably to each other, they both join in the creation of a rhythm, marked by stresses, nods, grunts, gestures, and sentence rhythms. . . . If the conversation is not going well, the discomfort will be manifested in arhythmic responses and repairs, until they get rolling again. . . . Our basic elusive unease in speaking to foreigners is in large part explicable because it is often in large part rhythmic.

Occasional lines of print run over where there is no intonational stop or pause whatsoever. These typographical run-ons are indented to the far right in the succeeding line.

Indentation has been used slightly differently to show the internal organization of quoted speech. When a character begins to speak, the storyteller's "He/she said" or equivalent marker occurs within a line in whatever place it was spoken. The quoted speech that follows starts with its own left-hand margin, inset from the regular margin, and the organization of full and semi-stops within the quoted speech is shown by the same principles as outlined above, with the new left-hand margin as base line. The purpose of this arrangement is to block out quoted speech so that characters' turns to talk, their juxtapositions, and their internal organization are easily visible within the texture of the whole narrative.

Working with a tape recorder with an automatic sound-level control which flattened out variations longer than a word or two, I could not trace volume changes as sensitively as some recent studies (Wiget 1987). Underlining and underlined capital letters with exclamation points indicate loud moments. Italics indicate untranslated Persian words and, inside brackets, designate speakers and describe qualities of speech, such as whispering. Parentheses enclose asides by the storyteller; remarks made by others during the story are in brackets, as are occasional words interpolated for clarity in translation which were not needed in Persian.

Segments of plot somewhat equivalent to scenes in a play as we conceive of them are set apart by a single line space in the text. I imposed these segmentations on the text, on the basis of auditory, syntactical, or lexical markers or a combination of them. Besides the intonational and pause markers just described, there are lexical segment markers, such as Karīm's frequent use of the word *khay*, "well," followed by full-stop intonation and usually a full-stop pause. There are also syntactical markers, especially of the variety I have called "chaining," in which the storyteller says something like, "So-and-so did such-and-such [*full stop*]. When so-and-so did such-and-such . . ." and the story goes on from there, usually with another actor responding to the just-described action. But the chain is used to divide minor as well as major segments (e.g., "Salīm," chapter 6, ll. 597–98). The Ākhond also uses a sort of lexical shorthand for this form of action summary, ending a segment by simply speaking the name of a principal actor in the foregoing scene, followed by a full-stop intonation and pause, before going on to the next scene, e.g., in "Black and White," chapter 13, ll. 37, 46, 86, 189. But these constructions are not always used as segment markers. At ll. 115 and 185, he uses them simply to clarify.

I have not yet worked out to my satisfaction an unambiguous system for hierarchizing these various kinds of segment markers. Sometimes they are used jointly, as Bright (1982) describes, and then one can correlate auditory and linguistic markers in a fairly confident portrayal of the storyteller's segmentation techniques and effects. In numerous places in these Persian texts, however, intonational and pause patterns seem to work at cross purposes (or better, counterpoint) with syntactical and lexical markers. Intonational run-ons of various kinds abound. Sometimes such accelerations seem to build excitement in conjunction with propositional content; at other times, the storyteller seems to be moving over material quickly in order to get on to other things. Often the texture of intonation and pauses changes dramatically within a single story: the storyteller starts out a narrative with short phrases separated by pauses, and thus elicits more numerous prompts from the audience, as if starting slowly to make sure they understand and are engaged by the story. As he builds toward a climax, the segments marked by full stops and semi-stops may get longer, and there may be more pause run-ons, accelerating his speech as he approaches a plot climax. In other stories in the series, e.g., "Women's Tricks" in chapter 10, the storyteller begins with rather long, rapidly narrated segments and with comparatively few opportunities for audience assent, as if in a hurry to get to the middle (where women's tricks begin to be discussed) right from the start. Such differences in internal auditory textures make it difficult to arrive at an objectively measurable distinction between full stops and semi-stops, long pauses and short pauses; the distinctions are situational and tactical within different parts of the same text, as well as significantly different among speakers.

Pauses can be used either to close a segment followed by a change of topic, or to foreground a climactic moment—"pregnant pauses." In fact, the pregnant pause derives its force from its paradoxical relationship to the topic-change pause. People generally stop talking when they have finished a topic, but in a pregnant pause, the topic is only on the brink of resolution, not completed, and the speaker's teetering on the brink intonationally increases the audience's interest in whether and when it will be resolved. In print, the pregnant pause and the segment-closure pause, like run-ons of different semantic force, are not visibly differentiated, and must be distinguished by their relationship to the propositional content of the utterances involved, if the reader is to understand the storyteller's particular auditory technique at the moment. I think it is helpful to try to show how the storyteller audibly builds and releases narrative tensions, but there is nothing mechanical about these auditory features, nor the choices made in deciding how to represent in translation their placement, magnitude, and significance within a syntax that is irreducibly different from our own.

As for characteristic patterns of segmentation and clustering in these stories, there seem to be a number of different configurations, some of which may be related to more formally recognized Persian verbal patterns, such as the folk quatrain and its literary cousin, the *rubāʿī*, and the literary extended verse narrative form, *mathnavī*. Wallace Chafe (1980) pointed out that all spoken narrative is produced in "spurts," consisting in the texts he examined of clusters of two to six words he called "idea units," typically bounded by pauses with a coherent intonation contour and usually one of a small set of syntactic structures. While these observations are generally apropos for Persian as well, with the possible exception of the length of the "spurts," the longer story texts reveal complicated interlocking clusters built on these principles. Patterns of twos, threes, and fours all occur with great regularity. Consider "Salīm the Jeweller" in chapter 6, ll. 597–601:

Once I got out, sir, he realized that I'd gotten out, and he hurled himself out
of the cave.
When he hurled himself out there, I was at the top of the mountain, and he
was below.
He's looking and looking for me, and I had a certain amount of strength, I
picked up a hundred-*man* rock,
and hit him on the main vein of his neck, and he fell on his face.
I hit him with another rock, and with the third rock I broke his head in pieces
and killed him and I left his body there.

Lines 597–99 form a triplet of triplets, immediately followed in l. 600 by a two-clause string and in l. 601 by a four-verb cluster. Lines 599–601 also comprise a propositional triplet, describing intersegmentally an assault with three rocks. The propositional structure of this entire, short climactic scene is thus both dual, attack and counterattack neatly dividing the five lines in the middle of the third line, and triple, in the hero's success with three rocks.

All through "Salīm," the Ākhond frequently pairs clauses, giving them isomorphic intonation patterns with no significant pause separating them, in which action and reaction, or action and verbal response are portrayed. On the one hand, this seems like a natural enough tendency in the binary, dialectic world of story plots, but it also invites closer inspection than given here because the main form of literary narrative verse in Persian is an elaborated binary structure, the *mathnavī*, which divides each line into two halves that rhyme with each other and have identical meter and sometimes additional internal rhymes (and in writing, sometimes visual isomorphism). The Ākhond's tendency to use bilateral balanced constructions in narrative may be due in part to basic cybernetics, but it is probably enhanced by his extensive exposure to literary Persian narrative verse. The poetics of *mathnavī* are a highly developed self-conscious system, and it is to be hoped that future work on the extended narrative of this and other Persian speakers with different known degrees of exposure to classical literature could approach a more sensitive understanding of the resemblances between such constructions in oral and literary narrative.

The quatrain form is another case in point. The quatrain is extremely popular in both oral and literary traditions, the literary form (*rubāʿī*) hav-ing stricter standards for rhyme and a more complex and rigidly calculated metrical system than its oral cousin, from which it probably derived. The quatrain is lyric, not narrative. Folk quatrains per se are embedded in some prose romances as the emotionally heightened poetic speech of the hero, his love object, and sometimes their allies. But the dualities of oral narra-tive readily lend themselves to doubling into structures of four, and prose speeches often acquire qualities of the *rubāʿī*, e.g., in "Salīm" at ll. 323–32, where two speeches are each divided into two sections by a full-stop. The second speech (Salīm's) is divided by its pauses into two halves with two segments each. Its third line (l. 331), unlike the others, is an Arabic idiom of praise, while the other three are all action propositions in Persian. This third-line contrast is an essential element in the poetics of *rubāʿī* and is also quite recognizable in many folk quatrains. The fourth line returns, in sum-mary fashion, to the subject matter of the first, now seen from a new per-spective because of the contrast introduced in the third line, a rhetorical pattern also basic to a well-formed *rubāʿī*. In this case, the Ākhond's audi-ble pause pattern outlines a *rubāʿī* configuration that would not have been visible on syntactical grounds alone, which would have suggested a five-line configuration with the two clauses in the fourth line separated. In the last line, the speaker's pause pattern compacts two clauses into one line, driving home the point of Salīm's speech and giving the end of the quatrain (if it can be so conceived) extra weight.

There are similar examples scattered throughout these texts, e.g., in Karīm's "Ill Fortune of the City of Rūm," ll. 192–95 and 196–99 form a neat isomorphic pair of these "syntactic quatrains." Another striking example is the edict which the mulla gives the Mongol at the end of chapter 3 (ll. 142–45):

"If a Mongol is an angel, he's no good »
if his name is written in gold, it's no good.
Don't take so much as a head of grain from the Mongol's harvest,»
because no matter who sows Mongol seed, it's no good."

At other points, the speaker's pause pattern seems to be at cross purposes to what would appear syntactically to be a quatrain pattern. In the Āk-hond's "Black and White " (chapter 13) ll. 42–44 would form a neat pattern of two pairs of parallel syntactic structures (a common form in folk qua-train), but the speaker's use of a very marked pause sequesters the second half of the second pair as a separate line (l. 44) for emphasis. In this transcription system, the quatrain form is obscured in order to honor the pause pattern, which actually accentuates the definitive last component of the four-part cluster, and thus sets the cluster off in speech. The storyteller reemphasizes it with a segment-terminal marker naming one of the principal actors (l. 45: "this merchant").

A thorough consideration of aural techniques and segmentation in Persian oral narrative would fill a book by itself. These are only a few examples of the complexities, drawn from the speech of only two individuals whose techniques, though they have much in common, are differently distributed through the texts. These differences in use of various intonational techniques, together with syntactical and other verbal stylistic variations, would bear exploration in light of the two men's different educational backgrounds and levels of literacy and in the context of a more general consideration of the relations between oral and literary stylistics. From the point of view of microanalysis, this series of stories is a vast sample, but from the point of view of individual versus general stylistics, it is too small for generalization. In any case, the main concern of the present study is the emergence, through intertextuality, of thematic congruency. What these stories mean is in no small measure mediated by the techniques outlined in the foregoing discussion, which have figured greatly in decisions made about the translation format, but the student of narrative segmentation will find this aspect of the analysis underdeveloped. This aspect is perhaps one of the richest for potential reinterpretation of these texts in the future.

The fine structure of these stories is certainly important to their effectiveness, but in the discussion which follows, fine structural observations will be presented only opportunistically in the pursuit of larger-scale observations about the storytelling session as a whole and the relations among its subunits, the individual stories. In tracing the fine structure of rhetorical technique, one sees anew that these stories are not closed texts, but flow into, echo, and evoke each other, comment upon each other by shared lexical, syntactical, and paralinguistic features, as well as topical linkages.

> *Īn nadārad ākhar, az āghāz gu,*
> *Rau tamām-i īn ḥakāyat bāz gu*
> This hath no end; tell of the beginning,
> Go, tell the rest of the story.

> —Jalāl ud-Dīn Rūmī, *Mathnavī* I:143

3. Khalīfah Karīm, "Mulla Mongol the Martyr"

Part 1: Interview

Mokhtār: Well, Ākhond, sir¹, [*Interruption to reposition the microphone*]
        All right—Ākhond, sir, first, if we may ask what your name is?   1
K: 'Abdul Karīm.
M: 'Abdul Karīm Khān². Where are you from, sir?
K: From Mīrabad.
M: From Mīrābād Village.   5
K: Yes, sir.
M: OK. About how old would you be?
K: I'd be about 65.
M: You're 65, sir.
K: Yes.   10
M: And have you been to school, or not?
K: I've studied in the home—the village schools, but not in the
        government kind.
M: OK. About how long is it that you've been telling these stories?
K: It might be 20 or 25 years, for these stories and jokes and
     gatherings, these—   15
     singing³ and such things—

---

    1. Mokhtār, the interviewer, is confused as to which of the two elderly men is the Ākhond (mulla), and mistakenly addresses the other man by this title. The two were not distinguishable by dress or demeanor to his observation at this point. A mulla is a Muslim clergyman, equivalent more to a rabbi than to a priest, since his responsibilities are for leadership in religious ceremonies and religious instruction but not intercession with the divine. The term "Ākhond" in Afghanistan refers to mullas who are also schoolteachers in the traditional Qur'anic educational system.

    2. Realizing that the man he addresses is not the mulla, Mokhtār adds the title *Khān*, a word of Mongolian origin which, in this context, is simply a respectful title addressed to an adult male, equivalent to "Mister." In other contexts it may designate, more specifically, a wealthy landowner or tribal chief.

    3. *khāndan* (literary, *khwāndan*): The verb means either to sing or recite poetry, or to

M: Who used to listen to these stories of yours, mostly?
K: These stories of mine, well, any group of people who were in the
                                  gathering, would hear them,
but they were more for the learned people,
    the Sufis, in the villages, because there aren't very many official
                              people in our village.   20
M: Yes.
K: So there were these people.
Sometimes I'd be on visiting terms
    with the headmasters or the teachers in the school, and I'd come
                            and talk with them.
M: In the schools.   25
K: Yes.
M: I mean, did more youngsters listen to your stories, or elders,
                              or—boys[4]?
K: Well, it used—used to be that the boys enjoyed it more, when I—
    when they had the same habits that I did, [were] my own age.
When I was younger and more ignorant,   30
    the boys were more interested in me.
Then when I got older and wiser, and like that,
    then the elders, my own age, mostly, they'd be interested
    and I'd converse with them.
M: What is your occupation? What do you do?   35
K: My occupation, sir, I used to sing[5] in the style of the old-
                             fashioned people,
    and then, I used to talk and joke.
M: That is, your daytime occupation,[6] during the day—
    do you farm?
K: I used to farm, sir.   40

---

read, silently or aloud (and by extension, to recite from written sources). In the context of Karīm's comment focusing on entertainment activities, singing and possibly recitation are more central.

    4. "Boys," *bachchehā*, may refer to males from about six years old to the early twenties, and the age range meant here is ambiguous. Karīm answers that his main audience tended to be his age-mates throughout his life.

    5. The word *khāndan* is used again.

    6. Occupation: *wazīfah*, "duty" or "occupation" in literary and city-dialect usage. The interviewer wanted to know Karīm's profession, but the term *wazīfah* in local village usage also refers to a private vocation for religious reading and study (see the discussion in the second part of this chapter) and Karīm took it that way in the context of his earlier stated preference for the company of elderly and learned men. He does not imply professional verbal performance by this remark.

M: Yeah.

K: Yeah. I was a farmer during the day,
    there were five fields[7] and I used to do my poor sort of farming.

I didn't have any other work.

M: You don't do any other work? [*K*: No—] But they call you
                          "Master[8] Karīm."   45

K: Yes, sir.

M: Why do they call you "Master"?

K: It's just that I know a hand's worth of masonry, too.[9]

M: OK, you do masonry, too.

K: Right, sir.   50

M: Is there work these days? For you?

K: Not in the winter like this, sir, you'd have to work with ice! [*laughs*]
    In midsummer there's work.

M: In midsummer there's work.

K: Yeah, during the heat there's work, but these days, sir,   55

a hundred masons aren't worth a beet! [*laughs*]

M: [*laughs*] There's no work.

K: No, sir.

[*Break in recording to check recorder function.*]

M: Well, Master Karīm.

K: Yes, sir.   60

M: Excuse me—uh—do you have children, too?

K: Yes, uh-huh.

M: How many do you have—by the gift of God?

K: Five.

M: Five.   65

K: Yes. Four you could say, of the weaker sex,[10] daughters, and one son.

M: Good, have you married them off, the girls?

K: I've married off two of the girls, and two remain.

---

    7. "Field," *pal*, a field of varying size, surrounded by low mud walls. Walls serve as boundaries for either irrigation or ownership purposes, and the size of fields varies according to water supply, terrain, etc. "Five" here is a vague quantity, as in English, "two or three." Not only is the amount of land vague, but Karīm's remarks are ambiguous as to whether he owned, leased, or sharecropped the land. One's exact economic status is not information freely shared with representatives of the central government.

    8. *Khalīfah*: A title given to a variety of skilled craftsmen. Mokhtār has realized that he is addressing the craftsman, not the mulla.

    9. "*Amtau yak panjah barnā'ī am yād dārom.*" Cf. the similar English idiom, "I turn my hand to a bit of . . ."

    10. Literally, "the weak," *ājezah* (Arabic feminine noun) is a common term for females.

M: OK, then you have sons-in-law, too.

K: Yes, right. Two of them. 70

M: Are you pleased with them, when they come to your house?

K: Yeah, well, a son-in-law is like this, that whether one likes it or not,
he comes, anyway! [*laughs*]

Ākhond [*off microphone*]: Sons-in-law have the nature of cats—they find
their way into every household! [*general laughter*]

K: That's why—so to say, the one who prays for a man's death, sir,
the death of the father-in-law—? [*M*: Yeah—] 75
—the truth is, it's the son-in-law.

And the thief of the father-in-law's property is the son-in-law. [*M*: Yes.]

And besides, kind sir, the one who wrecks the household of a man's
children is his son-in-law.

So how could a man be happy with him? [*Other audience comments
off mike, voices overlap.*]

M: OK, how many—how many times have you married? 80

K: —Twice. Yeah.

M: Both wives, sir, are they alive, or not?

K: No, sir. One has left this world, the other still remains.

M: A new one—the young one, have you just now married her, or earlier?

K: It's about ten years, fifteen years—it would be about fifteen years now. 85

Ā: She's young, sir—[*K*: Yeah—]

Others in the audience: Yeah, she's young.

M: Younger than he is—

K: Yes, sir. Yeah.

Ā: It's about ten years, she was the daughter of Hajji Shaykh, sir. 90

K: Yeah.

M: Do you have children from this new wife, then?

K: Yes, right. Two of the daughters are from her.

[*End of interview. Break in recording.*]

Part 2: Story: Mulla Mongol the Martyr[11]

Mokhtār: OK, uh—Master, sir—

K: Yes, sir.

---

11. No title was supplied by the storyteller. The name of a main character is affixed for convenience in reference.

M: First of all, where did you—learn this story? The name—
     first of all, what's the name of this story?
     This story that you're going to tell now—   5
K: This story, sir, it's an account about Mongol manners of speech,[12]
                                    that you could say,
     they had a gathering among themselves on account of someone
                                    who had died,
     and so we tell this story about them, that is, what they said and
                                    how they said it—
     they were burying their dead, how they were conversing.
M: Right, from whom did you learn this?   10
K: Well, this one, someone else told it before, so it was just handed
                    down from one to another, anyway. [*chuckles*]
M: Right—so you don't know who was the first to tell it, then?
K: Well, not like that! [*laughs*] God knows!
M: Right, so you didn't learn it from a book?
K: No, sir, no, it's not from a book.   15
M: Can you read, yourself?
K: Yes, sir, to a certain extent.
M: So you read books of stories, some evenings, too?
K: Yeah, some evenings I read, sometimes.
M: Fine. Let's go ahead and listen.   20
K: Yeah—this Mongol, sir, there were
          two brothers and they had an old, bent father,
          and by the will of Holy God his end came,
     and the father died.
The father died, and the two brothers sat down, one was younger
                                    and one older. [*coughs*]   25
The older brother said to the younger brother, »
     "Our father did us kindnesses,
          and took trouble on our behalf,

---

12. A remnant of the ethnic Mongol population, descendants of the armies of Genghis Khan, remained in certain villages in Ghūrāt province and adjacent eastern parts of Herat province, in west-central Afghanistan, in the 1970s. By the mid-twentieth century, the language called *Moghol* survived only among a few older speakers (see Schurmann 1962). Younger members of the community spoke as their first language a dialect of Persian which is one of the objects of satire in this story. "Manners of speech": *alfāz* (singular, *lafz*). Lexical meanings include "word," "vocable," and "pronunciation," but *lafz* in Herat usage regularly designated "accent" and/or "dialect," with reference to the well-recognized regional variations in Persian.

today, let alone that we expend his property, »
    we should also exert our own <u>bodies</u> for him, »   30
because he's our father."
He said, "Fine," he said, "What shall we do?"
He said, "We must take care of most of the work of his burial
        with our own hands,
    if it were left to other people, who would come for pay, to do it,   35
    it wouldn't be right." »
He said, "That's good."

So they did everything they had to do and got everything ready, pre-
                                pared everything,
this elder brother said, »
    "The logs that are needed for firewood for the pots, for the
                       cooking, 40
    I'll bring them."[13]
He said, "That's good." [*M*: Yeah—]

He said, "That's good,"
and after that, kind sir,
then he went off to the mountains, and the axe hit him in the leg and he died,
and <u>he</u>[14] was saying, »   45
    "He died a martyr for our dead," »
    and they announced at the funeral, and they said to him— »
        "Oh, Lord," [he said] "the dead, you could say
        he reached the rank of my brother, that he died a martyr."[15] 50
People said, "No, *bābā*,[16] he wasn't a martyr!" »

---

    13. The first local ethnic stereotype: Mongols are known as preparers and sellers of charcoal, for the making of which they gather firewood.

    14. That is, the younger brother.

    15. The construction creates ambiguity in the younger brother's speech: logically, he must be referring to his own, newly deceased brother, but the syntax implies he is now comparing some other person to the dead brother. See the commentary in the next section.

    16. Literally, "old man," "papa," but used for familiar address in a variety of contexts—here like the British slang expression, "old man," or American slang "buddy" or "man." Used, as at line 84, as an affectionate form of address for persons of any age, usually but not exclusively male. The term defies translation with any single English word or consistent combination of terms and will be left untranslated where it occurs. At line 84 it is used to address a young boy, the son of the deceased.

And that was it, and he came,
according to the story, sir, he said, »
    "I'm going to go ask for a decree from the mullas,
      if I tell the story of his death,   55
      if they attest
      that he's a martyr,
      that these [other] dead are of his same rank, for— »
      if they say 'He's not a martyr', I won't say any more."
◇
He came along,   60
came to the mulla's place and called out a greeting and was answered
                        and [went] before the ākhond,
gave greetings, said,
    "Ākhond, sir,"
he said, "Yes?"
He said, "Had you met our great patron of angelic disposition and
                        Islamic inclination?"[17] »   65
      —he spoke Mongol-fashion like that, sir—
He said, "No."
He said, "Yeah," [*to me*] sir, »
he said, "as he made his departure as a Muslim from the abode of mortality
                    for the abode of eternity,
    the horse of doom was led up for him and he died.   70
    You've seen our brother Mulla Moslem with the black beard
      thick as a log[18] and the bowed brows, with his white neck, and
                    his rare youth?"
He said, "Yeah."

---

17. Referring hyperbolically to the speaker's deceased father. At this point Karīm swings into a different, very rhythmic speech pattern, suppressing pauses and using rhyming parallel prose constructions which are a decorative feature of classical Persian belles lettres. He also makes some changes of vocalization (e.g., lowering and broadening terminal short vowel *a*) in imitation of vowel shifts between Herati and Mongol dialect, comically superimposed on the character's attempt to speak in an educated and elevated style. Rhymed prose (*saj'*) is the language of the Qur'an, in Arabic, and is used widely in Arabic-influenced classical literary Persian for decorative effect, as are parallel syntactic constructions (which rhyme in Arabic and to some extent in Persian). In oral storytelling the two devices are also used in tandem for comic hyperbole. Here, the language (expected to be comic in this context) lampoons the Mongol villager's attempt at elevated speech while he is making claims to religious sanctity for his dead relatives.

18. An ethnic joke encased in a boast: Mongols are stereotyped as thin-bearded or beardless, while the beard is a respected symbol of masculine maturity.

He said, "He went to the *dūgha*[19] of Khoāja Ghaybī[20] sir, for *tīrzad* wood,[21]
  mounted on a stud bull[22] with a *qashqa*[23] forehead, horned, tall
   in the *gowan*[24] and lean in the flank, with a three-kilo axe on
    his shoulder and twelve fathoms of rope on behind,   75
he went to the base of a *tīrzad* limb[25] by the Pear Road to
              Little Shoe,[26]
stopped there.
He lifted the axe to break a limb of *tīrzad*, and it went wrong
  and hit God-forgive-him[27] on the thigh, and there he fell.

  Afternoon came, he didn't come, »
  dinnertime came, he didn't come, »   80
  bedtime came, »
  bābā, what's become of him?!"
All at once we heard the bull bellowing behind the hut. »
We said, "*Bābā!*" »
The boy said, "Duh-whuh?"   85
We said, "Go see about that bull bellowing, whether it's God-forgive-him
     Mulla Moslem's bull or somebody else's." »

---

19. An as yet unidentified term.

20. "The Hidden Master," apparently a place-name, the meaning of which suggests a local saint's shrine, but no auditors recognized the name and the character's speech becomes progressively more obscure from this point on.

21. Possibly another place-name, but *gonda* (also *konda* in Herati dialect) means "log," "piece of wood," "firewood"; *tīrzad*, literally "arrow struck" might mean "marksman" (one whose arrows have struck the mark), but the phrase defied explanation or recognition among Herati-speakers reviewing the tape. The phrasing of its reappearance later (lines 40 and 42) suggests it might refer to a particular type of wood.

22. The folklorist Hafizullah Baghban, himself a native of the Herat area in the Injīl district, east of Herat City, explained that a propensity for using ungelded bulls as riding stock is one element in the humorous stereotype of Mongol people applied by their non-Mongol neighbors (personal communication, October 1980). Note the Ākhond's aside corroborating this at l. 89 and footnote 29.

23. Another as yet unidentified term—from the syntax, apparently a modifier on *pīnak*, "forehead, brow."

24. Another unidentified term, apparently a substantive.

25. *Shākh-tīrzad*—the word on the tape is somewhat unclear, but if this reading is correct, *shākh-e tīrzad*, "a limb of *tīrzad*."

26. A highly speculative translation of several words strung together, apparently highly esoteric and slightly nonsensical place-names. These lines are recited rhythmically, with increasing speed and decreasing comprehensibility.

27. *Khodā biāmorz*, literally, "God absolve (him or her)," a blessing invoked when a deceased person is mentioned. The young Mongol uses it, comically, as a name for the deceased and quotes himself using it thus even before he could know that the man was dead (see l. 86).

He said, "The horns are like the horns of Mulla Moslem's bull, and the
                            qashqa-forehead is like his qashqa-forehead, »
        but if it's Mulla Moslem's bull, I don't know whether it's
                            Mulla Moslem's bull or somebody else's."
[*The Ākhond makes a partly inaudible, laughing comment off mike*: . . .
                    that's stock with the testicles [left] on. . . .²⁸ *Others in
                    audience laugh.*]
"We said, 'God blind your eyes, if you're your father's seed, legitimately
                    born, and you can't recognize your own stock,
                    [yet] you want to be a bigshot²⁹!' "   90
I got up myself and looked, and it was God-forgive-him's bull,
                                            and we said, »
        "He must have fallen in White Creek," but once we went there, and
                                            he wasn't there,
and we went by the houses at Tāyerah Khosh and he wasn't there,
when we went to Dalīzak³⁰ we saw he wasn't there,
then all at once we saw, sir, in front   95
        of Khoāja Naṣrollah Mountain, when we got there, we saw,
        before reaching Tarīt-e Talkhakī,³¹ stopping there,
and we looked toward a dry wash and there's something white in that
                                            wash and we went and »
        there God-forgive-him had fallen,
the rope lying around, the saw lying around, the axe lying around, »   100
thorns and brush of the mountains fallen in God-forgive-him's eyes,
his head was fine, his back was fine, but now when we got our hands
                    on God-forgive-him's leg, it was going flop, flop!
We said, "Either the meat got busted or the bone got busted," and we
                    took in the situation, how early on, it just got cut off.

---

28. The Ākhond explains the Mongol term for bull, *bīqa* or *beyqa*, an unusual word
pronounced *bōqqa* in Herati dialect. Hafizullah Baghban identified the term; Kazim Alami, a
later auditor of the tapes and native to Herat City rather than the eastern village area, could
not and found the other dialect imitations largely incomprehensible as well. It is likely that
Karīm's dialect imitation was not perfectly understood even by some local members of the
live audience. The Ākhond realizes the difficulty and clarifies.

29. *Edʿā-ye walāyat mīkonī*, literally, "You lay claim to the governorate." At line 85, Karīm has mimicked the boy's inarticulate slow-witted response to a summons.

30. More obscure place-names. *Tāyerah Khosh* might be interpreted as "happy bird,"
Dalīzak perhaps as "little vestibule."

31. From the context, probably another place-name, so far defying further elucidation.

We said the prayer for the dead for the God-forgiven,

brought God-forgive-him,   105

tossed him bareheaded onto the bull,

and came

to the stream—to, to the houses at Tāyerah Khosh, when we got there

                his life's breath went into his chest and by

                Pūshtauah it reached his throat, it got stuck,

Behind the house it flew away.[32]

We said, "As for martyrs, he's a martyr, look and see whether he reached

                the highest level or a lower one."   110

When we opened the book of our fathers' Mongol lineage, »

    starting from *"aleyf,"*[33] *anānah, enenī, ondūr,* »

        "bī," banānah, bānenī, bondūr, »

        "tī," tanānah, tānenī, tondūr, »

        up to *"kāf," kānah, kannah, kūn,* »   115

    we read two prostrations' worth

for it is written in Shi'a,[34] *"Lāyakhsaleho ma'asob* for burials in the earth,"

---

32. This passage is somewhat unclear, but suggests that the martyr expired on reaching the house. This seems to contradict what went before, when they recited the prayer for the dead before moving him.

33. The Mongol pretends to be literate for the mulla, imitating reading from an alphabetized document. Both the individual speaker and the assertion that there are holy books in the Mongol language are satirized. This alphabetical recitation mimics the drill by which beginning school children learn to read the written (long) and unwritten (short) vowels in positions relative to written consonants. (See discussion below.) *Alef*, the first letter of the Arabic alphabet, is followed by nonsense words illustrating different vocalizations with that initial; likewise the letters *bī* and *tī*. *Tondūr*, the last rhyme word in *tī*, is a village dialect pronunciation of the word for bread oven. Under the letter *kāf, kānah* is a literary term (not common in everyday speech) for buttocks, with other meanings including "hypocrisy," *kannah* is the common word for louse, *kūn*, the common and impolite term for anus or backside. In this parody of a schoolroom drill, the speaker reveals that he has only the tiniest exposure to literacy, and the obscene content further insults the idea of Mongol "religious books." Given the importance of sound to the sense/nonsense patterns of this joke, an explanation seems more useful than a translation. "Two prostrations' worth," at line 116, implies that these recitations are being used as a prayer. Muslim devotional prayer involves a sequence of standing, bowing, and prostration coordinated with different recited verses.

34. The speaker, a Sunni Muslim, attributes Shiism to his Mongol target, and adds a (as yet undeciphered) bit of "Arabic." The speaker appears to be conflating one low-status minority group, the Mongol, with another, the Shi'a Muslim Hazārā who occupy the central mountain areas. Schurmann (1962:248) found all the inhabitants of Ghūrāt province, including the remaining Mongol population, to be Sunni. The Hazārā, who occupy neighboring mountain areas farther east, are predominantly Shi'a. Schurmann lists three Mongol villages in the district of Pashtūn Zarghūn (which Schurmann transliterates as *Pusht-e Zirghan*),

it indicated a description of that prayer in the Arabic tongue,
and so, unwashed, unbrushed,[35] »

> with a basket on his head, all dressed, »   120
> with his shoe-thongs tied
> and his leggings wound on,[36] »
> we put God-forgive-him underground.

With a flag at his feet, and the earth all nicely arranged over him,
Saturday nights and Tuesday nights,   125
we bring some kindling and some brush and thorn and light it and
                     make lawful requests to God-forgive-him.[37]
We say, "Wherever someone dies, may God elevate him to the rank of
                     our brother Mulla Moslem, for he's a martyr."
There was a relative of ours, who keeps insisting, 'He's no martyr.' »
What do you say?"
The mulla said, "Well, if he's gone to the Abode of Submission, still he
                     has no more moral superiority than a dog."   130

[*Audience laughs*]

He said, "What reason is, there, Ākhond, sir, to speak profanely of
                     our dead? »

---

where this story was recorded. Schurmann concluded that these were fairly recent migrants, not fully assimilated and predominantly employed as landless agricultural laborers (pp. 165, 172, 380, and 397). Schurmann's data suggest that they too would be Sunni, not Shi'a. Sunni-Shi'a tensions waxed and waned in the Herat area (see the Ākhond's personal experience narrative in chapter 11), the most tense period in recent memory being the early 1960s, when Sunni-Shi'a riots occurred in Herat City. The untranslated phrase is either a distortion of an actual Arabic phrase or a nonsense imitation of one.

35. A loose translation of the Persian, *nāshū, nārū*, where *nāshū* means "unwashed," but *nārū* ("un-faced") is a doublet word (the "Henny Penny" phenomenon, Dundes 1974). The next eight lines continue initial alliteration in several more pairs of words, which could not be duplicated in translation.

36. Muslim dead are ordinarily washed and wrapped in plain white shrouds for burial, not dressed in the clothes of the living, but martyrs can be buried in the clothes in which they died, still bloody from their wounds, as they are considered purified by the manner of their death. The specifics of dress here extend the ridicule of Mongols' hickish ways: the nomad-style shoes called *chāroq* are made of one concave piece of shaped leather, lashed on with thongs over the instep. Leggings are wrapped around the calves to protect the wearer from thorns while walking in uncultivated land.

37. Line 126 is a jibe at a wide variety of votive activities directed to saints at their gravesites in folk Islam, activities often criticized by clergy and those laity with more precise knowledge of orthodox doctrine. From this point of view, "lawful requests" (an oblique reference to eschewed opportunities for black magic) is itself comic, since in the eyes of the orthodox, *any* pleas for special intervention show deficiencies in faith and insufficient reliance on God's will and plan. Of the two nights mentioned for votive activities, Tuesday in particular is preferred in folk practice for petitioning *parī*, the nonsacred supernaturals (the word *parī* is cognate to English "fairy"). (Cf. chapter 6.)

You might as well doubt our Mongolness, with all the signs
of Mongolness present and manifest, »
the baggy eyes and squished-up nose »
and bushy beard and sawed-off height.[38]
Those are the signs of Mongol lineage.   135
We have our paternal lineage at hand, the Arbābdellā tribe,
and our original paternal residence at Nīlī and Zīrnī, »
and presently we're in Zamānābād.
What's your reason, for if my brother is no martyr, we're no
Mongols." »
He said, "Fine, [*laughs*] he's a Mongol martyr."   140
He gave him a decree, sir, a document.
It said, "If a Mongol is an angel, he's no good, »
if his name is written in gold, it's no good.
Don't take so much as a head of grain from the Mongols'
harvest,[39] »
because no matter who sows Mongol seed, it's no good."   145

So he gave him this decree, sir, [*laughs*] and he came back and gave his
kin their answer!

‹›

M: Is it finished?
K: Yeah, it's finished, sir."
[*Recording interrupted.*]

---

38. Another section of comic rhymed prose in this sentence. Dogs are considered unclean in Islam; hence, the ākhond's remark at l. 130 is a pointed insult. The "Abode of Submission" is the afterlife.
39. The village mulla, along with certain other specialists serving the whole village, is
entitled to a share of the annual harvest, which he collects by visiting the threshing floors of
individual farmers at harvest time.

From Interview to Story: Hicks and Sophisticates

Coming as it did, during the first two weeks of my fieldwork, this story-telling session reflects some procedures being tried out in this initial survey phase of my work but subsequently dropped as being awkward and unproductive. Yet the awkwardness of the question strategy and the occasional unease of Mokhtār, who conducted the interviews, were very important to the power relations established in this storytelling session, and in many ways, power relations were what this story session was about. Some observations concerning the particular inappropriateness of our conversational strategy, and the effect of that inappropriateness on the evening's conversations, are therefore germane to the analysis of the story performances themselves. Our awkwardness in these conversational transactions gave the storytellers greater control over the proceedings than they might have had in interaction with more skilled and experienced listeners. Audience reaction, whether sophisticated or not, becomes part of the performance to the degree that the storyteller, in turn, reacts to it. Privately sponsored storytelling lends itself to complex interactions among performers and audiences who know one another.[1] We as strangers entered a community in which the performers and the rest of the audience had long-standing acquaintances and complex relationships of which we were barely aware but which nonetheless shaped the performance.

From an outsider's viewpoint, a short biographical interview with each storyteller seemed a logical place for me, as a stranger and researcher, to start a conversation, but turned out to be quite anomalous in Afghan social context. In a conversational exchange between new acquaintances or acquaintances who see each other only intermittently, I later learned, direct questions requesting substantial information are avoided, at least in the initial stages of conversation, with the understanding that information necessary to any particular matter at hand will be volunteered or more circumspectly solicited, later in the exchange. Initial conversation in polite company usually takes the form of general inquiries after the health and well-being of the addressee and his or her family, and expressions of pleasure at having the opportunity to meet. More specific topics (e.g., daily happenings and news of mutual friends) are then explored, eventually

---

1. Susan Slyomovics's *The Merchant of Art* (1987) perceptively examines such relationships in the performances of an Egyptian Bani Hilal epic poet.

arriving at the purpose of this particular meeting, if any. When strangers meet through the mediation of a third party known to both, the third party will supply information to each about the other, either in advance or sometimes in the presence of the person discussed. Thus, our interview questions were more like official interrogation than social conversation.

Beyond the matter of direct questioning, a further aspect of etiquette affecting research strategy is a tendency in Afghan conversations to avoid the use of given names. Individuals may be addressed in conversation by a title: in the case of these two storytellers, "Ākhond Sā'eb" ("Mr. Ākhond" or "Ākhond, sir,") and "Khalīfah" ("master" or "representative," the title given to a variety of skilled craftsmen, such as Karīm the mason, here addressed). In the family or among close acquaintances, adults are normally addressed by epithets referring to their eldest living son (or daughter if there are no sons), "father-of-X" or "mother-of-X." When answering the door or the telephone, one is expected to be able to recognize acquaintances by voice (typical exchange in answer to an acquaintance's knock on a house door: "Who's that?" "It's I—" "Oh— [*opens door*] welcome, hello."). Personal names are not usually volunteered. A direct request for a given name, such as opens this interview, and further direct queries about personal history, family composition, and so on are therefore awkward by Afghan social conversational standards and put the exchange still more in the tone of an official interrogation, as in a government office. Thus, later in the interview (l. 61), Mokhtār asks pardon before he puts direct questions about the composition of Karīm's family. Certainly in comparison to American conversational etiquette, Afghan conversation employs a great deal of obliqueness and indirection, in referential as well as conative functions (cf. Beeman 1986 on public and private communicative dimensions in Iranian Persian).

Other aspects of respect relationships emerge, in fact are negotiated, in the course of this first extended exchange between Karīm, the less prestigious of the two storytellers, and Mokhtār, the interviewer (and, by implication, with myself for whom he acts as spokesperson). These negotiations take place not through anomalous conversational structures, but in subtle word choice of an idiomatic nature. For instance, as the interview progresses, Mokhtār, the interlocutor, uses the polite form of address, *sā'eb* ("sir"), more sparingly in conjunction with the interviewee's title and almost exclusively when taking control of the conversational floor to change the topic of conversation. By contrast, both the Ākhond and the mason liberally salt their responses to him throughout the evening with the polite vocative, sir. The overall effect is an asymmetry of respect terms, the storytellers showing more deference, in this conversational dimension, than their interlocutor. The storytellers maintain this measure of deference toward Mokhtār, a stranger and the guest of the subgovernor, even in the course of informal teasing and banter addressed to each other as the evening draws on. Mokhtār tends to use the respect terms to render his controlling moves less peremptory. In both usages, deference and polite control, *sā'eb* has phatic force as a request for solidarity with the addressee.

Yet at the same time, the interview questions allow for no reciprocity in information exchange. No information is requested or volunteered about Mokhtār's identity or profession. My identity as an American and at least my general purpose ("to make a book about Afghan stories") were known to the group through discussion prior to this interview, but in general, the flow of information and respectful address was one-directional, adding to the asymmetry of power and deference visible in other dimensions of the conversation. Partly on the basis of this experience in which power relations were more visibly at issue than in the three other recording sessions I had experienced hitherto, I later tried to develop strategies to avoid placing a general biographical inquiry at the beginning of any exchange but, instead, to incorporate such information-gathering in looser form, into conversations between stories.

Explicit interview-style information-gathering, as done here, established or enhanced nominal social dominance for the interlocutor (me or, in this stage, an assistant), while it temporarily shifted the tenor of the conversation from entertainment to interrogation. Yet in Afghanistan, traditional storytelling for entertainment can be construed as a form of hospitality, to amuse a guest, and was so described by some storytellers and hosts in the course of our conversations. Hospitality in general is a social good, the offering of which is a matter of pride for all Afghan adults, regardless of wealth or social status. Hospitality can be and frequently is played off against hierarchical relationships, allowing the weak a certain leverage over the strong. In this early session, the storytellers also had the advantage of fluency in a rhetoric which was unfamiliar both to me and, at a different level, to my government-educated research assistant and our host.

As my experience as guest and researcher accumulated, beginning within two or three weeks of this event, as soon as I could converse without an assistant, I sought to enhance the entertainment-hospitality tenor of my visits by moving as much as possible from official to informal contact networks, mediated by helpful acquaintances rather than government officials. I also tried to informalize biographical information-gathering from storytellers with somewhat mixed results. My inquisitiveness must always have seemed peremptory compared to the normally more indirect flow of personal information in everyday life. For this and all question-and-answer exchanges, it is well to remember Charles Briggs's general observation on interviewing:

> Interviewees interpret the meaning of both the past and the present, including the interview itself. Each query presents them with the task of searching through their memories to see which recollections bear on the question and then fitting this information into a form that will be seen as answering the question. (Briggs 1986:14)

This process of deciphering (one might say, deciding) the interviewer's informational needs and responding appropriately might seem straightforward enough, but can hardly be so when major discrepancies exist between the cultural knowledge bases and conversational etiquettes of the persons who interact in the interview, as in the present case.

In this interview, Khalīfah Karīm, questioned about his usual story audience, expresses a preference for male age-mates throughout his storytelling career. He also takes the opportunity to assert the superior wisdom of elders like himself. The then-present, all-male audience (numbering up to fifteen people, usually ten or twelve) was of mixed ages from about twelve years old upward, no doubt assembled partly due to the curiosity factor of the presence of a foreign woman, unveiled, with tape recorder and camera. Karīm's stated preference for the company of village "learned people" and those interested in Sufism (Islamic mysticism) is noteworthy in light of various themes which emerge in the storytelling session and is borne out by the friendly informality prevailing between himself and the Ākhond, who was by his own evidence well-read in Sufi as well as other Persian literature. Karīm's mention of "official people" (l. 20) may be a bow to present company but also recalls the tradition of court patronage for poetry, music, and other forms of entertainment in the heyday of the Muslim city-states, of which Herat was, at intervals, an important example.

Asked only about stories and tales (*qessah wo ausānah*), the Khalīfah associates several verbal genres with entertainment gatherings: *qessah* (stories), jokes (*mazāq*), and *khāndan* (literary *khwāndan*), a term whose total semantic field encompasses singing of various kinds of verse, plus recitation or reading aloud from written sources, plus silent reading. The entertainment-gathering context to which Karīm here refers favors the first meaning. In my experience, Herati notions of entertainment, public or domestic, often favored mixed genres, with prose narrative or folk dramas (or the stage dramas in the small vaudeville houses found in a few large cities) alternating with vocal or other music according to what talent was available. Indian popular cinema, very well liked in Afghanistan, offers a similar mix of story and song.

Given the many differences among regional dialects, even delegating the interview process to a native speaker of Herat City dialect did not enable me to avoid ambiguities and misconstructions of questions, though sometimes the misconstructions yielded more interesting information than was sought in the original question. One example is the misunderstanding between Mokhtār and Karīm on the question of "occupation" (*wazīfah*, in literary Persian, "duty, function," ll. 35–40). The term refers to profession or type of gainful employment in present Afghan urban contexts, but in village dialects of the Herat area, especially for older speakers, it can also refer to the reading and study of religious subjects for private self-improvement. Coming from the previous topic, in which he identified traditional elders interested in religious topics among his preferred storytelling companions, Karīm understood *wazīfah* in the latter sense but denied any claim to erudite activities, beyond the oral exchange of sung poetry (which might include mystical poetry), stories and jokes. The fact that he was willing to claim these activities as *wazīfah* confirms that he had some reputation as a raconteur. While storytelling was not a paid activity in the Herat area at this time, nor ever a prestigious activity, good storytellers' abilities were enjoyed and praised.[2]

Mokhtār, working from a rudimentary list of questions or topics we had developed to guide initial interviews, turned the slightly stiff exchange about the composition of Karīm's family in a more bantering direction by asking Karīm if he was pleased with his sons-in-law. As Karīm's response indicates, expectations for tension between the bride's parents and the groom were a cliché in popular thought and articulated through the issue of distribution of property. A more general, emotional resistance to giving women in marriage is indicated by the subject matter of chapter 15, "The

---

2. I compensated storytellers with whom I worked at any length, for their time. On being offered money, several elderly master raconteurs remarked with surprise that they had never before been paid to tell stories.

Destruction of the City of Rūm." On the matter of property, under Islamic law a daughter is entitled to half the inheritance of a son, but in some Muslim communities, the dowry furnished by her family when a girl marries is regarded as her share of family property, and she receives nothing further when her parents die, unless male heirs are lacking. In Herat, daughters did receive a share in family property, but the degree of adherence to the Qur'anic injunction varied among families. Sons often continued to farm their father's property collectively, sharing the produce among themselves and to varying extents with any sisters resident nearby, leaving the problem of actual division of the inherited land to a subsequent generation, at such time as joint farming arrangements would break down. A preference for cousin-marriage further encouraged corporate management of family property and added to the intricacy of the inheritance picture.

As in the case of Karīm's two marriages, multiple marriage was more likely to be due to the death of a spouse, rather than simultaneous polygyny, among Afghans of ordinary means. Wives contribute not only progeny but also essential services to the household, but despite the importance of the wife in the domestic economy, multiple wives in Afghanistan at this time were primarily the prerogative of wealthier men.[3] In this interview, the Ākhond steps in with comments about Karīm's second wife's youth and her family, partly teasing (and Karīm will respond regarding the Ākhond's marital history, when the topic comes up in his own interview) and partly as traditionally polite third-party information-sharing (see above) and oral witnessing in this predominantly nonliterate society, for which written contracts are a decidedly secondary form of record. The Ākhond as a community member may have been present at the wedding, but would in any case have been informed of it through normal information channels. The Ākhond's earlier humorous interjection, "sons-in-law have the nature of cats," also served to mitigate the awkward directness of the interview questions by generalizing the issue. Karīm readily picked up the more depersonalized tone the Ākhond established, expanding on his remark with several proverblike generalizations about the predatory nature of sons-in-law (ll. 74–79). Mokhtār attempted on my behalf to elicit personal

---

3. Two-wife households did occur among less wealthy families. An elderly or frail woman might encourage her husband to remarry, might even help recruit a co-wife, to help her with the household work, or a man might marry his brother's widow, to keep her together with her minor children, who normally become wards of their father's family, and keep her and her minor children's inheritance under family control. If able to finance the necessary payments for the bride's family and for the wedding ceremony, a man would remarry as promptly as possible after being widowed. Young widows without adult male children also remarried if possible.

expressions of traditional values from the interviewees by asking personal questions. The two men used aphoristic generalizations to turn the conversation away from personal interrogation, in keeping with the general etiquette of conversational indirectness in public.

Choosing and Introducing a Story

After this exchange, the momentum of the interview-conversation slackened, and following a pause to check the tape recorder, Mokhtār turned to the Khalīfah for a story. The Khalīfah, as the less prestigious of the two men, was called upon to speak first both as interviewee and as performer. Storytelling for entertainment, while it is greatly enjoyed, is not a prestigious activity. It is considered a pastime (sāʿattīrī) best reserved for relieving the tedium of travel or for times when productive work is impossible, such as evenings after dark, and especially winter days and evenings, when agricultural work is slack. According to a common folk saying, storytelling during daylight hours when productive work is or should be afoot "causes confusion" (sargardūnī dāra).[4] Fictional folktales (ausānah, literary afsānah) in particular are characterized as lies in the rhymed formulas storytellers often use to introduce an entertainment narrative. (The use of opening and closing formulas and their relation to the informational or didactic status or ascribed truth value of different kinds of narrative will be further discussed with reference to the Ākhond's storytelling in chapters 8 and 10.)

At this beginning point, Mokhtār opened the topic, as we two had planned, with some questions about the story, its title or subject and its source. This assumption or retention of the conversational initiative by an audience member during the lead-in to a story was awkward in the frame of normal Afghan conversational storytelling. The subject of the queries was also odd: genealogies for fictional stories, though of interest to folklorists concerned with transmission patterns and processes, are not normally of much concern to storytellers. For them, stories tend to enter a conversation by topical associations either to previous stories or to other conversational subjects which are on the floor.[5] That associative process, as

---

4. Hafizullah Baghban quoted a more colorful folk admonition, "If you tell stories during the day, your ass will grow teeth." (Cited in English in Baghban 1980.)

5. My goal in asking about the source of a story at this point in the research was as much (or more) to discover whether people did consider sources a remembrance-worthy kind of information, as it was to ascertain actual story sources, if any were recalled. In general, storytellers, whether or not they were themselves literate, could readily and accurately identify a

revealed in the series of stories told by the Ākhond and the mason, is of primary interest in this analysis. At the beginning of this session, however, the mason had the task of choosing and initiating a story in the context of a rather eccentric conversation, the flow of which had not developed in a normal way.

Asked for a name for the story, Karīm offered a précis instead, a common response to such a request. Narrators often did not supply titles as such for their short narratives, but rather characterized them by reference to one or more ideas or events within them. This tendency to identify a story by a selection of content features is in harmony with the process of conversational association whereby a given story may be relevant in a variety of conversational situations, and a gifted narrator may recall, and choose among, a number of potentially relevant narratives at any given performance opportunity. What a story is "about" depends at least in part on immediate conversational context.

Karīm identifies the story as being about the odd speech habits of a numerically small, low-status local ethnic minority, the Mongols (*moghol*). There are more than twenty distinct languages spoken in Afghanistan, plus various dialects (Wilber et al. 1962: vi, 1, 81–88). Pashto and Darī (Afghan Persian), are the official national languages, both of the Iranian branch of Indo-European. Dari speakers predominate in the Herat area. Languages identified by Heratis as spoken in the area include Pashto, Baluchi, Chahar Aimak dialects (languages of Iranian origin with substantial Turkic content), at least two Turkic languages (Turkoman and the language of the immigrants from Merv, which they designate as Turki), and (at this writing perhaps) Mongolian, by a small remnant of elderly speakers (cf. Wilber et al. 1962, Smith et al. 1973, and Schurmann 1962). Speakers of minority languages, especially males, often speak one of the national languages as well. Regional dialect differences in both the national languages are marked and remarked upon.

While the story with which Karīm chose to begin makes no overt ref-

---

story as either having a literary analogue or not. Some storytellers could also identify by name individuals from whom they had learned particular stories or whom they considered general models for their own storytelling, and so asking this question was sometimes productive of extended reminiscences about their relationships with other storytellers, but not usually so at such an early stage of acquaintance. Even when I tried to frame it in nonleading ways, such a question could also elicit flights of fiction: so queried, one of my primary informants named invented source-persons for several stories which were her own compositions. Only after several months of working together did she confide that certain stories were her own creations.

erence to the content of the conversation immediately preceding it, his choice of a dialect joke for his first effort focuses humorous attention on difficulties of speech and weird accents, well represented in the present context by myself. Certain of the story's features can also be seen to establish a ground for the story sequence which follows. Karīm chose a humorous story with an ironic relationship to the constitution of the conversational group, and indeed, humor and various kinds of ironic self-reference were strong through the whole storytelling session. The predominant type of humor in "Mulla Mongol the Martyr," the *blason populaire*, or ethnic joke, plays upon local dialects of Persian and other cultural features to build up a local stereotype of the ignorant countryman, in this case a member of the Mongol minority group. The Mongols, small tenant farmers living in villages remote from the urban center, are a common object of ethnic humor in the Herat area. The mason, himself a village-dweller, draws for the benefit of visiting city folk a comical picture of someone more rustic than himself. In the process he makes claim to sophistication in common with the urbanites, relative to Mongols; but at the same time, by focusing on language incompetence, his performance may also be an oblique joke on the so-called sophisticated foreigner(s).

In line with the theme of rustic foolishness, Mongol ways are here lampooned with particular reference to folk religious practice, the veneration of local saints. The Mongol's plea for his "saintly" dead brother is contrasted with the somewhat exasperated orthodoxy of the non-Mongol religious leader. The mulla hears the Mongol's story of his brother's death and furnishes him with an insulting decree which the Mongol cannot read. The Mongol is too ignorant even to grasp the insult inscribed in it.

The humor of the exchange in which the ākhond in the story presents the Mongol with an insulting document he cannot read has already been set up in the phase of their conversation when the Mongol, explaining his claim to the ākhond, imitates himself and his relatives reading from their "ancestral book" the directions for burying their "martyr" (ll. 111–15). The recitation of alphabetized nonsense syllables, resolving into obscenity, parodies the phonetic drills which mullas use for basic literacy instruction in traditional Qurʿanic schools.[6] Short vowels are not written in Arabic or Persian. The nonsense syllable drill familiarizes the young readers with the short (unwritten) and long (written) vocalic possibilities, $a, \bar{a}, e, \bar{\imath}, o, \bar{u}$,

---

6. I am indebted to Dr. Hamid Dabashi for this observation (personal communication, November 1986).

while simultaneously drilling them in the alphabetic sequence (*alef, bī,* etc.). In this portrayal, the Mongol, trying to impress the mulla with the traditional erudition and piety of his people, reveals that he has been only minimally exposed to the very first levels of traditional literacy instruction and suggests that Mongols treat literacy primers as sacred books.

In the process of this juxtaposition, Karīm's story asserts a distinction between "true," learned clerical piety and "folk" (ethnic Mongol, or "hick") religion and simultaneously constitutes an indirect compliment to the Ākhond who is present and establishes the storyteller as not a hick, in contrast to his subject (and thus, potentially in some kind of solidarity with his nonhick audience as well). Yet at the same time, the ranking member of the audience, who has arranged for the storytelling session, is an avowed atheist (as his behavior later in our visit illustrated; see chapter 16), a Marxist for whom all religious knowledge and authority deriving from it are false. Karīm's portrayal of an ākhond as the proper arbiter of superstition and knowledge is one that conflicts with the subgovernor's publicly demonstrated views. The solidarity which ethnic humor might promote between a storyteller and an audience, both desirous of proclaiming themselves not hicks, is undermined in this case by the difference in religiopolitical views between performer and performance-sponsor, just as the choice of comic subjects who "talk funny" resonated with my odd attempts at spoken Persian. The storyteller's offered solidarity, as one nonhick to another, is not unequivocal.

Furthermore, the humor directed toward Mongols, a very small remnant population not widely known outside Herat province, is regional and somewhat esoteric. Outsiders from Kabul would not necessarily be aware, for instance, that Mongols are known in the Herat area as makers and sellers of charcoal. Hence, they would miss a joke implicit in the type of service which the soon-to-be-martyred elder brother undertakes to honor his dead father. The collection of firewood is the first laborious step in the production of charcoal to cook the funeral feast.

Hafizullah Baghban (1977, 2:284–85), commenting in some detail on Mongols as an object of humor in the Magadi folk theater of the Herat region, noted that the clown-actors imitated Mongol speech as a separate language, rendered as formulaic nonsense syllables, rather than as a dialect of Afghan Persian (Darī). Karīm the Mason handles "Mongol" speech as a kind of Persian, rendered humorous by the inclusion of "Mongol" pronunciation of common words, and of words stereotypic of Mongol dialect *and* culture (e.g., l. 74, pronouncing as *beyghah,* a term extant but uncommon in standard Darī, *boqqa*, to describe the ungelded bulls which Mongols are said to favor as riding mounts). The esoterica thicken, as the younger brother tells his story to an ākhond using a few apparent dialect terms (*tīrzad* wood, ll. 73, 76) and a number of apparent place-names ("apparent" because two Herati auditors of the tape of the story, plus assorted Persian-speakers from Kabul and elsewhere, all declared themselves confused by the terms to varying degrees, were unable to explain their morphology, and interpreted them in different ways).

Disorientation among listeners was further provoked by the younger brother's tendency in two speeches referring to his brother's martyrdom to invert the expected comparison between the brother and other local "martyrs" ("the dead, you could say, he reached the rank of my brother, that he died a martyr," ll. 49–50), and addressing the mulla, "we say, 'Wherever someone dies, may God elevate him to the rank of our brother Mulla Moslem, for he's a martyr.' " (l. 127). Persian-speaking auditors of the tape have considered the storyteller himself to be confused at these points, but it seems more likely that the storyteller was portraying some sort of syntactic peculiarity in "Mongol" dialect or naive incoherency on the part of the character, since no such confusion about the issue of the "martyr" brother's status occurs, except in reported speech by the younger brother.

Taken together, the superimposition of "Mongol" accent, lexical oddities, possibly syntactical ones as well, and esoteric local color in Karīm's portrayal of the "Mongol" is a tour de force of local ethnic humor, but somewhat lost on the visitors (Mokhtār and the subgovernor, to say nothing of myself) for whom mere comprehension of some events of the story was a problem leading to confusion about the overall structure of the story and its "point." Hafizullah Baghban observed how the "utter strangeness" of incomprehensible language became an object of humor in the folk farce of this region but also found that the level of laughter at these nonsensical portrayals of the "other" was lower than at other types of jokes (Baghban 1977, 2:286, 289). In the present case, the outsider status of some principal listeners is a further obstacle to the success of dialect humor. At the end of the story, Mokhtār asks Karīm, "Is it over?" an indication that some aspects of narrative confusion, intentional or not, left him uncertain whether or not he had just heard the punch line, which would normally be discernible by a combination of a storyteller's pitch, rhythm, and other paralinguistic and kinesic patterns as well as more or less obvious closure with regard to content (either simply a punch line, as here, or perhaps a moral tag, summary statement, or closing formula, depending on the narrative genre and individual rhetorical strategy).

Though it may be safe to assume that this story, like other examples of ethnic humor, works to build solildarity among teller and listeners by lampooning the "otherness" of some third group, it is also possible that the teller perceived either in advance (perhaps) or in the course of performance (quite likely) that key outsider members of the audience were not well-equipped to grasp the fine points of the joke, in fact, were only half-getting it. With some others in the audience who could appreciate this performance as the tour de force that it was in the frame of local stereotypes, (especially the Ākhond, himself an accomplished raconteur in the same local tradition), the performer-audience relationship emerging in this first performance remains problematical. To what degree, one could ask, might the storyteller be pleased by the fact that an alien, atheist authority figure and his clients would have to choose among responses to the telling which would either reveal that they did not see the humor of the joke (though others in the group clearly did) or else express a generalized willingness to be amused, despite their inability to conceal some significant gaps in comprehension and their known disagreement with standards of social and intellectual legitimacy advocated through the portrayal of the ākhond in the story? While the offering of a dialect joke provides some clear opportunities for expressions of solidarity between this teller and his alien audience, it also provides a frame for a subtle test of the powerful but alien listeners' sportsmanship, their inclination to collude with the storyteller for the production of a lively performance, and ultimately, their willingness to be measured by the storyteller's own standards of wit and perception.

Mokhtār, in asking the storyteller to identify the end of the story, risked loss of face by admitting he had missed the nuances of a joke. Mokhtār's attempt to disambiguate (from his point of view) the end of the story was not, however, simply for his own comprehension. Here as elsewhere, the exigencies of my presence and recording activities affected the flow of conversational exchange. If native speakers of Afghan Persian (both Mokhtār and five subsequent auditors of the tape) had difficulty sorting out the fine points of this story, I was almost completely lost, not yet even familiar with the Herat village dialect in which Karīm himself narrated, the locally familiar background to the dialect humor. I comprehended perhaps ten percent of this narrative, taking my cue from others to laugh (a little late) at the funniest parts and striving to communicate my interest through an intent listening attitude which would not impede narrative flow. Technical difficulties with recording distracted me, complicating the matter somewhat.

Other aspects of local, "modernizing" culture were in subtle conflict with conditions I wanted to establish for recording. On the one hand, cassette tape recorders were by then a familiar item in the local culture, especially the subculture of younger men, who favored portable radio-cassette recorder combinations with shortwave capability. Young men carried their recorders around to social gatherings to play music tapes or the radio, and sometimes to record choice bits of the goings-on, if a musician or gifted storyteller were present. At public concerts, a veritable thicket of recorders, each with its microphone suspended from the radio aerial, would spring up in front of the musicians on the stage, as a number of audience members recorded the concert to take home. Recording was, however, very item-centered, in the sense that a story or song would be recorded and the machine then turned off during subsequent conversation, to be turned on again when performance resumed. My desire to record the intervening conversations at these events was thus not easily understood. The cost of batteries made continuous recording extremely extravagant by local standards. Additionally, conversation, even when not confidential or topically sensitive, was not a culturally appropriate object for recording, whereas a story performance might be.[7]

On this evening, just beginning my fieldwork, I was in any case taking cues on recording etiquette from my research assistant, who shared the prevailing item-centered concept of recording and who made it a point to tell me when to turn the tape recorder off. It is unfortunate for present analytic purposes that I was only able to ignore his cues on a couple of occasions during this sequence of stories. Mokhtār was assiduous to identify the end of the story for what he conceived to be my purposes, knowing how little I understood, and not fully informed of my ultimate goal of understanding the way stories are embedded and used in conversation.

---

7. A few storytellers who made the most overt claims to performative artistry preferred that their speech not be recorded unless it was a full-blown performance, as they understood it. One in particular refused over a six-month period to allow me to record our conversations about his life or his comments about stories and storytelling. I finally succeeded in pleading a severely impaired memory and the difficulties of rapid note-taking (in which I was perpetually engaged during interviews and performances once my grasp of local dialect improved) to persuade him to allow me to record some of our between-story talks. When he finally did consent to informal recording, some self-censorship was apparent relative to earlier conversations on the same topics.

Paradoxically, however, my lack of language skills and inability to participate actively in the conversation allowed the story exchange to develop in ways that it likely would not have, had I been capable of more active participation. The storytellers quickly understood that I was hardly a competent listener, and they addressed their performances more specifically to Mokhtār and their host, who presumably were competent listeners, and to each other, more or less ignoring the problem of my lack of comprehension. In any case, there was little they could do about it without extreme disruption of the story performances, and fortunately they showed no desire or capacity to turn the event into an elaborate language lesson. In his second story, Karīm turned away from the esoterica of local dialect humor, which in any case had enjoyed only problematical success with Mokhtār, to another example of ethnic humor, less reliant on dialect obscurities but directed primarily at the supposed sexual and social naîveté of the women of another group of local "hicks," the Sarhadī.

4. Khalīfah Karīm, "Rasūl's Mother"[1]

Uhh—there were some little old ladies sitting around— »
    dames have these sessions a <u>lot</u> when they haven't any work to do,
    or anything to worry about.
Some of them were sitting and talking,
these adult women, there were several of them   5
and with them there was this one—uh—girl, that is, kind sir,
    she was about at that age, too.
They were giving each other counsel and advice,
they had just gotten this little girl
engaged, and she asked this one old woman,   10
    "Uh, that is, how does it go, in the world,
    this 'housekeeping' business,[2]
    Uh—what are its difficulties, what are its duties, or its troubles?
    Describe it to me so I can get my heart up for when I go."
◇
[*Mokhtār*: Yes. (*barely audible*)]   15
The old woman said to her, "Dear lamb,[3]"—she was Sarhadī, from
                        toward Tūgeyshtūn,
    they have a different speech,
she said, "Lamb, it was the one time, and it passed on its way, anyway,
                    so don't bother me now,

---

1. The title was supplied by the storyteller in an untaped conversation. The title is an appellation for the old lady, referred to, as customary, by the given name of her son; "Rasūl" is a generic masculine personal name in this context.

2. The girl uses a common euphemism to seek information on sexual relations, about which women are supposed to be completely ignorant prior to marriage.

3. With his pronunciation of this common epithet, the storyteller sets out to lampoon another local group. *Sarhadī*, "borderer," refers to inhabitants of the mountainous eastern hinterland of Herat province (cf. Schurmann, 1962:421).

I don't know anything," but finally she really kept after her,—
she said, "Well, I don't know about other people,   20
    about my <u>own</u> experiences
    I can tell you that." »
She said, "Tell me."
‹›

She said, "I had reached the age of eighteen or nineteen, I was just new
        and green⁴ like that, the veils of my 'pistachio' had started
        moustaches, my little seeds had started to swell.⁵
[*audience laughing*]
They came, (saying) 'We're giving you to your father's brother's son.'⁶   25
I said, 'If you want to give a gift, give it, but I'm just new and green,
                                    my stream—
    my field, like,—put it off a little longer, till I myself can understand,

    don't sell me off all at once,
    like green fruit,
    before I can get my heart up for it,' »
they said, 'All right.'   30
They set a period of six years,
till I was twenty-five."

—Those people call it "fabrics and stuff,"⁷—
"They came and loaded my father up with fabrics and stuff, »
                                                            35

---

4. *korpah*, "green, fresh, and crunchy," a term usually used for alfalfa or other green plants.

5. Euphemisms for signs of developing pubes and breasts.

6. First-cousin marriage is a preferred choice in traditional Afghan families, not only to reconsolidate extended-family economic interests, but also to protect the interests of the young bride, who is expected to be better treated if her in-laws are also close kin than if she were sent to live among nonkin. "Cousin" as a generic term for the children of one's parents' siblings does not have an equivalent in Persian but is used henceforth in this text in place of the more precise Persian terms, which distinguish father's brother's son, mother's brother's son, father's sister's son, and mother's sister's son.

7. *bodah o pārchah*: the expression was unfamiliar to two native speakers of Herati. The storyteller identifies this as a Sarhadī dialect term for the bridegoods furnished by the groom's family. Among the expected goods are as many suits of dresses and trousers for the girl as the boy's family can afford and the girl's family can negotiate—hence, the clothes-buying trip. Her terminology for clothing-buying at lines 36, "get (my) coverings" (*jel estūndah*), sounds quaint to Herati ears, as the storyteller's explanation (l. 38) indicates. Karīm is making a more concerted effort to reproduce dialect lexical differences here than in the character's speeches previous to this point, but he is also taking pains to gloss them, as he did not in the preceding story.

and my cousin went to Herat City to get my coverings.
And I've got my eye on the road, thinking 'When will he get here?' "
   —We say "to buy clothes," they say "to get coverings"—
"He went and
then someone brought the good news, 'Your cousin has come.'   40

I opened my eyes and there's a big bright spot coming from the
                          direction of Naushūwah, »
a noble young man, and I said, »
   'By the power of God,
   such a full-fruited date tree, off there all by itself?!'
   I gave thanks. »   45
He came, with a <u>full</u> pack on his back![8]
[*Mokhtār, querying dialect word*: What's 'darrak'? *Ākhond and second audience*
                    member:'Full—' (*por*)—say 'full'—]
A pack—his shoulder-pack.
It's on his shoulders.
So I said, 'Cousin!' »   50
He said, 'Yes?' »
I said, 'How you've <u>killed</u> yourself, bringing a <u>load</u> like this with no
               donkey, <u>ten</u> *man*[9] on your back, and for <u>what</u>?' »
He said, 'I did it for you, I didn't mind.' »
I said, 'Well done!'

Now when he put it down, I open my cousin's pack, a garden of
               red and white flowers, delicate weavings,
               I don't know if it's chintzes or cashmeres!   55
They have white flowers, and black stripes all through them.
‹›
So there was that.
He'd had a ring made for me at the smith's, I put it over my finger and it
             came up, and I put my hand into it and it went right
             up to my shoulder." [*Audience laughter*]

---

8. The word for the traditional backpack, *tobrah* (in dialect, sometimes *torbah*), was not generally used for the western-style hiking packs carried by western travelers. With reference to their packs, the tourists were sometimes scornfully referred to as **khānah ba dūsh**, "house-on-their backs," i.e., vagrants.

9. One *man* equals approximately 3 kilograms or 6.6 pounds.

He'd had a ring[10] made, that guy. [*Audience laughter. Ākhond comments*
                              (laughing):—from the blacksmith!]
"He went and got nice tin beads, red-, gold-, and silver-colored,
                              twenty-two of 'em on a string, »   60
and he put 'em around my neck, and how they're shinin'!
I said, 'Cousin!' »
He said, 'My soul!' »
  I said, 'You've made a desert out of the Kalātah Mardak market,[11] and
                    brought everything for me, what will the rest of
                    God's people find for themselves?'
[*Quiet laughter. Mokhtār:* Yeah—]
He said, 'Aw, cousin, don't worry, that Kalātah is so FUL-L-L of shops,
                              there's no saying!   65
          And every shop has ten bundles of goods laid out,
          Chests leaned up against the walls,
          Burning charcoal glowin' under their balls![12]
          They'd take a poor man's hand off at the shoulder, the bastards!'[13]
[*Ākhond comments, laughing:* Shopkeepers—he's talking about those
                              shopkeepers!]   70

[*Others, laughing:* Yes—]
"Well!
The next morning came, and they went and
did the slaughtering and brought this and that.
They brought sweet singers there.   75
They made a party and put me on a donkey and took me to my
                              cousin's house, »
      and it got to be dinner prayer time.
‹›

---

10. In line 58, the old lady's word for ring is *kachchah*, a term common among some nomad groups but not in Herat city dialect. In l. 59, Karīm glosses *kachchah* with the commoner Dari Persian term, *angoshtar*.

11. More local color.

12. A reference to the small charcoal braziers used for heat in shops or in rooms of houses during the cold season. One sits close by to feel the heat. For greater efficiency, a brazier is placed under a low table, which is then covered with a large quilt to concentrate the heat. Those sitting next to the table draw the quilt up over their legs, sitting partly under the table. The whole arrangement is called *sandalī* in Afghanistan or *korsī* in Iran.

13. *Godar mordah:* Hafizullah Baghban (private communication, October 1980) explained this epithet as equivalent to *pedar mordah*, literally "dead-father," implying that their fathers have died or should die for offenses against religion and ethics. More common epithets of the same general form are *pedar soxtah* ("burnt-father") and *pedar sag* ("dog-father"), all roughly equivalent to English "bastard," "son of a bitch." *Godar mordah* was not a common expression in Herati; other native-speaker auditors could not identify it.

On the road to the house[14] I said, »
　　'It's practically evening prayer time, where're you going, anyway?' »
They said, 'We're going to your cousin's.' »　　　　　　　　　　　　80
'Well,' I said, 'I'll go, too.'
It's just ignorance—after all, I'm only 26!" [*Audience snickers.*]
"They said, 'Sit down, girl, this is your cousin's house.' »
So I said, 'But this house belongs to So-and-So's son,' »
and they said, 'No, this <u>is</u> your house.'　　　　　　　　　　　　85
Well, I sat, anyway.
Everybody went off on their own,
I stayed in this <u>deserted</u> room, and whoops![15] here came my cousin.
He came and sat down.
Now when he sat down,　　　　　　　　　　　　　　　　　　90
　　I saw that he spread out the bedroll, and threw down the black felt
　　　　　　　　　　　　　　　　　　　　　　　rug, and
　　put his wrap[16] over it, and set out the roll-up,[17] too, and
　　fastened the door of the room, »
　　and came over to this side of the hearth and took me under the arms
　　　　　　　　　　　　　　　　　　　and picked me up.
I said, 'Cousin, how you're weighing me!?　　　　　　　　　　95
　　This is no butcher shop, that you bought me by weight, like meat!'
[*quiet laughter*]
He said, 'That's all right, I'm just playin', it's affection!' »
I said, 'Go ahead.'
He brought me to the bed, and laid my head down, and now he's
　　　　　　　　pushing himself against me and me against himself.
[*louder laughter*]
It seems to me like there's something nosing and poking me in the
　　　　　　　　　　　　middle and then pulling <u>back</u>. 100
[*still louder laughter*]
I said, 'Cousin—' »
He said, 'My soul—' »

———————

　　14. House, or *sarāī*, a walled dwelling type which in isolated rural areas can reach the proportions of a private fort.
　　15. *bābey!* short for *bābeylah!*—a mild interjection expressing surprise or shock at finding herself alone with him.
　　16. *mūshau*: Herati speakers were unfamiliar with this word, but it appears to refer to a garment belonging to her cousin, possibly his shawl. Bedding is normally laid out over floor-coverings, such as felt or woven rugs or reed matting. During the day, bedding is rolled up and placed against the wall as a backrest for sitting.
　　17. *Lūlak*, "rolled-up" or "roll-up" (noun), probably a bolster-type pillow, but as with *mūshau*, the term is not common in Herati.

I said, 'What are you doin' these sl(aps)—these unfriendly kicks with?
    Have you got <u>three</u> feet?'
[*laughter*]
He said, 'No-o . . . .'   105
He put his hand on my face, and I said, »
    'Take your hand away, remember your limits, »
    don't you have a mother or sisters?' [*Much background laughter*]
‹›
He said, 'I'm playing,' »
and I said, 'OK, if you think so.'—Just then he puts his hand on my
          'bragging place'[18] and I said, '<u>Ayy</u>!! For <u>God</u>'s sake,
          mind the mullas, fuck you!'   110
[*Loud, sustained laughter*]
‹›
So who can you tell it to?[19]
He got his hand on my trousers-tie, and he got out that [thing].[20]
I said [*loudly*], '<u>There</u>, now, motherless and sisterless!
[*audience laughter*]
    Ay, they'll stone you to death, you <u>bastard</u>[21]! You put your hand on
                someone's daughter's privates, didn't you!?'   115
[*Laughter*]
‹›

He said, 'I'm playin',' »
and I said, 'OK, if you think so, then.'
Well.
Now he doesn't sit on this side of me, he doesn't sit on that side of me,
he came and he's sittin' right in front of me.   120
He didn't squat flat-footed, he didn't sit cross-legged,
he knelt right down on his kneecaps.
‹›
[*Mokhtār, quietly*: Yeah . . .]
He comes slip-sliding along toward me.

---

18. *Lāf qal'ah*, literally, "bragging house"? euphemism for genitalia.
19. *Be ki bogūī*: i.e., complaints are futile.
20. *ālghomak*: the term, so far, eludes exact translation, but in context, "penis."
21. *go mordah*: perhaps for *gūh mordah*, literally, "dead shit," but that expression is not otherwise attested, and this is probably a contraction of *godar mordah* (see l. 69 and note 13, above).

I said, 'Cousin—' »   125
He said, 'Yes?'
I said, 'If you're going to relieve yourself, then the room door is <u>that</u> way.
[*muffled laughter*]
     Have you lost your way, you?
     Going up some kinda blind <u>alley</u> like this?'
He said, 'No, I have to come along like this—'   130
He came along on his bent knees, he comes along, the wrong way, like
        that, he came, falling on his hands and knees, and
       that wild mule[22] of his kicking, in that crazy way.
[*muffled laughter*]
Well, this one is completely crazy, now—
'<u>Where</u>'s the way to get through here!?
‹›
[*muffled laughter*]
The mosque door isn't here!
[*audience laughs*]
The don— the donkey door isn't here, the sheep-pen door isn't here! »   135
You bastard, where <u>are</u> you goin'?!!'
‹›
Well, my lord, I put out my hand and he's got a <u>big</u> 'bragging piece'[23]
           like that in his hand!
‹›
[*Speaker pauses for sustained audience laughter*]
‹›
A 'bragging piece' with a burnt head.
[*more laughter*]
I said, 'Cousin—' »
He said, 'What?' »   140
I said, 'How come you brought this big pine root[24] in the bed,
     you'll be tearin' the covers, now—' [*laughter*]
‹›
He said, 'This is no pine root,' »
I said 'What is it?' »

---

22. *gūr*: in classical Persian, "wild ass, onager."
23. *Lāfchah-e bolandī*: clearly a euphemism for "penis" in context. Cf. *lāf qalʿah* (l. 110 and note 18, above).
24. *rīshah-ye khanjakī: Khanjak* in Herati refers to a gnarled, resinous evergreen tree whose roots are harvested for fuel.

He said, 'Well, it's my prick,' »   145
I said, 'Ey, your prick in your ma's cunt!' [*laughter*]
'This is no prick,' I said, 'a rough old log as big as that!'
‹›
[*quieter laughter*]
I put my hand down further, and it's got a lovely batch of long hair on it,
[*laughter*]
this big thick thing!
I said, 'Whose herd did you get this lead goat from? Take it away,
                              wha'd' you want to bring the butchers in here for?!   150
‹›
Some nomad's three-year-old stud—' »
He said, 'This is no lead goat,' »
I said, 'What, then?' »
He said, 'It's my cock,' »
'Ey,' I said, 'Your cock in your ma's ass! [*laughter*]   155
‹›
What are you doing?!!'
‹›
I put my hand down lower, and there's this pair of round things
                              hanging down under its head.
[*laughter*]
I said, 'Now, you bastard potato-seller! Where are you bringing this
                              under here?!'
He said, 'That's my yard,' »
I said, 'Your yard in your dead father!²⁵ [*laughter*]   160
        You're just one person, what are you doin' with three pieces?!
                              You must—you—[*breathlessly*]
[*audience laughter*]
        —have you gotten to be some kind of big committee, with all
              these "legacies,"²⁶ you bastard?!!' [*laughter throughout*]
‹›
So who can you tell it to?
Yeah, he's gotten the head of it a little bit wet, and he's creeping,
                              sneaking up.
‹›
Yeah.   165

---

25. *go mordah* again: Cf. lines 69, 115, 136 ("bastard"), and notes 13 and 21.
26. In a patrilineal society, a euphemism for male genitalia.

<u>All</u> at once he grabbed me by the shoulder blades and <u>thump</u>ed himself
                     down so hard the <u>cracks</u> in my head were ringing! »
I said, 'You bastard, take it out, you're <u>strangling</u> me, for God's sake!!
[*laughter*]
        You're so <u>mer</u>ciless, you <u>bastard</u>!
        Why're you <u>killing</u> people, and you a <u>Muslim</u>?' »
Who can you tell it to?   170
He did it <u>three</u> more times.
‹›
[*quiet laughter*]
Now when he pulled it out, this skinned camel neck, »
I said, 'Go on, hold the seventh-day mourning ceremonies for your
                     father, call the mullas, then—
        You've gotten your hands on some free meat.'[27]
I didn't know.   175
The little kids had those skinny little pricks. »
I'd said, 'A person could "eat" a thousand of those a day and it
                              wouldn't matter.'
I didn't know that a prick is one thing and a cock is another and a
                                  yard is another.
All three of them get together, and it makes a committee big enough
                     to bring people's houses down in ruins—!'"
[*laughter*]
‹›
‹›
Mokhtār: It's finished?   180
[*End of tape*]

---

27. "Free meat" here refers only to his penis, not to her own body, despite earlier references (l. 95). This remark, a composite curse and insult, combines an implication that his father is dead (as in *pedar mordah*, see note 13) and an accusation of cheapness, that he would offer as alms something acquired at no cost to himself.

Hicks and Women

Karīm's second story, "Rasūl's Mother," is another example of ethnic humor, directed at another marginal local group, the Sarhadī (literally "borderers"), who inhabit foothills of the Hindu Kush range to the east and south of the Herat valley[1] and speak yet another local Persian (which Karīm in his portrayal distinguishes both lexically and in details of pronunciation from his own speech). As Roger Abrahams among others has observed (personal communication), ethnic stereotypes and ethnic humor tend to focus on the target group's practices with respect to food and sex and accuse the group of confusion of basic categories and disorderly behavior around these topics. On the basis of the last story (and many other examples from Afghanistan; cf. Canfield 1977), one could add death and religious practices to the basic list of topics for stereotype construction in this population. In the present case, Karīm turns his satirical attention to sexual foolishness, and in the course of the story, what begins as ethnic humor keyed, as in the first story, to peculiarities of language as well as custom, veers toward a more generalized lampoon of the sexual ignorance and backwardness of rural women but also displays the sexual potency of men, for whom the Sarhadī bridegroom stands as a representative.

It is worth bearing in mind that this tale, which vividly and comically portrays female dismay at male sexuality, is here presented to a predominantly male audience by a male storyteller who would customarily find his audience among men. Sexual humor would by no means be unusual in his normal performance settings, but it has an added *frisson* of interest in this case due to the anomalous presence of an unveiled, foreign woman. Exposure to European and American films and the arrival in Afghanistan in the 1960s and 1970s of large numbers of young European and American overland travelers, male and female, with openly expressed attraction for each other and for hashish and opiates convinced many in the Afghan population of the promiscuity of westerners. Various Afghan auditors of this series of stories, including Mokhtār, at the time of the performance, expressed surprise at their sexual frankness, despite the official presence at the

---

1. Cf. Schurmann 1962:165, 172, 380, 397, 421. While Schurmann reported Mongol settlements within the district of Pashtūn Zarghūn, where this recording took place, and noted that "Sarhadd" refers to the mountainous eastern hinterlands of the Herat oasis, he does not list Sarhadī as a local ethnic designation. I found the term in common local use to designate people by their group and area of origin. If not strictly an ethnic designation, the term functioned within the system of such designations in everyday speech.

storytelling. Asked about the degree to which my presence as a female might have inhibited the proceedings, auditors' opinions varied, but there was a consensus that western women were known to be "free," and that the storytellers therefore may have assumed that I would not be offended. It seems likely to me that their frankness was encouraged by my manifest lack of comprehension of a great deal that was going on. My linguistic incompetence functioned to keep me about as much in the dark about the proceedings in this story as was its protagonist, and being in the dark sexually is, indeed, an appropriate condition for a single woman.

This humorous portrait is thus to a certain extent affectionate toward women, for women are expected to be sexually naïve at marriage. Nonetheless, comic sexual intimidation of women by men is not a theme one finds equally among male and female narrators. To the extent that women shared views of sexuality with me through their stories, fear or dismay was not prominent in their portrayal of everyday sex or male sexuality, though sexual danger was sometimes a theme in encounters with the supernatural.

While this tale in its present performance context presents a male view of female views of male sexuality, the attitudes of the young woman and the old lady who tells her story are comic exaggerations of views which both men and women expect women to express, if not actually hold. It would be highly unseemly for a girl to betray knowledge of the mechanics of sexual intercourse before marriage, though a thoughtful mother or aunt may offer some advice immediately prior to the wedding night, and young brides might joke and exchange information with their married and unmarried peers, on visits home. In rural Afghanistan in the 1970s, it was normal for girls to be engaged at or before puberty, and married soon after menarche at about age thirteen or fourteen,[2] so this portrayal of the young, engaged girl "of that age" querying an elderly woman about sexual matters, and being put off but finally indulged, is not farfetched despite its humorous treatment. Farfetchedness commences in the comic portrayal of hyper-rusticity, that is, the old lady's description of her advanced age at engagement, her portrayal of her state of development at that age, and the length of time her family made her fiancé wait (ll. 24–33). Eighteen or nineteen is

---

2. The groom would generally be several years older, especially in families who were not wealthy, because the groom, aided by his family to the extent they could, would have spent some years accumulating the money and goods needed to negotiate a marriage. There was sentiment against marrying young girls to elderly men. There was also strong sentiment against the marriage of a pubescent girl to a pre-adolescent boy, on the grounds that the age difference would undermine the customary and desired pattern of male dominance.

already a rather advanced age for a new bride in rural Afghanistan, where girls are often married at 14 or 16, and sometimes younger; the audience would expect her to be a little wilted by age eighteen. They laugh at the edible-vegetable euphemisms she uses to describe her pubescent state, yet these images are variations on a standard code of representation. A girl who is physically ready for marriage is called *pokhtah* ("ripe" or "cooked"). While confusion of food and sex is a common theme in ethnic stereo-typing, food metaphors are also common currency for euphemising sexual matters in everyday speech in Persian. Thus, the comedy of the old lady-narrator's use of such rhetorical strategies lodges not so much in any foolish confusion of food and sex, but in her euphemistic yet graphic reference to the politely unmentionable, her own bodily parts.

The scene of the fiancé's return from his shopping trip concentrates most of the themes of ethnic humor Karīm exploits in this narrative. To reinforce the rusticity in his portrait of the grandmother, Karīm inserts into her narrative a few terms which he identifies and carefully glosses as Sarhadī dialect, in lines 34 and 38 (*bodah o pārchah* and *jel estūndah*), lines 46–47 (*darrak*), and line 58 (*kachchah*, "ring," glossed in line 59). In contrast to the first story, he takes fewer chances here with his audience's comprehension of obscure terms, and the Ākhond's side comments (ll. 47, 59) help with explanations.

The old lady's glowing portrayal of her fiancé, in hyperbole suitable for a returning romantic hero, and her expressed surprise at the reappearance of her cousin (ll. 41–45), extend the joke about overelaborated naïveté conveyed in the earlier description of her advanced age at engagement and the lengthy engagement period. Only rarely do village couples see each other for the first time at their wedding. Particularly in cases of first-cousin marriage, such as this, the engaged couple has quite likely known each other as children, and normally families arrange for a couple to meet repeatedly in the girl's home during their engagement. The groom is customarily obliged to visit on major holidays, bringing gifts for his intended. More informally, *nāmzād bāzī* ("fiancé play"), a form of bundling, was practiced in the Herat area and allowed engaged couples to be alone together for purposes of courtship.

The bridegroom's actual cloddishness comes through in the description of the wedding jewelry: not the delicate filigreed gold of city bride-gifts, or the massive, engraved silver favored by nomads, but a huge ring forged by a blacksmith, so big it slips up to her shoulder, and "nice tin beads, gold- and silver-colored" (l. 60). Karīm exploits local color ("from

the direction of Naushūwah", l. 41; the description of the shops and merchants of a particular town bazaar, "Kalātah Mardak," l. 64) to reinforce
further the portrayal of the old lady's rusticity through her expressions of
amazement at the quantity and variety of goods available from such a place,
which from her remarks and her fiancé's reply, it is clear she has never
visited. More than in the preceding story, the Ākhond is ready with collaborative comments underscoring Karīm's humor (l. 70).

The next five lines summarize, without satire, a traditional wedding
among people of modest means, whether in the country or the city. The
humor of the wedding scene begins with and remains focused on the bride
herself: the rest of the party know what to do, she alone is comically in the
dark at the tender age of 26, confused about where she is being taken and
why, observing series of actions with no capacity to interpret them (ll.
78ff.).

In the second half of the story, Karīm makes progressively greater use
of pauses to accommodate, even encourage, the audience's ready laughter.
The limits of the recording notwithstanding, levels of audience response,
both laughter and comments, are audibly higher for the second story than
for the first. In the second story, Karīm uses fewer obscure words and is at
more pains to gloss them for the audience, which in turn encourages audience queries (e.g., at l. 47). Throughout the story, Karīm represents Sarhadī speech mostly by minor alterations in pronunciation rather than by
esoteric vocabulary, as in the first story. His main tactic is the use of pres-
ent-tense verbal contractions not found in Herat dialect, represented in the
English translation by dropped -g of terminal -ing and by copular contractions. The effect is more quaint than disorienting, and the higher level of
audience response suggests a greater ease of comprehension for the details
of the story, not only among the outsider guests, but among the local listeners as well.

Verbal play in the second half of the story hinges not on dialect esoterica, but on a demystification of sex through organic and food metaphors
extending those with which the old lady began her tale, and on ironized
sexual invective. In the wedding night scene, the organic metaphors have
shifted from the decorous vegetable euphemisms of l. 24 to vigorous animal and meat imagery, with reference both to herself and her husband's
sexual organs. The first simile, when the bride protests, "This is no butcher
shop, that you bought me by weight, like meat," (l. 96) draws on a standard image for the condemnation of commoditized sex, conceived as
bride-purchase (when a girl's family is judged to be handing her over to

the highest bidder, more concerned with the goods obtained than with her welfare in their choice of her spouse). Karīm will evoke the same image in defense of the Ākhond's marital history while commenting on his interview (chapter 5, l. 87). Indeed, throughout the last half of the story, the various metaphorical threads interwoven in the bride's comments have in common the deployment of conventional metaphors, expressions, and clichés which are literalized and thus ironized by her practical situation. This process of literalizing the figurative, a basic strategy of humor in this piece, culminates in the old woman's summary "punch line," as we will see. Her literalism is doubly humorous because it is utterly appropriate to the request which her young interlocutor has made, to explain what sex is "really" like, since sex has so far been represented to the young girl only in oblique and stereotypic references. (The standard, polite euphemism which the girl herself uses for conjugal sexual activity, translated literally as "housekeeping," l. 12, is *khānadārī*.)

Among the several interwoven metaphorical threads in the wedding night scene, the most obviously ironized are a series of remonstrances the bride makes to try to control the bridegroom's behavior, beginning at lines 106–8. The series breaks into two subsets. There are three remarks which are conventionally decorous ways for women to adjure strange men to practice sexual restraint. At ll. 107–8, she says, "Take your hand away, remember your limits, don't you have a mother or sisters?" Reminding a man of his mother and sisters is a common and effective way of demanding restraint, if a woman feels she is the object of sexual aggression, or more generally, insufficient consideration. She thus communicates her intention to be included in the category of sexually unavailable women for whom the male addressed has basic protective responsibilities. In public contexts such as the bazaar, if a man must speak to a strange woman, he communicates honorable intent by addressing her as *hamshīrah*, "foster sister," *mādar*, "mother," or *khālah*, "mother's sister." In this case, of course, her new husband's proper role of protector is untempered by sexual prohibition, so the bride's appeal for restraint is ironically naïve about the real terms of her situation. The bride repeats this strategy of invoking nonmarital kinship responsibilities again at lines 113 ("motherless and sisterless!") and 115 ("someone's daughter's privates . . ."), with equal lack of success.

Decorum having failed her, the bride resorts to highly indignant sexual invective, the second in this pair of rhetorical subsets. She responds to her literal experience with clichés of sexual aggression, beginning with "Fuck you!" (l. 110). The irony of a female using male-agent sexual invective is more explicit in Persian than in English, because the verb is in the first person (*tor mīgāyom*). The invective at lines 146 ("Your prick in your ma's cunt!"), 155 ("Your cock in your ma's ass!"), and 160 ("Your yard in your dead father!"), which turns on some of the same incest prohibitions as her earlier, more decorous appeals, is derived from idiomatic and stereotypic invective used by male speakers. (In ordinary invective, the elliptical ". . . in your mother's cunt!" implies sexual aggression by a male speaker.) The irony here is that the bride is only now acquiring a literal referent for the terms "prick," "cock," "yard," each time in response to a query of hers as she somewhat involuntarily explores her husband's privates. Up to now, she has had no direct experience of literal referents for any of the clichés of sexual aggression which she knows from daily speech.

In its small space, "Rasūl's Mother," as told by Karīm, develops a number of related, interlocked metaphor series in tandem with those just described. The bridegroom is metaphorically associated with butchering (ll. 96 and 150), then with murder (ll. 167–69), and his sexual activity finally yields him "free meat" from his own body (ll. 172–74). The imagery of butchering and meat links with that of eating and choking (ll. 167, 177). In Persian as in many other languages, references to food consumption are not infrequently utilized as metaphors for sex ("Come drink tea with me" being a not-very-subtle sexual solicitation offered in public contexts, such as the bazaar). On the one hand, Rasūl's mother's choice of figurative language to portray her sexual experience, like her choice of invective, is stereotypic and conventional. On the other hand, she pushes the representations over the edge in various directions, into naïve literalism or perhaps into a more evocative metaphorization than her naïveté ought to command. "Potatoes" are an unsurprising metaphor for testicles, but when the bride discovers them, her husband immediately becomes "potato-seller" (l. 158). She offers a complex metaphor: testicles are potatoes *and* he is a trafficker in them, not just a possessor of them, but she leaves unstated the simpler metaphor on which the complex one is founded (testicles equals potatoes). The complex metaphor connects not only with the food/sex series, but also with a series of reflections on public versus private roles and spaces, which began with the bride's reluctance to be "sold off like green fruit" (l. 28) and the bridegroom's return from the bazaar (l. 40ff.). In the latter scene, the bride's (expected) lack of familiarity with bazaars and tradespeople is contrasted with the groom's relative ease with them (ll. 64–69). The bazaar is foreign territory for her, secluded as she is, but so is her new home, to which she is taken on the wedding night (ll. 83–85). At this point, her confusion about what should be a domestic space already familiar to her is comically naïve. Thereafter, her extended series of remonstrances with her new husband all hinge on defining the new space and the behavior proper to it. She protests that the space (ambiguously, both the wedding chamber and her own body) is *not* a butcher shop (l. 96), a urinal (l. 127), a mosque (l. 134), a donkey stable or a sheep pen (l. 135), a place for firewood (l. 141), an abattoir (l. 150), or a potato-seller's (l. 158). These futile attempts to define her new space, by protesting the invasion of inappropriate objects, end at line 167, with the futile but conclusive "Take it out!" This is also the point at which the food and slaughter metaphors meet ("You're strangling me . . ."). Immediately thereafter, the death metaphor becomes funereal ("hold the seventh-day mourning ceremonies," l. 173), yet still alimentary ("free meat," l. 174).

Lines 173ff., following the consummation, also effect a semantic shift from denying and forbidding to acquiescence ("Go on . . .") and acceptance of the (metaphorical) presence ("you've gotten your hands on some free meat . . ."). Line 175, "I didn't know," constitutes the culmination of various image series, including all the foregoing metaphorical (mis)representations of male genitalia and sexual behavior, and also certain repeated statements which form refrains for different sections of the story. In the early part of the story, the refrain is some paraphrase of "I don't know" ("I don't know anything," l. 19; "I don't know about other people," l. 20; "till I myself can understand," l. 27; "I don't know," l. 55; "it's just ignorance," l. 82). Once she is confronted by her husband in the wedding chamber, the narrator's expressions of uncertainty temporarily modulate to paraphrases of "if you say so" ("Go ahead," l. 98; "OK, if you think so," l. 110; "OK, if you think so, then . . . ," l. 117). This refrain addressed to her husband is replaced, as matters get more and more out of her control, by the rhetorical, and hopeless, "So who can you tell it to?" (ll. 111, 163, and 170).

The purport of this last refrain is twofold: on the surface, it is obvious that protest is useless, for her husband does not heed her protests and no one else is there to hear them. But also, in the more general sense, explanation cannot substitute for experience: "Who can you tell it to?" yields to the final "I didn't know" (l. 175), and also links back to the original situation, in which a young girl is begging the narrator for precisely this, to tell her about sex. One burden of the old woman's story, mediated by the three refrains, is "I didn't know, and couldn't interpret, until I had direct experience." Narration is offered for its instructive value, but that value is hedged from the start:

"Well, I don't know about other people,
about my <u>own</u> experiences
I can tell you that." (ll. 20–22)

Even at the end, reality evades interpretation, as the narrator construes three common terms for penis (*chūl*, translated as "prick," l. 145; *kīr*, "cock," l. 154; *nar*, "yard," l. 159) as three separate entities brought into destructive alliance (ll. 178–79). She also ultimately portrays the subject of the young girl's inquiry, *khānadārī* (l. 12), "housekeeping," the common euphemism for marital sex (itself the mechanism by which households are created) as the ruination of one's "house" (l. 179), metaphorically, the female body.

The foregoing enumeration of connected images by no means exhausts the metaphorical dimensions of this tale. The pattern of images could equally be traced as developing series concerned with livestock as well as food plants, for instance. Explicit and metaphorical evocations of commodity exchange are also intricately woven into the portrayal of marriage negotiations and consummation. Rhetorical force lies in the richness of metaphor, not just in their number and variety but in the multiple, simultaneous linkages among series of conceptually related images, arrayed in parallel and contrast. The descriptive details of the story are immediately humorous and even explicitly instructive (one Afghan auditor of the tape remarked at about line 86, "If you didn't know how to do it before, you would after hearing this"). But at the same time, the interplay of conventional sexual metaphors, newly coined or extended metaphors (pine roots, potato-sellers), and naïve descriptions of actual experience, humorously illustrates the ultimate failure of language, as metaphor, to convey experience, particularly such a primary experience as sex.

One might complain that this is a weighty philosophical burden with which to encumber such a light-hearted piece of ribaldry. However, the next story, with which the Ākhond takes the narrator's stage, offers a second, even more direct portrayal of the chasm that separates representation from understanding.

5. Ākhond Mulla Mahmūd, "Ten Qerān"[1]

Mokhtār: First could you introduce yourself, your name?

The Ākhond: My name, sir, I'm known as Ākhond Mahmūd.

M: Ākhond Mulla Mahmūd.

Ā: Yes.

M: You don't say "Mulla" yourself, though?[2]   5

Ā: Well, then, for me to say it myself would be bad.

[*chuckles; audience chuckles*]

M: OK. About how old might you be?

Ā: Sir, if my wives aren't listening, [*chuckles*] I'd be up to seventy-five.

        In front of them, I won't say I'm over forty. [*chuckles*]

        Maybe I'm sixty, sir.

M: So it seems from this, that you've married a lot.

Ā: Sir, I haven't married more than seven times up to now. Seven.

                                    [*chuckles*]   10

M: God bless you. How many of them are alive?

Ā: Two are alive, sir, these—

other— [*Mokhtār, prompting*: —five—] five have died.

M: They gave their years to you.[3]

Ā: Yes.   15

M: OK. Have you children, too?

---

1. Title assigned for reference, not supplied by storyteller.

2. The interviewer attempts a joke. *Mulla* is a general term for learned religious in Islam. In Herat the term *ākhond* ("theologian, tutor": Haim, *Persian-English Dictionary*) was used for mullas actively engaged in teaching in traditional religious schools, including the elementary level ones described by this man. "Mulla" was a title of respect, and also, in colloquial speech, a synonym for "learned."

3. A commiserative remark, also a compliment and wish for the storyteller's continued long life.

Ā: Children, sir—I have seven sons. [*M*: In God's Name.⁴ *MM*: Ah—]
And I have two daughters, sir.

M: What do the children do?

Ā: My children, sir—one is a religious judge. 20

[*M*: Good.] One is a school principal.

[*M*: Yes— *MM*: Uh-huh.] One boy is at the state religious high school,
and reached twelfth grade this year.

[*M*: Yes—] One is at the teachers' college. [*M*: Yes.]

Three others are in the modern schools,⁵ one in fifth grade, one in sixth.
One in third grade. 25

[*M*: Uh-huh.] So that's what their activities are.

M: And did you send the girls to school, your daughters?

Ā: The girls, sir, they haven't gone to school, because there is no girls'
school in our village. [*M*: Oh—] You could say, they've all
read the Farsi-language books in the home schools.⁶

M: What's the name of your village?

Ā: Its name, they call it Koshk Haibāt, sir. 30

M: Fine, from Koshk Haibāt.

Ā: Yes.

M: And about—uh—studies—where did you study, yourself?

A: I sir, studies—you could say I started in our own village. [*M*: Uh-huh.]
I finished up in the city, sir. At that time there were no
teachers' colleges and such, it was in the mosques, under
Ākhondzādah Mulla Salāḥuddīn Sarhadī.

M: Yes, —Saljūqī. 35

Ā: Saljūqī, yes.

M: Mulla Salāḥuddīn Saljūqī.⁷

Ā: Yes.

‹›

---

4. A blessing invoked to avert harm when admiring someone else's good fortune.

5. The Ākhond refers to the state-run public schools.

6. *Maktab khānegī*: The traditional schools run by local teaching clergy, in which children learn Qur'anic literacy and, subsequently, Persian literacy as well if they remain in school long enough. One auditor of the tape guessed that the Ākhond had probably sent the girls to study with someone besides himself, since a father would be expected to be too indulgent to impose discipline on his own young children. In the Herat area in the 1970s, girls attended traditional schools with boys up to about age eight or nine, when there was a strong tendency to withdraw the girls, unless there was a woman teacher available in an all-female classroom. Government schools were segregated by sex, although shortages of women teachers placed some male teachers in girls' schools.

7. *Sarhadī* is a regional identifier (see previous story, n. 3), while *Saljuqī* is an ethnic one. Mokhtār differs with the Ākhond as to which name to use, but the subject probably was known by both (chapter 5).

M: OK. [*Consulting a jotted list of interview questions*] Your birthplace—
                                    [*A*: Yes?] Where was your birthplace?
Ā: It was the same Koshk Haibāt, sir. [*M*: Koshk Haibāt.] Yes.   40
M: What do you do now, yourself? Your occupation?
Ā: Well, sir, I myself am—right here, in my own village, I'm a mulla.
        [*M*: OK.] I give religious guidance. [*M*: Yes—] I have a little land
        of my own, too. [*M*: OK] So to say, sir, either my own sons or a
        sharecropper farms it, and they give me an income so to say,
it's shelter, enough to get by, anyway. [*M*: Enough to get by.] Yes.
M: [*consulting the list of questions*]: Fine. And do you have a radio, yourself?
        In your house? [*A*: What?] Do you also have a radio in your
                                                            house?
Ā: I don't have a radio myself, but my sons do, sir.   45
M: Don't your sons give you the radio?
Ā: Well, although there's a radio in my house, I don't know how to run it,
        sir [*laughs*], and when they go out, they take it with them,
                            and bring it when they come back.
M: These stories that you yourself tell, did you learn them from books,
                            mostly, or from other people?
Ā: Some are from religious books, sir, some from other people,
                                    and some from—like that . . .
M [*departing from the question list*]: Now, they say, it's remembered, there
                was once this Hājjī Esmāʿīl "the Black,"[8] do you tell about him? 50
Ā: Yes, sir.
M: Did you ever see him?
Ā: Yes sir.
M: It's possible you learned some of the— jokes about him, or not?
Ā: Yes, sure, sir.   55
M: Uh—and how long was it, since Hājjī Esmāʿīl's time?
Ā: It's been maybe ten years since his death.
M: Ten years since his death. [*A*: Yes.] And where—where did he live,
                                    formerly, then?[9]
Ā: Sir, mostly he lived at Kārokh. Kārokh in Herat.[10]

---

8. A famous wit and raconteur, native of Herat, who died in the early 1960s, according to this and other informants. A collection of his traditional satirical poetry was published in 1931.(Ghani 1988:451; cf. Sprachman 1988.)

9. A rhetorical question: Mokhtār is trying, unsuccessfully, to get the Ākhond to enlarge on the topic of Hājjī Esmāʿīl. Mokhtār himself is perfectly aware of where the man lived.

10. Kārokh is a market town and shrine pilgrimage site, with a locally famous Sufi community in residence, in Herat province about twenty-five miles northeast of the city of Herat, on the main road to Qala-i Nau and Maimana.

M: OK. How is it that he came— he had access to the kings' throne,
coming from Kārokh?   60

Ā: Yes, he had access everywhere.

M [*returning to the jotted question list*]: When did you start this storytelling,
with these stories?

Ā: Well, sir, I—

so to say, from the time I started studying, I was kind of fun-loving,
and from that time to this, no matter where—

even if it's a funeral, if I'm there I'll turn it into a wedding. [*M*: Good—
a laugh—] From the time I grew up, [*M*: Yes—]   65

—until this very date, sir, wherever I am, I'll be talking in the evening,
anyway.

[*coughs*]

M: Who likes your stories the best?[11]

Ā: Sir, my friend, now, these stories of mine, I'll tell you,

that the Prophet, peace be on him, has said, [*quotes* hadīth[12] *in Arabic*] to
qalb ol-monnāsa ʿalā qadar-e ʿoqolūhīn, [*Audience member:*
Inaudible comment]   70

"I speak to each according to his wisdom."

[*M*: Yeah—] To the young—if it's youngsters sitting around together,
a party of them, I speak like the youngsters. [*M*: Yes.]

Elders according to their own disposition. [*M*: Yeah.]

Sufis[13] that are of pure faith, according to the disposition of Sufis.
[*chuckling*] [*M*: Yeah.]

I speak to shaykhs,[14] some of them   75

    that are deficient,[15] according to their deficiencies.

    Warding off harm is canonically permitted, too.

I speak to <u>each</u> according to their disposition, »

    and everybody is happy with me.

---

11. This was an inaccurate paraphrase from the question list from which he was working: Instead of *Kī gūsh mīkashah*, "who listens to your stories?" (i.e., who is in the audience), the interviewer read *Kī khosh mīkonah*, "who likes your stories?"—probably a slip of the tongue, but a fortuitous one, given the answer elicited, which emphasized the situational, audience-dependent nature of adept storytelling in the mind of the speaker.

12. *Hadīth* are the sayings of the Prophet, as attested by his family and associates.

13. Muslim mystics—there are a number of orders, of which the Naqshbandīyya and Qādirīyya, both rather sober orders, are most active in the Herat area.

14. Charismatic religious leaders, often members of lineages descending from individuals to whom miracles of faith are attributed, who themselves are also often credited with various powers such as faith healing and efficacious prayer for other purposes. Cf. Roy (1983) on the same distinction of personal-devotional and charismatic mysticism in Afghanistan.

15. I.e., in religious understanding or learning.

M: And how do you speak according to the disposition of <u>women</u>?   80
Ā: I don't have much familiarity with the disposition of women, sir.
M: God bless you, you've married seven times—
Ā: Well, seven wives, now, sir, but [*laughing*] they didn't dance with
                              me at parties—[*MM laughs.*]
Women, now, sir, it would have to be night and lying with—a person
                    under the quilts, that's where one would show
                    whatever personality one had! [*Laughs*]
M [*laughing*]: God bless you, you've married <u>seven</u> wives, how did
                              you go about finding them?   85
Ā: Well, sir, it's over a period of sixty years, that these seven women—
          how important is it?—that they died one by one, poor things.
[*Laughs; MM and other audience members laugh.*]
Khalīfah Karīm: He didn't take these seven all at once, like the
          Soviets do,[16] the Ākhond wasn't running a butcher shop.
Ā: I wasn't, after all.
Another listener: One by one he married them, fucked them, and they
                    died, then he married another one, and she died—
[*rest of sentence covered by general laughter, with the Ākhond laughing along*]
M: Where are these stories fr— OK, —what's the name of the story
                              you're going to tell now?[17]   90
Ā: The name of the story, sir—
          this isn't a common story, now.[18]
The story is that there were seven brothers, sir, and their houses
                    were separate from each other. [*M*: Yes.]
They had one sister twenty-five or thirty years old. [*M*: Yes.]   95
She lived separately from them, too.

This one brother went, sir, and bought a cow from a village, for ten *qerān*.[19]
It started to come into milk a little bit, this cow.
So one brother came along and said, "Brother, let me have a share, too."

---

16. A common religiously-framed belief among Afghans is that unbelievers, and especially Russians because they are communists who deny God's existence, indulge in group sex and do not recognize incest rules (cf. Canfield 1977).

17. Mokhtār loses his place on the question note card, then finds it again.

18. I.e., the story is not so well known that it would have a recognized title. Only romances and the most common Märchen had titles that were generally agreed upon. Anecdotes like this would not require a title.

19. The *qerān* at the time of this study was an almost obsolete unit of currency, equal to a half Afghani or about one cent (U.S.), but elders reported that in their youth and in their parents' time, the *qerān* was the basic currency unit and had significant buying power.

He said, "If you want a share, too, you go give the owner ten *qerān*, too," 100
    —of course he should have given it to <u>him</u>.
[*M*: Yeah.]
He took the ten *qerān* and gave it to the cow owner. »
Another brother came and said, "Give me a share, too."
[*M*: Yeah]   105
He said, "Now you go give the cow owner ten *qerān*, too."
    <u>He'd</u> bought it for ten *qerān*, he was supposed to give it to <u>that</u> guy,
                                                                    <u>himself</u>.
[*Audience member*: Yeah. They give ten *qerān* (each), the brothers.]
So <u>every</u> brother came along and became a partner, »
        and he said, "Go give the cow owner ten *qerān*."   110
[*M*: OK, you said that . . . he bought it for ten *qerān*, himself?]
Yes. [*Other audience member*: He said ten *qerān*. Ten *qerān*.]
He went, sir, to the cow owner.
These— [*M*: OK, that's from the beginning, from the beginning of
                    the story, then] —yes—these—seven brothers, »
        he'd bought it for ten *qerān* and they gave the cow owner
                                        seventy *qerān* extra.   115

His sister, sir,
        she came, too, and said,
        "Give me a share, too, brother."
He said, "Well, you give your ten *qerān*, too."

Now the cow is really coming into milk   120
        she's about to calve, sir.
[*M*: OK.]
They said, "We—
        brother, what should we milk her into,
        once she's calved?"   125
They said—they all, all seven of them lined up and went off to the cow
                                                                    owner.
They said to the cow owner, "Once this cow of ours has calved, what
                                        shall we milk it into?"
        Out of their own stupidity. [*M*: Yeah, uh-huh.]
This guy said, "They've bought it for ten *qerān*, this bunch of
                                        bastard donkeys! [*laughs*]
        They gave me seventy *qerān* extra—"   130

he said, "Go milk it in your own ass."
They believed it, sir. [*audience laughter*]

The cow calved in the stable,
    and this one got out his asshole, and milked her,
    and this one,   135
    and the sister came and milked, too, the one place got full, and
        it poured over into the other one. [*muffled audience laughter*]
They knocked her down, said, [*chuckling*] »
    "Ooh, fuck the souls of your fathers, you heathen!
    You gave the same amount of money and now
        you're taking two measures of milk?!!" [*laughs; Mokhtār laughs*] 140
    "You give the same amount of money, your money—two mi—
[*stutters, laughing*]—
        you're taking two shares of milk?!!" [*laughs*]

They beat her, and the little woman said, "If—"
    they went, she said, "Well,
                what should I do?"   145
They brought an old man of their lineage,
    he raised his eyebrows,
    —he was a hundred years old—
    and said, "Why do you give an equal share of money,
        and take <u>two</u> measures of milk?" »   150
    She said, "Can <u>you</u> wall off half of it?"
[*Ā. laughs—audience laughs*] This girl said that.

The point is,
    that's what kind of people they were,
    they had that degree   155
    of stupidity, like that, that
it speaks in—in that respect
    about foolishness and intelligence. [*M*: Intelligence—]
    That people who
    in knowledge   160
    and wisdom[20] lack ad— advancement

---

20. *'elm o 'orfān: 'orfān* also designates gnosis or mystical wisdom.

are this kind of people, »
that they buy for ten *qerān* but give seventy.
[*M*: Seventy *qerān* . . .]
And they don't even know how to milk the cow! [*chuckles*]
[*Break in recording*]

Fools in General

When Mokhtār turns to interview the Ākhond, the interrogatory tone of the proceedings is not totally unexpected, Karīm having just been subjected to a parallel series of questions. The Ākhond readily invests the situation with wit, turns Mokhtār, the interviewer, into a virtual straight man at certain points and, in so doing, effectively gains control of the proceedings, though ostensibly he remains in a reactive role, responding to Mokhtār's questions as they are put to him.

Responding to the direct request that he identify himself on the tape, the Ākhond hedges gently ("I'm known as . . ."), allowing the interviewer to supply the omitted title "Mulla" and collaborating, chuckling, with Mokhtār's slightly ponderous reference to his modesty (ll. 5–6). The Ākhond follows up immediately with another joke: asked about his age, he voluntarily introduces the topic of his multiple wives in a joking reference to his years. Direct questions about wives are not appropriate in general conversation among male nonrelatives. The Ākhond was known not only as a wit and raconteur, but also for his vigorous old age and multiple marriages. Seven is a lot of marriages, even for a man of some means, such as the Ākhond reveals himself to be. Mokhtār in fact knew of his numerous marriages from talk with third parties before the interview, but the Ākhond anticipates the line of questioning even before it begins, and turns what could have been an awkward exchange into a field for jest (l. 10): "I haven't married more than seven times up to now . . ." Mokhtār responds politely with blessings on the Ākhond's good fortune, in both longevity and offspring (ll. 11, 14, and 17).

The Ākhond's description of his sons' activities provides an interesting picture of a family with a serious commitment to formal education, both religious and secular. Hafizullah Baghban (1977, 1:134) described a recent pattern of religious and secular education "in conflict at the folk level" in the Herat area. The religious elite of the Sufi center and shrine of Kārokh, in particular, were said to have used their influence to keep their children out of government schools, in favor of traditional religious education (ibid., p. 109, n. 71). The Ākhond, by contrast, takes manifest pride in five sons enrolled in secular government schools, as well as one who is a religious judge and another training for the clergy. With the revolution against the present Marxist regime, views on education have become further polarized. The directress of the Islamic Organization of Afghan

Women (a Peshawar, Pakistan-based group affiliated with the conservative Hezb-i Islami [Islamic Party] resistance organization), described to me the opposition they encountered in trying to establish schools for refugee children.[1] Some refugee elders argued that the government education system had created a group of Afghans who had sold out their country to the Soviets. The women's organization representatives countered that Muhammad the Prophet, at his initial revelation, had been enjoined by the Divine messenger, "Read!" and even though he was illiterate, the voice insisted, "Read: And it is the Lord the Most Bountiful / Who teacheth by the Pen" (*Qur'an*, Surah XCVI, v. 3–4; Pickthall p. 4). Muslims, the women argued, can do no less than follow the Prophet's example. In this way, she said, they ultimately gained acceptance for a curriculum which begins with Qur'anic literacy but includes general education topics as well.

The Ākhond's various strategies for the education of his sons bespeak a viewpoint akin to that underlying the current Islamic Women's Organization strategy. His observation about the lack of girls' schools is no lame excuse: apart from the *maktab khānegī*, the traditional Qur'anic primary school presided over by a local mulla like himself, girls' schools were few in villages in the Herat area, and it was socially unacceptable for girl students to travel outside their residential neighborhoods for schooling. In general, learned families favored at least basic reading and writing skills in Arabic and Persian for their own daughters, and expressed a preference for literate brides for their sons. Scholarly women, some of whom offered religious schooling to girls, were to be found among the families of the better-educated clergy and the saintly lineages attached to some shrines.

The fact that all the Ākhond's sons were pursuing high levels of education confirmed not only his support for a diversified educational strategy but also that he was a man of some means who could spare them from the family labor pool for a substantial portion of their time. After primary school, they would have had to travel one or two hours in each direction, daily, to attend regional high schools, or else relocate in the city for such programs as teacher training. People who did not own their own land, and those whose holdings were too small to support their families, most of whom also worked for others on a sharecropping basis, were usually hard pressed to spare the labors of male offspring after the first two or three years of primary schooling. The educational picture the Ākhond paints suggests a family of both means and influence. His own educational back-

---

1. Personal communication, July 1987.

ground, and his network of relatives in the city, which he describes later in the evening (see chapter 11), further confirm that impression. He is circumspect, as was Karīm, in describing his exact living conditions in the presence of the subgovernor. In this case, the subgovernor's prior jailing of the elderly man for nonpayment of property taxes is evidence that the Ākhond's net worth was a specific bone of contention between them.

Mokhtār and the Ākhond differ on the proper name of the Ākhond's famous teacher (ll. 34–38). It is likely that he was known by both names. *Sarhadī* is a regional identifier (see chapter 4, "Rasūl's Mother," note 3), while *Saljūqī* is an ethnic one, connecting the bearer to the Seljuq Turkish ethnic group and perhaps to its dynasty, which ruled on the Iranian plateau in the eleventh and twelfth centuries C.E. (fifth and sixth centuries A.H.). The Saljūqī family was still prominent in Herat in the 1970s. Attaching a regional or place-name identifier to a given name was a traditional practice with reference to prominent figures in Persian literature and history. Until recently, individuals of no particular prominence were also often given local or ethnic designations or nicknames, particularly when residing outside their place of origin. At the time of these recordings, the Afghan government, having imposed a system of identity cards for males in connection with mandatory military service, was encouraging men to choose surnames for themselves but frowned on the use of ethnic designations in particular as surnames, on the grounds that ethnic designations were politically divisive. It is possible Mokhtār favors the ethnic identifier because of the negative stereotype of Sarhadī people, which has just been displayed in the preceding story. At any rate, Mokhtār's twice correcting the name by which the Ākhond knows his own teacher (ll. 35 and 37) constitutes an assertion of authority of sorts.

Mokhtār's query about the radio (l. 44), taken from the interview question list, was the product of my desire to assess the impact of mass media on city and village communities. Electrification at that time did not extend beyond the immediate environs of the major cities. Even in Herat City, residential electricity was supplied only after dark. Despite the cost of batteries, portable radio-cassette recorders with shortwave capability were a very popular possession, especially among young men. Many men purchased them from the proceeds of stints as guest workers in Iran, whose booming economy offered a wage ten times that of the daily wage in Herat's small wage-labor sector. Not only the young but older men showed interest in news broadcasts. Some people I met said they also enjoyed the serial radio dramas in Persian and Pashto from Radio Kabul, and songs from the radio were widely sung and enjoyed. Radio listening was by no means universal, however, as the Ākhond's comments indicate. When he says (l. 47) "I don't know how to run [the radio]," the Ākhond may also mean that he does not understand the broadcasts very well.

Kazim Alami, a native of Herat City who helped edit and transcribe this and other tapes, said that the style of radio speech took a good deal of getting used to for the average Herati. Broadcasts from the city of Mashhad in Iran were in Tehran-standard Persian, which Kazim estimated might take two years of regular listening to master completely. Iranian news broadcasts in particular used a number of French and English loanwords not found in Herati or Kabuli Persian. Some wealthy families in Herat City were said to have television sets with limited reception of Iranian broadcasts from Mashhad, but television was basically nonexistent in Afghanistan at this time. Newspapers were little read in Herat City and nonexistent in the villages, so radio was the only pervasive mass medium. I did not develop reliable figures, but people I queried guessed that from 30 to 70 percent of households in their communities had radios, with considerable variation depending on the relative affluence of the community. As the Ākhond describes, young men frequently took their radio-cassette recorders on visits outside their homes to play music, copy others' tapes, or record performances (music and occasionally stories) at the gatherings, if any were offered.

The Ākhond had more to say later about books and reading (see chapter 11). At this point, he acknowledged more direct use of written story sources, especially religious works, than Karīm claimed. The Ākhond's conception of religious books is broad, as his later remarks showed, including didactic (but nontheological) works such as *Anwār-i Sohaylī* (*The Lights of Canopus*, a famous fifteenth-century Persian derivative of the Indic-origin story collection, *Kalila wa Dimna*; see chapter 10).

Mokhtār, departing from the interview question list, then queried the Ākhond about the famous Herati wit and practical joker, Hājjī Esmā'īl Sīāh ("The Black"). A widely known raconteur and satirist during the royalist period, Esmā'īl died in the early 1960s. Throughout their discussion of him, both Mokhtār and the Ākhond used the respectful third-person plural to refer to Hājjī Esmā'īl, a form of deference generally reserved for dignitaries. Hājjī Esmā'īl, a published satirical poet in the classical style, was portrayed in Herati oral tradition as a sort of folk social critic and improvisational satirist (see Cejpek 1968:687; Ghani 1988:451; Sprachman 1988). Hājjī Esmā'īl was renowned for having the ear of those in high places, despite or because of his tendency to satirize them. As a satirist of traditional elites, Hājjī Esmī'īl should have been a congenial subject for the iconoclastic subgovernor, and it may be that Mokhtār tried to elicit stories about him for that reason, as well as out of a personal interest which he expressed in other contexts as well. The Ākhond rather conspicuously declined to enlarge on the topic, even when Mokhtār framed very open-ended questions (ll. 50 and 54). Mokhtār, after a few unsuccessful attempts to get the Ākhond to pursue the topic of Hājjī Esmā'īl Sīāh, gave up and returned to the question list, at which point the Ākhond immediately became more expansive, talking animatedly about his own performances (ll. 64–66).

The Ākhond may have declined to take up the invitation to narrate from or about Esmā'īl Sīāh because he already had chosen a story to follow up on Karīm's first offerings or because he had already made choices about other stories he wanted to perform based on his prior assessment of more general audience-performer relations (see chapter 6). He shows a much greater inclination to expand on his own orientation as a storyteller; his voice takes on the cadence of sustained monologue only when he begins to itemize the different types of audiences (ll. 68–79). With his quotation from the sayings of the Prophet about speaking to everyone in ways they will understand (l. 71), the Ākhond places himself in good and ancient intellectual company. Plato, in the *Phaedrus*, quotes Socrates championing oral over written communication because in oral communication, "The speaker can vary his 'type of speech' so that it is appropriate to each nature . . . addressing a variegated soul in a variegated style, and a simple soul in a simple style." (*Phaedrus* 275d, 275c; 277c; Hackforth trans., quoted by Goody: 50–51). The Ākhond's portrayal of himself as an entertainer who could turn a funeral into a wedding (l. 65) invokes ambiguous aspects of the raconteur's social role; at this initial point, he seems to emphasize not the didactic but the entertaining and distracting dimension of storytelling. The raconteur, however skilled and however much his spontaneous performances are enjoyed, is not necessarily respected. Another gifted Afghan raconteur, western-educated and now residing in the United States, occasionally calls me on the telephone to share his stories, but he has so far resisted being taped because he says a general reputation as a storyteller would undermine his dignity in the Afghan community and annoy his wife. Particularly in this setting of cultural displacement, he is comfortable telling stories only with other raconteurs.

Mokhtār's misstatement of a question about the composition of the

Ākhond's audience (l. 67, n. 11) provoked the Ākhond's revealing short excursus on the storytelling art and the Ākhond's pride in his ability to adjust his performances to the disposition of different audience groups. To "speak to each according to his wisdom" (l. 71) is not only good performance practice but also imitation of the Prophet, toward which all good Muslims should endeavor. This valorization of raconteurship, by assimilating it to prophetic example, casts a more serious and respectable light on the Ākhond's self-professed power to redefine social situations through stories interpreted or constructed for the particular audience. Besides age, the discriminator provided by the form of the question, the Ākhond further distinguishes his audiences on the basis of their degree of enlightenment, construed in religious terms. His distinction between "Sufis of pure faith" and "deficient shaykhs" reflects an indigenous contrast drawn by those more formally educated Muslims who have mystical leanings, between those whose devotional tendencies are toward meditation and personal spiritual development and those more involved with charismatic devotion and the veneration of living spiritual leaders (cf. Roy 1983). In drawing out this distinction betwen "deficient shaykhs" and men of true faith, the Ākhond generalizes and removes from its ethnic context the distinction drawn in Karīm's first story, between the ignorant devotee-brother of the "Mongol Martyr" and the ākhond who sarcastically receives his representations of the martyr's sanctity.

Mokhtār reclaims the topical initiative with a follow-up question, asking, banteringly, "How do you speak according to the disposition of women?" This teasing query resonates both with the story just told (a male portrayal of the "disposition of women") and also with my own presence: "A woman is now in your audience: what are you going to say to her?" The Ākhond simply denies that he has women co-conversationalists, an opening which Mokhtār leaps on, but the Ākhond deftly parries (ll. 80–84), gaining the laugh. Bested in repartee, Mokhtār retreats, changing the subject to the logistics of courtship, a question of his own devising to elicit ethnographic information on traditional attitudes he thought would be of interest to me, as well as to extricate himself from an exchange in which he was increasingly being assigned the role of straight man. The Ākhond replies, matter-of-factly, that seven wives over sixty years of adulthood (he is actually about 75 years old), and the loss of several of them to death, is not remarkable. Karīm leaps to the defense of the Ākhond's marital history, pointing out that the Ākhond's marriage pattern was not promiscuous "like the Soviets" (l. 87). Karīm's butchershop analogy succinctly expresses the widespread Afghan popular contempt for the Soviets and what were presumed to be their amoral (because atheistic) habits. With this remark Karīm also reinvoked the analogy between excessive sexuality and butchery which he exploited for humorous purposes in the story just preceding. A second listener, a middle-aged man, then breaks in with the most daring and potentially cutting remark of the exchange (l. 89), suggesting that the Ākhond's sexuality was responsible for his wives' death, but the Ākhond joins in easily with the laugh.

The tenor of this last remark, indeed of this whole section of the conversation, is subject to interpretation. Both Mokhtār, at the time, and other Afghan acquaintances who audited the tape expressed surprise at the degree of frankness and disrespect, both for women in general in this formal a context and for the Ākhond's privacy. The sort of teasing the second audience member offers (l. 89) could occur among male friends in private, but not normally in as formal a context as that induced by the presence of the subgovernor and his outsider guests, including a foreign woman. This line of conversation certainly exceeded the bounds of decorum that Mokhtār found comfortable, but interpretations vary as to where the embarrassment was intended to lodge, and the degree to which the elderly speakers' breach of decorum was studied or strategic. I interpret the second audience member's remark (l. 89) as hostile to the Ākhond, perhaps expressing solidarity with the subgovernor, who as a Parchami Marxist was a Soviet sympathizer. Circumstances did not yield any further evidence to establish this audience member's intentions, but the general rowdiness of several subsequent stories permits further exploration of the storytellers' own strategies in this regard. The subgovernor, as host, was the individual most restrained by decorum rules which prominently include forbearance and accommodation toward guests.

Mokhtār, again losing control as interlocutor at this point, hurriedly interjected another question from the interview list, momentarily losing his placc in his haste and starting to repeat an earlier question about the sources of stories (l. 90). As with other parts of the interview, asking for the name of the story was not really culturally appropriate. Most short anecdotes and *afsānah* (approximately equivalent to European *märchen*, or wonder-tales) lack titles as such. A request for a title or designation often elicited a synopsis or, as here, introductory information leading into the tale proper. A few of the most widely performed *afsānah*, such as those belonging to the Cinderella and animal bridegroom cycles, have one or more widely recognized titles. The Ākhond's comment reflects the fact that only the most widely known short tales have recognized titles. The stories told in this session were unusual, to the extent that only two of them ("If/But" and "That Little Donkey and That Little Door") were told to me on more than one occasion. The Ākhond himself points out that the tale at hand is not a well-known item. These performers' lack of reliance on the core corpus of widely known stories which became familiar to me in Herat, bespeaks an extensive repertoire for both men and also, perhaps, an esthetic preference for stories which are less familiar to their audience, at least in this performance context, and perhaps in general.

The Story

The Ākhond's tale itself, when he is allowed to get on with it, succinctly reiterates and redirects some themes raised in Karīm's two stories. The central topic is still fools, with a major component of bodily humor, but there is no longer an ethnic stereotype underlying the ridiculousness of these characters: they are simply generic fools. Hafizullah Baghban pointed out (1977, 2:369) how ethnic stereotyping can serve as a distancing strategy and a cover for more generalized social-critical humor. Accordingly, Karīm made the victims of his satire ethnic and regional stereotypes. The Ākhond uses no ethnic distancing strategy, but does portray foolishness as a family affliction. Other tales from Herat also depict family stupidity, observed by an intelligent outsider who finally reacts with exasperation after repeated attempts to set them straight.[2] This family of fools is confused about the most basic principles of monetary exchange, and absurdly ignorant about the basic rural activity of milking. Unlike Karīm, the Ākhond takes no chances with audience comprehension in this performance. Initially, he keeps statements short, pausing often and thus eliciting frequent confirmations of comprehension from Mokhtār ("yeah" and "uh-huh" comments, ll. 94, 95, 102, 105) and carefully confirming the point about the family's financial confusion (ll. 111–12, 114). The second phase of the story, when the cow seller in exasperation tells the buyers to milk the cow "in your own ass" (l. 131), hinges on the same interplay of literal speech and metaphorical invective that Karīm exploited in the latter parts of "Rasūl's

---

2. One tale I heard more often concerned a bridegroom who discovers on his wedding night that his bride is a fool and then, to his dismay, learns as well that each of her relations is stupider than the last. He finally flees, abandoning the idea of marriage.

Mother." Lest the audience be left with the impression that the woman's physical inability to control her body, to isolate one body cavity from another (l. 151), is the main point of the story, the Ākhond turns after the laugh to a didactic explication: "it speaks in— in that respect / about foolishness and intelligence" (ll. 157–58), and not just any kind of intelligence, but *'orfān* (literary *'erfān*), which is more particularly the depth of wisdom that comes with spiritual insight. The Ākhond's invocation of *'orfān* in connection with such a seemingly profane story links back directly to his remarks about faith and "deficient shaykhs" (ll. 75–76) and his remarks about the use of storytelling to "ward off harm" (l. 77), in this case, warning against human foolishness in the particular form of overliteral interpretation. In the Ākhond's hands, the tale of fools moves from ethnic slur to a sly didactic admonition, aimed at anyone in the audience able to hear it, not to take the proceedings too literally. The Ākhond's familiarity with Sufi narrative strategy shows itself in his hinted readiness to move from the profane to the profound.

6. Ākhond Mulla Mahmūd, "Salīm the Jeweller"

[*The Ākhond is speaking as taping begins.*]
This . . . there's this one long story, it's a very big one, sir.
M: Even an hour is good—
MM: [*Off mike*] Fine—for me, <u>eight</u> hours is good, whatever you do—
Ā: Yeah— ? One time, sir,
This, —   5
‹›
there was this—whatsis—
‹›
M: What's the name of this story?
Ā: The name of it, sir, was—
    it was that—
    it was   10
    the story of—
    ‹›
    That—umm—that—[*pauses in frustration*]
(What was the damned name— ? There is no might [or strength but in
                      God]!¹)—right now it—
M: [*with prompting from MM*] That's OK, at the end, we'll ask again at
                            the end.
Ā: [*laughs*] Yeah—so to say there was this—amir, sir, that so to say—they   15
    called him so-and-so—
    That
    umm—
Hojāj bin Yūsof.²

---

    1. *lā ḥaula walā*: short for the Arabic expression, *lā ḥawla walā quwwata ʾillā bi-llāhī*, uttered in situations of anger, frustration, calamity, or amazement.
    2. Literary Hajjāj bin Yūsof, born ca. 41 A.H. (661 C.E.) in Ta'if, was governor under the

[*M*: Fine—Hojāj bin Yūsof.]   20
Ā: Hojāj bin Yūsof, sir,
   so to say,
      he was the kind of man
      that just going to his own court, whoever came his way,
         maybe ten people, sir, he'd behead.   25
He was severe to such a degree,
to such a degree that, sir, he was extreme, like that.

One time, sir, he saw a dream.
Because he was so tyrannical— [*M*: Yes—]
he saw a dream and woke up from the dream with a shaking in his
         body, and, sir, his dream went right out of his head.   30
He had a vizier at court—whose name I can't remember, what he was
                       called—
   <u>right</u> away he sent for him,
   because <u>all</u> his limbs were shaking
   and he couldn't remember the dream.
Someone went, sir, and brought the vizier.   35
He said to the vizier,
   "You know what?"
   He said, "No."
   He said, "I—this calamity has come upon me.
You go bring someone, because I can't sleep,   40
   I don't sleep at night
   and I can't fall asleep during the day,
   that's the calamity that's come upon me.
Bring someone—" —sir—
   "—who can tell me a story with both laughter and tears to it.   45
So that I'll both laugh and cry."
He said—

Omayyad caliphate of Mecca and later of Iraq, governing first from the city of Basra and later from the new capitol he built at Wasit, midway between Basra and Kufa. His authority later extended as far as Khorassan in eastern Iran. He died at age 52, in ca. 94. A.H. (714 C.E.), and was buried at Wasit. Arab historians characterized him as the epitome of cruel despots, and later tradition counted him "among the few Muslims for whom . . . eternal damnation [is] assured." See H. Lammens's article, "Hadjdjaj B. Yusuf," in *The Encyclopedia of Islam* (Leyden: Brill, 1927) vol. 3, pp. 202–4, for details of his tumultuous administrative career during a period of widespread opposition to the Omayyad caliphate as successor to the authority of the Prophet.

this guy went out, and came along, saying, »
    "He'll kill me over this guy.
    Where in hell am I supposed to get a person who can   50
    talk to him so he'll both laugh" —sir— "and also cry?"

He had a daughter, sir, she's about twelve years old,
    this—guy.
She said, "Papa, why are you so worried?" »
He said, "I'm getting away, dear, I'm going to Iran.   55
    Or maybe some other country.
    You see, this Hojāj is going to kill me,
        he's beheaded the whole world already.
Now he tells me, 'Go find a person to come to me and tell me a story
                             and—do that.
          And tell me a story,   60
          and for me—
          and it—should be both funny and sad.' "
His daughter said, "Pa—don't run away, Papa, now wait, I'll be back
                          in a minute."
She went out to the garden and came back.
She said, "Go tell Hojāj,   65
    'There's a Salīm the Jeweller[3]
    —in —the —in [*stutters*] —a prisoner in your jail.
    Bring that Salīm the Jeweller,
        he'll tell you a story that has both laughter and tears.' "
This little girl said that.   70
    [*M*: Yeah.]
He came back, sir,
    and said to Hojāj, "There's this Salīm the Jewel-seller right here,
        a prisoner in your jail, go and bring him."

And for the last fifteen years Salīm's been a prisoner in this jail.   75
They brought him, sir, and the vizier took—
    this court vizier cut his fingernails and
    fed him for a couple of nights
        and got him in shape
        and got him ready.   80

---

3. *Salīm-e Jawāyerī* (literary, *Javāharī*).

He came and
    said to him, "This man is called Salīm, sir, he's a jewel-seller,
        so to say, he'll talk so it's funny,
        and he can make you
            both cry and laugh."   85

He said, "Can you do this?"
    He said, "Yes."
"Can you tell my dream, too?"
    He said, "Yes, I'll tell it."

He said, "How did you find out about him?"   90
    He said that to the vizier.
He said, "Sir, I have a daughter twelve years old.
      This daughter of mine, so to say, told me this story."
He said, "Go get the girl,"
He brought the girl,   95
    and Salīm is a man fifty years old,
    and the girl is twelve.

He said, "How did you know?"
The girl said to him, "Sir, I knew it because
          when I was in my mother's womb, in my
              father's garden   100
       my mother went to this sitting platform—[4]
       right there on the platform, my birth took place.

God gave me [to her], a daughter,
    and up in the tree there was a *parī*,[5]
    and God gave <u>her</u> a son.   105
That *parī* brought her son and placed him at my mother's breast,
    and took me and put me at her own.
For two and a half years she gave that boy—that brother of mine milk,
    and <u>she</u> gave <u>me</u> milk.[6]

---

4. A *takht* is a wooden platform used both as bed and sitting area, indoors or out.

5. The word is cognate to English "fairy." Generally benevolent, occasionally vindictive supernaturals.

6. The two mothers thus make their children foster-siblings, who are expected to have all the loyalty to one another that blood siblings have. Incest proscriptions also pertain between foster-siblings of the opposite sex.

When we parted from each other, she said to me,   110
    'Whenever you have a hardship,
        so to say, you knock these sticks together,
    I'll appear
        and remedy your hardship.'
So I knocked those sticks together and the same *pari* who had given
                             me milk came   115
    and told me,
    so to say,
    about that Salīm—the jeweller.
I spoke on that account."
This— this girl said that.   120

After that he said to Salīm, "Brother, tell your story, whatever you
                                  have to say."
He said, "My father was a jewel-seller
    by the name of so-and-so,
    very well known,
    very well supplied,   125
    very knowledgeable,
    very wealthy.
My father got sick, and called me, »
    and said, 'Oh, son, —'
    —I said, 'What?'   130
    he said, 'Relying on God,
        ‹›
        after you have
        buried— [*stutters*] —enshrouded me and carried me away,
    relying on God, take care not to sit down
        with unheeding people,   135
        with wisdomless people,
        with honorless people,
        with unheeding people.
    Sit down with people of wisdom,
    sit down with those who govern,   140
    sit down with the Muslim man,
        the seeker of God,
    sit down with the man who, so to say, dedicates himself
        to governance and the nation and the land.'
‹› [*coughs*]   145

When my father died, he'd left <u>great</u> wealth, beyond sense
                                                    or comprehension.
        Beyond <u>anything</u>.
When I'd buried him, the Lord made me—hopeless of His Court,[7]
        wherever there was a hash-smoker or a gambler or a bugger or
                                                    a lowlife,
        on any evening, for ten thousand or twenty thousand or forty
                                            thousand, and   150
        'Let's get some gypsies to dance,' or 'Let's get some boys,' or
                                    'Let's find a game.' —
I hit that property of my father's so hard that after three years of
                        spending, sir, that I got so I couldn't command
                        one *qerān*, not <u>one</u>! —for daily bread.
        Completely!
I came and sat my wife down, saying »
        'You've been with me for a while,
        now I've become penniless and helpless,   155
now you have your choice whether to stay or go marry again.'
She said, 'I was with you while you were wealthy, now I'll go to work.
            ‹›
            I'll do laundry,'
My wife was doing laundry for a bite of bread,
and of those friends and companions and   160
        those who had been around me,
        every one who saw me, needled me,
            and I stayed flat broke.

One day, sir, my wife said to me,
        'You go on, act like a Muslim,   165
        go get some
        work,'
—I was a young guy, of that age, able-bodied,
        and I went out, sir, where I saw people were
        carrying those sacks.   170
        They had ropes for doing porterage.

---

7. The now-penitent ex-apostate in telling his story attributes even his apostasy to God's will, just as his return to faith (*Islam*, literally, "submission to the will of God") should properly be credited to God's grace.

I went among those porters,
    sneaking here and there,[8]
    and I got hold of two or three *qerān* a day,
And I lost my shame,   175
    in the extremity of my courage and zeal
    and the fact that I was very strong,
so much so that, sir, for me—
    it got so nobody gave any of these porters seven pounds' work
                         as long as I was there.
All the porters got together, saying 'He's taken our arms off at
                       the shoulder.'   180
    They gave me three or four thousand *qerān* a month,
they said, 'You sit home, we'll give it to you. —
    If he's here no one gives us a turn.'
They came, sir, and gave me four thousand *qerān* a month.
◇
Those porters.   185

One day I went out and a horse had fallen, sir, in—
    —in the street.
The load lay on top of it, no matter how the porter tried to lift it,
    and I reached under, called on God,
    and dragged the horse out from under the load   190
    and heaved it into the square.
I saw someone up there [*stutters*] washing for prayers, red-eyed[9] and
    with a staff and garments of green.
I was right there
    when I happened to think, [*hoarsely whispering*] 'What
                     great strength I've got!'   195
All at once he called out,
    'Hey, Salīm the Jeweller! Now you've blown it all,
    you looked not to God's strength but to your own!'
Just as I came along there, I was laid low, sir.
    ◇
    For two entire years   200

---

    8. To conceal his identity, out of embarrassment.
    9. A mark of extreme piety: red-eyed from night vigils spent praying and weeping while meditating on God. Green is the color of the Prophet and of sanctity.

I was so sick that the very breath was chilled in my body.
One day—those porters were bringing the money, —
one day I let one of them into the house,
    he bro— the one who brought it, went and told the porters,
    'The guy is about to die,' and then the money was cut off.   205
It got, sir, so that my wife and I were left stripped bare, hungry, all was
                            in vain.
It got so that, on an evening, I—
    —I was lying there like that, —for one bite of bread
    if only someone gave it to us,
    we would draw a thousand groans."   210

And here whatsisname wept.
    Hojāj.
At this
    asceticism of his he cried a little.[10]
"After that, one time in the evening I came, extremely weak,   215
    I begged pardon before blessed God,
    and I saw a young man in green
    who came to the bedside—I had fallen asleep, —
    I begged pardon of him,
I said 'Who are you?'   220
He said, 'I am the Master of the World[11],' »
he drew his blessed hand over my head, so that when I woke up," he said, »
"*Bābā*, my neck was <u>this</u> thick, <u>this</u> big, and there wasn't a <u>pain</u> in my body!

‹›

I got up from there, kind sir,
    went out into the city,
    where Hojāj's caravan was coming
    from Mashhad,[12] headed for the House of God.   225

---

10. *Zāhedī* ("asceticism, piety") would seem an odd term for involuntary misfortune, but the enforced poverty functions for Salīm as an exercise in remembrance of God. The point here is not simply poverty, but poverty which reminds one of God's power and of the transience of human strength. A warning to the tyrannical Hojāj, the listener, is of course implicit.

11. *Sarwar-e 'ālam*: an epithet for the Caliph 'Ali, the Prophet's cousin and son-in-law, a revered martial hero of Islam who frequently figures in folk belief as a divine messenger and an intercessor with God.

12. A major city and Shī'a pilgrimage site in Khorassan, in present-day eastern Iran. It is the burial site of the martyred Imam Reza, seventh in the lineage of twelve imams de-

I went there, sir,
    and brought the pilgrims water
    brought this and that,
    brought the camels,
    did this and that,   230
took care of their camels, and they, they were pleased,
    they gave me a lot of money, »
    and I brought it and gave it to my wife, »
    and went off with them to the Holy House.
Once we had finished   235
    with all the holy pilgrimage duties and the sanctuaries,
we came to Holy Medina,
    for the caliphate of Holy Omar was there in its radiance.
After that, sir, the people—this—King Negus or whoever,[13]
    he had seventy thousand commanders   240
    and they came to surround Holy Medina.
I saw all—
    sixty thousand of—of, of those—partisans,
    they got outfitted from Medina,
    and Hojāj[14] released me and I got myself clothes and got an outfit,   245
    and I went into combat with these sixty thousand people.
    ‹›
To face that
king.
‹›
We went out like that, sir,
    till we came to a halt   260
    and we saw that this—
this king has sixteen nephews,[15]

---

scended from the Prophet who are revered in Shi‘a Islam as his spiritual heirs. The "House of God" is the Kaaba, the supreme Muslim shrine, in the city of Mecca. "Hojāj's caravan": the governor sponsors the expense of caravan guides and guards as an act of charity; pilgrims can then join a guarded and organized party for the journey.

13. *nejāshī*: title of an Abyssinian king (Steingass: *Persian-English Dictionary*).

14. By extension; he would logically be released from service by the functionaries conducting the caravan sponsored by Hojāj.

15. Literally, "sisters' sons," among the most loyal of natural allies. The reference to the mountain in the next line apparently refers to the size and weight of their weapons, most likely maces which are often the first weapons employed in the stereotyped sequence of single combat encounters common to Persian epic and romance. Single combats are followed by general melees in this sequence, as in Persian and European traditional epic.

it's as if each of them could pick up Davandar Mountain in one hand,
and toss it onto the field.
They're that kind of champions.   265
One champion rode out, and the hos—
of sixty thousand of this Muslim host not one had the will to ride out.
I got down all at once,
tightened up on my horse's saddle and bridle, and all,
rode up to the chief,   270
and said, 'I'm going.'
He said, 'You're a poor man, you don't have the strength of body.'
I said, 'I'm going, by God!'

As I went, sir,
by the power of God,   275
this, this, this—nephew of the king,
as he came in, like that,
he lifted that Davandar Mountain[16]
and rushed at me, and
with one blow I took him,   280
struck him, sir,
took his head off his body.
On this same day, sir, by lunchtime, I beheaded all sixteen champions
who were serving him."
‹›
This — guy said that.
‹›
[*M*: Yeah. Salīm the Jeweller— ?]   285
Yeah—Salīm the Jeweller.
He said, "Eighteen thousand— [*sic*]
and eighteen [*sic*] heroes who could tear up Davander
Mountain with their bare hands,
I cut off all their heads at once."
[*Break in recording—tape change*]

Ākhond [*To M and MM about where to restart the narrative*]: Back
a little farther?   290
[*M*: Yeah.]

---

16. Another metaphorical reference to the size and weight of his weapon.

"Well, so to say, sir, I killed eighteen of these heroes and
     the entire army poured down on my head
     and I struck the army on every side,
     and they <u>all</u> took off,   295
     <u>gone</u> completely!

That evening when I came back, sir,
their king had said, 'You dig forty pl— pits,
                    cover them with brush,
               and tomorrow morning go to the battle field,   300
                    Don't you make any more attacks,'[17]
[*M*: Yeah—]
He said, 'This champion himself will come on, the way he does, and
                              fall in a pit amidst you all.'
‹›
I came riding along, sir,
     and the horse balked.   305
     I spurred it,
     and I fell into the fortieth pit.
     Along with the horse.
When I fell, dirt and brush and everything they had, sir,
     they poured into the pit.   310
And I held my spear in my hand up in the air, to make it so that I
                              could breathe,
     and they filled the pit to the top, but the spear was still up in the air."
‹›
Hojāj wept a little here, too.
‹›
Because he had fallen into the pit.

When Hojāj wept, after that [he said],   315
"Next morning
     they came and were busily opening up the top of the pit.
     They dragged me out of the pit.
     They took me before this—Hojā—this guy—
     uh—the king.   320

———————

17. Other invincible heroes defeated by the pit trick include Rostam of the Iranian national epic *Shāhnāmah*.

[*M*: Negus—]
Yeah, —he said, 'Brother, I'll tell you something,
        for someone like you,
        even if you did slaughter my army,
        my heart burns that I would have to kill you.   325
        So come on, accept our religion.
        If you accept our religion,
        I'll set you at the head of an army of the whole world.'
I said, 'Even if you tear me apart piece by piece,
        I abso<u>lute</u>ly refuse to accept your religion.   330
        Praise be to God,
        whether you kill me now, or whatever you do!' "

He said, "They took me to prison, sir.
        He sent that delegation again,
            'Go on, tell him.'   335
        When the delegation came to me,
            they said, 'Accept this religion.'
            I said, 'I won't,' like that and
        there was this
            piece of iron lying in the prison,   340
            that weighed a hundred *man* or fifty *man*,[18]
        they hit me over the head with it and split my head open.

There were a <u>lot</u> of Muslim prisoners, there, too, in this prison.
After that, then, I don't know what happened, it was three nights later,
        —these prisoners put poultices on my head, sir, and   345
        bound the wound up with handkerchieves.
        I came to three nights after that.
And my head is all swollen up, and no matter what they did, I didn't accept
                              their religion.

One night when I was lying there, again
        I saw that blessed messenger in a dream drawing his hand over my
                         blessed head.[19]   350

---

18. In Herat, a *man* equals approximately three kilos, or almost seven pounds.
19. The storyteller inverts the phrase, making it (literally) "drew his hand over my blessed head," but the epithet belongs to the hand, not the head. He corrects himself in the next sentence.

He drew his blessed hand over my head.
I got up, sir, and my head was cured, mended!
In the dream, he'd said, »
  'Take that pillar,
  that piece of iron.
  You go out,   355
  hit those who are on guard,
      kill them all at once.
  Let these men loose, and you, too, flee, go!'
I picked up that iron
  and hit all the guardsmen and killed them,   360
  and freed the Muslims, too,
  and I, too, with the iron on my shoulder, ha! Run, if you're
                                      running!!![20]

I went, and went, and went, like that, sir, to an island.[21]
  And I'm completely dead from hunger.
  I went onto the island and ate something,   365
  ate some fruit, and ate this and that.
I stayed there that night and there were a lot of wolves and lions,
and I took
  and made a boat.
  From the bark of these trees.   370
I cast myself out to sea.

I went hungry for sixteen days at sea.
After that I got caught in a whirlpool that wouldn't be believed.
  There are all these ships in the whirlpool, sir,
  and everyone on them dead.[22]   375

By the power of God all at once an opposing wind came up,
  and cast me on an island, sir.
When I went into this island, sir,
  there were a lot of trees

---

20. *Bejīh keh mījīh!* literally, "Flee, for you're fleeing!" a variation on a more common storyteller's idiom, *Bejīh keh nemījīh!*—"Flee, you're not fleeing [fast enough]!"
    21. *jazīrah*: In landlocked Afghanistan, the concept often seems to be of an island or peninsula in a river or delta, surrounded by water which is fordable at certain points.
    22. The idea being that the whirlpool catches ships and whirls them around in circles indefinitely.

and a lot of wild animals,   380
    and in the evening I climbed up,
        there were such trees that every branch had a spread of one parsang.[23]
I was sitting there,
        it was the middle of the night when I saw a bull come out of
                                                            the sea, sir,
        and it let out a bellow, and that bellow made the whole valley echo.   385
It came to the foot of this tree, and dropped a night-glowing
                                            jewel[24] out of its mouth.
        So that all that area was illuminated.
After that it grazed on that grass till dawn, all the grass around there,
        then it came back, picked up the jewel, and left.
And I was a jewel expert.   390
I became avid to have that jewel.
That morning, I said, 'It will come back tonight.' »
I was up in that tree, and I went and prepared ten or twenty *man*
                                            of mud, out of the mud there.
I came back and put it there, and when it put the jewel down at the
                                            tree, under the tree,
it went off to graze and I dropped the mud glob by glob down on
                                            top of the jewel.   395
I dropped the mud down so that it hid the jewel.
When the jewel was hidden, sir, it got dark,
the bull came and hit the tree,
        hit this side and hit that side,
        and me up in the tree.   400
The bull quieted down, and in the morning I came down, after the
                                            bull was gone, it had just died.
Once the jewel fell from its throat.
I pulled out the jewel, sir, and cut a slit at my shoulder and hid it there.[25]

---

23. *farsakh* (literary, *farsang*): an ancient Iranian unit of distance, also used in Arabic texts, one parsang equals 6.24 kilometres, or about 3.75 miles (Haim, *Persian-English Dictionary*).

24. *gohar-e shab cherāq*: also a metaphorical term for any spectacular gem, not only those which are thought to emit light. In the next clause, the co-occurrence of two rather bookish terms shifts the diction of the previously quite colloquial narration.

25. *sar-e shonah-e khor chāk dādom haminjī īr dafn kardom*: it is not quite clear whether he cut a slit in a garment or actually concealed it beneath his skin, but probably the latter, on analogy from nonambiguous uses of this motif in other stories.

I left that valley, and came along, and came along, sir, I went for
                                           a while, till I got to another valley.

I went there and there were monkeys,   405
    it was a valley of monkeys.
I went into this monkey valley, sir,
    I was there that night.
The monkeys were picking little fruits and throwing them at me,
                               and I went here and there,
    until this one place, sir,
where there were a hundred million monkeys.   410
They had storage chambers where they were gathering fruit to store
                                    for winter.
They saw me and came up to me laughing,
    and I passed by there.
Sir, I went,
    and the king of the monkeys has a daughter.   415

These, sir,
these girls—all these girls[26] who saw me came up to me, laughing,
    and I, a young, brave man,
they brought me up
this—   420
to, to this platform where that girl is sitting, brother dear that I
                                  consider you,[27] and
    there's this area, this place,
then she kissed me and did this and that, and showed me great honor,
and ordered me milk and food and did this and did that,
and right there that evening" —it's like the Khalīfah said about that
                                 other dame—[28] 425
    [M: Yeah—]

---

26. That is, young female monkeys.
27. *Barādar gol keh shomār dārom*: literally, "flower-brother that I have [in] you," a friendly address to the listener, more intimate than *sāyeb* or *sā'eb*, "sir, master," which the storyteller has used to Mokhtār and Salīm has used toward Hojāj hitherto. As the topic takes a more intimate turn in the story within the story, the speaker's changed manner of address asks the listener's indulgence for greater informality.
28. Reference to the earlier story, "Rasūl's Mother" (chapter 4).

he said, "She's an unmarried girl who'd never seen a human in her
                                                        whole life,
        and she had a great interest in men"
        —monkeys are just like people, anyway.
[*M (murmurs)*: Yes . . .]   430
"She's very beautiful and I'm single, too, sir, and she started from the
                                        bottom of my foot,
        stroking, she came along and came along, up the special tool of mine.[29]
[*M*: Uh-huh.]
She massaged it and did this and that and rubbed herself against it,
and she was well aroused and I was single, too, sir, and I took hold
                        of her shoulders and [*claps*] came <u>down</u> like that!   435
I <u>hit</u> so she was hollering 'Cinnamon two and a half *man*, one *qerān*!!'[30] »
        She fainted there and I fainted here."
This — king laughed a <u>lot</u>.
Right here where he fucked the monkey girl. [*laughs*]

"Sir, I was there for about two years, God had given me a son from
                                        this monkey.   440
[*M*: Yeah.]
He gave me a son, [but] one day I thought, 'My wife got left there, and
                I came here and got hitched up with monkeys, this bastard,
<u>every</u> day, <u>every</u> day,
she liked it and twelve months of the year I'm fucking a monkey, me,
        —I'm a <u>human</u>, after all."   445
[*M*: Yeah . . .]
"So <u>all</u> at once I picked up that club, that iron, and ran.
And that dame came along hollering, with my child on her shoulders.
Ho! I raised the club, and she tore my child in two and threw one part in
                front of me, and picked up the other—picked it up, and left.

I came along and came along and came along, kind sir, to this—   450
I came, sir, and arrived at an island,

---

29. Somewhat more euphemistic terminology than in the earlier story.
30. Her loud and enthusiastic yelling is compared in an idiomatic expression to that of a street vendor selling very cheaply.

and I'm so tired I'm just ready to die, there's a tree here, sir, and in the
                    hollow of the tree, I lay down my head and fell
                    asleep, and before dawn—
     there was a pool right there—
three pigeons came along,
took off their (feathered) skins[31] and jumped into the pool.   455
Then I went, without a sound, like that,
     and picked up the feathers of one of those sisters
     and came and hid in the hollow of the tree.
When they had bathed,
     the *parī*s were putting their feathers back on.   460
     The youngest sister,
     no matter how she searched, she couldn't find her feathers.
She came back. »
The other sisters said, 'Come on, let's go,' »
but she said, 'Until I find my feathers, I'm not leaving.'

They left.
This one girl came,   465
     with her hair wrapped around her,
she came up near me and said, 'Ah, Salīm the Jeweller, at such-and-such
                    a place, you did thus-and-so, and so on,
                    treated your wife so and so, and so on,
                         did this and that,
                    and in such-and-such a place you prayed . . . ,'
this girl told me every <u>bit</u> of my <u>entire</u> past.   470
'Now give me my feathers.'

I said, 'I've fallen in love with you, "Give me my feathers" doesn't
                    mean a thing.'
She said, 'If you've fallen in love, come along with me, I'll take you
          to my father, my father is a good person, doubtless he'll
                         give you—
     —give me to you in marriage.'   475

---

31. *Parī* often travel in the guise of pigeons or other birds. *Jeld*: "skin, covering," here refers to a removable "pigeon suit" of feathers which enables a *parī* to fly.

Well, I gave her back her feathers and from there she took me on her
                         wings, and took me behind the veil of Mount Qāf.[32]
    To her father.
Her mother saw me, and her sisters, and the point is,
I'm a noble young man, there was this spring there, king sir, she dipped
                         me in the spring and I became a youth of fourteen.[33]
The Spring of Blessed Solomon, peace be on him.   480

In short, to make the story shorter, I'll say that they took me to her
                                                   father so—
    the point is, they negotiated the marriage with the father—
                                                   engaged her to me,
    her father engaged her and gave her to me.
God gave me a son, the next year, a very handsome, fine son,
They swaddled him, kind sir,   485
and this lion came
    and they—put him in the lion's mouth, and it picked him up and left.

My child.

The next year, God gave another son,
a wolf came, and they swaddled him and put him in the wolf's mouth.
It picked him up and left.   490

Some while later, one day I started to weep and mourn, and
she said, 'Why are you weeping?' »
I said, 'I'm remembering my wife,
        I came here so long ago,
        besides, you're such pitiless people
        that in my own presence you gave one of my children to a wolf
                                    and the other to a lion.' 495
She said, 'Oh, well, those were their nurses.
        They were going about in those skins. — [M: Yeah —]
        Go and bring the children!' »

_____

    32. The *parī* world lies behind Mount Qāf, the mountain at the limit of the human
world (sometimes conceived as a huge mountain ringing the known world).
    33. Fourteen is considered the age of maximum beauty and romantic promise through-
out Persian literature and popular thought.

They brought my children, one seven years old, and one five, and
                    each one has the strength of a lion-fish.³⁴
She said, 'They were nurses.'

After that, I spoke with her,   500
I said, 'Now, I'm going,
        this one time,
        to—find out how my wife is,
        in my own country.'
This woman gave me a great deal of wealth, and said, »
    'Be careful my father doesn't find out.   505
    On this condition, that you come back within one month.'
She gave me a great deal of money, sir, and she set me on a *deyb*,³⁵
    as a mount.
She said, 'It's two and a half years' travel to that place of yours.
        He'll carry you in a day and a night.   510
        Now as he carries you, be careful,
        if my father finds out,
        he'll send an army after you.
        You'll have to throw down oil and things,
        so he'll turn back from following you.   515
        As you go, be careful that you don't mention the Name of God.
        If you mention the Name of God, wherever it is, this *deyb*
                        will throw you down.

        ‹›
[*M*: Yeah—]
    Don't mention it at all. ' "

_____

34. In Herat, the term *sheyr mohīn* (for literary, *sheyr māhī*) ordinarily referred to a particularly large fish occasionally caught in the Herat river. Haim's, *Persian-English Dictionary*
offers other meanings, including "walrus." The simile, which is an odd one, is lacking in the
current chapbook version of the story in my possession.
35. Literary *dīv*: the word is cognate to Sanskrit *deva* and Latin *deus*; they are the
demons of Zoroastrian cosmology. In modern popular Muslim thought in Afghanistan
and Iran, the *dīv* are generally competitive or malevolent toward humans and *parī*, but subject to taming through various means. *Parī* generally have *dīv* as servants. The activities of
dīv, who are of pre-Islamic Indo-European origin, are generally confined to traditional
fictional narrative, whereas *jinn*, supernaturals of Semitic origin who figure in Islamic religious legends, also appear as dangerous forces in people's personal experience and belief
narratives.

So it's like his place was at Qorīyān, and he got as far as

Khojah-e Chisht.[36]   520

This, this Salīm.

The *deyb* put the guy down to catch his breath, and he said,

"Thank God!"

Said, "Lord, praise be to God, thanks!" »

As soon as he said, "Thanks," »

[the *deyb*] said, "Blessings on mine, and peace upon yours![37]

Let's go!"

He said[38], "He set out and went, anyway." [*M: Inaudible comment*]   525

He remained. "So I got up and looked around,

I saw a thou— a guy herding about three thousand sheep over at the

foot of the mountains.

And he has <u>ten</u> *man* of wool in his hand.[39]

‹›

A *deyb*,

sir.   530

[*M*: Yeah—]

He's <u>such</u> a *deyb*, sir, that his nose, sir, is the size of this house.

So that when he glanced over, each of his eyes is like the roof-dome

of a house.

When he saw me, he said, 'Hey, come here!'

And I didn't want to, »

but he could reach his hand out and get me, »

he could reach a whole *parsang*.   535

I went up to him, »

and he said, 'Where are you going?' »

---

36. Qorīyān is a town about twenty miles west of Herat City, and Chisht, a market town, Sufi center, and pilgrimage site, is approximately 100 miles up the Herat River valley to the east of the city. The total distance by present roads is perhaps 120 miles. Chisht is the original home of Muʿinuddin Chishti, a disciple of Abu Najib Suhrawardi who migrated to Delhi in 1193 C.E. (A.H. 589) and founded the Chishti Sufi order, a key force in the Islamization of India in the twelfth and thirteenth centuries C.E. (sixth and seventh centuries A.H.; Schimmel 1975:344 ff.).

37. A formula for parting when the other party has no choice in the matter (equivalent to the English, "Goodbye and good riddance!"). The *deyb*'s second expression, "*Yallah!*" (l. 524) literally means, "Oh, God!" but is normally used to prompt others into motion, as in "hurry up," "let's go," or "let's get on with it."

38. The storyteller returns the narrative voice to Salīm.

39. Spinning yarn as he follows the sheep.

I said, 'I'm just going to my own country,' »
He said, 'Let's go
        to my place, tonight.'

He headed up the flock and whistled to the sheep and
he set me in front of him and came, and there was a stone in front of
                                                his cave, kind sir,
‹›
that weighs a hundred *kharwār*[40], a thousand *kharwār*.   540
He took hold of it by a handgrip, and moved the stone to one side,
                                        and put the flock into—
        the — cave.
        In there.
When he put the flock in, »
        I went in and there were about twenty thousand young men,
                                                there, sir, »
        hanging in chains.
When we sat down right there, »
        after that he easily set the stone back, »
        and put the flock in the back of the cave.   545
He brought a cooking pot, kind sir, a great, big pot, and put a lot of
                                                oil in it.
He took one of these youths and his head—
        —cut off his head,
        threw him in the pot »
        and fried him.
        ‹›
[*Audience member*: Just like a chicken . . .]   550
Just like a chicken."
There where he said, "He cut off his head and
                fried him,"
whatsisname started to weep again.

Hojāj.   555

———————

40. *Kharwār*, literary, *kharbār*: literally, a donkey-load, a unit of weight measurement,
which in Herat, equals 100 *man* (about 650 pounds).

[*M*: Yes—]
"After that, he ate him, and then he parboiled and boned a sheep
                                        and roasted it on iron spits[41]
        and gave it to me and to them,
        and gave us raisins and sweets
        and this and that.   560
The next day he took the flock out, set out, and left, shut the door
                                        of the cave.
The youths said, 'Oh, brother, you can weep for years,
                but when [your] forty days are up, your turn will
                                        come to be killed.
                Until he fattens you up good, you won't end up
                                        in the pot.'

‹›

Brother dear that I consider you, [*coughs*]   565
these iron skewers, sir, they were skewers this long,
these ones, sir, that he makes the kebab on,
        he gives it to the youths and to us people so we'll get fat,
        that we—umm—for him to eat.
When he was eating, he'd drink wine, too, sir.   570
After the wine, he'd pass out.

This—I said this to these young men, »
        'Oh, brothers, I'll free you all from these bonds.
        When he drinks the wine,
        let's put these iron skewers in the fire, and this—
        —[while] this bastard is sprawled on his back,   575
        I'll take one, and you take one,
        and—we'll run them into his eyes, so they come out the other side.
        And one can cut open his stomach, and we'll kill him, anyway.'
Not one," he said, "had the courage.
I called on God, brother,   580
        and when he passed out and I had put the skewers on the fire before—
[*M*: Yeah—]

---

41. *Qau kardan*: Kazim Alami identified this cooking procedure as a special one, often
used for entertainment of guests or for preparation of food to be given away in charity as a
votive offering (*nazr*).

then I took them up and stood over his head, sir, and those two skewers,
   I stuck them both at once into his eyes so they came out the other side.
He was blinded, sir.   585
   As soon as he was blinded, I ran into the midst of the flock.

Now he's searching the sheep to find me—and his eyes were blinded, OK.
Right away I killed a sheep and skinned it, sir,
   and put on the skin.
◇
The <u>whole</u> thing, <u>head</u> and all, and me on all fours—I stood among
                                                        the sheep.   590
◇
As I stood among the sheep, he came behind
   —he took hold of the stone and lifted it, picked it up, sir.
I'm standing there on all fours, and the sheep are coming along to pass by,
   so then, I'm feeling my way around the cave,[42] so he can't get me.
And I got out, too, along with the sheep.   595
He thought I was a sheep, too.
Once I got out, sir, he realized that I'd gotten out, and he hurled himself
                                                        out of the cave.
When he hurled himself out there, I was at the top of the mountain,
                                                        and he was below.
He's looking and looking for me, and I had a certain amount of
                                        strength, I picked up a hundred-*man* rock,
and hit him in the main vein of his neck, and he fell on his face.   600
I hit him with another rock, and with the third rock I broke his head
                                        in pieces and killed him and I left his body there.

I came, and the door of the cave was open.
I freed all those people, and gathered up all his worldly goods.[43]
So we came along, like, to Obeh.[44]
Some of these people were from Obeh,   605
   and there's a jail there.

---

42. Inside the skin on all fours, Salīm cannot see, either.
43. The *deyb*'s.
44. Local color: Obeh is the main market town on the road between the shrine town
of Chisht and Herat. See note 36 above, and Map No. 1.

We sold the sheep and divided the money, »
    and we came to Pashtūn Zarghūn, »
    came to the city, »
    came along.
So that very evening I arrived at Qorīyān at my own house.
At the dinnertime prayer I went and knocked on the door.
My wife came, 'Who is it?' »
I said, 'Salīm the Jeweler,' »
she said, 'Salīm—it's been thirty-two years he's been lost, now you
                        come and say, »
       'I'm Salīm,' —as young as you are?'   610
'God's truth, I'm Salīm!'

This cousin of mine[45] came and we got each other's scent,[46]
she said, 'We—we don't have a thing, even a light tonight!'
I took the money, and went, sir, to the bazaar to buy that—kerosene.
I came and went up into this guy's shop, and he grabbed me, [saying]
                        'You're a thief.' 615
He hit me.
A soldier came, sir, and they took me to prison, »
    and it's sixteen years I've been a captive in your prison, nobody's
                        called my name.
And I haven't seen my wife, either.

So now you called for me, those are my circumstances."
[*M*: Yes—]   620
This Salīm the Jeweller spoke.
[*M*: Yes—]
After that, the king gave him a house and, sir,
    he brought his wife and children
    and then he sent him and brought that other wife, that *parī*
                        of his, and 625
so all of them, sir, it was some time that
God gave her offspring, »
    and gave offspring to that other wife, »

---

45. Literally, father's brother's daughter—his wife. Cousin marriage is preferred by many traditional Afghan families, as it is in many other parts of the Middle East. Use of the term at this point reaffirms the special loyalty arising from consanguineous ties.
    46. Metaphor for recognition among intimates.

and so it was that Salīm the Jeweller and his cousin died
and that—
parī took her children and went back [*claps once softly*] behind
                          the veil of Mount Qāf.
M: [*prompting the storyteller with a closing formula*] "And our desire
                         and yours . . . " 630
Ā: [*laughing*] —Yes?
M: "And our desire and yours . . . "[47]
Ā: Oh, yeah—his desi— the story of Salīm, that's the story that's told, sir.
M: Good.

——————

47. The entire formula is, "And as God gave them their desire, may He give our desire and yours."

"Sit down with people of wisdom . . ."

When the Ākhond takes the performance floor again, he expands the generic scope of the storytelling session, offering a lengthy, framed, multi-episodic novella-type adventure tale, replete with religious themes and supernatural encounters which school and test the hero in patience, fortitude, and faith. No conversational comment explained the Ākhond's choice at this point or explicitly tied this story to what had gone before, either in interview or in story. The Ākhond introduced the story only by a hesitant alllusion to its length (l. 1). Yet a consideration of the complex content and structure of the tale reveals a number of possible associative links, as well as rhetorical potentialities, which may have influenced the Ākhond's choice.

Mokhtār's request for a title while I sat poised, pen in hand, to write it down created a momentary stumbling block for the Ākhond, as he tried to recall the name of "Hojāj," or (more properly), Hajjāj bin Yūsuf (ll. 8–19). The name is important, not only to understand the content and historical background of the tale, but also in the context of present company. Hajjāj was a seventh-century C.E. governor, in what is now Iraq during the Omayyad caliphate (see note 2, to l. 19). A staunch opponent to the ʿAlid faction (who were partisans of the Prophet's son-in-law and his descendants, and the founders of the Shiʿa sect), Hajjāj was vilified by several later historians as an exceptionally cruel despot, damned in the eyes of Islam. Down to this day, Sabra Webber reports, Hajjāj is famous among schoolchildren in Arabic-speaking countries for his remark, "I see some heads ripe for harvesting" (personal communication 1989). It is his error and injustice, and their at least implicit correction, that frame the adventures of Salīm the Jeweller and provide a reason internal to the narrative for the telling of those adventures.

The Ākhond's choice of a tale concerned with unjust rule and the rehabilitation of a despot who, himself Muslim, oppresses and wrongly imprisons other Muslims, cannot easily be dismissed as accidental in the subgovernor's presence, still less so considering that the hero, Salīm, is the victim of unjust imprisonment and the subgovernor was, by his own admission (to Mokhtār in private), responsible for locking the Ākhond up several months previously. Now the Ākhond, possessor of special knowledge, has been summoned like Salīm to tell a story to his oppressor. Thematic connections are reinforced by stylistic ones. The Ākhond addresses

Mokhtār with titles of respect at virtually every other line in the first part of the story ("sir," "kind sir," etc.). Once Salīm begins to narrate his own story to Hojāj, the fictional storyteller showers the tyrant with the same honorifics, and the fictional and actual narrators and audience almost merge, rhetorically. At certain points (e.g., ll. 529–30), distinctions made in the written translation between reported addresses to the tyrant and actual addresses to Mokhtār, as marked by punctuation necessitated by literate convention, are in fact arbitrary and artificially disambiguate the spoken words. Prompted by the Ākhond's use of eye contact, Mokhtār responds with murmurs of assent as if words attributable to Salīm (addressing Hojāj) were addressed directly to himself.

In addressing his words to Mokhtār, the honored guest, rather than to the subgovernor himself, who was also present, the storyteller both observes rules of hospitality and also potentially increases the obliqueness of his didactic strategy. We never discussed the events of his imprisonment with him (indeed, I did not hear the story from Mokhtār until after we left the town). Thus, the Ākhond had no overtly acknowledged responsibility for knowing that Mokhtār or I had heard about his prior imprisonment, hence, no overt reason to expect that we would detect a pointedness in this choice of subject matter, though he may have surmised that the subgovernor would have told Mokhtār the story. Thus, the etiquette of indirectness, whereby information about other people is not solicited from them directly, leaves a margin of deniability for statements which may be interpreted as critical of them. The tactic of addressing an "innocent bystander," appropriate to the guest-host relationship then prevailing, also allows a storyteller to speak to someone who is an object of commentary indirectly, through (perhaps) unsuspecting third parties.

Assuredly, it remains arguable how consciously the Ākhond chose the themes of imprisonment and injustice, since none of this topical linkage was made explicit. It must be stressed, however, that didactic storytelling makes extensive use of oblique implications and implicit connections, especially from adult to adult, in communities where circumspection is a basic ingredient of polite conversation among nonequals in public, of which this was certainly a case. Making points through narrative absolves the speaker of responsibility for direct confrontation. It is up to each listener to infer to what present persons or events the story might relate. While the storyteller avoids the rudeness and risk of direct confrontation, a listener may save face for him or herself by not directly acknowledging possible applications of a story which third parties may see as a comment on his or her own behavior. All the while, the subtle game of indirect comment and criticism proceeds.[1]

The implicit social power of didactic storytelling is nowhere better portrayed than in the story of Hojāj and Salīm itself. This is a classic "talking cure" (cf. Clinton 1986). As in the frame tale of *The Thousand and One Nights*, a despotic and troubled ruler is induced to listen to narrative when he should be sleeping, and the narration, in order to succeed (at saving the teller's life among others'), must amuse the despot and move him to pity (ll. 45–46), but also must finally enlighten him about the causes of his affliction, which lie in his own behavior. The predicament of the vizier, assigned on pain of death to discover a man who can resolve this mystery, becomes a kind of neck-riddle, a puzzle that must be solved to save one's own neck.

The parallels between the story at hand and the frame tale of *The Thousand and One Nights* extend to details as well as general themes: in both cases, a vizier, under threat for his life if he cannot meet the demands of his sovereign, is saved by his wise, virginal daughter.[2] Though the tyranny in question is not sexual in Hojāj's case, and the vizier's daughter only plays a transitory role, the judicious and innocent young virgin who arranges for Hojāj's deliverance is still a powerful foil for the tortured tyrant. The uniformly positive roles of women in Salīm's own sexual history round out a highly complimentary portrait of the feminine, somewhat of a departure from what has gone before in this storytelling session.

This story is a major departure from the stories that preceded it in several ways, not only in its handling of sexual themes but also in its treatment of religious issues and of the supernatural, in characterization and the

---

1. For an excellent discussion of this dimension in Apache storytelling, see Keith Basso (1984). Susan Slyomovics (1987) found the performance of Egyptian Bani Hilal epic in private settings to be rich in innuendo as the poet used the traditional poetic device of punning to comment on the personal lives and character of his patrons and other members of the audience within the frame of the epic verse recitation. Nor is context-based inference confined to narrative in traditional speech communities. Lila Abu-Lughod (1986:173ff.) describes poets' use of ambiguity, and the traditional audience's ability to disambiguate a poem based on their knowledge of the speaker's circumstances, in her study of Egyptian Bedouin women's traditional poetry. For a discussion of relevant literature and reexamination of proverbs in context, see Briggs (1988).

2. As might be expected, episodes in Salīm's story share content of varying specificity with tales within the *Nights*, e.g., a vizier who, under threat of death, must identify a man to resolve a mystery ("The Tale of the Woman Cut to Pieces"), abstaining from naming the Holy Name in order to keep supernatural transport working ("The Third Qalandar's Tale"), and a Polyphemus variant in Sindbad's third voyage, to name a few. Appendix A lists relevant international tale type and motif numbers.

degree of constructed distance and/or potential identification between the teller or listeners and the main characters in the story. But perhaps the most striking departure concerns scale, structural complexity, and the allusive resonance of the story in the wider oral and literary narrative tradition. The frame tale has a number of affinities with *The Thousand and One Nights*, as has been shown. The frame tale construction itself characterizes the great literary tale collections of India and the Muslim world, such as the *Pancha-tantra, Kalila wa Dimna* (which the Ākhond will shortly discuss under its other title, *Anvār-i-Sohaylī*), *The Thousand and One Nights*, and other still-popular later collections such as the *Tūtīnāmah* (*Book of the Parrot*) or the *Seven Viziers*. In each case, the tales narrated by characters within the frame tale have didactic purposes. Aside from the colorfulness of their predica-ments, the fictional narrators within the frame tales reconstruct a common psychosocial dynamic of actual storytelling in Middle Eastern contexts: stories may be offered as entertainment, but they are selected for reasons particular to the audience at hand, and often interpretable as interpersonal comment, critique, or admonition. The more apt the selection, the more powerful the storyteller's performance.

Nor is the frame tale strictly a literary device in imitation of socially contexted oral storytelling. People who told stories for me prided them-selves on the length and complexity of the stories they could recount, and framing and other types of chiastic structure are well represented among stories that have no known literary existence. As has just been pointed out, framing can be a useful distancing technique in everyday didactic expres-sion. In the present case, however, the story of Hojāj and Salīm does have a literary life as well, and by introducing this story, the Ākhond brought us into the realm of written tradition. The Ākhond did not volunteer that his source for this tale was a book. It is not found in any of the famous literary story collections just mentioned. It is quite possible that the Āk-hond learned it orally from another teller, with or without direct knowl-edge of any of the written versions. In fact, it was only several years after hearing it that I encountered a printed versions of Salīm's story, in a small lithograph on pulp paper printed by Khorshīd Publishers in Tehran, sell-ing for eight rials (twelve cents U.S.) in the 1960s (Sharkat-e Nasabī Kānūn-e Ketāb, n.d.). Such books, printed in Iran and Pakistan, were widely marketed in the bazaars of Afghan cities and towns. I did not find this book in either Herat or Kabul bookstores in 1974–76, despite a fairly general search for published stories of this kind, so it may not have been in distribution in Afghanistan at that time. Yet Harvard's Widener Library had acquired it from Tehran in 1970.

It is possible that the Ākhond had encountered the little book, though that is unlikely since he did not identify Salīm's tale as a "book" story, despite our expressed desire to discuss such connections. Since Hajjāj is an historical personage, the Ākhond may have assumed that this story would be found somewhere in the written histories of that period, whether or not it "had a book" (in local terms) of its own. In 1984, Roxanne Haag-Higuchi published a description of an eighteenth century C.E. (twelfth century A.H.) manuscript story collection in Persian from the Shrine Library in Mashhad containing another version of the story of Salīm, which like the lithographed chapbook, names Salīm and Hajjāj. The formal resemblances among these various versions of Salīm's story will be explored at the end of this chapter, as they raise some questions and challenge certain assumptions concerning the workings of joint oral-literary traditions in the Middle East and elsewhere where such a long-standing symbiosis has prevailed. Haag-Higuchi's evidence together with the Ākhond's performance and the Tehran chapbook establishes at least a 200-year currency for the tale in Khorassan (the historic region encompassing present-day eastern Iran and northwestern Afghanistan). The simple, unornamented style of the eighteenth-century version, like the subtitle of the twentieth century version, which calls itself "the best stories for reading (*khvāndan*)," suggests that the compilers expected the written versions to be read aloud. Reading aloud was and is a recognized form of entertainment in the Middle East, whereby literates, though few in most communities, were called upon to exercise their skills on behalf of those who did not read. Both entertainment and didactic purposes were regularly so served, down to the present day in Herat. This story, however, was not widely known during my time in Herat. The Ākhond was the only one of about eighty informants who performed it for me or even mentioned it as part of a repertoire.

Before undertaking the comparison of oral and written versions, let us first situate the oral story in the immediate proceedings, for the form it presents in the oral version is interpretable within and partly dependent upon its performance context. The tale is sufficiently complex and richly detailed to preclude an exhaustive analysis, should one be contemplated, but the purpose of analysis here is in any case not to exhaust the text (to say nothing of the readers) but to demonstrate aspects of its thematic organization which form parts of a larger, emergent structure encompassing the whole complex performance sequence. In this regard, certain themes are already familiar, and still others which appear in this story for the first time are picked up and elaborated later by either the Ākhond or Karīm. Story structures in general should be viewed as open-ended sets of potential patterns, developing differently in different performance settings, differently received by different listeners, rather than closed entities manifested in sets of variations.

Two topics that dominate Salīm's story, religion and sex, were also prominent in the preceding stories. But in the case of Salīm and Hojāj, each man's failure of religious consciousness is attributed not to foolish ignorance (as portrayed in all the previous stories, especially the first, which focused on religious matters), but to culpable forgetfulness (the technical term for which is *ghaflat*) on the part of an intelligent person who should know better. In this tale, the main characters of the story are not distanced from the listeners by being portrayed as grotesquely foolish or foreign. They are Muslims, they are intelligent, and they are members of a community which is regarded as historically real, belonging to a known time and place important in Muslim history. The Ākhond brings the tale into more immediate reference by using local color, place-names of the Herat area, instead of the locales of historical Iraq and Syria where the written versions place the story's events in consistency with records of the historical Hajjāj's rule.

The tyrannical Hojāj has an influential dream, which he cannot remember when he wakes (l. 30), so terrifying is it and so out of touch is he with the demands of righteousness. Yet the dream continues to afflict him with sleeplessness. For a cure, he appears to seek only diversion (ll. 40–46), but when Salīm is presented, Hojāj asks, "Can you tell my dream, too?" (l. 88). In the Ākhond's handling of this detail (not in the written versions), Salīm's role assimilates to that of the Qurʿanic-Biblical Joseph (Yūsof), whose interpretation of Pharaoh's dream and subsequent release from prison are prominent in the very well-known Persian Yūsof legendry.

Salīm agrees to interpret the dream as well as tell his own story, but in the event, he never does reveal Hojāj's dream. Instead, in the course of his story he tells several dreams of his own in which he has received divine guidance and admonition. Hojāj's final act, to repair the injustice done to Salīm in his own prison, is implicitly one of self-redemption since Hojāj's own affliction is to be relieved by hearing Salīm's story and being moved to pity him. Hence, the content of Hojāj's dream is implied to have been an admonition to the redress of wrong, but Salīm never reveals that admonition directly. Salīm is the direct beneficiary of divine admonition and punishment, Hojāj the indirect beneficiary of Salīm's experience.

Salīm's own forgetfulness is of a much less enigmatic kind: he forgets his father's deathbed advice and becomes a prodigal youth of a kind quite standard in Persian (and for that matter, world) folktale. Salīm's father's advice, as retold by the Ākhond, is detailed and develops themes of more than casual concern to present company. Not only should the boy rely on God, but he should avoid the ignorant (cf. the preceding three stories), and seek out "people of wisdom," "those who govern," and "the Muslim man, the seeker of God, . . . the man who . . . dedicates himself / to governance and the nation and the land" (ll. 134–45). In such scenes in other stories, the son is commonly enjoined to keep the faith and associate only with the honorable and wise, but explicit advice to seek out those who govern was not, in my experience, a common ingredient. The words in Salīm's mouth can be construed as a compliment to Hojāj, if the despot chooses to take them so, or an admonition to be like the righteous governors.

In the Ākhond's mouth, the explicit connection of Islam with good governance in a story performed at the behest of a Marxist civil servant can hardly be random. The subgovernor would surely count himself among "those who govern," with whom Salīm's father advises him to consort. One of the main stated ideological goals of Afghan Marxists at that time was to demonstrate that ethics in government are not dependent on religious affiliation. According to Mokhtār, the subgovernor was trying to demonstrate this principle at his present post by making no secret of his apostasy (e.g., not participating in daily prayer, not wearing a head-covering; see chapter 16) and at the same time pointedly refusing to take bribes.

Later in the story, rescued from the effects of his initial foolhardiness by hard work and the divine gift of health and strength, Salīm once again forgets his debt to God, is cast into abject helplessness by way of a lesson (ll. 195–201), and not released till he thinks to beg pardon of God (l. 216). Thereafter, having established a direct line of communication with divine messengers by his submission to God's will, Salīm the man gains what Hojāj the governor lacks: an ear for divine guidance, at least while he is asleep.

On the basis of overt content, Salīm's story divides into two major segments. The first is dominated by the lessons he receives in religious obedience and hard work, culminating in his successful pilgrimage and his heroic exploits, virtuous suffering and subsequent divine rescue in the aftermath of the holy war. The second half of the story is dominated by sexual and other adventures in otherworldly realms, through which Salīm is eventually motivated to seek his home and human wife again. Two encounters with murderous monsters bracket Salīm's travels in the supernatural world. The first monster is a supernatural herbivore, a dangerous cow or bull from the sea (the Persian *gau* does not specify the monster's sex), the other a supernatural eater of men, a huge *deyb*. Both encounters entail Salīm's being cornered by the monster (up in a tree or down in a cave), and result in Salīm taking measures by night to deprive the monster of sight, thereby bringing about its death and acquiring its treasure. In both cases, his tactics include throwing earthly matter (mud, then stones) down from above. In the first instance, it is Salīm's own avidity to possess a night-illuminating jewel belonging to the bull which involves him with the monster, but in the second instance, Salīm wants nothing other than to get away. In the first instance, Salīm the outward-bound, solitary adventurer acts on behalf of himself alone. At the conclusion of his otherworldly travels, Salīm the homeward-bound father and husband acts as a member of a social group, on behalf of himself and a number of fellow prisoners who have also been prevented from returning home by the monster, and shares the spoils with them once he kills the monster. The direction of events is toward Salīm's social reintegration after his interlude in the non-human other world.

In each of these episodes, Salīm is brought into proximity with the monster through a supernatural transportation problem. In the first instance, Salīm's little bark boat is caught in a monstrous whirlpool that captures whole ships and keeps them till the occupants starve to death (ll. 373–75). Salīm is only released by the power of God, which raises a wind sufficient to overcome the whirlpool and casts him up on the shore of the sea-cow's meadow. Conversely, in the second instance, Salīm prematurely calls on God's name in thanks for what he thinks will be a safe arrival, thereby causing his demon mount to desert him in the man-eating *deyb*'s neighborhood (ll. 520–30). However important the power of God is in Salīm's (man's) life, it is not to be invoked at will even by the righteous.

Food imagery is another dimension of the counterpoint between these two episodes. In the first instance, vegetable imagery predominates: Salīm survives by foraging for raw, wild fruit and shelters in a tree from the grazing sea-cow. In the later episode, animal flesh predominates: Salīm has elaborately cooked meat (mutton) pressed upon him, in preparation for becoming meat himself, and takes shelter among the sheep, even disguises himself as a sheep, while escaping from the man-eater. The reappearance of meat (a festival food for the average Afghan) seems an ambiguous element, even an ominous one, in Salīm's transit back to human society.

The above are only a representative selection of the total array of reflections and resonances between these two episodes. The patterns set up hint at a system of distinctions between fully human (i.e., Muslim) society and non-human, non- or semi-social worlds outside it. The geography is moral as well as physical. Yet the intricate contrapuntal pattern of parallels and contrasts between the two episodes within the present story will not obscure for western readers the striking fact that the episode with the man-eating *deyb* is a binocular version of the Polyphemus story, famous to us from Homer's *Odyssey*. This episode is common in written and oral adventure tales in Persian-language and adjacent traditions down to the present day.[3] Its similarities to the Homeric version are set off for us by certain differences, characteristic of Persian variants of this episode yet intricately woven into the present story, as the previous summary of its resonances with the sea-cow episode serves to illustrate. Major differences from the Homeric version include the fact that the hero himself, not his adversary, is the rock-thrower, and that he succeeds in killing his opponent, without bringing divine reprisals down upon him as Odysseus did for blinding the giant. Eaters of men do not have divine sponsors in Muslim tradition. Likewise, wine being a polluting substance, it is the infidel monster, not the Muslim hero, who is responsible for the wine supply and the drunkenness through which he is overpowered. As in the Polyphemus episode, the hero overpowers the monster with a weapon made out of a tool belonging to the monster himself. In Odysseus' case, he fashions a huge pikestaff from a green olive trunk the technologically primitive giant has cut and left to season. Salīm, like other Muslim heroes of binocular versions of the story, uses two forged iron skewers which the monster has been using to roast his human meat. Polyphemus eats men whole and raw, not even cut up or gutted; the *deyb* prepares them in a monstrous version of human festive cuisine (ll. 546–51), and furthermore, in the Ākhond's telling, prepares even more elaborate mutton kebabs to fatten his human victims (l.

---

3. The sea-cow story also has literary reflexes, and the likelihood that the Ākhond specifically associates that episode in Salīm's story with its appearance in Jalāluddīn Rūmī's mystical *Mathnavī-e Maʿanavī* will be explored in chapter 8.

557 and note). The piercing of this monstrous chef with his own cooking skewers in this version thus adds a layer of poetic justice.

Odysseus can rely on aid from four of his shipmates, chosen by lot, but Salīm, like other Muslim heroes of these Cyclops-type adventures, must act alone, because none of his fellow captives has the courage to attack. Salīm's solitary heroism here recalls his two earlier exploits, in battle and then in prison, when in each case he acted alone on behalf of numerous other Muslims who appeared to lack the will or ability to fight. By acting as he does, Salīm puts an end to a godless demon, manages to continue his own journey to his home city, and saves numerous other prisoners, whereas Odysseus, approaching the monster out of mere curious adventurism, angers a god and indefinitely prolongs his own return, at the eventual cost of the rest of his companions' lives. Salīm and his companions, like Odysseus', escape with the monster's herds (ll. 401 and 404). Several aspects of this Persian form of the episode, as distinct from the Greek one, thus suit it for its present position toward the end, when the hero is being gradually returned to society rather than the beginning of the hero's trials,[4] when his isolation is increasing.

Internally to this narrative, Salīm's cave adventure not only resonates with the episode of the sea-cow, but also shows symmetries with the episode of the holy war, particularly Salīm's incarceration by a heathen adversary, and his heroic physical action on behalf of other, more passive Muslim prisoners. Those two episodes in turn are bracketed by two episodes of his own physical helplessness and confinement at home among Muslims, the first brought upon Salīm by his own fault (illness and confinement in bed brought on by his pride and forgetfulness of God), and the last an imprisonment through others' tyranny and error, his unjust incarceration in Hojāj's prison and resultant physical wasting away.

The whole chiastic series of paired episodes, with their repetitions and inversions of detail, brings Salīm from the loss of his father through a series of ethical and physical trials and exploits back to a state of health, wisdom, prosperity, and familial wholeness, won not by his own strength but by reliance on God and by the grace God ultimately shows. Yet remembrance of God is not a constant protection: Salīm's thanking God at the wrong

---

4. An occasional detail which had important functions in the Homeric version, such as the deceptive story which the hero tells the monster, survives—enigmatically and with no particular plot significance—in the modern Persian chapbook version but not in the Ākhond's telling.

moment causes the premature departure of his demon mount, and post-pones the hero's final homecoming. The problem of unjust suffering, introduced through the cave episode and Salīm's imprisonment under Hojāj's misrule, is attributable not to Salīm's own defects of faith (by now corrected) but to the godlessness of the perpetrators, the *deyb* and Hojāj himself. Salīm, caught up by their evil, ultimately becomes the agent of their correction.

The two sexual adventures which are bracketed by the monstrous and warlike encounters form the pivotal center of the tale's overall chiasmus. Their relationship to each other develops through a series of parallels and contrasts, and eventually links back to the wife Salīm has left at home, and to whom he ultimately returns. Salīm, leaving the sea-cow's valley, walks along carrying the huge iron club which he brought with him out of prison, and the jewel, which he has sewn into his shoulder (l. 403 and note 25). Salīm then passes from sheltering in trees and foraging like an animal, to residence among animals who would normally live in trees, but in this other world live in a city-like community with a royal court, and practice horticulture. The valley of monkeys which he encounters seems to him at first another land of wild beasts (l. 409), but it soon appears that these monkeys have a virtually human technology and social order: storage chambers into which they are putting their harvest of fruit, a courtly elite (ll. 411–15), prepared and served food (l. 424), marriage-like attachments and families (l. 440) and, not least of all, very effective habits of seduction (ll. 431–35). The Ākhond explicitly connects this ribald scene with the tone Karīm has set in the tale of Rasūl's mother (l. 425). The effect of the telling is to make Hojāj laugh—as he has demanded that the story should—and to invite the present audience to do the same, which they did.[5]

The Ākhond does not dwell on the earthy delights of Salīm's liaison with the monkey princess, but eventually, a son is born. Some time later, Salīm tires of his too-enthusiastic lover (ll. 443–45), who, though monkeys are "just like people" (l. 429), is nonetheless just "a monkey" in the end (l. 444), inferior to the human wife Salīm has left behind (l. 442). When Salīm abandons her, however, the monkey, "that dame," reveals her more-than-animal attachment, following him with their child in her arms, pro-testing. When he threatens her with the club, she tears the child in two and throws one half after him, taking the other half back with her in a brutal

---

5. Baghban notes bestiality as a humorous subject in the folk theatre of the region (1977, 2.377ff.).

reflection of the family separation he has initiated (l. 449), perhaps also implying the ultimate unnaturalness of their union and the impossibility of its having positive issue.

Salīm's next place of refuge is a hollow tree, from which he encounters a *parī* princess, immortal and magically powerful, as much above human nature as monkeys are below it. Unlike his monkey bride, this love-object would fly from him, but he immobilizes her by stealing her shape-changer's suit of pigeon feathers. Animal nature is something quite external to the *parī*'s being, assumed only for purposes of mobility and disguise. Left naked and vulnerable when physically separated from her avian disguise, she tries to bargain it back with a display of clairvoyant knowledge of Salīm's past (ll. 467–71), of which the Ākhond mentions just two points explicitly, his treatment of his wife (whether monkey or human is unspecified) and his recourse to prayer.

Opportunities for recapitulation are a common feature of Afghano-Persian folktale: either the hero or someone sympathetic to him or her (a guide or a love object) retells the hero's experiences in the course of a pivotal recognition scene or a test. The extent of actual verbal recapitulation by the storyteller varies, depending on external conditions, such as the state of the audience's attention and their familiarity with the story (known or assumed), as well as the importance of the particular recapitulation scene in interpreting the basic structure and significance of the hero's adventures and motivating further action. The Ākhond's use of the recapitulation device here is pared down, brief in comparison with that of the chapbook version in the same position (see below) but sufficient to demonstrate the *parī*'s special powers and affinity for the hero, and to point out two main issues of the hero's past and future, marital loyalty and reliance on God.

Salīm has already demonstrated that he has learned the lesson of submission to God's will (*taslīm*, the basic duty of a Muslim). His treatment of female dependents up to this point has been more problematical. His human wife is also his cousin (l. 612), a preferred marital choice in many traditional Muslim societies. As befits a spouse who is also blood kin, she has been unswervingly loyal to him, even in hard times (ll. 153–59), but she also has the strength of her position as his lineage-mate and status-equal, when necessary, to admonish him to "act like a Muslim," to go out and get an honest job instead of shamefully living off her labors (ll. 165–67).

Once Salīm repairs his relationship with God and is healed, he uses his first earnings to provide for his wife while he sets off on a pilgrimage of thanksgiving (l. 234). It is incumbent on pilgrims to provide properly for those left behind, and Salīm does so; wife-neglect does not recur as a topic until his adventure with the monkey princess comes to a close (l. 442). No themes of sexuality figure in the episodes concerned with pilgrimage and holy war, nor is there any implied competition between familial and religious duty. This is appropriate: pilgrims should be celibate, and, Afghans stress, should have provided for their families before setting out, as he has done. When Salīm encounters the *parī*, the two duty themes are restated in tandem. *Parī*s are both loyal and God-fearing. When this one is caught by Salīm's ploy (and also, in the logic of the story, by fate and God's will), she acquiesces gracefully, and her father and family do the right thing, marrying the couple to one another properly (ll. 481–84). In contrast to the monkey bride's nuptials, the Ākhond does not exploit the erotic potential of this very proper wedding with a beautiful supernatural: a son decorously appears a year later.

With the appearance of offspring, Salīm receives an ironic test of his own loyalty, as each newborn son is handed over to a wild beast and not seen again. Salīm's response to this pattern is to mourn for his human wife and accuse his *parī* wife of cruelty (ll. 491–95), a reversal of the circumstances of the separation from his monkey lover. After the apparent sacrifice of two *parī* sons born in succeeding years, Salīm despairs of his *parī* wife's hard-heartedness. It was also after two years that the monkey wife's excessive affection had aroused his disgust and caused him to remember his human wife. His hostile departure goaded the monkey bride to the actual destruction of their only child, which caused him no visible regret. Hypogamous otherworldly marriage threatens him with monstrous offspring, whose death at the hands of the mother he does not regret, while hypergamous otherworldly marriage gives him immortal offspring whose death he wrongly fears.

Salīm's suffering over the apparent loss of his *parī* offspring may be configured in other tellings as punishment for his abandonment of his monkey family, but not in the Ākhond's telling. Yet in this telling, too, the experience of loss acts as a reminder of neglected loyalties. Even after the *parī* has reassured him that the wild animals are only *parī* nurses in disguise, and he has seen with his own eyes the miraculous growth of his two sons, Salīm still wants to see his first wife again. The *parī*, unlike his monkey bride, agrees to part with him, if only temporarily (ll. 505–6). The net effect of both nonhuman alliances seems to be to remind Salīm of his own human nature and his ties to the human world. In the wider folktale tradition, the incident of the supernatural wife turning the hero's children over to animals usually figures in the husband's breaking an injunction attached to the marriage, that he, a mere mortal, not question the actions of his supernatural wife. Marzolph identifies the incident with Tale Type *832A ("Feenfrau durch Ungehorsam verloren"), and locates this particular incident in Elwell-Sutton's collection of oral stories from Iran (cf. Marzolph 1984:149). He also remarks on the often unhappy nature of human-*parī* marriages.[6] In other versions of this motif from my own collection, the *parī* shows the husband that the children are unharmed, as here, but then banishes him for doubting her, and he can win her back only after a long quest. In Salīm's case, the departure is the husband's own idea, on account of his homesickness in this alien world, and the *parī*'s injunction pertains only to his travel arrangements and his prompt return to her, which she tries to facilitate (ll. 509–17). Salīm's violation of her injunction concerning travel removes the means of his return and subjects him to further dangers, but his doubting her is not the direct cause of their separation. This *parī*, an exemplary co-wife and as personally devoted as Salīm's other ladies, never sets herself up as an authority over him, despite her superior powers. The Ākhond's telling of this incident mutes the theme of retribution for marital disloyalty, only hinting at the possibility of the enraged father-in-law's magical pursuit (ll. 512–15), a traditional element which is narrated in detail in other versions of this incident, including the Tehran chapbook's.

The lack of emphasis on retributive themes in the *Salīm* version of this episode, in contrast to other folktales where it is the core incident, serves the coherency of the larger plot, and especially the symmetry between this incident and Salīm's other experiment with marvelous marriage to the monkey bride. Salīm and the *parī* must part, at least temporarily, for the working out of his and Hojāj's joint fate. Nevertheless, Salīm's womenfolk are uniformly devoted and ultimately submissive (even the monkey princess), despite moral qualities and, in the *parī*'s case, powers that are superior to his own, especially in matters of commitment. Thus it is Salīm's choice, not the *parī*'s, that they should part, and he lives to regret it (ll. 562

---

6. Marzolph, p. 29. In legend from the Muslim world, human males' alliances with *parī*s have varied outcomes. R. A. Nicholson comments on the story of the "pious Abdu'l-Ghawth," in Rūmī's *Mathnavī* (VI:2977–3113), who forsook his human family to join the *parī* world for nine years, returned briefly to the human sphere, then rejoined the otherworld forever because they were his true spiritual congeners. Tamīm al-Darī is a well-known companion of the Prophet who, in legend, traveled to the world of the *jinn* for a period of years, had various adventures, but returned to claim his human family, including his remarried wife. *The Encyclopedia of Islam*'s (1st ed.) article on *djinn* describes other legendary otherworldly marriages.

and 618). Remarks by Salīm's human and *parī* wives both suggest a complementarity between the themes of marital devotion and religious duty in Salīm's history (ll. 165–67 and 468–69).

When Hojāj is called on at last to correct the injustice and so heal his own divinely imposed affliction, it is precisely by reuniting Salīm with his two wives that he acts out his new role as a just ruler (ll. 623–25). At this final stage, the Ākhond glosses over such marvelous plot details as the logistics of travel to and from the otherworld. What he finally stresses is the symmetry of personal and ethical relationships which must be restored, the web of connections among Islam, familial loyalty, and good governance, not the marvelous, imaginary aspects of the story. Unlike King Shahryār in *The Thousand and One Nights*, Hojāj's personal sexual fate is not at stake, but in restoring Salīm to his family, Hojāj heals himself and, by implication, heals his own misruled society. Both the Ākhond and Karīm continued to pursue the connections between Islam and good governance in subsequent stories. Karīm's final story, "The Destruction of the City of Rūm," in particular returned to an even more explicit and dramatic portrayal of connections between religion, private morality, sex, marriage, and the well-being of the state.

"Salīm the Jeweller" in Written and Oral Tradition

While the generally interdependent relationship of oral and literary traditions in Persian is readily discernible in people's conversational citations of literary and oral narrative, poetry, proverbs, and sayings, the one oral and two written versions of "Salīm the Jeweller" available for comparison here provide a cautionary example against facile assumptions about particular relationships between oral performances and literary texts.[7] The primary obstacle to obtaining a meaningful comparison between the Ākhond's performance of "Salīm the Jeweller" and written versions of the story, even a more or less contemporaneous version such as a chapbook datable to the late 1960s, is the indeterminate processual relationship, if

---

7. Blackburn and Ramanujan (1986:5) suggest a sensible descriptive schema for cycles of transmission of traditional literature, in which literary and oral transmission channels intersect and interweave freely. The particulars of such intersection for any given story or story tradition remain complex and difficult to trace. Matters pertinent to the interrelations of oral and literary transmission mechanisms in Islamic societies are raised more specifically by Zwettler (1978), Street (1984, especially chapter 5), and Eickelman (1978).

any, between the Ākhond's telling and this particular chapbook or any other written version of the tale, despite his self-confessed interest in books. Therefore, the two available written versions of this story constitute simply alternative traditional versions, not verifiable antecedents for the Ākhond's own performance. Yet a comparison is useful, to highlight aspects of the Ākhond's telling that differ from the other two versions, but resonate with the context of this particular performance.

What follows also demonstrates that degrees of formal resemblance among versions do not necessarily mirror degrees of proximity in space and time of the productions, oral and/or written. A comparison of the Ākhond's telling of this story and the two available written versions raises questions about the assumptions both of historical-geographical studies of tales and of that basic of Middle Eastern literary-historical scholarship, stemma-constructing historical studies of manuscript traditions. Questions arise particularly when those manuscript traditions are symbiotic with large oral traditions, as in this case. The basic problem with both such lines of study, and with the evaluation of the performance at hand, is potential inaccuracy in inferences made, because of the lack of detailed knowledge of the stepwise changes which occur between individual performances of a story, let alone between multiple written versions derived in part from such individual performances. Lacking the Ākhond's direct identification of a written source, or other tellings of this tale by him, it is impossible to specify which aspects of the Ākhond's telling, whether or not shared by a chapbook or other version, are relatively stable features of his version of the tale, and which are variations occasioned by the present performance context. Even a single step in the transmission of a traditional tale, between one teller and one learner, can occasion key changes in structure and content, after which the learner's version of the tale may be altered in subsequent performances either toward or away from the source version due to repertorial or other influences (Mills 1978, passim). Story versions both diverge and converge over time.

Joint oral-literary tradition being a multiconduit affair, even if the Ākhond had seen fit to identify a written source as his primary model for the story, it would still be hard to rule out supplementary influences from other people's performances or other sources, before or after his contact with any written version, in shaping his performances. Neither is it possible, without direct evidence (e.g., repeated performances over time before different audiences), to gauge the range of variations in the Ākhond's own renditions of the tale, making any generalizations about what constitutes "his" version or his debt to different potential sources of such a tale risky (cf. Mills 1978, chapters 3 and 4).

Despite the availability and ready sales of chapbooks throughout the Persian-speaking world, there has been virtually no research either on this form of vernacular literacy in general, or on the specific contribution of chapbooks to oral performance and vice versa. Chapbooks printed in recent years on high acid pulp paper, stapled together and paperbound, are unlikely to survive physically for more than a few years, as they readily disintegrate with exposure to light and use. Though these texts are much more numerous than their manuscript predecessors, they are also more ephemeral, making their influence on oral tradition-bearers hard to gauge. My own preliminary inquiries among self-avowed book readers suggested a widespread pattern of borrowing or passing on both books of a sturdier kind and these more fragile booklets, so that any one reader's access to any one fixed text may be transitory, after which the reader's access to that text becomes memorial, like access to orally mediated "texts."

Even a casual survey of the market reveals that printers often reprint from older plates, either their own or those of other presses legitimately or illegitimately acquired. What is not clear is the extent to which printers in recent years have availed themselves of oral performers to produce, by transcription, new texts or new versions of out-of-print stories, a process which constitutes the most direct influence of oral on written transmission. Wilma Heston (1991) has begun an exploration of author-publisher relations in chapbook production in Pashto language (including some of the same publishers who produce books in Persian for the Afghan market), but no such work has yet been presented for Persian. My own cursory investigation of a few of these publications in Afghanistan in the middle 1970s revealed that alternative editions of the same story, if they existed, tended to be obvious lineal relations of each other, either from the same plates or lightly edited, suggesting that if the option of reprinting was available for a given item, printers were more likely to avail themselves of it than to recruit an individual to create a new written version. The use of chapbooks as a source for oral performance, more of an issue for the present discussion than the books' dependency on oral tradition, is as yet unexplored.

In particular, one might ask whether the Ākhond, if he was aware of *Salīm*'s existence as a chapbook, would even consider it *ketābī* ("literary") in the same league with the famous, highly didactic literary narrative collections, such as *Anwār-i Sohaylī*, for which he expressed so much admiration. As the Ākhond's discussion of his children's education illustrates (see chapter 5), literacy in recent years was available from two major institutional sources, the traditional religious schools (by the 1970s, to some extent government-regulated), starting with the *maktab khānegī* and carried on in centers of learning associated with mosques and pilgrimage sites, and the secular government school system, kindergarten through university, based on European models. In neither system would popular chapbooks be regarded as learned or prestigious. Some of those with religious education avoided such material as frivolous, while to the government-educated, it was old-fashioned in comparison to cinema and the translations of modern European fiction which appeared in the more western-oriented book shops.

Necessarily, given the lack of data, the significance of the written versions of *Salīm* for the present discussion centers more on questions of formal variation than on questions of oral-literary processes, still undocumented. While one cannot discount the likelihood that other versions of the tale, besides the Ākhond's, were in written or oral circulation in the Herat area at the time, a comparison of those alternative versions which are available underlines the difficulties attendant on trying to deduce matters of narrative process and intention from isolated performances unglossed by the performer. Peculiarities of the Ākhond's present performance which suggest unfinished editing processes, such as narrative threads mentioned but not taken up, or omissions of detail in the resolution of certain major plot sequences, would suggest this is a pared-down telling, subject to considerable ad hoc editing, such that those dimensions deemed pertinent to the present performance context were favored for more expansive development, other themes which were deemed less pertinent or perhaps distracting being kept sketchy. As Albert Lord (1960:94ff.) observed with regard to folk epic, however, narrative inconsistencies can be very stable in a narrator's repertoire over time.

Taking all the above into consideration, the comparison of the Ākhond's performance to another version (in this case, written) supplies some insights on formal alternatives, tantalizing us with what might have been learned had multiple performances by the Ākhond before different audiences been recorded. This discussion must be limited to pointing out possibilities: themes and overall structures that the Ākhond did develop, which are or are not developed in the written versions, and opportunities for elaboration suggested in his telling but not pursued, which can be seen in more developed form in the more leisurely, detailed written versions of the tale. One or two elaborations in the Ākhond's telling not present in the written versions stand out, in light of the overall terseness of his performance in comparison to the written versions. Yet any observations about the *process* of shaping a performance must remain speculative, in the absence of specific editorial comments and other performances from these storytellers. Literary connections to performance processes can be more fully explored for two other stories the Ākhond told later in the evening ("Mahmūd of Ghaznī and the Thieves" and "Women's Tricks," chapters 8 and 10). The present instance mostly illustrates the problematic and speculative nature of many oral-literary studies. But since much of current literary studies (Goody 1968; 1978; Havelock and Ong, in particular) engages in generalization on the basis of untestable inferences about literary processes (untestable because based on literary artifacts, not on observed processes; cf. Street [1984] and Harris [1986] for critical overviews), perhaps a cautionary tale like this has some utility.

Generally speaking, the modern Tehran chapbook is the most expansive of the three versions in physical descriptions and scene-setting, such as the battlefield scene when Salīm goes to war, or Salīm's description of his own youth and upbringing prior to his father's death. The manuscript seems less wordy than the chapbook overall, because less description is lavished on physical detail, but it does offer fuller dramaturgically motivational or circumstantial descriptions of certain actions and events. For example, after Salīm has righted the porter's load, in the chapbook and the Ākhond's telling, he simply looks up and sees an elderly man of ascetic appearance, who is washing for prayers, and who chastises him for his pride and forgetfulness of God, after which he is taken ill (chapter 6, ll. 192–98). In the manuscript version, Salīm has been covered with mud in the process of righting the load, and so goes to wash up in the mosque precinct, where washing facilities are provided for all to make their ablutions before prayer. Salīm is washing and thinking pridefully of his accomplishment when he meets that first divine messenger. Similarly, the scene when Salīm returns to his human wife and must then go off to seek a light is more logically elaborated in the manuscript than in the other two versions. In the chapbook, they are simply at home together after dark, when the light goes out. The wife wants to go to a neighbor for a light, but Salīm volunteers to go to the nearby bazaar instead. There, a shopkeeper somehow mistakes his efforts to light the lamp for attempted theft, and he is arrested. The Ākhond's version (ll. 613–15), equally brief, offers different detail which allows for a brief reiteration of the theme of marital responsibility (discussed more fully below) which he has already developed early in the narrative: the wife has become so poor in Salīm's absence that she has no kerosene for a light, so Salīm goes off to buy some and is somehow taken for a thief. The manuscript version makes the greatest dramatic use of circumstantial detail of the three. In it, Salīm and his wife are sitting up late talking when their light goes out. All the neighbors' houses are dark, so Salīm proceeds to the bazaar to get a light from a lamp which a storekeeper has left lighted outside his shop (a few lights would be kept burning in the bazaar, for security purposes and the use of night watchmen). A shopkeeper, sleeping in his shop to guard it as some shopmen do in traditional bazaars, hears Salīm moving around outside and not illogically takes him for a thief trying to extinguish the lamp. The manuscript outlines these circumstances succinctly but precisely, drawing on the audience's familiarity with the conditions of bazaars. Neither the chapbook nor the Ākhond's rendition undertakes such exactness.

These are two of probably a dozen similar comparisons to be made among the three versions. The Ākhond's rendition, like the chapbook, makes less use of such circumstantial and motivational detail to context actions, but the Ākhond's telling, like the manuscript, also lacks the richness of description for description's sake (e.g., of the battle scene, or the *parī* court) which is to be found in the chapbook.

Of the three versions, the Ākhond's is thus the tersest, leaving tacit both motivational and descriptive detail. At this level of composition, his succinctness sometimes makes his tellings of action sequences more resemble the relatively terse eighteenth century manuscript version than the twentieth century chapbook. But the variety of details shared by the Ākhond's telling and the chapbook, but lacking in the manuscript, suggest (as would seem logical) that the Ākhond's story is closer to the twentieth century written version. In the Ākhond's telling, such action sequences as Salīm's departure from home, the circumstances of the holy war, the jailbreak scene, the meeting with the *parī*, many but not all elements of the cave episode, and Salīm's meeting with his wife more resemble the chapbook's treatment than the manuscript's. Yet at the level of gross structure, particularly in the omission of a pivotal episode (discussed below), the Ākhond's telling more closely parallels the manuscript version.

The Ākhond tends to omit marvelous detail in the story. In particular, the denouement of the Ākhond's story, in which Salīm is reunited with his wives, is elaborated in the written versions but very briefly told in the Ākhond's version. In the concluding scenes of the narrative, the Ākhond omits details which, if not absolutely crucial to narrative logic, nonetheless enhance closure and are implied by previous goings-on. One such omission is the "obstacle flight" (Motif No. D672 in Thompson's *Motif Index of Folk Literature*). The *parī* princess, instructing Salīm for his journey home, warns him that her father will pursue him with an army, and that Salīm must "throw down oil and things, / so he'll turn back from following you." (ll. 514–15). This reference to the casting down of magical objects to create barriers between the hero and a pursuing supernatural might seem cryptic to those unfamiliar with traditional storytelling, but it is a motif common to many folktales I recorded in the area, and probably the audience was familiar enough with it to understand the offhand reference. In the actual flight scene, the Ākhond omits mention of the irate father's pursuit altogether.

The Ākhond also slights other such folkloric commonplaces as tokens and magic words. In both written versions of the story, the *parī* tells Salīm a verbal charm with which to summon her in a month's time, when he has agreed to return from the human world, but the trauma of imprisonment drives the word from his head and he cannot remember it till after he is released and restored to health. In the Ākhond's version, it is unclear how the *parī* wife is summoned (l. 625), though Hojāj appears to do so. Also in the written versions of the story, Salīm is required to prove the truth of his marvelous narrative and does so by producing as a token the night-illuminating jewel which he took from the sea-cow and had sewn under the skin of his thigh (not his shoulder). Hojāj buys the jewel from him at a huge price, thereby restoring his fortunes. The Ākhond makes no mention of the jewel's reappearance as a recognition token, a common folktale closure device. He has Hojāj give Salīm a house as compensation for his story and perhaps for unjust imprisonment (and perhaps, again, an oblique reference to debts owed in connection with the Ākhond's own imprisonment). The Ākhond manifests little interest in elaborating these and other traditional folktale elements, just as he resists the use and denies knowledge of the opening and closing formulas for *afsānah* (wonder tales) or other common tale formulae. See, for example, l. 362: his perfunctory *Bejīh keh mījīh!* (literally, "Run, if you're running!") for the commonplace *Bejīh, keh nemījīh!* ("Run, you're not running [enough]!").

There are some points at which he does develop such traditional elements fully, however, and these stand out in the context of the general lack of development of such elements. One is Salīm's meeting with the *parī* and his theft of her pigeon suit while she is bathing. Only the chapbook shares this incident, the manuscript omitting it entirely, and in the chapbook, it is not a shape-changer's guise that he steals, but simply her clothes.[8] This is a rare instance of a magical motif which the Ākhond develops but which is lacking in the generally more elaborated written versions of the tale. In the eighteenth century manuscript, Salīm simply arrives in *parī*-land, makes his way to the court, and is offered the king's daughter in marriage. Salīm never compromises the girl, and thus, the scene in which she demonstrates her clairvoyance and reminds Salīm of his treatment of his previous wife is lacking in the manuscript, but retained in the Ākhond's telling (ll. 467–71). In the chapbook, the *parī* explicitly chastises him for abandoning his monkey bride and son; the Ākhond (l. 468) leaves it ambiguous whether Salīm is being accused of abandoning his human or his animal wife. Loyalty to both emerges as an issue most clearly later in the chapbook and manuscript, when he accuses his *parī* wife of wanton cruelty in relinquishing their sons to animals. She retorts that it is only humans who abandon their loved ones, that *parī*s mate only once, and being immortal, resign themselves to an endless future of loneliness when they consent to marry mortals like himself, who will surely forsake them in death if not sooner. In the world of *afsānah*, *parī*s pointing out the brevity of human commitment are a commonplace, one that the Ākhond does not bother to mention. Yet his retaining the motif of the *parī*'s capture by the theft of her pigeon suit and her clairvoyant confrontation with Salīm concerning his past (the latter not a commonplace ingredient of this motif) allows the Ākhond to invoke the theme of marital loyalty and family responsibilities, which emotionally drives the concluding episodes of Salīm's adventures. The Ākhond portrays magic in the service of transcendent ethical values. The righteousness of the *parī*s, who are Muslims and therefore marry Salīm off to the princess in a proper manner, is a related element spelled out in the written texts and suggested by the Ākhond's telling.

The generally reduced detail of the Ākhond's performance makes those moments when he indulges in more expanded description stand out. The advice of Salīm's dying father is a case in point. The eighteenth century manuscript has only the following:

"I left you all this wealth so that you would suffer no grief in the future nor remember the past [with regret], and do not seek faith from women or tell

---

8. The Ākhond's version of the *parī*'s capture more closely resembles the version in *The Thousand and One Nights*, "How Hasan Captured the Bird-Maiden" (Lane 1927:775–76).

them your secrets, and do not sit down with base or bad men, and don't trust every person." When he had presented these precepts and advice, after three days, he died. (Haag-Higuchi ms, p. 254. Translation by this author.)

The twentieth century chapbook has the following, typically expansive:

> He called for me and said, "Oh, child, while I lived I had my share of the world, I tasted the warm and cold of the world, I saw profit and loss, till I acquired property. Now I entrust it to your hands. Keep my advice constantly in your ears, so that you are successful in the world, recognize the one God and maintain gratitude to Him, do not exchange faith for farthings, know that the day of good fortune is a windfall, do not deprive the beggar, give thanks for safety and health, strive to preserve the powers of your monarch, honor your country, give the prescribed alms to the dervishes, do not lie, abstain from [the company of] base persons, mix with persons of knowledge." My father bade farewell to life in that same hour. (pp. 6–7)

Not all of this advice is fine-tuned to the subsequent plot structure of the tales. Given that sons in folk narrative can generally be expected to violate the injunctions of dying parents by way of initiating the action sequence of their stories,[9] the father's explicit advice in the manuscript version, to avoid confiding in women, sets up an expectation that one of the hero's failings will be overconfidence in women, which is not in fact the case in any version of this tale (though it is a central theme in some other traditional adventure tales). Similarly, the chapbook version stresses the Muslim duty of charity and the avoidance of greed, but the hero's failings do not include niggardliness or rapacity. The chapbook version does make repeated mention of the remembrance of God, which along with extravagance is Salīm's major failing in the first part of the tale, in all versions. The manuscript does not mention matters of faith, even though they are central to Salīm's story as it unfolds. While the manuscript version only briefly warns against base company, the chapbook also advises loyalty to king and country and seeking the company of the knowledgeable (*dāneshmandān*).

The Ākhond's version of the death scene is striking for its brevity, focus, and declamatory use of measured parallel phrasing:

---

9. Cf. Propp (1968:26–28) describing the initial sequences of folktales, one variety being, as in Salīm's story, absentation of a family member (in this case the death of Salīm's father) / interdiction addressed to the hero / interdiction violated.

He said, "My father was a jewel-seller,
     by the name of so-and-so,
     very well known,
     very well supplied,
     very knowledgeable,[10]
     very wealthy.
My father got sick, and called me »
     and said, 'Oh, son—'
     —I said, 'What?'—
     he said, 'Relying on God,
         after you have
         buried—[*stutters*]—enshrouded me and carried me away,
     relying on God, take care not to sit down
         with unheeding people,
         with wisdomless people,
         with honorless people,
         with unheeding people.
     Sit down with people of wisdom,[11]
     sit down with those who govern,
     sit down with the Muslim man,
         the seeker of God,
     sit down with the man who, so to say, dedicates himself
         to governance and the nation and the land.'
When my father died . . ."
                                                (ll. 122–46)

    The Ākhond's arrangement of this scene is a particularly elegant example of his overall tendency to construct balanced pairs, pairs of pairs, and chiastic arrangements of syntactic and conceptual units. Both Salīm's description of his father and the father's speech are made highly declamatory through parallel syntax and intonation. In the Ākhond's telling, this is all we know of Salīm's life before his father's death. The Ākhond focuses entirely on the death scene as the opening event of Salīm's narrative, whereas each of the written versions first describes Salīm's childhood strength and precocity, a theme common to epic and romance

---

10. *Fahmīdah*, "possessed of understanding."
11. *Ahl-e 'orfān*.

heroes which the chapbook in particular develops at length. The Ākhond's omission of such heroic description makes Salīm more of an Everyman.

In the Ākhond's telling, the father enjoins four things: (1) reliance on God (as preface to all), (2) avoiding base persons, (3) seeking out those with religious faith and wisdom (*'orfān* [literary, *'erfān*], which is not just good sense, but wisdom based on the knowledge of God, gnostic wisdom, the same word he used in describing the deficiencies of fools in "Ten *Qerān*"), and (4) seeking the company of those who govern with the welfare of the community foremost in mind. Salīm violates the first two injunctions straightaway but, once having learned his lesson, sets out on the hajj pilgrimage which should gain him the company of believers, only to fall involuntarily into the clutches of irreligious oppressors of Muslims (the Negus who captures him in battle, the man-eating *deyb*, and finally, Hojāj). The Ākhond's handling of the father's death scene resembles the manuscript's for brevity, but as to content and topical sequencing has more in common with the more prolix chapbook. Salīm's failings as a manager of property are not foreshadowed in the Ākhond's version of the injunctions, as they are in the chapbook, but are one conspicuous effect of bad company on his character (ll. 146–52).

The pertinence to the present audience of the Ākhond's emphases in the injunction scene has already been observed, but emerges clearly in comparison to the more generic, less tightly logical injunctions of the two written versions. In particular, the chapbook merely enjoins loyalty to the king and state, while the Ākhond's telling enjoins Salīm (twice) to seek the company of those who govern righteously. The manuscript version is less akin than the other two in this regard, omitting any mention of wisdom or governance. The Ākhond's choice of the word *'orfān* for wisdom, the same word he used at the end of his previous tale of fools (chapter 5, l. 152), inextricably joins the idea of wisdom to religious enlightenment, in fact to mystical insight or gnosis in this word's more technical applications. The chapbook's term for wise persons at this point is *dāneshmandān*, which refers to general knowledge or learning, without religious overtones.

The emphatic rhythms of the Ākhond's declamatory phrasing add weight to the scene in counterpoint to the less measured clusters of phrases surrounding it. The list of injunctions in the chapbook offers similar weight, but without as clear a focus and direction in connection with the sequence of events to follow. The Ākhond's rendition of this scene combines content selection and ordering, measured parallel phrasing and even individual word choice to focus the interpretation of Salīm's experiences and interaction with Hojāj on the conjoined themes of the private faith and honor of the individual, religious enlightenment, and righteous governance.

The latter two themes are central to the Ākhond's (implicit) critique of the Wolǝswāl. The first, individual honor, establishes his credentials as critic of the powers that be. It is basic to Islam's egalitarian ideology that private citizens, the Salīms and Ākhonds, are morally situated to observe and critique, perhaps to correct, but failing that, violently to reject the excesses of unrighteous ruling powers (cf. Asad 1973:110). At the outset, it is Salīm's dying father, an elder like the Ākhond himself, who lays out the architecture of social responsibility. Salīm has yet to grow into his father's wisdom.

Salīm's relations with females, especially his first wife to whom he was married before his father died, figure prominently in the working out of his personal fate and ethical condition. As mentioned before, only the manuscript foreshadows this pattern of themes in the injunction scene, and then with doubtful relevance, since Salīm never errs by overconfidence in women. Instead, his general profligacy includes neglect of his wife, most graphically portrayed by the Ākhond's mention of dancing girls and homosexual prostitutes, ll. 149–51. Once his fortune is dissipated, Salīm offers his wife a divorce, to go home to her wealthy family (Salīm's uncle, since the girl is his cousin), in both the Ākhond's and the chapbook's versions. The wife loyally refuses to leave him, vowing to stand by him in bad times as she has in good and counseling reliance on God. In the chapbook, it is she who decrees that they will both seek work. The manuscript likewise portrays the girl as loyal, wise, and hard-working, but as an orphan who loves Salīm in spite of his neglect of her. Thus Salīm does not offer her a divorce (which would constitute abandonment if she had no family), but does ask whether she can tolerate being married to a humble porter; she announces in reply that she, too, will go to work as a servant in the households of relatives (thus sacrificing her pride by appearing poor before their wealthy connections, but respectably avoiding contact with nonrelatives). Generally speaking, here and elsewhere, the manuscript, among the three versions, employs the most detail for the purpose of spelling out motivations and transactions among characters in terms which are consistent with everyday sensibilities. Yet here the Ākhond includes a bit of detail unique to his own rendition, and significant: Salīm is paralyzed by shame and does nothing after losing his fortune, until his wife, who has already gone to work to support them, chastises him and tells him to go look for work (ll.

159–68). In Herat, very few women work outside their own households. For a man to live off his wife's earnings is shameful, and this arrangement of the sequence in which the two go to work compounds Salīm's moral failings, from a Herati perspective. The Ākhond alone gives Salīm's wife an assertive, morally admonitory voice. In the absence of Salīm's father she, his cousin as well as his wife, speaks for the family honor, not just for his own. The moral power of women becomes visible in Afghan society in default of appropriate male authorities, but it also operates behind the scenes when not forced into the open by male default. The moral quality of Salīm's wife's assertiveness is unusual, for a male narrator, but rather normal in women's narratives from the area.

By the same token, when Salīm is miraculously cured and sets out on the hajj, the Ākhond reiterates the theme of marital responsibility. The two written versions portray Salīm leaving town suddenly, without informing his wife. The chapbook says only, "I entrusted her to God," a rather sudden change of direction after its extended description of the couple's mutual hardships and joint efforts to overcome them. The manuscript, characteristically, spells out Salīm's motivation more fully. Salīm explains that he set out as soon as he woke from his healing dream, without waiting to tell his wife, because he was afraid that she, practical soul, would persuade him to delay his departure, perhaps not go at all, in order to repair their material condition with his new-found health. He has vowed to make the pilgrimage in gratitude for the cure and dares not defer the journey. By contrast with the other two versions, the Ākhond details Salīm's handing over to his wife an advance on his earnings, given by pilgrims whose caravan has employed him (ll. 222–34). This money is to keep her while he is away. In Afghan thought, pilgrimage loses merit if it works a hardship on those left behind, and so pilgrims must provide for their family while they are away. The theme of marital responsibility resurfaces in Salīm's interactions with the *parī*, and his first homecoming scene, in which the Ākhond portrays his human wife as indigent. At this juncture, before his departure, the Ākhond portrays Salīm as a rehabilitated provider, not as a renouncer of worldly responsibilities. '*Orfān* (gnosis) as a basis for righteous action does not, in the Ākhond's telling, cause one to reject the world. The Tehran chapbook has a more Shiite, world-rejecting flavor in this regard.

Salīm's pilgrimage and exploits as a holy warrior are devoid of sexual content, as such religious activities should be. His next conjugal encounter, with the monkey princess, is the great comic interlude in the tale, at which both Hojāj and the real-life audience laughed heartily. The monkey bride in her physical way is as loyal to Salīm and as dedicated to his comfort and well-being as his cousin-bride was. All three versions portray their sexual pleasure in comic detail; the manuscript Salīm even confides that it was the best sex he ever had. Yet Salīm cannot remain in this world of physical pleasure and material security: in the chapbook, he says that he feared his monkey-son would grow up to destroy him, while for the Ākhond, himself married sixty years, sexual fatigue plays a major role in Salīm's decision to leave (ll. 442–45).

This is a world of the purely physical, and also of the purely female: although the Ākhond describes the monkey bride as "the daughter of the monkey king," there is no male authority present, only other female monkeys in her retinue. In the written versions, she is the queen of the monkeys, with no male present except Salīm. The monkey bride's role as the initiator of sexual activity also reverses the ideal order of patriarchal society. Perhaps it is the absence of a masculine principle which causes the animal bride to destroy her own child when she and Salīm separate. She lacks either will or wisdom to carry on child-rearing for an absentee husband, as Salīm's *parī* spouse, superior in wisdom, will do. In the manuscript version, Hojāj finds the monkey's destruction of her son as uproariously funny as he found the sex scene and the child's birth. In the chapbook, Hojāj is noncommittal at this scene, but Salīm expresses relief at this severing of the tie between himself and the monkey. The Ākhond offers no emotional gloss on this scene at all (ll. 447–48). In the written versions, Salīm lives to express regret for not appreciating the monkey bride's hospitality more, when his life is endangered in subsequent adventures.

The structure and implications of Salīm's liaison with the *parī* princess have already been explored in some detail above, with reference to the overall structure of the Ākhond's tale. The *parī*, like his human wife, is loyal, intelligent and God-fearing, in all versions, and helps him to return home. In a detail omitted by the Ākhond but present in both written versions, the *parī* later arranges for Salīm's human wife to be bathed in the same youth-restorative in which she has dipped Salīm, rather exemplary behavior in a co-wife. Co-wives are generally unfriendly rivals in Afghan popular thought, but *parī*s are above human rivalries. The Ākhond, much married, then had two wives at home. If he had complaints, he did not voice them, but perhaps his attention to Salīm's attempt to balance his responsibilities had some personal biographical relevance. Husbands are enjoined in the Qur'an to treat wives absolutely equally, if they marry more than one. The chapbook, like the Ākhond, tells that the *parī* eventually took her children and returned to her own land much later, after Salīm and his cousin died (according to the chapbook, the two died together on the same day, as they had asked in their prayers). This bit of incidental detail, lacking in the manuscript, links the Ākhond's telling to the print edition.

This closing scene of polygamous harmony completes a general pattern of positive roles for females in the Ākhond's telling, indeed in all three versions of the tale. The Ākhond's portrayal of female solidarity with the hero(s) extends to the smallest details: the vizier's young daughter, when she asks her *parī* foster family for help in her father's predicament, is aided by her foster mother (ll. 110–19). In the manuscript, it is her foster brother who responds to her need, while in the chapbook, it is both mother and son who appear. The manuscript version, which alone among the three ends with an extensive gloss on the moral messages of the story (of which, more later), explicitly points out the value of loyalty and wisdom in women, as exemplified by the vizier's daughter and Salīm's human wife, without reference to the dying father's warning to Salīm to avoid confiding in women. The Ākhond's telling conveys a similarly positive image of women amidst all of Salīm's travails (even the monkey is loyal and seeks in her way to honor and care for Salīm and give him a family), but the Ākhond omits any reinforcing moral commentary. Through small details of action and circumstance, the Ākhond does reiterate, more than either of the written versions, the theme of Salīm's marital responsibility and the problem of providing for his human wife. As will be explored in chapter 7, the story of 'Ādel Khān, with which Karīm responds to this performance, projects a rather more negative role for the female in miraculous masculine adventures.

The chapbook includes one additional adventure, set between the monkey- and *parī*-bride episodes. It is lacking in either the Ākhond's telling or the manuscript version but adds a dimension to Salīm's sexual adventures. This is the encounter with the "Strap-Legs" (*dawāl-pāī*), which has an analogue in the fifth voyage of Sindbad the Sailor in *The Thousand and One Nights*. Leaving the monkey's valley, Salīm arrives in another land, similarly rich in fruit trees, and encounters an old, white-bearded man with weak legs who asks him to raise him up on his shoulders so that he can take Salīm home and feed him meat and bread, which Salīm has not eaten in some time, the monkeys having given him only milk and fruit. Once aboard, however, the old man wraps his strap-like legs around Salīm so tightly that he cannot be dislodged, and turns Salīm into a riding mount. If he fails to follow the old man's orders, the old man chews on his ears, jabs him with a bodkin or "squeezed my testicles so hard with his heels that I was almost destroyed, my soul was at my lips." Nor do the promised meat and bread ever materialize, but only bitter dried fruits, at the nadir of Salīm's adventures in the vegetable world. It is at this point that the chapbook Salīm first regrets deserting the monkey: "I never knew her worth, the bride's curse has affected me." Indeed, the scene both resembles the monkey kingdom, in its horticultural abundance and semi-human population (there is a community of these creatures, of whom the old man is king), and inverts it: the population seems to be entirely male, Salīm is now fed on bitter dried fruits rather than lush fresh ones, and "ridden" not by an oversexed bride but by an old male who subjects him to sexual abuse (poking him with a bodkin and squeezing his testicles).

These and other themes developed in this episode make it logically as well as spatially pivotal in the sequence of otherworldly adventures. The old man, promising meat and bread but supplying only dried fruit, promising hospitality but in fact a predator, stands between Salīm's encounters with the threatening, then nurturant vegetable world (the sea-cow, then the monkey kingdom where he is lodged under trees and fed on fruit and milk) and the elegantly civilized, courtly world of the *parī*, where even apparent carnivores are actually benevolent wet nurses, and, subsequently, the violently hypercarnivorous one of the *deyb*, where Salīm will be offered mutton in preparation for his becoming meat himself. The culinary transitions—from foraged fruit to uncooked vegetarian foods provided by others, to a court so refined that food is not mentioned and predation is an illusion, and finally to hyperconsumption of cooked meat—are interwoven with changes in the sexual dimension. Sexually, Salīm has forsaken the bestial world of unbridled lust but passes through status *as* a beast, subject to sexual abuse by another male, before he contracts a decorous and supernaturally hypergamous marriage. Giving tit for tat to his captor, Salīm escapes the Strap-Legs by a deceptive manipulation in the culinary realm, getting the old man drunk on wine he has prepared by fermenting fruits in a gourd. Yet wine is unclean for Muslims, and Afghans are more categorical than many in their rejection of fermented beverages, so Salīm's resort to this ploy creates ambiguity in his own ritual and ethical status. Habitual use of wine by the carnivorous *deyb* Salīm later encounters is one aspect of the *deyb's* godlessness and also, as in this episode, the monster's undoing.

The Strap-Legs episode, in its pivotal position in the chapbook, is the apogee of Salīm's otherworldly travels, polar opposite to the home world of conjugal companionship, physical prosperity, and secure governance which is his starting point and ultimate goal. The other two versions of the story lack this pivotal incident, but since its main themes—cuisine, sex, and tyranny—are integral to other episodes shared by all three versions, it mainly reinforces thematic possibilities common to all, rather than introducing new structural features.

The intratextual aptness of its content, and its potential for enriching and reinforcing the tale thematically, tell little about its durability in tradition, however. The presence of this episode in the twentieth century chapbook, taken together with its absence from the Ākhond's twentieth century oral version and from the eighteenth century manuscript, illustrates the problem of convergence and divergence among variants in a joint oral-literary tradition. In respect to gross structure, the two versions more distant from each other in time more closely resemble each other than the two which were more proximate in provenance. On the basis of existing evidence, one cannot know whether the Ākhond consciously or unconsciously edited this episode out when he learned the tale, knew this episode and included it in other performances of this story, though he omitted it on this occasion, or whether his sources lacked this episode. Any of these is possible, on evidence gleaned from multiple performances of individual stories I later recorded with other performers (Mills 1978, passim). At the same time, a variety of details shared by the Ākhond's telling and the chapbook, but not the manuscript, suggests a closer relation between the former two. In still other aspects, such as the circumstances of the cursing of Hojāj or of Salīm's return to *parī* country, the chapbook and manuscript agree but the Ākhond differs.

The reader has been subjected to this extensive content review to stress the following point: The fluidity of oral tradition must not be underestimated, even when supposedly "fixed" written texts are an element in the tradition. Oral tradition is too protean to make straightforward genealogical inferences on morphological bases. Historical-geographical "mapping" of variants, when dependent in part or in whole on single, scattered examples, some of them summaries and some from written sources distributed over broad time periods, is from this perspective a highly dubious activity. The literary historian's construction of "genealogical" maps, or stemmata, for a collection of manuscripts whose production was scattered over space and time presents related problems, because of the possibility of convergence effects when the manuscript tradition is symbiotic with an active oral one, as in the case of *The Thousand and One Nights* or, more modestly, *Salīm*.

Religious Sensibility: Performance Coherence and Meaning

Where full-length narratives, not summaries, are available, one may pursue the matter of proximity of variants at the level of narrative and stylistic details, but like gross structure, details are systematically malleable under the influence of narrator personality and performance situation. One dimension of detail on which the Ākhond has clearly put his own stamp in Salīm's tale is that of religious sensibility, which the Ākhond fine-tunes in harmony with issues raised in Karīm's "Mongol Martyr" tale and to which subsequent stories in the performance sequence return. In particular, both the chapbook and the manuscript portray Salīm's relationship with his divine sponsors as a votive one: devastated by illness, Salīm vows to mend his ways and make the pilgrimage *if* God will heal him. The Ākhond avoids any suggestion that Salīm is bargaining with divine authority. In his telling, Salīm simply despairs and acknowledges his human weakness (ll. 206–19), and through that submission (*Islam*, in its basic sense) he receives grace and healing.

The Ākhond's omission of any hint of a votive element in Salīm's transactions with the divine guides who visit his sleep, is in keeping both with Karīm's negative portrayal of votive folk religion and saint veneration in "The Mongol Martyr," and with the distinction the Ākhond himself made in his interview (chapter 5, ll. 74–76) between "Sufis of pure faith" and "deficient shaykhs," who receive offerings and veneration from simple people by virtue of their supposed powers to intercede with God, to heal, and to divine. The chapbook and manuscript portrayals of Salīm's clearly votive relationship with his heavenly guides are unacceptable to the Ākhond's religious sensibility, which is less charismatic and indeed more orthodox, in keeping with his rather sober, probably Naqshbandī Sufi spiritual orientation.[12]

The Ākhond calls Salīm's suffering *zāhedī*, "asceticism" (l. 214), as if it were voluntarily undertaken for the sake of spiritual advancement, because poverty and helplessness, properly viewed, remind one of God's power and the transience of human strength. Salīm's complete submission to God's will in his penitence is reflected in his subsequent explanation of his fall

---

12. Naqshbandīyya and Qādirīyya, both rather sober disciplines, were the two most active Sufi orders in Herat at that time, according to other informants. The Ākhond never explicitly claimed a mystical affiliation, but his Sufi sympathies are obvious from his interview comments. Naqshbandī was the most likely choice, given his location, background, and the general tenor of his remarks.

into error: "The Lord made me hopeless of His Court" (l. 148). This is not to blame God for his own apostasy, but to acknowledge the role of God's grace in every individual fate. In the larger sense, it is Salīm's entire history, told to Hojāj as a lesson masquerading as diversion, which will ultimately reform and redeem Hojāj. A fall from grace may be ultimately redemptive not only for the individual but for others, just as Salīm's unjust suffering at the hands of tyrants (the Negus, the *deyb*, and Hojāj) becomes a catalyst for the rescue of others and, in the last two cases, for the neutralization of tyranny.

The *jihād* (holy war) the Ākhond portrays is the classic form, defensive warfare against a force which threatens the Muslim community and its faith, not aggressive warfare against non-Muslims (Shahrani 1984:28–30). If the religious commitment of such a hero, his willingness as an ordinary man, inexperienced in battle, to die in holy war, and the use of his outlandish experiences to illustrate the place of suffering in ethical development, seem far-fetched or artificially idealized, one must consider that four years after the Ākhond's story was recorded, residents of the Herat area, armed with hunting rifles, handguns, and farm implements, initiated the local revolt against the Marxist government, which was equipped with tanks, mortars, and aircraft. Witnesses report that several thousand were killed in the street battles of that initial confrontation in the spring of 1979. Kazim Alami, a Herati refugee who was present in Herat during the first years of the war, listened on tape in 1984 to the Ākhond's description of how pits were dug to ambush Salīm and remarked, "Maybe that's where the people of Pashtūn Zarghūn got the idea for the tank traps they built," camouflaged pits dug in the roads as a line of defense against advancing tanks. He went on to explain that the villagers of the Ākhond's own district, Pashtūn Zarghūn, were credited with taking the first violent action against the government in Herat City.

The chapbook text, like the Ākhond, portrays the holy war as a defensive action. The Ākhond identifies the adversary tentatively as Abbysinian (l. 239), perhaps by analogy to the Qur'anic account of the unsuccessful Abyssinian siege of Mecca in the year of the Prophet's birth (Surah 105, "The Elephant").[13] The chapbook identifies them as Byzantines, attacking not Medina but Damascus and Aleppo. The manuscript, by contrast, por-

---

13. Pickthall n.d., p. 634. Roxanne Haag-Higuchi (1984), in her description of the Mashhad library manuscript containing Salīm's tale, describes another tale, not Salīm's but No. 5 in the same collection, entitled "Qasim and Gauhar Banu," with Habāshī (Abyssinians) named as adversaries of the Muslims.

trays the action as an aggressive raid by Muslim forces from Tūs, "city of warriors" (in present-day eastern Iran), against the Byzantines in "Rūm" (Byzantium and/or Anatolia). In the manuscript, these Muslim warriors are primarily interested in the booty or ransom to be gained from a successful campaign. Salīm alone, asked what share he will claim, asks simply for the right to be first in single combat: he alone is seeking martyrdom. In the manuscript, Salīm's eagerness for martyrdom is highlighted by the venality of the Muslim forces. The Christian king, devastated by Salīm's attacks, prays to God to be allowed to capture "the Wāsiṭī" (Salīm being from Wāsiṭ, Hojāj's city), pledging if successful to make peace with the Muslim forces. He captures Salīm and pays a sizeable tribute to the Muslims, after which they all go home, making no attempt to rescue their hero.

Salīm's eagerness for martyrdom correlates with a more specifically Shiʿa sensibility common to both the manuscript and the chapbook, which is understandably lacking the Sunni Ākhond's performance. In the manuscript version, when Salīm goes into battle he pronounces the statement of faith (*kalīmah*) in the Shiʿa form, adding veneration of ʿAli to that of God and the Prophet. In both the chapbook and the manuscript, Hojāj's affliction is brought upon him not just by his general murderousness (as the Ākhond portrays it), but also and specifically by his historically documented persecution of ʿAlids (precursors of the Shiites) in Wāsiṭ and his pursuit and execution of Saʿīd bin Khabīr, "one of the companions and loving friends of the imams" (Sharkat-e Nasabī Kānūn-e Ketāb, p. 2). The manuscript (Haag-Higuchi ms, p. 251) calls this victim "Abū Saʿīd." It goes on to explain that Hojāj first killed a sympathizer who sheltered him in his home, then sent an army after Abū Saʿīd himself to the Kaʿaba, where he had taken refuge. The tyrant then extracted him from the sanctuary by force and had him killed. For this outrage not only to his person but to the holy precinct, Abū Saʿīd's dying curse brought on Hojāj's affliction of terror and sleeplessness.

Both the written versions more closely approximate details of Hojāj's career, as recorded in historical sources, then does the Ākhond's telling. Both of the former are also of Shiʿa provenance, which makes the historical Hajjāj's persecution of ʿAlid sympathizers more audience-pertinent than it is for the Sunni Ākhond and his listeners. The Ākhond substitutes local Herat-area placenames for the written texts' evocations of Omayyad caliphate history and geography; he also places the events during the earlier caliphate of ʿOmar, a companion of the Prophet (l. 238), removing it from the political context of the historical Hajjāj's activities.

Haag-Higuchi in her analysis of Salīm's story (1984:144) points out the frequent appearance in this and other story collections of the theme of the hero's reliance on God (*tawakkol*), as the source of his powers and ultimate good fortune. But she also raises questions about this story's conceptual unity, perceiving a thematic discontinuity between the first, religiously framed sections, concerning Salīm's apostasy, rehabilitation, pilgrimage, and heroic deeds, and the sequence of otherworldly adventures beginning with the sea-cow episode. This perception of disunity may, however, be an artifact of a European conceptualization of narrative generics and thematics. Hojāj has demanded that someone tell him from their own experience a true story, previously unknown, which will make him both laugh and cry. The juxtaposition of laughter and tears itself rationalizes the difference in tone between the two parts of the story, but Hojāj's additional demand that it be the teller's own true experience, means that the ludicrous and the tragic are to be integrated not just as entertainment, but in a single person's life in a deeper way. Not to put it too grandly, Salīm is to perform an act of witnessing to the unity of these two dimensions of life, which will be therapeutic to the tyrant who has let himelf be separated from his own humanity as well as from divine guidance, from love as well as justice.

Haag-Higuchi sees the problem of unity as being one of disparate material. She assumes, according to European notions of artistic unity and our tendency to hierarchize belief systems, that devotional religious themes are antithetical to fantastic material concerning *parī* and *dīv*. This is not a distinction that troubles traditionally educated Afghans, however. *Parī* and *deyb* are etymologically members of a pre-Islamic Indo-European supernatural order, their names respectively cognates to English "fairy" and "deity" (Sanskrit, *deva*). Persian-speaking Islam, rather than marginalizing these beings as the Christianization of Europe did their cousins, integrated them with Semitic tradition. In popular religious consciousness, they are otherworldly, but not unreal creatures, the same general class of beings as the *jinn* whom, according to religious tradition, Solomon subjugated and, in part, converted to Islam. There are Iranian popular religious rituals (*sofreh*, "votive meals") dedicated to righteous Muslim *parī*, just as there are *sofreh* dedicated to the relatives of the Prophet as intercessors (see Jamzadeh and Mills 1986, and associated bibliography).

With all this in mind, the diversity of Salīm's adventures becomes less a defect of conceptual structure than an assertion of an essential unity behind the apparent diversity, in this case extreme, of human experience.

Salīm explores and displays his own humanity not just by carrying out the duties of husband and pilgrim in the world we recognize, but also in his negotiations in otherworldly realms with creatures operating by different rules. The Ākhond avoids votive themes in presenting Salīm's experience, without rejecting the fantastic elements in his story. To him, the notion of alternative creations does not threaten the logic of God's sovereign order over creation, rather it confirms God's limitless power, but the idea of bargaining for grace does constitute a threat to the notion of divine sovereignty. To a religious teacher of his background and inclinations, such bargaining compromises the idea of unconditional submission to God's will (*taslīm*) which is the most basic tenet of Islam.

Salīm's Story in the Present Context

The complex possibilities of this text, particularly in comparison to other available variants, can easily divert analysis from the central question for present purposes, what is the story doing *here*? But at the same time, a discussion of what the story achieves in its present position is enhanced by our knowledge of alternative possibilities, which the foregoing was meant to supply. The many angles from which the story can be viewed, give radically different perspectives on its generic status. Haag-Higuchi in her analysis pointed out the affinity Salīm's story has with popular Islamic heroic (*sīrah*) literature ("Ritterromanen" in Hagg-Higuchi's terminology), especially with regard to the pilgrimage and holy war sequences. In aspects of its gross structure, the tale also resembles other romantic quest tales popular in the area at the time of this performance. The story's attachment to the romantic quest genre, or subgenre, is evident in the structure of Salīm's marriages, both of which constitute double wooings, the basic structure of the short popular romances performed by other storytellers I met. In these tales, the hero first identifies and woos a spouse, only to be separated from her by forces beyond their control. In the first wooing, he seeks and wins her by his own efforts. They are then separated, usually by the intervention of a hostile male principle, who may be a rival to the hero or a hostile father figure to the love object or a combination of the two (here, the *parī* king's hostile pursuit of Salīm after he leaves *parī*-land inverts that theme, and Hojāj, the ultimate agent of separation, is a more generalized form of a hostile male authority figure). After their separation, the hero is so incapacitated (often nearly or actually dead) that their reunion can only be accomplished by the intervention of others, either divine intervention, the intervention of the woman herself, using special powers, or occasionally, the intervention of a hero's companion or substitute who has not been incapacitated and acts to rescue the hero. In the latter half of Salīm's story, the intervention of females with access to special powers (the vizier's daughter, the *parī* women) plays the key role in rescuing the incapacitated hero and reuniting him with both his lost spouses.

To say that this story partakes both of religious heroic themes and of romantic quest literature is not to say that the tale is generically hybrid but only that the generic categories we might want to impose on Islamic popular literature do not capture unities which operate across our distinctions. Nonetheless, from the point of view of form and scale, this story is quite a departure from the short anecdotes about fools which preceded it in the story session. The Ākhond distinguished it at the outset from what had gone before, on the basis of length (l. 1). The only explicit association he made with what had gone before was his somewhat apologetic reference to sexual humor (l. 425), connecting the scene of Salīm's seduction by the monkey with the defloration scene in "Rasūl's Mother." While the explicitness of the sexual humor in these and subsequent stories during the evening surprised Mokhtār, my assistant, "Salīm the Jeweller" is not *about* sex in the way the Karīm's anecdote was set up to be.

The lack of close associations between this story and the preceding anecdotes, together with its thematic connection with the prior history of the Ākhond and the Woləswāl (as subject and governor, prisoner and captor) leads me to suspect that the Ākhond had thought in advance of making this tale a major part of his evening's performance, if circumstances would permit. Stories which the Ākhond told after it, especially "Mahmūd of Ghaznī and the Thieves" (chapter 8), can be seen to be more intricately associated with "Salīm" than can anything which has gone before. The Ākhond's emphasis on certain elements in Salīm's father's dying injunction, particularly "Sit down with people of wisdom . . . , with those who govern . . ." (ll. 139ff.), is an invitation, conscious or unconscious, for present company to consider what they are about in gathering to hear these stories under these auspices. One might see Karīm's two stories as a warm-up act which the Ākhond could use to gauge his audience and to determine levels of comprehension and appropriate degrees of license, but from the start, the Ākhond's turn away from the *blason populaire* and his more restrained presentation of sexual humor indicate that his sense of the situation differs from Karīm's.

From this point of view, the Ākhond's choice of "Ten Qerān" (chapter 5) as an opening story can be seen as a courteous pursuit of the generic and thematic line established by Karīm, but also as a generalization of the issue of fools, to be followed in the larger story by a more complex disquisition on right guidance and right action. "Salīm" is far from a sermon, and the Ākhond was quite willing to dwell on its amusing elements, but his paring down of the descriptive details of the heroic adventure literature and fantastic romance—both potentialities of the story's structure more fully realized in the written variants—narrows the focus of the performance toward the frame tale of Hojāj's tyranny, his affliction, the rent in the social fabric caused by Salīm's unjust imprisonment, and its ultimate repair through the telling of his story.

The Ākhond has given a clue to what he was about by glossing his tale of fools, however briefly (ll. 159–64):

That people who
    in knowledge
    and wisdom ['orfān] lack ad— advancement
    are this kind of people,
    that they buy for ten qerān but give seventy.
And they don't even know how to milk the cow!

In the case of "Salīm the Jeweller," the Ākhond offered no gloss at the end of the tale but simply said "That's the story that's told." Mokhtār's immediate demand for a closing formula (chapter 6, l. 630), which amounted to a reassertion of his own place on the conversational floor, effectively deflected any supplementary comment which the Ākhond might have offered.

The chapbook, like the Ākhond's telling, ends with a simple "Thus ends the story of Salīm the Jeweller." The manuscript alone undertakes an extensive gloss of the story, to identify its fāïdah (usefulness or moral). The moral mirrors and expands somewhat on the injunctions of Salīm's dying father as given in the beginning of the story:

> One should not be beguiled by wealth and gold of this world, or rely on them, and one should keep an agreeable, suitable woman well, and make her happy, and should ask God (blessings on Him) for pious children, and [even]

if all are daughters, suitable children are an aid and assistance to their fathers and mothers, like that daughter of the chamberlain who answered his cry for help. And strength in battle and bravery are needed, like that which Salīm had, that carried him through difficulties and deserts, and every prisoner who pledges to God and keeps faith, will doubtless arrive at his heart's goal. Know also that the Decrees of the Truth, glory to Him and may He be exalted, no matter on whom they have run their course, at every time and hour and place, will necessarily come to pass, and [trying to] avert [fate] is an absurdity, and the attempt is fruitless, whether it be in the seventh heaven or the depths of the earth, as with Salīm's experiences marrying the daughter of the *parī*, and those circumstances of his that were told; and 100,000 praises of God on the writer and the reader and the listener and the compiler and the book-owner, and on that faithful and monotheistic one who says, "Amen, oh Lord of the Learned." (Haag-Higuchi ms, p. 276; this and other translations by this author)

The manuscript follows directly with the title of the next tale. In classical Persian, tale collections organized by a frame narrative, such as *Anwār-i Sohaylī* (also known as *Kalīla wa Dimna*) or the *Tūtīnāmah* ("Book of the Parrot"), to name two which still have currency in Afghan oral performance, the tale-teller in the story often engages in lengthy didactic glosses of individual tales, but such glosses were seldom, in my experience, carried over into the oral performances which derived from written texts.[14]

Omitting explicit glosses in live performance helps keep the narrative interpretively open, and any critical content implicit and thus deniable. In the present case, various didactic potentialities of the story are indicated by the manuscript gloss, but not all of these need have been on the mind of the Ākhond in his choice of this tale. One theme which the manuscript does not mention, but which the Ākhond made much of in the father's dying injunctions, is that of righteous governance and the desirability of keeping company with righteous rulers. Not to supply a gloss at the end of a story of this complexity assigns interpretive responsibility to the audience, which, given the delicacy of the Ākhond's relationship to his host, would have been a strategic move, however conscious or unconscious. In the Ākhond's telling, only Hojāj's tears and laughter supply moral commentary to Salīm's tale. The tyrant, whoever he may be, is left to his own interpretations.

---

14. I assume such derivations only when the storyteller identified a written source. Even so, the storyteller may not have read the story, but may have heard it read by another person, or just heard it told and attributed to the book or literary author named.

7. Khalīfah Karīm, " 'Ādel Khān 'the Just' "

. . . One time, sir, there was a king, 'Ādel Khān,[1]
they called him 'Azīz[2] "the Just Khān," because of his great righteousness.
He went to the baths.
Early in the morning.
[*Mokhtār*: . . . went to the baths?]   5
Yes, uh-huh.

He went, went to the baths and,
sir, this vizier of his went with him, too.

They came to the baths, and when they'd washed and cleaned
                        themselves from head to foot,
after that,   10
the vizier said, "Sir, if we wait half a min— half an hour, uh—
        here in the bath chamber, in the outer chamber,
           then go out, it's better, because the weather is cold and
           they say it's harmful." »
He said, "Fine."   15

They came and sat in that room and
uh—they talked there,
the vizier said—ah— m — »
the king said, "It's a fine thing that we sat down here and
           since we're sitting here, let's call the barber, too,   20

---

    1. *'Ādel*: "just, righteous", masculine personal name; *khān*: title of Mongolian origin, previously used to designate traditional nobility or tribal leaders, now often used in Afghanistan as a respectful title approximately equivalent to "mister."
    2. *'azīz*: "dear, beloved," a popular masculine personal name as well as an ordinary adjective.

so he can dress our heads and beards,"³ »
and he said, "That's fine."
They called, and the barber came.
The barber came, sir,
and when he'd dressed and arranged their heads and beards in
the manner he knew,   25
after that, the king put his hand into his purse,
to give something to this barber.

Now, a king's purse doesn't have small change, but there was
a precious gem, and he took that out
and gave it to the barber.
When the vizier saw that, it troubled his heart.   30
He couldn't <u>say</u> "Don't give him that," [so] he said, "Sir, he's a barber."
When <u>he</u> said, "He's a barber," <u>he</u> put his hand back in his purse
and gave him another.
He said, "Sir, I say to you, he's a barber."
He took out another one, three all together.
When he gave him all three of them,   35
it really troubled [the vizier's]⁴ heart,
[thinking] "If he gives one little barber-guy three of them,
and <u>one</u> is <u>so</u> valuable,
this king [will give away] the wealth— uh— of the whole
treasury all at once,
by the time he's washed his hair a couple more times—   40
or, God forbid, if he goes somewhere else this time,
and there's some other guy —life just can't go on
this way, now—"
It really troubled his heart.
He said, "Sir,
Uh— you gave these three jewels to the barber,   45
but a barber doesn't <u>get</u> that kind of pay, now—
You should give him a hundred rupees or so."
The point is, he made the king regret that, what he'd done.

———

3. Normally, this would include shaving the head, which is covered by a turban, and trimming the beard and moustache, which are worn full, with parts of the neck shaved.

4. Use of the third-person singular pronoun is disambiguated by pitch variations in the storyteller's speech. Names are supplied in the translation to avoid introducing ambiguity not present in the original.

Once he made him regret it, the king couldn't just take them back
                                                    from the guy,
    he didn't get high-handed.   50
He said, "We— let's say, uh— let's arrange something, now that I've
                                        given them to him." »
This vizier said, "Sir, we—
            this—
            time, we're having a pleasant time here, now stay
                                a minute, or maybe five.
            Come on, let's tell each other a story, or a joke,   55
            let's see— whoever has had the worst past experience,
            can keep the three jewels.
            Let's say we're three brothers.
            Without any distinctions, like that." »
He said, "Fine."   60

The king was figuring in his own heart, "Worse things happened to me,
                            these two have never seen the like—
                            —and [the jewels] will be
                                    back in my purse."
The vizier said, "Worse things have happened to me,"
    —in his heart—   65
                "so I'll get them."
The barber said, "OK, so maybe I won't get them, after all.
            Still, I've seen some of the hardships of the world.
            Perhaps I'll get my hands on them."

Each one of them had the same misconception and   70
they put [the jewels] down, and said, "Come on,"
they said, "who'll talk [first], and who [next]?"
Finally they turned to the king, saying, "Since you are highest in rank
                            no doubt you are also higher
                                        in honor,
                            whether or not you are in age,   75
                            so it's your right to begin,
                                    and start this off."
He said, "Fine."
The king said, »
    "When I
    was young and haughty and   80

in those days when I had either just taken the throne, or was about to,
    or a little after that,
one day I went out, I wanted to go to the desert, to go hunting,
so I came and
I was riding around the mountains, hunting and passing the time
                        with my friends.   85
All at once by the power of God a dust storm and
a sudden cold wind and
all that came up, it was wintertime, [and] I lost track of my friends.

When I got lost," he said, sir,
"No matter where I rode that day, I couldn't find my horse any
                        watering place. »   90
Evening came, and I passed the night dirty,
filthy, like that, morning light came," kind sir, »
"I came to this place,
where there was this—in this one place, a marshy meadow, and
                    the sun had come out a little,
there's a spring of water.   95
When I looked down into that spring of water, »
I thought, 'How can I make ablutions here, how can I wash my
                        face, how
        can I get a drink?'
Since the—water—the springs were all dirty, muddy and cruddy, »
    they've got a whole lot of stuff in them.   100
I saw there was no way here, my clothes would be ruined, »
and I look along a little further, and a wheel appears.[5]
I went over to the wheel.
I saw the wheel, that there's a well,
it has a bucket   105
has a rope,
has all the parts like that.
Well, now, I threw that bucket down into the well, »

---

5. That is, a winding-spool apparatus for a well-rope. The narrator is switching tenses, back and forth between simple past and historical present, in an informal, conversational style parallel to similar tense-switching tendencies in American English anecdotal narrative. The translation attempts to preserve the conversational tone of those tense switches which are nonequivalent to colloquial English, by placing a tense switch as near as possible to its original position. In this sentence, for instance, "saw" is actually present tense and "look" is actually past.

I said, 'I'll draw some well water and wash,
     well water is warmer[6] and cleaner, too,   110
     compared to what's in these wet spots.'

I let it down.
When I let it down and the bucket went down into the well,
whether it got to the middle of the well or not, a really
                                       terrifying voice
came up out of the well,   115
saying, 'Just as you broke my sleep,
     and woke me up, wouldn't let me rest,
     if you're a man, become a woman!'

As <u>soon</u> as I heard that voice, I took fright, jumped back,
[and] I saw that my body,   120
that place with the 'special limbs' of mine just started to burn
as if with an <u>ant</u>-bite, like.
     'Bābā, what's <u>this</u>?!'
Well, I backed off some more,
then once   125
involuntarily, like that, my hand went down inside my pants,
     'Was that a wasp there, d— a scorpion, a worm, or what?'
I put my hand down,
[and] I saw my hand went in for about a meter.
And it's warm. [*muffled laughter and sotto voce audience comments*]   130

Well!"
Sir!— "How could <u>that</u> happen?
Again my awareness—I, I investigated.
Then when I investigated, there wasn't a <u>trace</u> of that tool [and balls]!"[7]"
Yeah!   135
[*Audience member comments*: He became a woman . . .]

Ye—eah, a <u>wo</u>man!
Yeah, "—just like a pull-on hat, an open mouth right there, face down.

---

6. A generalization made about well water by Heratis; in winter, well water remains unfrozen even when freezing occurs at surface level.

7. *sāmān-e sāgerdā*: the second element has not yet been identified; translation is tentative.

[*continued muffled laughter*]

    I thought, 'What's going on?' [*more laughter*]

    Well!   140

    What am I to do? »

    Well, I was really upset and

    right there,

    lost in my own thought, right there in the mud and crud,

        I'm wandering around, »

    forgot all about clothes and such,   145

    suddenly, now, a fine-looking young man

    riding on a horse, now, he came up, and dismounted.

    As soon as he spotted me, it was as if before—

    —two months <u>before</u> all this, they'd read the words over me,[8]

    And he came along with his bag and things,   150

    grabbed me around the middle, in the midst of all this mud

                                     and crud, »

    didn't even worry about his clothes,

    fuck, fuck! went right at it," —kind sir— "down in this meadow.

    Lord, what am I to do? Well, any—

    whatever he [wanted],[9] he satisfied himself,   155

    and said, 'That's for starters,[10] let's go!'

    And there was nothing I could say.

    I mounted my own horse, and he mounted his, and took me—where?

    He had a winter pasture[11] there, and he took me right there.

    For something on the order of forty days and nights,   160

    he kept me right there, and if it was twice, it was eighty times

    that guy did that thing to me.

---

8. *faut khāndah* (from literary, *fāti ḥah khwāndan*): to read the opening lines of the Qur'an in ritual context, for personal rites of passage, e.g., funerals or, as in this case, the *nekāḥ* marriage contract.

9. *har sūlsūlī keh desht*: the second element is so far unidentified. One Herati auditor suggested *sūlsūlī* was an onomatopoetic sound of some kind.

10. *bismillāh yē*: literally, "That's [to say], 'In the Name of God,' " the formula uttered at the beginning of any enterprise.

11. *qeshlāq*: transhumant pastoralists in Afghanistan and Iran maintain established summer and winter grazing territories, the latter sometimes with permanent shelters of stone or mud and thatch.

After that, kind sir,
this one day I said to him, 'Oh, don't—
               whatever people you're from, now,   165
               you <u>are</u> God's servant.
          That is, I won't get out of this
                    marriage with you,
          I won't leave your house.
          It might be there's three or four
                    babies in my body,
          and when will they be born?   170
          Oh, take me
          out on the plain, give me a turn around,
             because my heart is breaking,
             after all, I was in a
                    well-watered place!'[12] »
He said, 'Fine.'   175

I mounted up along with him and we came, kind sir, riding here
                    and there, »
     we came up to that same well.
     When we arrived there,
     he said, 'Come on, let's you and I have some tea, or a bit of
                  breakfast, right here.' "
—In those days there wasn't any tea and—   180
Well, they sat down for tea and breakfast—
He said to her, "Now, you—
       I'll gather some wood,
       you bring water."
"I said, 'Fine.'   185
He went to gather wood,
to bring it,
he has to put a kettle on, and do all that, and I came to the head
                  of this well,
when my eye lit on it, that it's the very same well and the very
              same wheel and the very same bucket,
when my eye lit on that, it frightened me, I gave up hope,   190
I just <u>wept</u>, because God comforts the helpless.

---

12. In contrast to the campsite on the dry plains, without trees or green growth.

I said, 'Lord!
At the head of this very well you rendered me hopeless,
and now it's <u>forty</u> days and nights that you've cast me into
the clutches of this shepherd,
and even a <u>bear</u> couldn't stand it in this heathen's grip!' "   195
[*Muffled laughter*]
Fine.
" 'That is, if you give me rescue,
give me my wish,
whose loss is it? What loss would it be to you,
you who are without need?' "   200
Yeah.
"I came along weeping and hopeless like that,
picked up that bucket and threw it into the well.
<u>Right</u> when it reached the middle of the well, or [maybe] not even,
it struck the side of the well.   205
When <u>it</u> clattered,
this
voice came up.
It said, 'Just as you've awakened me from sleep at the time of prayer,
and my heavy sleep has gone,   210
Oh <u>Lord</u>! may you have your wish!
What<u>ever</u> desire you may have!' "
<>

Yeah.
"So I <u>saw</u> that my body—ouch!
It scratched, like a burning,   215
and I put my hand down quick,
down inside my pants.
And it's like the crossbar on a 45-pound scale, hanging there, and
its nose reaches the bend of my knee! [*Muffled laughter*]
I said, '<u>Lord</u>! If I— if you were going to give [me] limbs this big,
if only you'd done it sooner!'
[*Inaudible background comments*]
I was satisfied, delighted.   220
I gave thanks."
Yeah.

"After that,"—
he said, "I gave a —great deal of praise to God,
    and gave thanks,   225
    and the point of this is,
    a— mm— uh—
    I touched this—
    this new blessing,
    took pleasure in it,   230
    yeah, I came up to this guy, and before the guy could say anything,
    yeah—I lowered my pants-band and raised my shirt tail,
                                            [*speaking rapidly*] »
    'There, now,' I said, 'if you have any shame or modesty,
                                        then run for it!
    'Cause now it's my turn! Now do you remember,
                                  what you did?' »
    The guy said, 'Goodbye!'   235

    He ran for it, his father[13] —ran, anyway,
    yeah!
    He ran for it.
    He ran for it, and then I was back to my own form and
                               that same youthfulness, »
    the Great God has these ways—   240
    Now, then, I came back to my own throne and my own place.
    And so I am to this day.
[*Partly inaudible prompt by the Ākhond*: That kind, that kind of hardship . . .]
    That is, who's seen that kind of hardship?
They said, "Sir, friend, you have seen severe hardship,   245
    but don't take these up right away, till everyone tells his own
                                  experience, anyway!"
He said, "Fine."

The vizier said, »
    "I—

---

13. An oblique reference to a common male curse in Afghan Persian "I fuck your father['s soul]!"

in the days of my youth, I was engaged, and the point is,

they married me to a lovely wife,   250

and gave her to me.

When I brought her home, I saw that she was miserable, like that,

in a way that

uh— she's set against affection, and for one night and two nights

and ten nights

well, whatever the conditions, I spent them with her—   255

My heart's really troubled.

I came to my mother and said, 'Ma—' »

She said, 'What is it?'

I said, 'That wife that they just brought for me—

that is, it's not possible to <u>live</u> this way!   260

Yeah, most of the time she's annoyed when she talks to me,

with me,

it's like she's always angry or vexed or up to some trick

or excuse,

and it's all that kind of thing.'

This old lady was very elderly, »

she said, 'This   265

has some basis.

Do you know about her situation?' »

I said, 'No.'

She said, 'Now, tonight don't fall asleep,

or else go off somewhere,   270

tell her, 'I'm going somewhere, I won't be back tonight.'

Come back and hide in some corner of the house, »

see what happens in the evening when you're

not there.' "

He said, "Fine."

"I came back here, that is, kind sir, in the evening   275

I hid up on my own roof[14], in—

_____

14. Traditional housing in the Herat area is flat-roofed mud brick. Roof tops are used for drying and processing foodstuffs, sleeping in hot weather, and other household activities, as well as for routes of passage for women visiting between contiguous households. Passage over the roofs allows women to avoid traveling in the streets where they might encounter strange men.

in a loud voice I said, 'I'm leaving, I'm invited somewhere else.'
Then I came back there.
I sat down on top of the roof, I was hidden in this place and
                         the point is, toward—
    it wasn't yet midnight,   280
when I saw my wife
put on her veil and
—arrange her limbs and all,
and there she went out of the house and went off toward the
                            edge of the desert.
I came along after her, and there was a fortified house[15] there,   285
    the door opened and she went in,
and I stayed outside.
I was there till dawn, and she came out and came back to the house, »
    and I came in after her.
I came back to my mother and said, »   290
    'Ma, last night I saw <u>thus</u>-and-such of a situation.
    ◇
    What shall I do about it?'
She said, 'Lamb, do as I tell you—
        In this *qalah*,
        there's a *deyb*,   295
        she's gotten attached to him,
        she goes and does that thing there
        and then she comes back. »
        In the end he'll[16] kill you.
    ◇
    It's better if you take thought for yourself.' »   300
I said, 'What shall I do?'
She said, 'You go,
        [get] some special, excellent friends,
            who are friends of yours from the heart,
        gather them around you,   305

---

15. *qalah* (literary, *qal'ah*): A typical residence-form in many parts of rural Afghanistan, a high-walled complex of mud-brick buildings, including stables, storage rooms, etc., around an open central court. Size ranges from large extended-family compounds up to palace-fortresses.

16. The verbal inflection does not mark the gender of actor. It could also be translated, "In the end, she'll kill you."

take them and go.   305

In front of that *qalah* there's a spring, and right next to

       that spring, at the edge of the road,

take and dig a great, deep pit, heap up the dirt from it

       on one side,

conceal it right there.

Come and tell her this plan, say "I'm going off

       somewhere for two or three nights."   310

‹›

Go there and hide. »

Toward dawn he'll come out to wash in that spring,

when he <u>does</u> that with your wife, he also washes

       according to his own custom.[17]

He'll fall into that pit. »

When he falls in,   315

tell your friends, "By the Four Friends![18] Strike [now]!"

       Throw the earth down on top of him any way you can, then.

After that, when you go into his *qalah*,

‹›

everyone can pick up whatever his heart desires for

       himself, from among the goods that he has,

but don't you pick up anything.

When you go into this one isolated, empty room that's

       there,   320

right there,

there's this one little boxlike thing,

like a little box, that's been put there.

Pick that up.

be careful you don't give it to anyone.' "   325

He said, "Good."[19]

He, sir, came to see his friends and informed them, and they went and

---

17. Sexual intercourse is polluting, according to Islamic law, and necessitates complete ablution (*ghosl*) before prayer can be performed.

18. The "Four Friends" (*chahār yār*) are the four "rightly guided caliphs" who immediately succeeded the Prophet as leaders of the Muslim community. They were close companions of the Prophet and one, 'Ali, was his cousin and son-in-law, through whom Shi'a Muslims trace the lineage of the twelve Imams, spiritual guides of the Shi'a community. A particularly appropriate invocation, this assimilates the vizier's friends' loyalty to the ideal model of Islamic history.

19. Especially in the vizier's tale, where there is a great deal of reported speech, Karīm

Yeah— "We went," he said, "and dug that pit.
   After that we were hiding there, at around midnight, when there,
            now, [my] wife
  came and went inside the *qalah*.   330
  The hour came when they were coming out,
  this —wife went off, with her head high, toward home,
  uh— he came toward the pit. »
  When he came along, he fell in the pit, and we struck him
           and killed him.
 We went into the *qalah*, and when we went in, sir, »   335
   everyone took away whatever his heart desired of
        [the *deyb*'s] wealth,
 and I came along some, to that empty room that she had told
         me about,
 and I looked around a little and there above the door of that room,
 about the size of a pomegranate or a little bigger, there was this thing
 put there, as if it were a little box, like.   340
 I picked that up, and I didn't open it, either, I came home.
 When I came back, came home, and my friends had gone off
       about their own affairs,
  when I came back,
  my wife,
  her mood was very jealous, like—   345
  she's sitting there with a troubled heart,
  uh— and she hasn't let herself be washed and dressed up at all and
  so I came, 'What's this?'
  That is, 'You weren't here, I was beautifying and adorning myself
    on account of you,   350
    when you weren't here, whom would I do it for? »
    My jealousy was on account of that. »
    Thank God you've come.' "
Yeah.
  "When she talked like that and   355
  after that she said,
uh— 'Where were you and where did you go? What's <u>that</u> in your <u>hand</u>?'
  ◇

———————

is having difficulty keeping the narrative in the first-person voice of the vizier. Discrepancies
in Karīm's use of voice are preserved in the translation.

I said, [*softly, mumbling*], 'Noth— a thi— just a little thing.'
she said, 'No, tell me, what, huh!? Where is it? Give it here!'
And I handed it to her, just that once, 'cause I didn't <u>know</u>!   360
As <u>soon</u> as I handed it to her and she took it from my hand,
she <u>hit</u> it against me, and said, '<u>Down</u>! bitch! Get out of the house!'

As soon as she said that, put it that I grew fur and a tail and
I've got long ears and teats,
and in this condition I followed along.   365

The neighbor's dog came running and the <u>other</u> neighbor's dog
                                                                                        came running, »
the point is, whap![20] they poked and they prodded,
who can you tell about it? To—
[*Ākhond: one or two-sentence comment, inaudible under narrator's rapid speech*]
—the <u>bazaar</u> dogs came, the curs started in,"
Man, what can I do?
[*This latter apparently in response to Ākhond's comment. Ākhond laughs in*   370
                                                                                        background]
"Well, the point is, kind sir,
my life became infinitely bitter,
they rolled me around in the mud and the crud, the dogs chewed on
                                                                                        me, they did all that kind of thing,
God knows how many of them there were, there are so <u>many</u>
                                                                                        dogs in a village! And they <u>all</u>—
for <u>one week</u> I was trailed around, for a week   375
they all did that thing to me.
                              ‹›
If it was <u>forty</u> days for you, it was only <u>one</u> person,"
—he turned to his master. [*Ākhond and others: muffled laughter*]
"Woe for my condition!
After that,"   380
he said,
"Whimpering and crawling and trying to stand up, like that, »
I got myself back to the house, »
went to my mother, and when my mother saw my condition,
she said, 'What's wrong?'   385

---

20. *labbīnah*: not a word, but an onomatopoetic sound, according to one Herati auditor.

when she said, 'What's wro—' I jumped up on my hind feet,
and my mother understood quick enough.
She dashed into the house, God knows where that woman was, »
[but] she picked up the box, and hit me with it
and said, 'Get up, oh vizier of the king!'   390
The fur fell away, the teats disappeared, the tail fell off, sound
                                                                                    and well,
the same person I was,
in my own clothes, perfectly beautiful, clean, and even a kerchief
                                                                    around my neck,
good,
everything right again.   395
‹›
I turned out like that, and she said, 'Good.' "
He said, "After that I took myself into the house.
      I said, 'This time it's <u>my</u> turn,'
      I picked up the box,
      I said, 'Now even if she's on the prayer mat, I won't let her off,
                                                                    fuck her father!'   400
      As soon as I got there, I hit her with it.
      I said, 'Down! Bitch!'
      and the fur came out on her, a bitch just like I was,
      yeah, she went out. »
      I said, 'My heart won't be satisfied with just this.   405
            What does it matter if these little village puppies fuck her?' "
Yeah.
      "I made her follow me, 'Ha, go on, go on!' partly by force, partly
                                                                    by consent,
      I led her around by the houses off in those streets, put it that
      Hājjī Walī's dog came and Borānak's dog came [*background laughter
            as audience members recognize names*], and this other one,   410
      every one from the smaller mastiffs up to the size of a cart-horse."
Yeah.
      "I put her in such a state that up to now there isn't a sound out
                                                            of her about that experience, »
      as long as I don't mention it, and I wouldn't mention it in a year."
They said, "By God, the hardship that—happened to you, and what
                                                            happened to him—   415
            Yeah, you had more," and the king agreed,
but just as he was going to pick up [the jewels], »

the barber said, "I, too, am a friend of yours,
        and <u>I've</u> seen something of the world." »
They said, "Tell!"   420

He said, "One day I was sitting in the barber shop
      right there, shaving some guy's head,
   when suddenly a lady passed by the door.
   Just as she passed by, she raised the corner of her face-veil[21],
   all my <u>sense</u> and <u>consciousness</u> was wiped <u>out</u>, and following
                          after her, 425
   [wondering] 'She—what group of people is she from?'
   ‹›
   I just left the barber shop and the whole layout behind,
          'Goodbye!!' and fell in behind her.
   Put it that the shop was there open, no one in it, in the middle
                   of the bazaar, »
   and somebody took the sharpening stones, »
   somebody took the razors, »   430
   somebody else took the decorations,
   somebody took the towels, they cleaned it out, 'Goodbye!'

   I came to the house.
   I came there, she went to this one place, went to this one
         house, and I came to the door of the house,
         came to the door following her.
   When I went there,   435
   and she was sitting there in the house, on a couch, I came
                 and wished her peace.
   She said, 'And peace be on you!
      It's a blessing you're in these parts.'
   I said, 'I came for a moment's conversation,[22]
      if it's possible.'   440

---

21. *rūband*: In the older-fashioned woman's veil, this short cloth piece covering the face was separate, tied above the ears with strings, and a second, body-enveloping garment was draped over the head. The *chāderī* worn in Herat at the time of this performance was in one piece, with an embroidered lattice over the eyes and nose. For a woman to show her face this way would be interpreted as an intentional sexual invitation.

22. *sohbat*: Between two adult nonrelatives of opposite sex, this is a euphemism for sexual intercourse.

She said, 'You're very welcome, it's wonderful, a blessing, you
                                    did a fine thing to come,
    I've been wanting you to for some time,' —lying in her teeth.[23]"
Yeah.
Yeah, then— " 'Now, I—never—despite the fact that I do these things,
            I took an oath that would make it a sin for me unless
                                there's an ablution, I won't do it.   445
            Yeah, go and do the ablution.'[24]
    I said, 'Where, here, there's no well, there's no pool, there's no stream,
        where can I make the ablution?'
    She said, 'Go there, like, into the vestibule, there's a water pitcher
                                            and bowl there,
            go there and make the ablution, and come back.'   450
    ‹›
    So I said, 'Good.'
    I came there,
    and I saw that there's a pitcher and bowl set there, with water—
    I took it up and
    I lowered my pants so I   455
    could wash my privates,
    and just as I poured the water at the moment of washing my
                                privates, put it that this old tool just—
    whoof!—was cut off and fell on the ground.
    ‹›
    A smooth, clear field
    I was left with,   460
    this—[*muffled laughter*], what now?
    'Cause there's nothing, if only there were one pin or needle left of
                                    it, there's nothing—
    it's just like on some Mongol guy's cheek, without hair or fur or
                                    the whole business!
[*Audience laughter*]
    'Man, what a miserable *kosah*[25] I've become, out of this place.' "
Well!   465

---

23. *Be wojūd dorūgh mīgoft*: literally, "lying with her whole being."
24. *wozū'*: the lesser ablution, required before all prayer.
25. A loanword from Turkish, *kosah* is distinguished physically by a thin beard. In Persian and Turkish folklore the *kosah* is usually also a double-dealer who is caught out in his
trickery, an unmanly and untrustworthy individual who is usually bested by a trickster-hero
(cf. Marzolph 1984:25).

" 'Now how can I heap dust on my head?²⁶

If I go home, what do I say?'

I quit worrying about my wife, I just turned back the way I came,

‹›

I came back.

I came back, because there wasn't a <u>bite</u> to eat in the shop.   470

‹›

I came back all hopeless, and it was already afternoon prayer

time,²⁷ I came to the house, »

and there's just enough in my purse to buy some organ meats²⁸ [for

supper].

Oh, Lord, what shall I do?

As fate would have it, this same evening,

it's Thursday, too, and I—   475

now, it's about to be my day off at the shop, and I »

this evening the wife has

sort of an appointment with me.²⁹

'How am I going to answer to that bastard [woman]?'

[*Muffled laughter*] »

Well, at any rate, we came and had our food and drink,   480

she said, 'The evenings are

getting short, compared to before, yeah, let's go to bed,

then, m—

—and day before yesterday I did the washing—'³⁰»

—('Oh, you *kūni*,³¹ if you did the washing day before

yesterday, »

---

26. Ironic: "How can I disgrace and harm myself any further?" To heap dust on one's own head is to harm oneself or bring oneself into disgrace by one's own actions.

27. Approximately 4 P.M., though the time varies according to the length of the days at different seasons.

28. *delband*: Heart, lungs, and sometimes liver of a sheep or goat, sold as a unit. A cheap and somewhat low-status food.

29. Thursday night was a popular time for conjugal relations in Herat. The husband would then visit the baths on Friday morning to make the greater ablution before going to communal prayer at a mosque. A flurry of activity among married women, dressing up and applying make-up if available, was apparent and the subject of jokes on Thursdays in some households I visited.

30. A feeble excuse to plead for extra time in bed, as the barber's unspoken response indicates.

31. Passive partner in anal intercourse, a common insult applied to either men or, sometimes, women. This sentence is not spoken aloud but addressed by him to his wife in thought.

you, what does that— have to do with being tired
tonight?')" 485

Well.

"I said, 'I've got such a heartburn, oh God! Im dying, aagh!
the way it's cramping around my navel!
I can't even move or bend!'

She said, 'What did you eat?' »
I said, 'Peaches, unpeeled and unwashed.[32]'   490
‹›
She said, 'If you haven't been killed—that's serious—'
I said, 'It's yet to see, maybe I will be, bring *manjūlak*,
     bring *kalpūrah*, brew some *bū-ye māron*![33]'
I took seven pounds of bitter stuff out of dread, [just to say] I'm
sick tonight.'

Put it that with all this uproar, I got myself out of that,   495
lest God forbid my whole life would be ruined.

Well, that night passed. When the next night came,
I came home, and around afternoon prayer the woman went— pu—
p— put everything down,
all nicely put away, and the house was clean, and   500
the point is,
she'd done up everything on her 'lists,'[34] even fresher
than yesterday!"

Yeah.

"And so as soon as we'd eaten,
she said, 'Last night you were without sleep and exhausted
and half-killed, » 505
     with that sort of stomach-ache that you had, come on,
let's go to bed!' »

---

32. *shaftālū nāpost o nāshū*: "Peaches," *shaftālū* in Herat dialect is a euphemism for female genitalia, "eating peaches" a euphemism for sexual intercourse.

33. Apparently, traditional medicines, but more specific identification is still pending. Steingass, *Persian-English Dictionary* has *manjol*, "The fruit of *ficus oppositofolia*"; *-ak* is a common diminutive suffix, but here probably not for the same fruit. Kazem Alami identified *kalpūrah* as a stomach remedy available from traditional herbal druggists. He also pointed out that in the household setting, as in this scene, it is women who prepare and dispense herbal medicines, and who know the ingredients and methods of preparation. The traditional druggists are male.

34. *hesābāt*: "accountings, tallies."

I said, 'Wait till I
    say the evening prayer,' »
she said, 'Good, say it,' and right away she brought the pitcher,
        and I made the ablution,
I made the prayer, »   510
and she said, 'Come on, let's go to bed,' she said— »
'Aw, woman,' I said, 'Don't ask it of me!' »
She said, 'How's that!?'
I said, 'I've got such a migraine that <u>two</u> ākhonds wore out their
    asses [praying] [*Ākhond and others laugh quietly*], and
    <u>couldn't turn</u> it,[35] I'm <u>dying</u>!' " [*muffled laughter*]

    ‹›

[*sighing*] Yeah.   515
    ‹›

"She said, 'Why didn't they do the *badrah* recitation?'[36] »
I said, 'It's too late for *badrah* and all that, I'm thinking about
        my <u>present</u> state, aagh!
    By God, br— um, brew up some *bū-ye māron*, pound up some
        rue incense, fix up some something-or-other!'
        —and so on until dawn.
I wore her out with all this migraine and pains in the eyes,
and when dawn came, she fell asleep, and so did I.   520
'Oh, Lord, if you could make it easy tomorrow night, — »
—how could I throw dust on my own head!? What else can I say?'

In the morning I came, hopeless, and sat at the shop door, »
and <u>now</u> that— woman came again and passed right by there.
This time when she passed by and raised the corner of her
        face veil, » 525
I said, 'Oh, by God, may He rip you out by the roots! You've
        set fire to
    the graves of seven generations of my ancestors, »
    there's not a needle left in my shop, »
    and still with your face—' "

---

35. *gard nazad*: the translation is an approximation.
36. *badrah khānī*: apparently a special prayer.

[*Tape change caused a short break in recorded narrative. In the missing sentences, the barber describes his decision to follow the woman back to the same house, hoping for revenge or restitution, and his being let in at the gate.*]

"—This same house and this same layout and   530
the same couch. »
I gave my greetings, there, »
and she said, 'It's a blessing, your being in these parts.'
I said, 'Yeah, right, it's a blessing, I came for a moment's conversation,
                                                            if I can.'
She said, 'Of course it's possible, it's been so long since you came
                                    here, you're very welcome,   535
            now that you've honored [us] with your presence,
                        something I wished for,' — »
        I said, 'I too, have a wish—' "
Yeah.
            "('You've really wrecked me,[37] how could I not have a
                        wish!? I have this request to lodge in the
                        hands of so–and-so—')[38]
Yeah, I went to the door,   540
into the back room, saying 'I'll do the ablution.'
This time when I went,
I'm looking, kind sir,
for these
special limbs, that staff of the old and the blind, lying there, and
                                    I picked it up,"   545
he said, " 'Ah,' I said, 'May the heathen never see you in this condition!'
        'Clean the dirt and dust off it, kiss it, look it up and down,
                        'cause you were my support!
        You, who were the sign of my ability! You who were my
                        legacy! You, than whom none was closer kin
        or dearer to me, how could God have taken you from me!?[39] »

---

37. *Ītau sanadī to be mā dādī*: The barber in his soliloquy here uses the same term for hardship or disaster, *sanad*, which the three storytellers have used in setting up their contest, but the expression in this construction has a special idiomatic force: "You've really done it to me this time!" in the sense of a particularly vicious and ill-meant trick.

38. This line is not spoken aloud, but thought by the barber.

39. Throughout this comic lament sequence, the barber speaks more and more rapidly, till his speech culminates in the vehement prayer which follows.

Oh, Hidden One of the saints, flower-adorned Lord, for
                    the honor of the Blessed Scion of the
                    Prophets,[40] grant my desire!   550
For hopeless of here, hopeless of there, hopeless of my own
                    home, where can I go? »
You who—
after all, m—, b— you comfort the helpless anyway—' I <u>wept</u>.
I put it back on, saying 'There was a day when you were sitting
                                right here,
          what bravery you had, what counsel
                                you gave,   555
          what sitting and rising up you had,
          fine,
          what a shadow you cast, what a body
                                you had, »
          how you looked in clothes!
          If you, if I got you a jacket, it looked
                                beautiful, »   560
          if I got you a hat, it looked beautiful!
          Woe, woe, woe, woe! how bent
                                and withered!
          Like some kind of
          chili pepper that the hotel guy[41]
          picks out of the bottom of the pot
                                the morning after!   565
          Bent! withered!
          So twisted, broken, covered with dust that
          it's hopeless!' "

                    <>

Yeah.
     "I put it there like that, saying, 'You were thus-and-so,' and I poured
                                out water, »   570
     and I said, 'Oho!
                God! With this same water you cut it off.

---

40. Mohammad is the "Seal of the Prophets," who completes the line of Biblical prophecy, in Muslim thought.
41. A manager in a native "hotel," a bazaar eatery.

If you will make it flourish with this same water,

you <u>are</u> able.

If you will grant it,' and when I poured out the water,

<u>there</u>! It started to move like a baby fish when it hits the water!   575

It starts to live and move and

the point is, it bobbed its head and its nose and

I looked it over from bottom to top, and I kissed its face

and began— »

I said, 'Lord, be merciful to it!' "

‹›

Yeah, " 'Now where's a mulla, to get a sniff of this [miracle], anyhow!' "   580
[*Audience laughter*]
<u>Well</u>! "I came back" —he said, —

"back there.

The woman started in, and I <u>threw</u> myself out of the door, »

I said, '<u>Bastard</u>! Are you <u>still</u> calling me!? Good<u>bye</u>!' "[42]

Yeah.   585

"I came back,

on the road I said, 'I'll fuck the little father of that dame,[43]

that my excuse—I— »

twice she wouldn't give me respite!

Even if she's on the <u>prayer</u> mat, I'll fuck her!"

[*laughter*]

‹›

Yeah.   590

"Yeah, I arrived at the house. »

I arrived at the house and as fate would have it, the woman

is working over the bread-dough trough,

and just as she said, 'Peace be on you!' »

I said, 'I don't need to give you any 'peace' back, I'm gonna sit down,

I've got something to do.' "

Yeah.   595

"Yeah, I knocked her over, and now when I knocked her over, I look,

---

42. *be 'amān-e khodā*: literally, "God protect you!" the standard "goodbye" in Herati and approximately the fourth highly ironic use of it in this text.

43. *Pīārak-e az ī zanakar gām*: a common curse, now directed at his own sexually demanding wife.

to see if it—putting it back on, I <u>put</u> it on, »
and it <u>took</u> hold, »
<u>stuck</u> on there <u>good</u>— »
backwards!!"   600

    ‹›

[*Prolonged general laughter*]

Yeah.
    "Like a treasurer wearing his satchels slung around his neck,
                                    coming along there—
    My saddle bags around the head and the, th— lumber underneath!
                                          [*laughter*]
        'Oh, no, no, no, what do I do with <u>this</u>?
        Well, to black dust with it,'[44] I said, 'Whatever disaster this is,   605
        all right,
        He <u>granted</u> it, anyway, <u>whatever</u> happened.'
    The point is, I was hopeless, burning up,
    so with its saddlebags and satchels
    I just put it on in, kind sir that you are,"   610
there, <u>he</u>—it was the king—said, "Brother,
                    for you and me, Vizier,
                    whatever happened, it passed.
                    <u>This</u> man is <u>still</u> trapped in the disaster,
                        if he speaks the truth.   615
                    Take the loincloth off his waist."
                ‹›

Yeah.
When they took off the loincloth, like that, they said, "Yeah . . ."
Like [somebody][45] with a backpack around his neck. [*laughter*]
‹›
He said, "Give the jewels to him."   620
They gave all three of them, sir, gave them to him.
The barber got up, and went about his own affairs, and they sat there. »
So hand me your waterpipe, son!
Come on, Ākhond, sir, your turn in the shop! [*Ākhond laughs; others laugh.*]

———

    44. A mild curse, equivalent to a disgusted "to hell with it!" in English. The reference
is to the dust of the grave.
    45. *bīgor-āteshūn warī*: an as yet untranslated reference.

"... and it *took* hold, *stuck* on there *good—backwards!*"

Besides its rowdy sexual humor, the most obvious connections between " 'Ādel Khān" and what has just gone before are of scale and style: it is a complex tale involving substantial indirect speech, in the form of narration within the narration. Karīm acts on the permission the Ākhond has secured to tell a longer story and one which demonstrates powers of narrative organization not entailed by the previous short anecdotes. He also sustains the major parallel between the fictional situation and the actual one, that of storytelling at the behest of a ruling authority to resolve a lapse of justice. In his closing remarks at the end of this story (l. 624), Karīm expresses his sense of the storytelling session as exchange and/or turn-taking: "Come on, Ākhond, sir, your turn in the shop!" To him, turns at talk should in some sense match or answer each other.

In content, Karīm chooses a tale which pursues and intensifies the theme of sexual adventure (here, more precisely, misadventure) developed in the second half of Salīm's story. In his introduction of this tale's main character, Karīm rings a change on the Ākhond's theme of good governance. The opposite of Hojāj, 'Ādel Khān is a king so renowned for righteousness that his given name, 'Azīz ("dear one") is replaced by the epithet 'Ādel, "the just" (l. 2). His first act is one of excessive generosity, which causes his vizier to despair for the royal exchequer (ll. 28–43). In the catalogue of traits included in the Afghan concept of manliness (*javānmardī* or *mardānegī*) which Hafizullah Baghban assembled for his discussion of Herati folk humor (Baghban 1977, 1:211, note 32), generosity heads the list (followed by piety, hospitality, bravery, and several other qualities[1]). The king is not a fool but errs in the direction of too much virtue. Yet beneath the reversals are parallels between the two tales: as in the case of Salīm and Hojāj, ethical conduct is at stake here, and the telling of stories is undertaken to enable the protagonists to choose ethically, to avoid tyranny ("He didn't get high-handed," l. 50) and to repair a type of misrule. The enlightenment of rulers is still at issue, high-handedness versus respect for the

---

1. Frankness, loyalty, support of the weak, protection of one's womenfolk, spending one's own legally earned money. The qualities of the *nāmard* (unmanly or base person) are, by contrast, miserliness, inhospitality, cowardice, slyness, disloyalty, not caring for one's women's honor, taking bribes or stealing, suppression of the weak, and impiety. Baghban develops these lists directly from the prologues on the theme of manliness recorded in his collected corpus of folk plays. These values are reflected explicitly or implicitly in a wide range of traditional expressive forms.

governed as a fellow human, but with a gentler picture of the potentially errant ruler and with no direct mention of the Ākhond's loaded term for right-thinking, 'orfān, with its burden of religiosity and mystical wisdom. Honor and deference among the three protagonists, rather than tyranny and raw power, are illustrated in such details as the polite negotiations over who shall tell the first story, once they have lodged their wager (at ll. 58–59, "Let's say we're three brothers. / Without any distinctions, like that," and also at ll. 71–76).

Karīm's tale departs somewhat from the veiled allusion to actual events to which the Ākhond's tale was interpretively open. Yet the ambiguities of narrator-listener address in reported speech remain, blurring the boundaries between fictive and actual listeners. While the king tells his story, each vocative "Sir" in the text definitively breaks the frame: it is Karīm the narrator addressing his main audience member, Mokhtār, for the king would not use such a formal term of address to a familiar such as the vizier or a lowly subject like the barber. When the vizier and the barber speak, later, the boundaries of address are once again blurred: it is often not clear whether the "Sir"s are addressed by the fictive narrator to the king who listens or by Karīm to Mokhtār. In a second ambiguating effect, the emphatic, summative, and anticipatory "yeah," which forms a frequent unit marker and a breath pause for Karīm (ll. 135, 201, 213, 222, 231, 232, 237, 328, 354, 407, 412, 443–44, 503, 515, 538, 569, 580, 585, 590, 595, 601, 617), usually sums up an action or an attitude in anticipation of a crucial event immediately to follow. It sometimes seems to be uttered by the fictive narrator, summing up what he has just said (especially as the narration gets more hectic and charged), and sometimes seems to be Karīm's own marker, inviting his live audience to savor and reflect briefly on the goings-on. Written translation, unable to represent an utterance simultaneously as quoted and not quoted, does the audience boundary-blurring mechanism an injustice by disambiguating it.

Other linkages to previous tales are more explicit. The pit that the vizier and his friend dig to destroy the *deyb* (ll. 302–9, 328–34) recalls the trap the unbeliever adversaries laid for Salīm the holy warrior. 'Ādel Khān, sexually exploited in his converted state, is speechless since, as Karīm's Sarhadī bride found, female protest is useless (l. 157, "There was nothing I could say"), and the vizier, raped by village dogs in his converted state, uses exactly the same words of frustrated complaint as the deflowered bride in "Rasūl's Mother": "Who can you tell about it?" (l. 368). Karīm also reinvokes ethnic humor. When the barber finds himself castrated by the demonic woman's ablution water, he exclaims that the former site of his private parts is "A smooth, clear field ... just like some Mongol guy's cheek, without hair or fur or the whole business!" (ll. 459–63), recalling both the comic stereotype of Mongol physiognomy ("Mulla Mongol the Martyr," chapter 3, ll. 71, 132–35, where the Mongol speaker implausibly claims thick-beardedness as a racial trait, against the prevailing stereotype, the beard being a sign of manliness), and the Sarhadī bride's alarmed discovery of her husband's hairy privates ("Rasūl's Mother," ll. 148–50). When the barber finds his private parts restored by God's grace, he exclaims "Where's a mulla, to sniff this [miracle]?" (l. 580), recalling amidst audience laughter the brother's attempt in "Mulla Mongol the Martyr" to get a mulla's proclamation to attest to his dead brother's sanctity and also poking gentle fun at Karīm's fellow-performer, the Ākhond.

Comedy has a higher profile in "'Ādel Khān" than in the previous story, with a tighter link between the horror of misfortune and its humor. This story like the other is not widely performed in the Herat area. Karīm's performance of it is unique in my collection and it does not, to my knowledge, exist in written versions (despite the similarity of the vizier's story to such literary items as the Third Merchant's Tale in the complex "Tale of the Merchant and the Jinn," with which Shahrāzād begins her performance in *The Thousand and One Nights*.)[2] The Afghan audience's laughing response to this tale establishes the prominence of its humorous qualities for native listeners and, especially when juxtaposed to *The Thousand and One Nights* tale, demonstrates the difficulty of determining the traditional reception of a tale from its text content alone without any indication of audience response. On paper, in the story text's catalogue of castration and abuse alone, there is little to distinguish sexual humor from sexual paranoia. Kazim Alami, a native of Herat who helped to transcribe this tape, expressed special delight with the humor and plain speech style of this story, a new one for him, and took a copy of the recording to play for friends. He subsequently reported that it had been copied and circulated in the male Afghan refugee community in California, further testimony to its humorous appeal (personal communication, 1984).[3]

---

2. Marzolph (1984:89) lists from oral collections "Die Treue Hund," Tale Type 449, in which a man follows his wife to a rendezvous with her lover, kills the lover, and in some versions, is subsequently turned into a dog by her. Sympathetic people discover his state and restore him, and in retribution, he changes his wife into an animal and keeps her caged.

3. Indeed, it was the special appeal of this tale to some Afghan listeners, together with a project to explore the distribution of gender roles and role reversals in stories, which drew my attention back to the entire story session as an object of analysis. The content of this story

Sexual comedy is certainly more intense and relentless in this story than in "Salīm the Jeweller," even while its themes of bestiality and sexual servitude form links to the monkey bride episode, sexual servitude in particular regard to the barber, who like Salīm is exploited by females rather than inflicted with female form. The barber is tormented not just by the witch-woman who lures him away but by the sexual demands of his own wife. The wife as sexual aggressor is a staple of humor, represented also in the folk plays reported by Baghban, particularly in the "Polygamous Husband" play (Baghban 1977, 2:370).

As I have explored elsewhere (Mills 1985), " 'Ādel Khān" presents a hierarchy of male misfortune, all of it sexual in nature. The first misfortune, the king's, was merely to *become* a woman for a brief period. This transformation occurs purely by chance, when the king has the ill luck to annoy a supernatural. His misfortune is also more than compensated (ll. 220–21, "I was satisfied, delighted. / I gave thanks."). In fact, his private parts when restored are larger and better than the originals, and his first use of them is to terrify his sexual tormentor into headlong flight. The female position here portrayed, as in "Rasūl's Mother," is one of powerlessness, captivity, and rape, and the king counts it the greatest misfortune of his life that he was briefly female. No hint of feminine acceptance or enjoyment of sex appears. Male sexuality is portrayed as pure aggression.

The vizier's misfortune, also involving a sex change, occurs through the disloyalty of his wife. Seduction of women is interpretable as a form of male-male aggression in Afghan male thinking (Nazif Shahrani, personal communication, 1976). Even in orderly transfer of sexual partners through marriage, the superiority of wife-takers to wife-givers as a psychological theme is linked to pre-Islamic Arabia and thence to Muslim thought. Mohammad is said to have sought to eradicate the idea that men should be ashamed to give their women as brides by giving his daughter Fatimah to 'Ali at a public party (Knabe 1977:43). A reluctance to furnish women, even legitimately, persists in Afghan thought, expressed in the direction of marriage payments from the groom's family to the bride's, among other things (see chapter 15).

Through a wife's misbehavior, a man's own sexual self-determination is compromised: in the case of the vizier and his wife, he himself is rendered feminine and raped. This specifically sexual dimension of honor, the

---

is examined with particular reference to sexual roles in Mills (1985). Circulation of oral performances in taped form also occurred regularly in Herat and Kabul at the time of my stay.

honor of men that depends on the virtue of women, is called *namūs*. The dishonor is amplified by adding an aspect of pollution to the humiliation (from the male point of view) of sexual vulnerability: the vizier is changed to a bitch, and to Muslims, dogs are unclean. As the vizier points out, the fact that his abusers were many is an additional source of grief (l. 377). The vizier, like the king, has full restitution and revenge, however, thanks to his mother, the only positive female character in this tale. Even she is a bit sinister, conversant as she is with her evil daughter-in-law's magical techniques and sharing with her an ability to see beyond appearances. The vizier's wife apparently knows without being told that her lover is dead, and takes on the trappings of mourning, refusing to wash or adorn herself, but she cunningly attributes her demeanor to her husband's absence (ll. 345–53). The vizier's mother, in turn, instantly recognizes her son in the abused and beleaguered bitch (ll. 385–90). At any rate, the vizier is ready enough to condemn his wife to similar torment. As in the king's tale, the female physical state is deplored, and this episode adds the themes of female moral depravity and sexual disloyalty. It is not clear, in the end, whether the vizier has converted his wife back to her human state, or whether the word which has yet to be spoken in the one which would unspell her (ll. 413–14). In either case, the female is silenced. In Marzolph's Persian Tale Type 449 and the Third Shaykh's Tale from *The Thousand and One Nights*, the disloyal wife is left in her animal form.

When the various representations of female sexuality and male experiences of it are summed up, this tale presents a male view which neither envies nor admires the female state. The female role in sex is experienced by these men as rape victims, while those women who show sexual initiative are portrayed as importunate (the barber's wife), castrating (the barber's seductress), and/or murderous (the vizier's wife). The message of this tale concerning female sexuality, taken by itself, seems to be that it is tragic to be female and that one would have to be depraved to want to act like a woman. The only exception to this pattern is the vizier's mother, who is both intelligent and capable of action supportive of a man. She completes the whore-mother dichotomy, but her role is relatively unstressed. She is also an old woman, presumably postmenopausal, who has "become a man"[4] and yet remains socially attached and loyal to her family. In this, she

---

4. One common Persian expression for passing menopause is *mard shodan*, "to become a man." Women of menstruating age avoid mosque attendance in Afghan Sunni communities, but in some communities elderly women, who cannot pollute the sacred precinct by the onset

departs from one stereotype of old women in folktale, that of panderers and spoilers, disruptive social isolates. The other major role for older women in story is as advisors and allies of the hero, often with special knowledge. They usually identify themselves as foster mothers and are transient figures in the hero's life, however.

The third episode, the barber's tale, is another permutation of the masculine trapped by the feminine. The peril comes not as an inflicted sex change through inadvertant contact with a supernatural force nor from the disloyalty of a female relative but from pure, impersonal female sexual aggression in the form of a seductress with apparent supernatural powers. This episode manipulates the ideology of pollution connected with human sexuality. For Muslims, both men and women, sexual contact is polluting and must be followed by ritual ablutions before praying or entering a sacred precinct. The seductress asks the barber to wash *before sex* to render himself ritually pure for what is itself a polluting act (and in this case, an illicit one, but even licit sex is polluting). This inversion of normal ritual order has a disastrous effect: his penis falls off. While the barber clearly sees her as aggressive (ll. 442 and 539 and note 37), it is not clear that the woman actually intends to castrate him. When she reappears outside his shop and he follows her for the second time, seeking restitution, she is as inviting as before, seemingly unaware that he is unable to perform sexually (ll. 533–36). Her supernatural power, if indeed she controls the power of the ablution water to castrate, seems nonpurposive, certainly not intelligent, but simply a force for disorder and destruction.[5]

It is also significant that the final victim, and the victim of the worst misfortune, is a barber. By his profession, he is in an ambiguous position vis-à-vis pollution. His duties (besides shaving, circumcision, sometimes cupping and bleeding for illnesses, and minor surgery) while polluting to himself, render others clean. In Afghanistan, barbers are almost a separate class within a theoretically classless Muslim society. They are conceived by the general population to be hereditary members of a low-status endogamous group called *jat*, to which blacksmiths, sieve-makers, hereditary musicians, play-actors, entertainers, prostitutes, and certain kinds of traders are also assigned.[6] Making a member of the *jat*, a familiar but alien group,

---

of menstrual bleeding, are more free to attend communal prayer, sitting separately from the men.

5. A similar folktale portrayal, by a male narrator, of female supernatural power which threatens men with diffuse and apparently nonpurposive danger is examined in Mills (1983a).

6. Baghban (1977) discusses at length the complexities of these groups' actual profes-

the ultimate victim of the most comically horrific sexual misadventure distances this non-*jat* audience from his predicament. Yet the first Persian-speaking convert to Islam is reputed to have been Salmān, the Prophet's Iranian barber, a castrated former slave and yet a revered figure among Shi'a Muslims. *Jat* entertainers also have license for social criticism and satire of the elite and powerful in the context of their performances. In this connection, the *jat* barber is an appropriate figure to act as both foil and judge of the king's behavior. The fact that it is the barber around whom the manipulations of the ideology of pure and impure concatenate in this tale resonates with a complex set of beliefs and practices concerning purity, pollution, and power with regard to the barber and his professional group.

The bath which is the barber's workplace and the site of the story exchange is one which often figures, in folktale and legend, in complex and sometimes dangerous mediations and exchanges. Public baths, operated by people regarded as *jat*, are also believed to be the haunt of *jinn*, especially after hours. Women as well as men use attendance at the baths as an occasion to meet and exchange news and information. In Herat, the women's baths are one of the few locales where women can regularly interact with nonrelatives, and highly fastidious women avoid them for that very reason. Women may visit the baths to look over, discreetly, young women whom they are considering for marriage to their male relatives. Marzolph in his Persian tale type index identifies the bath as a site of storytelling with particular reference to his Tale Type *425D, in which the heroine, separated from her supernatural spouse, has a bath built and asks visitors for their stories in lieu of payment for the bath. Eventually, a traveler brings news of her lost spouse. The public bath is a place of unpredictable meeting and exchange, between humans and, in folktale and legend, between the human and the supernatural.

Water, as a substance which mediates both purification and pollution, seems implicated in the unpredictability of these exchanges. All three sexual transformations, the two sex changes and the castration, are associated with water sources and ritual bathing. The king's takes place because he disturbs the supernatural inhabitant of a desert well when trying to wash

---

sional and ethnic/kinship arrangements. Rao (1982) presents a similarly complex analysis of the kinship relations and economic roles of another selection of the itinerant groups collectively called *jat* by outsiders. Sakata (1983), in a study of music and musical concepts in three different areas of Afghanistan, reports (p. 78) that *dalāk*, the lexical meaning of which is "bath attendant, barber," is also the most widespread term for professional musician in Afghanistan. Both professions are considered members of a single endogamous group.

for morning prayers (ll. 114ff.). The vizier's ambush of his wife's demon lover at a spring (where the *deyb* goes to wash after intercourse with the woman, ll. 312–13) precedes her vengeful transformation of him. The barber wants naturally flowing water, considered pure (ll. 447–48), in which to perform the ablutions his seductress demands. Her house offers no flowing water supply, and the pitcher of water she provides takes its disastrous toll.[7]

The three episodes vary systematically in the degree to which the victim's own will is implicated in his sexual predicament. The king is concerned only with getting clean, with making the morning ritual ablution. His misfortune occurs through no will of his own. The vizier in turn is trying only to assert his legitimate sexual rights to his new wife and to protect his own life by removing his rival. The barber, by contrast, shows illicit sexual initiative when he follows his temptress. According to the Qurʿan (24:2), both partners in adultery are equally culpable. Thus, this tale presents a spectrum of suffering, righteous and unrighteous, but the progression is from innocent to implicated, rather than the other way around, as was the case in Salīm's history.

As in Salīm's case, though, sincere appeals to God, whether by the righteous or the repentant, are not ignored. Given that, they still may not be answered in an entirely straightforward way. 'Ādel Khān's rhetorical approach injects a note of humor into his acknowledgement of God's infinite power, the essential ingredient of a petitionary prayer:

That is, if you give me rescue,
     give me my wish,
whose loss is it? What loss would it be to you,
     you who are without need? (ll. 197–200)

In contrast to his "What's it to you?" approach, the barber's appeal is more straightforward, more ostentatiously submissive, and more florid:

"Oh, Hidden One of the saints, flower-adorned Lord, for the honor of the
                    Blessed Scion of the Prophets, grant my desire!

---

7. Sex changes frequently occur at water sources. Cf. Haag-Higuchi (p. 115), regarding Tale No. 22 in her manuscript and other examples, and Stith Thompson, *Motif-Index of Folk-Literature* (1955–58, 2:9), which lists Motif No. D10.2 as "Change of sex after crossing water."

For hopeless of here, hopeless of there, hopeless of my own home, where
>
> can I go? »

You who—
after all, m—, b— you comfort the helpless anyway—" I <u>wept</u> . . .
"God! With this same water you cut it off.
If you will make it flourish with this same water, you <u>are</u> able.
If you will grant it . . ." (ll. 550–53 and 572–74)

His fervent prayer is interwoven with a comic lament for his lost member.[8]

If his pious resignation is more vehement than the king's, the low-status barber is also the only one whose misfortune is brought on by his own somewhat clownish misbehavior, and also the only one of the three whose suffering is not completely reversed. Nor is he able to punish his tormentor, unless escape constitutes revenge. Whereas the king has made his tormentor flee in terror, and the vizier has kept his captive, the best the barber can do is to flee the castrating seductress. When he escapes, it is on his sexually demanding wife that he attempts to vent his rage, by raping her, only to discover the error he has made in hastily reattaching his privates (ll. 586–600). He is permanently marked: having inverted the purification ritual, he has also accidentally inverted the cure, attaching his penis behind his testicles in his haste to escape (ll. 597–604). Although the barber is not forced to perform as a female, he is sexually maimed and permanently marked by his encounter *with* a dangerous female, and the permanency of his injury earns him the prize for the greatest misfortune by consensus of the king and vizier (ll. 611–21).

The lowly and afflicted barber's role as the one who definitively tests the king's sense of fairness, by the telling of his story, conforms with the role of his fellow *jat*, especially the actor-entertainers, as traditional social critics. Baghban (1977) discusses in detail those activities of actors that test and pronounce on the generosity of their patrons and the ways they use play scripts and surrounding improvisational dialogue to praise and blame elite patrons and members of the general audience for whom they perform. Although " 'Ādel Khān" is gentle in its portrayal of authority figures, it asserts as directly as the tale of Hojāj and Salīm, the right of the ordinary

---

8. Parodies and other representations of spontaneous lament can be found embedded in narratives such as this, in classical poetry (Rūmī 1927–40, 1:1691), and in folk plays (e.g., "Ahmadak the Well-Digger," in Baghban 1977, 3:733–35).

citizen to hold the ruler to account. This implication of the tale may be somewhat obscured by its rowdy sexual humor, but in this story as in others in the session, themes of sexuality and gender roles, Islam, legitimate and illegitimate authority, politics and governance, and ethnicity emerge contrapuntally, none being wholly obscured for long and each providing an opening into one or more of the others. To try to isolate one from the others would be like trying to listen only to the B-flat chords in a fugue.

8. Ākhond Mulla Mahmūd, "Mahmūd of Ghaznī and the Thieves"

Mokhtār: . . . the name of this—now, that "Whereas the reciters of news
and the narrators of remains,"
and those things, if you would say a few of them, so that—
Another listener, perhaps the Woləswāl: Yes, say them for them—[1]
Ākhond: Those, sir—the Khalīfah says them, I don't know them well,
by God—   5
M Mills: Oh, all right—
M: You say a few of them, too—
Ā: No— I didn't say them, anyway—
M [*loudly*]: The reciters of news
so recite that . . . [*Ākhond*: No-]   10
—and so forth, the beginning— [*audience member laughs*]
Ā: [*laughs*]
M M: [*laughs*]
◇
Ā: Well—
M: The name of this story that you are going to tell, what—?   15
Ā: The name of
the story, sir,
it's the story of His Excellency the King, Sultan Mahmūd, sir,
he used to go o- out walking, in dervish dress.
[*M*: Yes.]   20
[*M M*: Yeah.]
The story is that story.
That's the beginning of it.
[*M*: Concerning Sultan Mahmūd.]

---

1. Encouraging the Ākhond on grounds of hospitality to accommodate the guest's request for story-opening formulas.

Mahmūd of Ghaznī.[2]   25
His Excellency Sultan Mahmūd used to go out, sir, walking—
[*M interrupts with an exasperated, laughing tone:*
Say the "reciters of news," anyway, now that you're starting—]
Ā [*laughing*]: "Reciters of remains, and narrators—" [*laughing*]
        —"drinkers of gems"[3]—
His Excellency the Lord Sultan was going out, sir, to walk around.   30
[*M*: Yes.]
He[4] used to go about at night,
        in dervish dress.
He came along near his own treasuries, and he saw some seven or eight
                                        people standing there, »
with something [*inaudible word—audience coughing*] in their hands.   35
[*M*: Yeah.]
They're thieves.
[*M*: Yes.]
‹›
His Excellency the Sultan, when he got close to them[5], the thieves
                        said to him, "Brother, who are you?"
        —they said to Sultan Mahmūd.   40
He said, "I'm a thief, I always go around by myself, thieving."
[*M*: Uh-huh.]
They said, "What kind of thief <u>are</u> you, that you go around <u>alone</u>?"
He said, "I—
If I'm alone, if I'm there first, I get away.   45
If I were with friends, and they catch my friend, he'll give me away— I've
                                thieved alone my whole life."
‹›
[*M*: Uh-huh.[6]]

---

    2. The famous fifth century A.H. (eleventh century C.E.) king and founder of the Ghaz-
navid empire (see discussion below).
    3. The Ākhond garbles the formulaic phrase, substituting *gosār* "-drinking," for *gostar*,
"-strewing."
    4. The Ākhond continues to use the honorific third-person plural pronouns and verbs
to describe the king's activities, in addition to his consistent use of honorific titles. The translation converts these to singular forms for clarity in English.
    5. The Ākhond drops the plural verb form for the Sultan at this point, using third-
person singular hereafter, but continuing to use honorific titles to refer to him.
    6. The Ākhond is speaking in a leisurely fashion, with lengthy pauses after some full
stops, which Mokhtār takes as pauses for confirmation that he has been understood. The
longer stops tend to close off clause clusters, or as here, to isolate a summary statement for a

"I've never been caught and never gotten into a trap, either."

<>

He said to these thieves, "Who are you?"

They said, "We're thieves, we're going to steal something."   50

   "What are you going to do?"

   "We're going to hit the king's treasury."

He said, "Seeing that you're going to hit the king's treasury,

   even though I've thieved alone for my whole <u>life</u>, brother(s),

   I'll go with you tonight, too, to the king's treasury."   55

His Excellency the Sultan said that.

[*M*: Yes.]

They said, "If you go with us,

   each one of us has a special ability,

   we have specialties," —that's what the thieves said.   60

[*M*: Yes.]

   "If you have a specialty, too, tell it, and we'll take you,

   if you don't have one, we won't take you with us."

He said, "What special abilities do you have?"

(One) said, "Do you see this rope?"   65

  He said, "Yeah."

  He said, "If I tie this down to the ground, I can raise my friends

            up to the North Pole."[7]

[*M*: Yeah . . .]

The one thief said that.

Another one said, "If a dog barks, I— I understand what it says."   70

One thief said, "In the fa— in the dark of night, if I see someone,

          I'll recognize him by day."

One said, "I can smell a house and I know whether there's gold or

            silver inside."

[*M*: Yeah. What they have, that is—]

Yes. [*M*: *Additional, inaudible comment*]

---

narrative subunit. Mokhtār's murmured responses are low-pitched and nonintrusive, signal-
ling the Ākhond to go on.

 7. *qotb-e shomālī*: Kazim, one of the Herati auditors of the tape, opined that this reference to western-style geography would not be understood by illiterate listeners. While the
idea of the North Pole is not a folk geographic concept, the idea of a reference point around
which other things or people organize themselves—a *qotb* in the larger sense of *axis mundi*—
has a place in indigenous terminology.

"There, now if you have a specialty, —" —I don't know what's become of the
Āqā, maybe he's not coming.[8]   75

[*Others listeners*: We'll see. He's coming.]

"If you have a specialty, we'll take you, too," they said to the king.

He said, "I have a special ability, too."

    They said, "What special ability do you have?"

[*Audience members to entering guests*: Shut the door. *Muffled greetings.*]   80

If only—you weren't here at the beginning of what I said—

[*New audience member*: Well, that's OK.]

[*Other audience members*: No harm done.]

All right—

He said, "I have a specialty, too."   85

    They said, "What kind is it?"

      He said, "If I go like this, with one gesture of my beard,[9]

          I put a <u>hundred</u> people to the cannon,[10]

          and if I do like this — [*strokes one side of his moustache*]—

          I can save a hundred from the cannon."   90

<>

[*M*: Yeah.]

His Excellency the Sultan said that.

[*M*: Yes.]

"By God, your special ability is useful, too!"

They took the rope, and climbed up.   95

A dog barked.

The one who understood the language of dogs said, "Oh, brothers, (you
know) what the dog says?"

    he said, "The dog says a king, the king of this very city, is amongst
these thieves."

[*M*: Yeah.]

---

    8. The Ākhond notices that an expected audience member, a local notable (from his title
a *sayed* or descendant of the Prophet), has not yet arrived. Several men arrived and departed
in the course of the evening.

    9. The Ākhond points with beard and chin.

    10. An idiom for execution: public executions in Afghan cities where there were garrisons were carried out in the nineteenth and early twentieth centuries by strapping the condemned across the muzzle of a cannon. One cannon shot was fired from the central garrison of major cities, including Kabul and Herat, daily to mark the hour of noon, and routine criminal executions were carried out at that hour.

[*M M*: Oh-oh! (*laughs*)]   100
   "The dog says the king of this very city is amongst the thieves."
[*M*: Yeah.]
[The king] said, "The dog is mistaken, brother, are you crazy? Where
                                       is he, if the king is here?"

They got to the top of the roof-dome, and the one smelled around, sir,
                                                 like that—
they let one man down, and hauled up fifty or <u>sixty</u> sacks of gold.   105

They got down, and his Excellency the Sultan said, like,
     "Go to the desert,
          to such-and-such a place, a hollow,"—he described it to them
          "—and you sit there—
     Now, I'll come at eight o'clock tomorrow   110
          and we'll divide it,
          each one take his share."

He came back—got dressed in the morning—to his court. »
He said to a troop of soldiers, "Go to such-and-such place, there are
                                       thieves there, pick them up."

They came and surrounded them on both sides, caught them, <u>nice</u>
                                                 and neat.   115
They got these guys up out of the places where they were sleeping,
     loaded the gold on their backs,
     and when they got near and saw,
     the one who could see in the dark of night and recognize by day
said, "Brothers, the dog spoke the truth.   120
     Don't so much as twitch your <u>tails,</u>
          because God's truth, he's the same one.
     This king [*laughing*] was the one that was <u>with</u> us!
[*Audience laughter*]
     He's the king! <u>Watch</u> it, now, d— don't offend." [*M*: Mm-hmm.]

They came forward, sir,   125
     and he said, "Why did you steal?"

He said, "Sir, God made our faces black, and we did it."[11]
He said, "Take them to the cannon."
When they'd taken them a little way away,
  he said "Ba— Bring them back."   130
  He said, [*laughing*] "My specialty has had its turn."
[*Laughs. Audience laughs.*]
They said, "Yes."
He forgave them, sir.
  He established each one in some j— job.

It is said that in that day,   135
  if a person was, for example,
  deserving of being killed,
  without even such proof as this
    that the king <u>himself</u> was present,
    when they hit his treasury,   140
  they would have had to testify, "The camel is small."[12]
On account of the fact that four hundred—
  that Sultan Mahmūd was (such) a righteous king,
  and he had been their companion,
  he forgave them.   145
If a person, for fifty years or forty years,
  or ten years, acknowledges the Excellent Lord God, [*M*: Yes—]
  and has faith in Him, anyway,
at the Throne and the Gathering[13] He will accept him,
  on what account would he go to Hell?   150
[*M*: Ye-es.]
With <u>one</u> twitch of the eyebrow of the Prophet, on Him be peace,
  a thousand Zoroastrians,[14] sir, go to Paradise.

----

11. The "seeing" thief speaks. *Rū-siāh*, literally, "black-faced," blushing darkly with shame, shame-worthy. The sense of the statement is not so much to try to transfer the blame to God as it is to allude (and accede) to the completeness of God's power and thus invoke one's own weakness, while at the same time admitting one's own fault.

12. A most unlikely statement. The sense is, "it would have been hard enough to escape deserved punishment in those days, even without the king as a witness. One would have had to swear to a manifest untruth (camels are large, not small)."

13. *arsh-e nashar*, probably for literary *'arsh o maḥshar*: the Throne of God and the gathering place on Judgment Day.

14. *gabr*: Zoroastrianism was the state religion of the Sassanian empire in Iran before the Muslim conquest in the seventh century c.e. (first century A.H.). Remnant communities of Zoroastrians survive in Iran and India to this day. The term *gabr* is derogatory in Persian

A thousand saints go to Hell.
There now, you could say, this—   155
    just like this, sir,
    well-tuned stories[15] were like this.
M: It was good—
M M: Very good.
Ā: I'll tell you another story, sir, that there was a guy . . .[16]   160

---

and in Afghan parlance may refer to unbelievers in general. Sunni speakers also occasionally
use it to refer to Shi'a Muslims.

   15. *qeṣṣahhā-ye sāzī*.
   16. The Ākhond immediately launches into the next story.

"Well-tuned stories were like that . . .": The Ākhond as Sufi Didact

The thematic connection of this story to previous performances seems straightforward from its opening lines. As in the two previous stories, the Ākhond introduces this tale with the name of the ruler who will be its main character. There is, however, a more specific and intricate thematic linkage for this particular tale back to the story of Salīm, which implicates the Ākhond's knowledge of major works of Sufi mystical literature, and will be explored below. But for the Herati general listener, the mention of Mahmūd's name is enough to invoke once again the theme of royal wisdom and righteousness. Mahmūd of Ghaznī, the famous fifth century A.H. (eleventh century C.E.) king and founder of the Ghaznavid empire, directed campaigns against the Indian subcontinent and consolidated power over the East Iranian culture area from his capitol of Ghaznī in what is now southeastern Afghanistan. The descendant of Turkish Mamluk slave-regents, he installed ethnic Turkish commanders in place of ethnic Iranians in his military. Besides being an extremely effective military campaign leader whose affluent court was supported by the proceeds of his raids on the subcontinent (the Czech scholar, Jan Rypka 1968:173 styles him "one of the most wicked despots"), he was a legendary patron of poetry and the arts. Probably most famous is his (reputedly, somewhat belated) patronage of Ferdowsi, author of the Iranian national epic, *Shāhnāmah*.

A considerable body of legend has thus gathered around Mahmūd as the "greatest Maecenas ever known in the literature of Persian" (ibid.) and as a king of exemplary *noblesse oblige*. Whereas 'Ādel Khān "the Just" is a generic but otherwise unknown antithesis to the despotic Hajjāj, Mahmūd is Hajjāj's antithesis *in* Islamic legendary history. By choosing another historical figure as his subject, the Ākhond sustains his claim to erudition, whereas Karīm's presentation of the otherwise unknown 'Ādel Khān makes no such claims.

Mahmūd's legend includes credit for being a poet himself (which Rypka considers misplaced) and also a place in Sufi mystical poetry as the king-lover who renders himself a slave to his own beloved slave, Ayāz. This role-reversal element in the slave-descended king's legend developed as a powerful metaphor for the mystical love relationship of God and man, a particularly mystical extension of the generally understood connection between good government, religious consciousness, and kings who heed their subjects. Mahmūd's legendary habit of going out among his subjects in disguise at night to check on the welfare of his realm, which he exercises at the outset of this tale, is a virtuous proclivity which he has in common with Shah 'Abbās, the Iranian Safavid king who shares legendary honors with Mahmūd in Persian-language tradition as a righteous monarch[1] (and also with Noshīrvān "the Just" in Zoroastrian Persian tradition), and of course, with Hārūn al-Rashīd, the fifth Abbasid caliph, of *The Thousand and One Nights* fame.[2]

Eschewing the opening formulas for fictional folktale which Mokhtār tries to persuade him to use (ll. 1–12 and 27–30) and repeatedly referring to the king with the honorific *hazrat* ("excellency," a title also used for saints and prophets), and with deferential third-person plural verbs and pronouns (ll. 18, 26, 30, and 32; cf. English royal "we"), the Ākhond begins this story with a more solemn air than what has just preceded it, and with a reverence for the monarch which is at odds with the antimonarchist, antireligious ideology of his host. Only three years previous to this, the Woləswāl's Parcham party had actively supported Mohammed Daud in the overthrow of the monarchy, in the person of Daud's cousin, Zaher Shah. Mokhtār, a senior English teacher in the western-style high school system who had briefly studied abroad (University of Hawaii's East-West Center), used no such honorifics in discussing Mahmūd.

There was an ongoing struggle between Mokhtār and the Ākhond over the use of opening formulas, which became evident in this performance. Mokhtār, pursuing what he perceived to be my interest in things folkloric, pressed the Ākhond (but not Karīm, for some reason) to repeat formulas colloquially called *būd-nabūd* ("was-and-was-not"), rhyming phrases which are used to begin entertainment narratives and frame the narrative as fiction. The Ākhond on his part denied knowledge of these formulas (l. 5) and, in so doing, avoided framing his narratives as simply entertainment, *dorūgh* ("lies") or *sā'attīrī* ("pastimes"), as nondidactic taletelling is called. These formulas are in such common use that it is hard to

---

1. Cf. Marzolph (1984:26) who finds that Shah 'Abbās predominates in this role in Iranian oral tradition. Marzolph connects this motif with Hārūn al-Rashīd's portrayal in *The Thousand and One Nights* and considers it to be the product of Arabic influence in Persian, but he does not take into account the figure of Noshīrvān as the archetypal just king in pre-Islamic Zoroastrian tradition or the more general theme of righteous versus unrighteous kingship which is central to Ferdowsi's *Shāhnāmah* and no doubt was at issue in the Sassanian courtly precursors to that work. Adrienne Boulvin (1975, 1:ix) notes the popularity of Shah 'Abbās and his habit of going about disguised as a dervish, in oral traditions in Khorassan, the culture area which historically encompassed Herat and areas to its north and west.

2. For example, in the "Story of the Three Apples," Night No. 19 in Burton's edition.

imagine that a storyteller as experienced as the Ākhond could avoid having knowledge of them, whether or not he chose to use them. The particular forms of the formulas which Mokhtār tries to press on the Ākhond are those found in chapbook romances and written story collections (placed after the opening invocation, "In the Name of God, the Merciful, the Compassionating," with which any enterprise should begin). These rhymed prose sequences generally simply assert that the contents of the book have been received from traditional sources.[3] It may be that Mokhtār sought them from the Ākhond, but not from Karīm, because Mokhtār himself associated them with literary material and considered the Ākhond more conversant with such material or its verbal style.

In fact, there are two different styles of opening formula. The one just described (see note 3), whether recited aloud or written, is associated with written material and comprises a generalized appeal to authoritative tradition of one degree or another of formality (within this category, Haag-Higuchi notes two different styles of attribution, the oft-used one quoted in note 3 above and another, which I did not find in common usage, which "emphasizes the literary tradition"; both are associated with written texts, but one seems more to emphasize written, the other spoken, tradition). The second group are nonsense formulas, also in rhymed prose, but with humorous content, in the form of non sequiturs or preposterous brags, often ending with a specific denial of the truth of the tale to follow (e.g., "and tonight it's our turn to tell lies"). They can go on for twenty or thirty lines. In my collecting experience there appear to be male- and female-favored versions of these formulas, with slightly differing subject matter.[4]

Baghban (1977, 1:223 and 2:276), identifies rhymed material in the folk

---

3. A typical example, quoted by Haag-Higuchi (1984:1) from the tale collection she edited, and similar to those I heard used in oral performance, translates as follows: "But the relaters of news and the narrators of tradition and the measurers of the time and the sugar-breaking parrots, sweet of speech (i.e., eloquent speakers), have thus related, that . . ." (Parrots are thought to love sugar and their breaking lumps of sugar with their beaks is metaphorically connected to their eloquent speech.)

4. Marzolph (1984:22–23) distinguishes between the formulas of the "once there was, once there was not" variety (a disclaimer or fiction marker), preferred for "Volksmärchen," and opening formulas similar to the one quoted from Haag-Higuchi's collection (note 1 above), which Marzolph rather found associated with "Volkserzählungen." He does not directly define "Volkserzählung" for the Persian corpus. The difficulties Marzolph encountered in reconciling German ideas of the "Märchen" and other oral genres with English typologies of the "folktale" are further compounded when one tries to take into account Iranian or Afghan performers' ideas of form, genre, and the appropriate use of markers such as different types of opening and closing formulas. One or two storytellers I recorded used both types, strung together, to introduce a single story, further complicating the formulas' identification as genre or subgenre markers.

plays which is similar in form and function to the nonsense variety of tale-opening formulas. Journey poems which are found in some plays resemble nonsense formulas I recorded in form and content. The nonsense-rhyme prologues of plays, which generally run six or seven lines in length, in Baghban's view "entertain by the silly nature of their expression," and constitute "art for the sake of art." If they do not, in the plays, make as overt an assertion of the fictive nature of what is to follow as the *yakī būd yakī nabūd* ("once there was, once there was not") or similar disclaimer openings used for stories, they nonetheless set a tone of nonsense humor for what is to follow, and so perhaps deflect the pointedness of jokes that may be taken as comments on current affairs. Baghban contrasts the nonsense prologues with didactic prologues, of which he gives a number of examples (pp. 198ff.), which generally or specifically praise proper behavior and admonish the audience to right actions and attitudes. Baghban further notes the occasional use of literary poetry for didactic prologues and epilogues to plays.

By eschewing framing his narrative performances with either a book-style attribution to unnamed traditional authorities or an oral nonsense verse, the Ākhond does not avoid attribution but rather keeps the intention of his performance, entertainment and/or admonition, open. With regard to literary attribution, there is, in fact, a specific and rhetorically powerful literary antecedent for this story, and it is a work that the Ākhond knows and reveres highly, the *Mathnavī-e Maʿanavī* of the great twelfth to thirteenth century C.E. (sixth-seventh century A.H.) Sufi poet, Jalāl ud-Dīn Rūmī. Such is the work's spiritual authority and poetic power that it is known as "the Qurʾan in Persian tongue." The poem, running to over 25,600 rhymed couplets in Nicholson's 1925–40 edition, is a huge compendium of narratives from a wide variety of oral and literary sources, framed in didactic and meditative mystical verse.

The Ākhond's association of this particular story with Sufi discourse remains implicit. The Ākhond did not directly attribute this tale to the *Mathnavī*, and like many of Rūmī's tales, this story of Mahmūd also circulates in oral tradition.[5] The Ākhond's later remarks indicate that he is familiar with the *Mathnavī*, and furthermore, an associative pattern emerges between this story as it stands embedded in a series of narratives

---

5. Marzolph (1984:178–79) identifies it as Tale Type 951C, notes its identity with Aarne-Thompson Type 951A*, and cites examples from Kurdish and Arabic (where it is Type 494 in Nowak's type index).

in the *Mathnavī*, and the Ākhond's placement of it in his own performance sequence. Specifically, the episode of the sea-cow which figured in Salīm's otherworldly adventures is told as an independent tale and placed in the *Mathnavī* directly after this tale of Mahmūd and the night-thieves.[6] What is more, the story directly following Rūmī's version of the sea-cow episode is the legend of 'Abdul-Ghawth "and his being carried off by the *parīs* and staying among them for years, and how after years he returned to his (native) town and his children but could not endure to be parted from the *parīs*, because he was really their congener and spiritually one with them" (Nicholson 3:422). The resemblance between that legend and Salīm's marriage with the *parī* princess is very close with the exception that 'Abdul-Ghawth voluntarily forsakes the human world for good after a brief visit home to return to his *parī* companions, a metaphor for Sufi disregard for worldly attachments and pleasures.

Since one who is destined for Paradise is (inwardly) homogeneous with Paradise, on account of homogeneity he also becomes a worshipper of God.
(Nicholson 1925–40, VI:2981).[7]

This sort of exegesis, typically exceeding in number of lines the actual lines of narrative, is a staple of Rūmī's *Mathnavī*, but generally lacking in these tales as they appear in oral tradition.[8] What links this sequence of stories in Rūmī's poem is the interpretive theme of the witness to God, and the affinity of such witnesses for the company of the divine and the divinely inspired. In Mahmūd's story, it is the special faculties of the thieves that Rūmī focuses on, as versions of human affinity for the divine, through which the mystical quest can be pursued. In the case of the sea-cow, it is the image of the illuminating jewel concealed in earthly clay (the mystically inclined spirit encased in flesh), that introduces and closes Rūmī's telling of the traveler's tale:

---

6. The story of Sultan Mahmūd and the Night-Thieves is in Book VI, ll. 2816–2921; the story of the sea-cow, ll. 2922–40; the story of 'Abdul-Ghawth and the *Parīs*, ll. 2974–84, with a lengthy meditation on the theme of spiritual congeniality following the narrative proper.

7. All *Mathnavī* line references are to Nicholson's edition; quotations from Rūmī are Nicholson's translations, unless otherwise noted.

8. Mills (in press) compares the Ākhond's prose performance of the Mahmūd story with a verse performance of another section of the poem by another individual, and explores the general phenomenon of Sufi storytellers' editing in oral performance, especially the omission of the poet's meditative and exegetical commentary.

Oh, many a piece of gold is made (like) black polished iron in order that it
    may be saved from pillage and calamity. (VI:2921)

Every piece of clay in the heart of which there is a pearl—its pearl can tell the
    secrets of another (piece of) clay;
While the clay that has not been illuminated by God's sprinkling (of light)
    cannot bear the companionship of the pieces of clay that are filled with
    pearls. (VI:2938–39)

With regard to the story of Mahmūd and the thieves, the Ākhond
reveals his interest in refocussing this story to press the connection between Islamic faith, rightly guided government, and social order, by his
return to that subject in the course of four other narratives, three stories
and a lengthy personal reminiscence (see chapter 11) about a religious debate he had with a Jewish rabbi in Herat City many years before. His emphasis on these themes in his telling of the Mahmūd story is particularly
striking when juxtaposed to Rūmī's own introduction to this story. Rūmī
initiates the story with a discussion of the role of the senses in the spiritual
search:

Since Thou givest to each sense the means of access to the Unseen, that (spir-
    itual) sense is not subject to the frailty of death and hoary eld.
Thou art the Lord of the kingdom: Thou givest to the (spiritual) sense some-
    thing (peculiar to itself), so that that sense exercises sovereignty over
    (all) the senses. (VI:2814–15)

In Rūmī's treatment, the thieves' special physical abilities become vehicles for discussion of the spiritual senses and their importance to seekers
of union with the divine. The thief whose gift receives the most ecstatic
description at the outset of the story is the one who can smell gold hidden
in the earth. In a typical example of Rūmī's use of piled-up similes, drawn
from legend, proverb, and other traditional expressive fields, the thief compares himself successively to the one who knows the secret of "men are
mines," (i.e., the Prophet Mohammad), to Majnūn scenting the earth of
Laila's land, to one who can tell the shirt of a Joseph from that of an Ahriman by its smell,⁹ and again to the Prophet, who smelled the scent of

---

9. Referring to the Islamic Joseph legend, in which Jacob, having cried himself blind
over Joseph's disappearance, recognizes him and has his sight restored by the scent of a shirt

sanctity emanating from Yemen (all references to Qurʿanic and Muslim legendary subjects) (Nicholson 1925–40, VI:2825–32). In the next few lines, the last thief to speak, the lasso-thrower, who has only a tributary role in the plot, is given a brief coda to the longer meditation by the olfactory thief, in which he too likens himself to the Prophet because he, the lasso-thrower, is enlightened by the divine admonition, "Thou didst not throw when thou threwest (but Allah threw)" (Qurʿan VIII:17). This coda structure is also typical of Rūmī, as though the poet were unwilling to relinquish the meditative exploration of a section of narrative until the metaphorical potential of each of its elements is at least partially realized. Rūmī so elaborates upon the gift of the thief who can smell gold, at the outset, that the audience's attention is focussed on that individual, and one is led to expect this gift to play a pivotal role in the tale's resolution, but it plays no role at all. It is, however, an excellent example of how Rūmī expands, even explodes single motifs within stories, building them up with a rich proliferation of scriptural, legendary, proverbial, and other associations, not letting the audience's notion of what is at stake rest simply or securely with the main story line.

In this way, the poet opens up yet asserts strong mastery over the interpretive dimensions of the tale which is about to unfold. Thus, the thieves, not Mahmūd, become the loci of identification for the poet's consciousness and, invitationally, that of the audience as well, since it is to the differently gifted thieves that the poet gives long monologues on the spiritual quest, not to the king who is its metaphorical object. The concentration on the thieves is even more striking in the scene at court which ends the story, where one thief's soliloquy and appeal to the king (combined) run fifty lines. Before that point, after the introduction of the thieves and of Mahmūd's saving gift, the actual narrative events of the raid on the king's treasury, the subsequent arrest of the thieves, and their arrival in court are related swiftly and succinctly in only fourteen lines (VI:2841–54).

By contrast, the Ākhond in telling the story builds up dramatic moments in the plot in order to foster identification between the audience and the king as story hero and omits the kind of meditative excursus that dominates Rūmī's narrative. At their first meeting, the Ākhond's thieves challenge the solitary stranger's credentials as a thief and demand that he show a special ability equal to theirs before they will accept his companionship.

---

which Joseph has sent him from Egypt. Ahriman, the evil principle in the Zoroastrian cosmology, is assimilated as Satan in Persian Muslim terminology.

The king, as portrayed by the Ākhond, explains himself in the pragmatic terms of a professional criminal, an exchange which has no place in Rūmī's telling:

They said, "What kind of thief <u>are</u> you, that you go around <u>alone</u>?"
He said, "I—
If I'm alone, if I'm there first, I get away.
If I were with friends, and they catch my friend, he'll give me away—I've
⟨⟩   thieved alone my whole life."
[*Mokhtār*: Uh-huh.]
"I've never been caught and never gotten into a trap, either." (ll. 43–48)

Rūmī's thieves do not challenge the king (VI:2836). When the dogs bark a warning and the thief who understands them reports that they are saying a king is with the thieves, the Ākhond dwells on that dramatic moment, whereas Rūmī passes over the thief's remark without comment, and his king makes no response to it. By the end of the raid on his treasury, the Ākhond has the king acting as the practical leader of the group, telling them where to go to divide the spoils (ll. 106–12), directions which they obey. The deference which Rūmī's thieves show to the king is mystical rather than practical. When he describes his special talent, to save with a motion of his beard, they reply:

"Thou art our *quṭb* (supreme chief), for thou wilt be the (means of our) de-
    liverance on the day of tribulation." (VI:2840)

The "day of tribulation" in this discourse always suggests the Day of Judgment, together with whatever less ultimate tribulations may be immediately at stake. *Quṭb* ("axis, pivot, pole") has a specialized meaning in Sufi parlance, referring to the spiritual guide through whose attachment the devotees pursue the quest for mystical union. While the Ākhond does not employ this word in the Sufic sense that Rūmī does, it is interesting that it pops up in one thief's speech, in an anomalous reference to the North Pole, a bow to western geographical concepts (l. 67 and note 7). It seems to be a demystified echo of the poet's language, further suggesting that the Ākhond's main source for this tale was the *Mathnavī* itself.

    In the throne-room scene, the Ākhond's night-seeing thief, who can recognize by day the night's companion, tersely warns his friends to be circumspect because the king has witnessed their activities (ll. 120–24). There is no indication of the thief's inner state of mind, to which Rūmī dedicates a number of lines of eloquent soliloquy on witnessing, merging into his appeal to the king who is addressed as God (VI:2858–2905). This rapturous theosophical flight, comprising some fifty lines, almost twice as long as the preceding narrative proper, is the longest mystical meditation within the story, and its emotional climax. In an inversion typical of Rūmī, the thief reconstrues himself, rather than the king, as witness. The thief then mounts a direct appeal which ultimately shames the king into exercising his gift of rescue for the sake of their night's companionship.

The time has come, oh king of concealed ways,
> That out of mercy you move your beard for weal. (VI:2909, M.M.
> trans.)

The king felt shame before [the thief] on the day of audience,
> For his gaze had been on the king's face in the night. (VI:2915, M.M.
> trans.)

This last verse is the only indication, in Rūmī's telling, of the story's ultimate outcome and the King's mercy, a simple, hopeful, and very brief assertion that the seeker's devotion will be recognized and rewarded, in vivid contrast to the outpourings of the seeker, just preceding it. Rūmī then closes the episode with an observation on the value of the ear, that the talent of the listening thief who understood the dogs is also not to be despised, nor even the discerning dog who recognizes the king, comparable to the dog who guarded the Companions of the Cave for righteousness.[10] Thus, in ending this narrative, Rūmī reiterates his emphasis on the mystically attuned faculties of seekers and witnesses, which was his point of entry into the tale.

The Ākhond gives the audience no such opportunities for identification with the thieves, except perhaps in a final remark (l. 146). He shows the seeing thief in court as a circumspect prisoner, anxious not to antagonize the king, his only statement in his own defense emphasizing his human weakness. The thief makes no direct move to remind the king of their

---

10. The reference is to the dog of the Seven Sleepers, whose story is related in Qur'an XVIII:8–25, and associated by western scholars with the legend of the Seven Sleepers of Ephesus (Pickthall n.d., p. 275).

compact to share their talents (ll. 124–26). It is the king himself who reminds the thieves, after they have submitted fully to his authority and God's (l. 127), that his talent has yet to play its role. The king first toys with the thieves, pretending to condemn them to death with a motion of his beard before he makes the saving gesture which carries out his part of their bargain. Whereas Rūmī's king had described his special power as one of rescue only, the Ākhond's king described motions of his beard and moustache which can either kill or save, and finally demonstrates them both. His comment, "My specialty has had its turn" (l. 131), raises a laugh from the Ākhond's audience. The drama of the recognition scene has been carried not by ecstatic theosophical meditations, as in Rūmī's poem, but by suspenseful action. Then, practical earthly monarch, the Ākhond's Sultan Mahmūd gives the thieves honest jobs, a detail which did not occur to Rūmī. By giving him more action and initiative, the Ākhond develops a more down-to-earth portrait of the king than does Rūmī, and by the same token, his thieves are a pragmatic lot, hardly the pious, mystically minded crew that Rūmī introduces. In the court scene, the Ākhond gives the thieves an idiomatic admission of guilt and submission, "God made our faces black " (l. 127).[11] Rūmī's thief offers the excuse of human weakness in rather more elaborate terms,

"We have been bound like the spirit in its prison of clay; thou art the Sun of the spirit on the Day of Judgment." (VI:2908, translation adapted by M.M. from Nicholson)

This anticipates the metaphorical use the poet will shortly make of the story of the sea-cow and its jewel concealed in the clay.

Only after the king's reprieve of the thieves does the Ākhond offer a short exegesis, which definitively reveals his debt to Rūmī in the framing of this narrative. First reminding his audience of the legendary justice of Mahmūd, a commonplace in Herati oral tradition, he follows immediately with observations on God's merciful acceptance of those who have believed in him and on the power of the Prophet to save or condemn regardless of sectarian alignments (ll. 146–50 and 152–54). By juxtaposing these observations, he implicitly links righteous rule with the justice of God and the Prophet. Were one not aware of the gloss on this story in Rūmī, the

---

11. Baghban (1977, 2:432) describes the same excuse as one of a class of excuses used by the buffoon-thief to transfer his guilt, with comic effect in folk plays.

Ākhond's topical shift from Mahmūd's justice to the grace of God might seem abrupt. This connection the Ākhond makes is virtually conclusive evidence that his main source is Rūmī (this connection does not figure in other recorded versions of the tale). The tone of Mokhtār's hesitant "Ye-es" (l. 150) suggests that the Ākhond's line of argument has taken a slightly unexpected turn for him. The Ākhond closes with a final, brief critical observation, "Well-tuned stories were like that," implying that he finds a special aptness of suggestion in the story he has just related. What that suggestion is, for him, is indicated by his juxtaposition of Mahmūd's just behavior and God's grace.

If the Ākhond renders a more mundane Shah Mahmūd than Rūmī, who identifies Mahmūd metaphorically with the divine King who is the object of the mystical quest, the Ākhond has not entirely separated Mahmūd from the idea of divine mercy and acceptance, and in his final exegesis of the tale, he reconnects them. Thus, he redirects Rūmī's interpretation of the story but retains its central element. The parallel between the adventures of Salīm, the Ākhond's previous hero, and narratives adjacent to the story of Mahmūd in the *Mathnavī*, together with his somewhat muted mystical exegesis of the story, strongly suggest that the *Mathnavī* was his primary source for this story, and that Salīm's adventures with the sea-cow supplied the mnemonic for this particular story, together with the surface congruency of the topic of righteous and unrighteous kings in this particular performance.

These inferences do not rule out the possibility that the Ākhond had also heard the story in oral versions without the mystical gloss that Rūmī gives it.[12] Even if the associative pattern to Rūmī's *Mathnavī* does operate in this performance as suggested, it is also possible that the Ākhond made the connection not in the process of performance but in advance, with a tactical eye to exploring the topic of righteous rule under the Woləswāl's nose.

Having claimed during our earlier conversation to be able to "talk to anyone according to his disposition " (in which context he specifically distinguished "Sufis of pure faith" from "shaykhs . . . that are deficient," in chapter 5, ll. 74–76), the Ākhond uses a story which he does not attribute

---

12. The Ākhond's version of the story does differ from Rūmī's in some narrative detail. There is a tunneling thief in Rūmī's version, omitted from the Ākhond's, who uses his talent to break into the king's treasury after the rope-throwing thief has gotten them over a high wall. In Rūmī's version, they do not enter the treasury from the roof, but by tunneling from below.

to its spiritually authoritative source (one of several possible sources), to address the problem which the Woləswāl as government authority and atheist offers to the Ākhond's religiously based value system. Though he does not attribute this tale to a religious source, later in the visit the Ākhond does single out the *Mathnavī* (the "Noble Mathnavī," *Mathnavī-e Sharīf*, as he calls it, using the same honorific used for the Qur'an when it is mentioned by name) for praise. While the *Mathnavī* may not be the Ākhond's sole source for this tale, the spiritual authority of that work is such that it must, for someone of his background and sentiments, constitute a supreme interpretive guide. The secularly educated Woləswāl would not likely be familiar with the *Mathnavī* and would probably not spontaneously recognize this story's place in that work or its theosophical dimensions which, though edited out of the Ākhond's narrative statements, still operated in the Ākhond's understanding of the story, as he indicated in the juxtaposition of his brief closing comments.

Nor was the Ākhond addressing the Woləswāl alone. While he was relating the thieves' attributes, just before he repeated Mahmūd's own claim, the Ākhond looked around and asked for one particular person he had evidently expected to join the audience, a *sayed* (descendant of the Prophet) (l. 75 and note 8). When the man entered a moment later, the Ākhond expressed regret that he had not heard the beginning of the tale, giving him the opportunity to request a repeat (l. 81), but the *sayed* gave him permission to continue instead. The Ākhond plainly wanted this man to hear this story. Resuming the performance floor the next morning, the Ākhond told a long personal reminiscence about the visit he once made to a Herat rabbi (see chapter 11) in the company of another *sayed* and his comic disgust when he found the Prophet's kinsman unable to hold his own in religious debate with the Jew. Thus, in closing the extended performance, he transported the audience from the world of fiction to the world of glossed personal experience. Veiled admonitions to present company other than the Woləswāl cannot be ruled out. A story less than flattering to *sayeds* reiterates the skepticism about saintlike charismatic figures which figures earlier in the performance sequence.

Judicious selection and editing of stories of deep and complex meaning accommodates both the degrees of understanding of different members of the audience and the political conditions of the performance context. The Ākhond's voice can be heard differently by different listeners at the same performance based on their familiarity with different source materials and prior contexts of performance of any given story. In this case, the Ākhond can simultaneously allude to esoteric theosophical ideas turning on the topic of worldly kings, and continue the exposition of righteous government which he began with the story of Salīm, a critique of present company made safe in part by his adversary's lack of familiarity with the rhetorical resources at the Ākhond's command. Precisely imitating the Prophet and Rūmī himself, the Ākhond converses with ideological adversaries who cannot fully understand him (but think they do) and, in the process, takes their measure and perhaps points out their deficiencies to more perceptive bystanders:

> He would speak his meaning wrapped in a parable, in order that the adversary might not know foot from head,
> He (the Prophet) would receive his answer from him while the other would not catch the smell of his question. (*Mathnavī* I:1053–54, translation adapted by M.M. from Nicholson)

As the Ākhond "tunes" it, this tale alludes indirectly to transcendent spiritual truths encompassed in Sufi witnessing, while explicitly continuing to develop themes of worldly justice and injustice.

9. Ākhond Mulla Mahmūd, "The Old Thief with Five Sons"[1]

[*The Ākhond is speaking, continuing directly from the previous tale of Sultan Mahmūd and the thieves.*]

  . . . Let me tell you another story, sir, that there was this guy with low habits,
      corrupt behavior, and his beard—
        a beard like this. [*Points to a distance halfway down his chest.*][2]
        Sir, a turban as big as this. [*Gestures to designate a turban about
                                 two feet in diameter.*]
      He was an old man who had five sons.   5

He himself, at the gate of the sheep bazaar—if these ones[3] understand—
[*Mokhtār*: Yeah—]
So you explain to them— the bazaar for sheep and cows and—don't they sell
                                them there?
      —to the people?
The father, sir, with his white robe and his white beard, as if, like me,
                              brother, 10
      with his turban and—
he's just like Kheyzr,[4] peace be on Him, sitting at the gate of the bazaar.

---

1. Untitled, title supplied in translation.
2. A man's beard is a symbol of his manly nature and honor. Elders cultivate long beards, and the generic term for the respected elders who generally arbitrate affairs in traditional village communities is *rīsh-safīd*, "white-beard."
3. A third-person plural, polite reference to me. Questions and comments about high-status persons present are, in politeness, not addressed to the person directly, but to his or her closest associate in the group.
4. Kheyzr (Arabic, *Khidhr*) is a much-revered figure in folk Islam, a wandering saint whose activities include aiding righteous travelers and childless couples and other needy suppliants. The blessing the Ākhond speaks after mentioning the name of the saint is customary, even when the real saint is not being invoked or discussed. Cf. l. 61 below and the discussion in chapter 9.

His sons are along the road, sir.
Every two parsangs along the way one of his sons is sitting, and he has five
                                                                    sons. 15
And none of them have any wives at home.
‹›
He came and— sir,
they're sitting there now, when you bring an animal to the bazaar,
if ten people put a low price on it, you say (to yourself) »
        "It must not be worth much, they must be giving me the right
                                                    price, anyway." 20
These guys' habit was that when some guy would bring an animal,
        the first son would say, "How much is that horse of yours?"
        He'd say, "Ten thousand,"
        and he'd say "Two hundred *qerān*."[5]
        [The next] one would say "A hundred *qerān*." »   25
        [The next] would say "Fifty *qerān*."
Until they got to the front of the bazaar, [*belches*]
        with their father—they would all be there together,
        and they'd say to their father, "Old man, you put a value on it," —the
                                                    father of these sons.
That guy would say, "A hundred 'papers,' "[6] and they would—   30
this guy would be reassured
        in his heart, »
he'd say "That must be right."
He'd sell his horse for a hundred "papers."
Now, that same one that was worth ten thousand. [*Mokhtār*: Yes . . .]   35

One person, sir, had an old mother, he's young, a boy, fresh-faced, with
                                                    clothes that were very—
        —a fine person, and he had a milk cow. »
His mother said, "My son, it's the Feast of Sacrifice[7],

---

5. One *qerān* equals 0.5 *afghānī*, or 50 *paisa* (approximately one cent U.S. in recent years) in the modern currency. The purchasing power of one *qerān* has declined greatly in the last century, according to elderly informants.

6. *kāghaz*: colloquial term for the smallest unit of paper money, equivalent to 10 *qerān* (or 5 *afghānī*). The unit was no longer in circulation at the time of this recording, but the term was still in general use.

7. *'Aīd-e Qorbān*, the greater of the two major Muslim feasts, commemorates the sacrifice of Abraham. Afghan families slaughter animals at this time and give meat to the poor, as well as outfitting the family with new clothes, to the extent that family finances permit.

take this milk cow and sell it,
      that will take care of the sheep for sacrifice, »   40
      take care of other things,
      take care of clothes for us.
  Take it and sell it."

He put the cow, his milk cow, on a lead and came along,
that first son said, "How much is the milk cow?" —that old man's [son].   45
  He said, "Four thousand."
  He said, "It's [worth] two hundred *qerān*."
He got to the second son, and he said, "How much is it?" »
  He said, "Three thousand."
  He said, "It's [worth] a hundred—a hundred rupees."[8]   50
He got to the third one, and in the end, sir, when he got to the fifth person,
  he said, "How much is your milk cow," »
  and he said, "Four thousand."
  He said, "I'll buy it for three thousand."
They all ended up together, and they said, "Let's go to someone—   55
  with white hair,
  a Muslim,
  whatever value he puts on it."
They came along—he didn't <u>know</u> they were his sons.
[*Mokhtār*: Yeah.]   60
They came along to that old man, that "Kheyzr" —peace be upon Him.
  They said, "How much is this cow?"
  He said, "In fairness, it's worth four thousand *qerān*."

That guy said [it].

Sir, they don't have any wife at home. [*Mokhtār*: Yes.]   65
They brought the cow to the house.
He said, "Give me my money."
They said, "In <u>three</u> installments.
    We'll give you your money over <u>three</u> weeks."
He said, "Brother, my mother will curse me," »   70
    —they <u>beat</u> him up and threw him out of the house, sir.

---

8. *rūpīeh* is the colloquial term for the present basic monetary unit, the *afghānī*, which equals 2 *qerān*.

The dinner prayer time came, and he set out, alone, crying, and came
                                        to his own house.
To his mother—she said, "What did you do?" —
He said, "They took the cow, like that.
        They said, 'In three weeks, in <u>three</u> installments.' " [*with a*
                                        disgusted intonation]   75
[*Mokhtār*: Yeah–]
She said, "You lost the cow, —by God, if ever you'll see good fortune!" »
So anyway, sir, this boy went to the baths.

He said to the bath-guy, "I'll give your wife a hundred rupees, you
                                        and I are neighbors."
He asked the wife to come to the bath, and said, "Pluck[9] the hair
                                        on my face.   80
                Give me long
                                hair, curls—"
—everything she did, she fixed him up <u>really</u> beautifully.
He came back to his house, that boy.
He put on garments and bangle-bracelets[10] and put gold-embroidered
        slippers[11] on his feet and a full veil[12] over his head, so he
        shone like the light of day. [*muted audience laughter*]

---

9. *nakh ko*: literally, "do the thread." Women traditionally use a loop of thread in place
of tweezers to remove unwanted facial or other hair.

10. *lebāshā-ye karrah*: use of the *ezafeh* makes this appear to be a noun plus attribute
construction, but *karrah* as an attributive could not be identified. *Karrah* is the usual term for
bangle-type bracelets in Herat.

11. *kaushhā-ye qorṣ*: literally, "sun shoes," old-fashioned ladies' shoes, flat leather-soled
slippers with pointed toes, the tops entirely covered with gold-colored couched threadwork,
are now worn almost exclusively by Pashtun nomads in the southeast of Afghanistan and
northwest Pakistan and, of them, mostly the older generation. They were formerly also popular with villagers in a wider area.

12. *chāder-e boghrah*: The full veil or *chāderī* worn by adult women in most Afghan cities,
a solid-color, full, ankle-length enveloping garment pressed with a hot iron in many small
vertical knife-pleats, stitched to an embroidered, tight-fitting cap. The facepiece, which is
unpleated and hangs to somewhat below the waist, is sewn to the main body of the garment
and has a lattice of embroidery over the eyes. The shorter length of the front piece allows it
to be lifted so that one can expose the face if necessary, or insert infants or bundles for carrying
under the veil. The cut, fabric, color, and pressing of the *chāderī*, as well as the type of panta-
loon-cuffs which show below its hem, are all taken as clues to the age, attractiveness and
possible availability of the woman wearing it, in the imaginations of men. Young men joke
about the possibility of an old or ugly woman affecting an attractive, well-cut *chāderī* and
thereby fooling her male observers.

He set out on the road, this same boy who'd sold the cow.   85
[*Mokhtār*: Yes.]
He showed a corner of his face to one of that old man's sons.
He said, "Who are you?" »
He said, "I'm a single girl, I'm going to get married."
He said, "How much is the brideprice[13] for you?" »   90
He said, "I have need [only] of wealth and property, and youth.[14]
        I don't need any brideprice."
"Let's go—" he said, "Take me."
'She'[15] said, "Let's go look at your property." »
The next son fell in after him, and the next son, they all went to the
                                                        old man, sir.   95

They all came together,
he said, "This girl wants to get married, she says 'I want wealth and
                                property, I don't want a brideprice.' "
They're six people, the father and sons.
They brought him to the house, and they have no wife at home.[16]
<>
They said to him, "Brother [*sic*], <u>which</u> one of these sons of mine
                                        will you take?"   100

---

13. *pīshkash*: generally, "gift," but more specifically in Afghan usage, the money actually paid to the bride's father by the groom's family, in compensation for the expense of raising her (not the money promised to the woman in the event of divorce through no fault of her own, or the bride's own portion, called *mahr*). Some families take pride in spending the entire sum on outfitting the bride; in others the father to varying extent treats it as income or applies it to the acquisition of a wife for his own son. "Daughter-selling," accepting the offer of the highest bidders, is regarded as shameful, but the brideprice itself is also regarded as a token of the value in which a family holds its womenfolk and its ability to protect them from casual or unsuitable offers (see chapter 1). Two families which each have marriageable sons and daughters sometimes arrange a sibling exchange, to obviate the need for brideprice and to develop multiple marriage alliances between the families, both desirable outcomes in traditional thinking. Brideprices were substantial in Herat, typically the equivalent of perhaps two years' wages for a laborer working in the city's small wage-earning sector. Travel to Iran and the Gulf states as guest workers facilitated young men's accumulation of the capital needed to marry at the time I lived in Herat (1974–76).

14. That is, "she" is looking for a good family and a young husband, and no brideprice will be demanded in such a match.

15. The third-person singular pronoun in Persian *ū* (he, she, it) is not marked for gender, so the tension between apparent and real sexual identity is not reinforced in Persian in quite the same way that it is by necessary use of gender-marked pronouns in English.

16. If there were women in the household, "she" would have been expected to visit them in the private part of the house, and unveil, perhaps revealing "her" identity.

He said, "Tomorrow I could get blind, get old, I—'ll take a head of hair.[17]

      <>

      You're young and tomorrow you'll take another wife on me, »

      I'll land in a disaster—no, I'll take this <u>father</u> of yours."

And from being single, their father was ready to fuck his own sons.

[*Brief audience laughter*]

His cock goes up and down like a dredge-plow[18] —those things they

                         do the smoothing with.   105

[*Mokhtār, laughing*: OK, yeah . . .]

Their father was very happy, anyway, and

they said the *fātah*[19] for their father, said "In the Name of God."

He said, "Now that you've said the *fātāh* for me,

      <>

      you bastards have to go get me the bridegoods."[20]   110

He took and wrote it on a piece of paper for the boy.

This 'woman'.

He sent one of them to the New City[21], and one for foreign shoes,

                         one here, one there.

After they left, he came and

      locked the house gate.   115

He put the veil down over there! [*Claps once.*]

[Hit him] one right on the father's arm! and one on his thigh, and one for »

      "<u>Give</u> me the first payment for that milk cow of mine! »

      My prick in your 'wife's' ass, by God if I let you be!"

They [*sic*] <u>beat</u> him to a paste, »   120

he said, "<u>Ayy</u>, for God's sake!"

---

17. *ma-m kallah-mūi mīstonom*: Apparently opting for a more mature bridegroom. The expression was perfectly audible, but unfamiliar to Persian-speaking auditors of this tape. The intonation is declarative, not interrogative, with a deliberative drawl.

18. *zanjīrmālah*: a large plate of wood, slightly curved, attached with chains and dragged behind a draft animal to level the furrows and break up clods of earth after plowing.

19. Literary, *fātehah*: the opening verses of the Qur'an, are read for personal rites of transition, as in this case to seal an engagement, or at funerals.

20. *Rakht-e 'arūsī*: Usually including a number of sets of garments, shoes, etc., plus kitchen and other household equipment, perhaps also carpets, furniture, etc., which the groom's family agrees to supply for the bride. The number and quality of items are negotiated as part of the engagement agreement; hence, he writes them down for the "bride."

21. The more westernized part of each major city, where imported luxury goods were marketed and traditional architecture was replaced by more international styles of construction, was called the "New City."

"Well, I'm the <u>cow</u> owner, I came after the <u>first</u> payment, I'll fuck
your <u>father</u>!"
He said, "There's twelve thousand *qerān* tied up in that kerchief, heed
the Lord, don't do anything else to me!" »
He picked up the money and left, and the sons came back around
afternoon prayer,
each one of them brought goods, and said, "What became of that
bastard (woman)?" »   125
He said, "Yeah," he said, "<u>Bābā</u> it was the <u>cow</u> owner, <u>where</u> was there
a woman?

He got his <u>first</u> <u>payment</u> out of me! [*laughs*]
Pissed on my grandfather's grave!"[22]

‹›

He left, kind sir, but he didn't go back to the village, that boy.
He went to the New City, dear brother that I take you for[23], and got
a <u>good</u> suit and   130
a necktie and the finest Persian lamb cap[24] and such stuff, and
came, sir, and got the stuff for
a surgeon's kit,
—he <u>knew</u>, because he'd beaten their father to a <u>pulp</u>—
[*Mokhtār*: Yeah—]   135
Anyway, sir, with a sign in his hands and this and that, <u>right</u> before
prayer he came and walked around outside their house.

‹›

He, —kind sir— he— his sons came out to go after a doctor, »
and said, "Who are you?" »
He said, "I'm a doctor, and I came here on my way to—
—my place."   140
He said, "We have a sick person here, come on, let's go!"

---

22. This sort of scatological aggression is characteristic of female cursing styles (the equivalent of male threats to rape one's dead ancestors). The "woman's" revenge takes a metaphorically female form.

23. *barādar gol* (literally, "flower-brother") *keh shomār dārom*: a formulaic address, but a less formal, more affectionate one than sayb, sa'eb ("sir"), *sayb-e-mehrābān* ("kind sir") or *yār-e sayb* ("friend, sir") which have been used hitherto.

24. A flat-folding hat made of the pelts of unborn Persian lambs, its shape like that of the cap worn by Jawaharlal Nehru or the U.S. Army cap of the World War II dress uniform. The headgear was the alternative to skullcap and turban for "modernizing" adult males in the middle decades of the twentieth century in Afghanistan but was no longer fashionable with younger men by the middle seventies.

They didn't recognize him, that he's that cow owner.
They took him in, and as he passed the gate, he <u>knew</u> where the wounds
were from the club.
He said, "It's on that arm," —and from the door to the room
[he said]—
—"and on his thigh—"   145
and who knows where, but right there where <u>he'd hit</u> him, anyway.[25]
"<u>There</u> now," [the other] said, "Saints! This is a doctor for the saints!"

He sent them away, one after plasters and one for this and one for that,
all at once
he sent the sons away.
When they left the house, dear brother that I take you for,   150
he dragged out the club, saying "I'll fuck your father, give me the
second payment, »
by God if I let you be!"
He lifted up that club, hit him <u>once</u> and <u>he</u> said, "Ayy, I've eaten shit,[26]
heed the Lord!
Heed the Prophet!
There's six thousand qerān
in that box, » 155
take it and go." »
He picked them up, too, and left.
That's eighteen thousand <i>qerān</i>. [<i>Inaudible audience comment.</i>]
Yeah.
After he left, kind sir, he came back the next day.   160
Like to the Qandahar Gate,[27] for instance.
At prayer time.
He said to some guy, "Son, I'll give you two hundred rupees— »
Can you <u>run</u> to Gozārah Center?[28]
<u>Five</u> people, one after the other, will be after you."   165
He said, "They won't catch my <u>dust</u>."

---

25. By describing the wounds before laying eyes on the patient, he gains credence as a brilliant diagnostician.

26. That is, "I've disgraced and confounded myself by my own actions."

27. One of four historical "gates" to Herat, the Qandahar Gate is a market area on the south side of the city, which is no longer walled (see Map No. 3).

28. The district administrative center for Gozārah District is on the main road to Qandahar, 7 or 8 kilometers south of the city.

He gave the guy the money and said, "Go set fire to²⁹ the door of that house.
     Say, 'I'm [*laughing*] the cow owner, »
     I've come for the third payment.' »
     Five will come after you, one after
         the other. 170
     Then you run for it, and they'll
       come after you, anyway."

When he went and knocked on the door and said to the sons, "I came
       for the third payment,"— »
"Great God!" they thought it was the cow owner!
They took off after him, and [the cow owner] ran for it and threw
      himself into the house and locked the door.
He said to their father, "Give me the third payment, fuck the souls of
       your grandpa(s)!" » 175
He said, "Heed the Lord, I don't have anything!"
Whatever rugs or carpets or copper pots that were in the house,
  he gathered them up and tied them <u>all</u> together with rope, and
      set out, took them away.
The sons came back at afternoon prayer time, [*laughs*] sir, saying
       "What happened?" »
"That bastard got his <u>third</u> payment, it was the <u>cow</u> owner, he pissed
     on the graves of nine of my grandfathers!" [*laughing*] 180
That's all!

So right there, sir,
ah—um—the treacheries that their father had done, [came down] on
       their heads to that degree.
[*Mokhtār*: I say, everything that he'd saved up—]
Yeah! <u>Everything</u> that he'd saved up, he took it all. [*Claps once*] 185
[*Mokhtār*: —he took it all at once.]
‹›
[*Ākhond sighs.*]
[*Mokhtār*: That's the end.]
That's the end, anyway, sir.

———
 29. Hyperbole for knocking loudly and making a great disturbance.

"With his . . . white beard, like me, brother . . .": The Ākhond on Private Justice

Moving directly from the story of Shah Mahmūd and the thieves into this one, without intervening conversation, the Ākhond retained the performance floor, and continued to do so for the rest of the evening and into the next morning. Indeed, Karīm did not reoccupy it until after the Ākhond's departure at midmorning. Nor did Karīm show any signs of wanting a turn on the floor during the Ākhond's presence, but deferred to the Ākhond's seniority in age, education, professional status, or some combination of these. No longer performing contrapuntally with another narrator, the Ākhond was free to construct a story series according to his own chain of associations and readings of audience response.

This story, like the previous one, opens with a view of the human underworld, not a gang of thieves in this case, but a corrupt family, headed by an old man whose respectable appearance the Ākhond ironically compares to his own (l. 10; for more of the Ākhond's views on physical appearances, see "Black and White," chapter 13). Whatever their threat to his treasury, Mahmūd's thieves are of the honorable variety, bound to one another by voluntary commitments of reciprocal help which ultimately bind the king himself and thus rescue the repentant thieves from destruction. The old man's bonds to his accomplices are not of honor but of blood and, in his own case, apparently more exploitative than noble (ll. 104 and 110; an elderly widowed father would ideally address his own adult sons' need for marriage and offspring, before indulging his own desires).

The threat to social order presented by an old man who can falsely assume the badges of elderhood and piety (white beard and turban) is unmitigated in this story by the presence of any higher authority who could bring him to justice. Instead, retributive justice falls solely in the hands of one of the little men who are the old man's victims, and a particularly unlikely one. The hero's everyman status, his lack of institutional power or connections, or even older male allies, is compounded by his youth and inexperience. But if he begins as the perfect victim, afraid even of his mother's anger (l. 70), the young boy soon develops into that staple of world folktale, the trickster hero. This tale is one of a group of comic revenge tales with young heroes, in current oral circulation in the area. Though it does not conform precisely to any of Marzolph's identified Persian Tale Types, in keeping with the fluidity of oral tradition it combines major elements of his Tale Types 1539 (Part I concerning deceptive animal-trading practices) and *1525 S, "Der listige nimmt Rache," which in several of the variants he lists involves a young male hero in female disguise contracting marriage with the object of his revenge and in a second disguise, as a barber or physician, completing his vengeance.[1]

After the last three tales, with their portrayals of kings and governors dealing (or at first, misdealing) justice, the absence of any higher authority in this tale, either governmental or religious, the lack of divine intervention or even of any appeal to the divine, makes justice a matter of self-help. Even appeals to interpretive authority, as in "Mulla Mongol the Martyr" and "Ten Qerān," are lacking, giving the hero a social autonomy which is characteristic of Afghan (and other) trickster-heroes. It is doubly fitting that the element of arbitration by legitimate authorities is missing from the resolution of this tale, since the very idea of reliance on just arbitration by elders is compromised by the old man's habitually exploitative behavior. This tale's events are played out in an environment where elements of social order and authority structures which figured in the satisfactory resolution of the preceding tales have broken down.

In setting that scene, the Ākhond's aside that the old man looked "like me" (l. 10) humorously brings the problem of false authority home to present company. Not only does he look like an Ākhond, the villain looks like a saint, specifically Khoja Kheyzr, who is a legendary guide figure (ll. 12, 61).[2] This old man, dispenser of deceptive assessments and advice, reverses the customary role of the Kheyzr of Afghan oral narrative tradition, who provides advice, guidance, and magical protection to deserving wanderers and innocents (especially young males) met along the road. Kheyzr himself is extremely widely venerated in popular Islam and alluded to in the Qurʿan[3] but his veneration is a folk rather than an orthodox element of

---

1. For an overview of transvestite disguise themes and their import in the whole corpus of stories recorded in Herat, see Mills (1985).

2. See entry under *al-Khadir, Encyclopedia of Islam*, 1st. ed., 1924, vol. IV, pp. 861–65. His name in Arabic means, etymologically, "the Green One," and he is connected through his legend with the Waters of Life and thus with the resolution of fertility problems and the fortunes of male children. He is believed to be eternally alive and wandering about the earth. Iranian ethnographers report a wide variety of popular religious votive activities dedicated to him. His tradition is generally recognized to predate Islam. He is identified in some literary sources with the Prophet Elias. For beliefs and activities concerning him in the Persian culture area, see, e.g., Anjavi Shirazi (1973, 2:125ff.).

3. Not by name but as "one of [God's] slaves" who travels with Moses, and reveals to him some aspects of divine mystery, after Moses tries to find and drink from the spring of the Waters of Life (Qurʿan XVIII:65).

faith. His miragelike presence, connected only in simile with the deceptive persona of the old man, is the sole explicit reference to religious guidance in this tale, until the (equally misguided) exclamation of the old man's sons, "Saints! This is a physician for the saints!" (l. 147), regarding the hero's apparently clairvoyant diagnostic abilities. In this story (unlike, e.g., the "Mongol Martyr") the object of the humor is not gullible folk piety, as such, but the complementary problem of deceptive sanctity and venerability turned back on itself.

The old man is guilty not of simple theft but of "treacheries" (*khī-yānāt*), betrayals of trust. His dishonest advice on the price of the cow is compounded by his sons' later insistence that the payments will be made in three future installments over three weeks' time (l. 75), which would make it impossible for the boy to use the price of the cow to pay for the 'Aïd festival expenditures for a sacrificial animal and new clothing, as his mother intended (ll. 38–42).

Having clearly described in a generic way one price swindle that the old man and his sons are in the custom of carrying out (ll. 21–35), the Ākhond slightly obscured the particular dealings over the price of the cow by his references to alternative units of currency, the *qerān* and the *rūpīeh* ("rupee," now the "afghānī," which is worth two *qerān*). In the first exchange, between the boy and the old man's first son (ll. 45–46), the boy offers the cow at "four thousand," apparently 4,000 rupees, but the son scoffs that it is only worth 200 *qerān*. The second son offers 100 rupees, the same as 200 *qerān* (l. 50). The third son, surprisingly, offers not an absurdly low sum but "3,000," apparently 3,000 rupees (l. 54). In any case, they agree to abide by the old man's arbitration, and he sets the price at 4,000 *qerān*, or 2,000 rupees, half the boy's original asking price.

Compounding the slightly confusing handling of this two-currency bargaining scene, the Ākhond leaves unclear the process of the boy's disillusionment. At the point when the bargain is struck, the boy does not realize that the old man is the father of all the bargainers. The Ākhond does not really indicate when the boy realizes he has been swindled and when he begins the metamorphosis from swindled innocent to vengeful trickster. It seems logical that their collusion would have become obvious to the boy while going to the house together with all six purchasers, before they commit the additional offense of refusing to pay him the money at once. The violence suggests that they have no intention of paying him at all. Despite (or even because of) the defects of logic and lack of clarity in its detail, the sequence of the boy's initial dealings with the swindlers amply conveys his confusion and helplessness in the face of their manipulations of him.

The father and sons, always out for a dishonest superbargain, are natural victims for a "girl" who offers marriage without a brideprice. Their vice, more than lust, is greed and willingness in its service to bypass legitimate exchange systems, including those established for marital exchange. But just as they are out of control, a young girl like this (were she really female), negotiating marriage for herself without the intervention of her relatives (who should be looking after her interests and her family's), would also be dangerously out of control. The lack of decorum in her seductive approach to the first son, showing her face from the corner of her veil (the same technique that the castrating seductress used on the barber in " 'Ādel Khān"), signals a major, perhaps dangerous, breach of social rules. The old man and his sons, antisocial and opportunistic themselves, are not equipped to detect the danger or protect themselves from it.

Whereas Karīm has tended in his performances prior to this point to portray women as sexual victims (except when they are dangerously out of control and victimizing others), the Ākhond here introduces the idea of the power of female sexuality as a weapon, and a weapon that can ultimately be used to restore order, through judicious use of the disorder female display can produce in men's psyches. As has been pointed out in chapter 6, the females in "Salīm the Jeweller" are each, in their way, advocates of order and responsibility vis-à-vis the hero. Even the one confused woman the Ākhond has portrayed, the sister in "Ten *Qerān*" whose brothers complain that she has taken twice her share of milk by filling up two bodily orifices, challenges the male elder who arbitrates, "Can you wall off half of it?" (chapter 5, l. 151). Even though a fool, the woman challenges the male authority, by asking him whether he can control her physiology himself, if he presumes to hold her responsible for doing so. The basic logic of male dominance is challenged, even ridiculed.

The hero's mother, like the vizier's mother in " 'Ādel Khān," presents another face of female power, that of the older, perspicacious (and not incidentally, nonsexual) woman. Elderly women in tales are often tricksters themselves, frequently antisocial panderers or, more positively when they are working on the hero's behalf, effective go-betweens with his love interest. But whether on the side of order or disorder, elderly women tend to be portrayed as seeing through tricks and deceptions. The hero's mother in this case is quick to blame the hero for being swindled (l. 77, where the verb "to lose," *bāy dādan*, implies loss through gaming or wagering). Apparently stung by her cursing his future luck (". . . by God, if you'll ever see good fortune"), the hero then pursues his strategy for revenge, which depends on assuming the guise of a female trickster. He trades his real vulnerability as a young and inexperienced male for the false vulnerability of female disguise.

In his portrayal of the hero's transformations, the Ākhond shows a good eye for fashion detail, though understandably a few years out of date, given his own age. The "girl's" finery, and especially her "sun shoes" with their gold embroidery, are village fashion of twenty or thirty years before. The "full veil" (l. 84) with its many elegant knife-pleats is still, as it was in former years, a city-based institution, an item that village women would don when going to the city or traveling outside their immediate residential area. The "foreign shoes" the sons are sent out to purchase for the "girl" as part of their father's bridal gifts (l. 113) are still part of city trousseaus, but no longer an exotic item for wealthier city women. The karakul cap that the boy dons in his "physician" disguise (l. 131) was the fashion of "modernizing" Afghan city dwellers of a few decades before, to be seen mainly on somewhat westernized men over fifty years of age in provincial cities at the time of this performance.

In keeping with the egalitarian, self-determinative cast of this story, once the hero begins to extract his revenge the Ākhond begins to address Mokhtār as "brother" or "dear brother that I take you for" (ll. 130 and 150) occasionally, in place of the more deferential *sayb* (literary, *sāḥeb*, "sir"). His pacing also speeds up and speech pauses are reduced in number and length as his narration accelerates toward its conclusion. At the end, the Ākhond offers a summary statement reiterating that the misfortunes of the old man were brought on by his own actions (l. 183) and that the boy's revenge was complete (l. 185). The private revenge of the little man restores social balance, at least temporarily. But there is no overt or covert critique of traditional authority itself in this portrayal of the little man acting autonomously against a fraudulent authority figure. Private individuals, such as Salīm and the barber, may remind kings and governors (and in the next tale, judges) of the duties entailed by their power, but in the world of the Ākhond's tale selection, ordinary men do not challenge that power. The ordinary man's critique of authority is not a revolutionary one.

As with other performances during the evening, Mokhtār at this point shows concern about closure. He does not demand formulas this time, but offers a summary statement of his own (l. 184) and then repeats the Ākhond's paraphrase of it (l. 186). The Ākhond then pauses and sighs, showing his fatigue at the late hour. Mokhtār again solicits an ending statement (l. 188). Unlike the conclusion of "Mongol Martyr," there is little here to confuse Mokhtār as to whether a conclusion has been reached, and his solicitation of an ending statement was primarily directed as a signal to me to turn off the tape recorder.

This story ended the evening's performance. After we thanked the storytellers, they were shown out and several of us retired to sleep in the guest room. (Without a woman present in the Woləswāl's house who could chaperone by sharing sleeping quarters with me, propriety was judged to be served by Mokhtār and two or three of the Woləswāl's assistants "guarding" my sleep in the guest room.) On waking and breakfasting the next morning, we were again joined by the storytellers. The Ākhond waited with us for the local-service transport truck which would take him back to his village, and as we chatted, the topic turned to proverbs. He soon began to narrate.

10. Ākhond Mulla Mahmūd, "Women's Tricks"

[The recording begins with the author (rather tellingly revealing the language dif-
ficulties she had when newly arrived in the area) struggling to understand the des-
ignation of the next story.]

M. Mills: . . . *azmak-e zan?*

Ākhond: Yeah

Mokhtār: *Az* **makr-e zan**. *[In Persian]* He's talking about "*makr-e zan*."

MM [In Persian]: What's that?

M [In English]: It's about the —ladies' —tricks? *[smiles]*   5

MM: Ohhh— *[writes title]* "*makr-e zan*"?

M: Yeah— *[laughs]*

MM [laughs]: All right—

Ā [smiling]: Yeah—

The reciters of news and the easy[1] *[sic]* narrators so relate that there was a

shaykh,[2] sir, sitting in his retreat.   10

He was in his retreat, and a thief—some person brought him ten

thousand *afghānī*, sir,

as a pledge to God.

He took it, sir, and put it under his cushion.

---

1. *Nāqqelān-e āsān* for *nāqqelān-e āsār* ("narrators of traditions"): a slip of the tongue which makes the second phrase in the formula nonsensical and spoils its rhyme, either out of intentional carelessness or because the Ākhond really does not know these formulas, as he protests he does not.

2. A charismatic Muslim religious mystic (*sufi*) and teacher. There are a number of different mystical schools or orders in Islam, distinguished by their history and by the partic-ular devotional emphases and techniques of their founders. The two most popular in the Herat area at present are Naqshbandīyya and Qāderīyya, both of which are among the more "sober" orders, which downplay or eschew the use of music, dance, or acts of extreme self-mortification in devotional practice. Sufism attracts devotees from both Sunni and Shiʿa branches of Islam. All orders make great use of poetry and narrative exempla in devotions and teaching, and a great proportion of classical poetry in Persian is connected with the mystical tradition (cf. Roy 1983).

A thief found out that they had brought him ten thousand *afghānī*.
He came to him,   15
    offered to act as his servant.
He served him for two or three months and one day the shaykh went to
                      perform ablutions,
    and he gathered up his books and the ten thousand *afghānī* and ran
                            off, left.
The shaykh came back and his heart really burned for those books,
        and following his trail, he picked up his walking stick
        and set off after him.
He came along and came along, and saw two wild animals fighting
                        each other.   20
    Wasn't it the wild animals that have those big horns?
[*M*: Those —things —stags.]
[*Another listener*: Rams.]
Yeah — rams.
They're hitting their horns together, like that [*claps*], and they were
                          hitting »   25
    so that the blood flows down onto the stones, »
    and there's a fox, sir, just licking along
    on those stones.
This fox got that blood in his eyes, and he started to—
    lick their bodies, their necks.   30
And he licked right up to the roots of their horns, and this one from
        this side, and that one from that, they <u>hit</u> [*claps*] together
        so that the fox's head, in between, was torn right off.
His body fell on the field.
The shaykh went on his way.

He came along and came along, sir, to a city.
When he got to this city, sir, there's a woman   35
    and she's got a lover.
She has a servant girl who is more beautiful than the woman herself.
The servant girl got involved
    with the lover.
The guy came, sir, and she's lying there in another room with the lover,
                    they're fooling around.   40

It got to be dinner prayer time, and this dame climbed up on the
roof,³ [thinking] »
"My lover hasn't come,"»
and the shaykh came along in the dark, passing right by their house.
This dame got it into her head that—
[*New guests arrive and are greeted and invited to sit down.*]
This dame, sir, it got into her head, this dame,   45
that— [*More greetings and welcomes interrupt*]
The dame got it into her head that he was her own lover, and said,
"Please, come into the house."
And the shaykh saw that he —he was stymied, anyway.
So the shaykh went into the house,
    this dame in front and him behind,   50
    they went right into the room where [they were],
    the servant girl and her lover.
They had been peacefully fooling around, and their asses —their hearts
were carried off by sleep.⁴
This dame, the fire of rage and envy⁵ gripped her lower parts,
    because she saw her lover there.   55
She found a little powdered poison and put it in a hollow spindle,
and brought it to blow into the servant girl's nose, to kill her.
And while she was setting it up, »
    the shaykh was in the midst of his prayers, too.
[*M*: Yeah . . .]   60
Just when she was setting it up, the woman sneezed, sir.
And the poison got into this woman's own body.
She fell over immediately, and died.
After she died, they woke up,
    and she had died and there was the shaykh, praying.   65

That's the way it was, around dawn.
The shaykh picked up his prayer mat⁶, and ha! "Run, if you're running!"⁷

---

3. To scan the nearby roads to see if he is coming.
4. The Ākhond opts belatedly for the more decorous phrase.
5. Reading *ḥasrat* for the Ākhond's *nasrat*, evidently a slip of the tongue.
6. The shaykh has spent the night in prayer and meditation.
7. The Ākhond's version of the idiomatic expression describing precipitous flight (cf.
"Salīm the Jeweller," l. 362 and note).

He left, sir, and there's a shoemaker

 that was a devotee[8] of this shaykh.

He caught sight of his master.   70

He said, "This evening, sir, you are my guest."

  —The shoemaker said that.

  —In this same city.

And the shoemaker's wife was fooling around, too.

They said—that evening the Sufis were all getting together for some

           mumbo jumbo[9], a big to-do. 75

  There's a gypsy[10] dame, sir, working for this woman.

  For the shoemaker's wife, a gypsy woman.

She said to the gypsy dame, »

  "Tonight so-and-so's son[11] who's my friend —tell him to come.

  Because the Sufis are having their dissolvings and their resolvings[12] » 80

  I'll go there too and beat my breast." [*laughs*]

She came and, kind sir—

[*Door opens. Tea is brought in. Audience members:* Put it down.

            —is he coming? —Yeah.]

He said, kind sir—

---

  8. *morīd*: one who takes a particular shaykh as a spiritual guide and teacher.

  9. *haqq o hūqq*. The Ākhond speaks with comical familiarity of Sufi gatherings, which in different orders involve varying degrees of vocalization in the process of group devotions and meditation. Some orders, like the Naqshbandīyya of which the Ākhond is probably a member, prescribe silent meditation; others make extensive use of music and dance.

  10. *Kherrāt*: in Herat, approximately synonymous with *jat* (cf. note 16 below and note 6 in the second part of chapter 7).

  11. Adults are routinely referred to not by their given names, but by familial referents. Parents are ordinarily called after their eldest son (or daughter, if without sons), "Mother-of-so-and-so" or "Father-of-so-and-so" in preference to their given names. Those without children may be called after their father, as here.

  12. *hall o hūll*: both this and the previous expression (note 9) make comic use of distortions of Sufi terminology; *haqq*, "truth" or "right" in the previous phrase, means among other things, God as the Revealed Truth. The Sufi martyr al-Hallāj was executed for heresy, in part for allegedly saying, "I am the Revealed Truth," (*Anā al-haqq*), a claim to spiritual unity with the divine which was interpreted by his orthodox opponents as a claim to personal divinity. *Haqq* is one of the words used in *dhikr*, a meditation focusing on the repetition of one or more of the names of God or other verbal formulas. *Hall*, "dissolving," in Sufi terminology may describe emancipation from the sense of the separate, bounded, and finite self, which is sought through contemplation of the divine. Steingass's *Persian-English Dictionary* lists only one meaning for *hūqq*, "margo glandis," and translates *hūll* as "conceiving (a camel)" or "camels not conceiving in the first year," but it is virtually certain that the storyteller had neither of these meanings in mind for the second elements and was simply making doublet words for the first elements, a common humorous strategy in colloquial Persian.

They gave the people food, and the Sufis and all left, got lost,   85
    the shaykh was left and that guy's wife and—
    that shoemaker.
The shaykh is praying by himself.
In the shoemaker's house, sir, there's this
    piece of wood, hanging up.   90
[The shoemaker] laid his head down to sleep and said to his wife, »
    "You bastard, people are talking about so-and-so's son,
    if you're not taking it up the ass, when did I ever invite him,
    why was he here?" »
He said that to his wife.   95
His wife said, "He's one of God's creatures, and he came here, what's
                         it to me, bastard?"
He took and brought a rope, sir, and tied her up to the hooks,[13] hand
                        and foot, standing up.
That shoemaker guy.

He went off and fell asleep, and the shaykh was praying.
Then, sir, that dame came.   100
That woman —that one who was working for her.
The gypsy woman.
She said, "Bastard, why don't you just go to that 'mine [of delights]'?" »
She said, "Ah, you *kūnī*, I—" she said, "Because he's tied me up!"
—she said—"Give me your clothes, I'll put them on,   105
      I'll tie you up, and go off and beat my breast!"[14]
She tied up the gypsy woman [*laughs*], sir, and she went off to her
                    lover, the shoemaker's wife.
[*M*: —to the Ākhond.]
Yeah—
—in front of this— it's the shoemaker's wife, and the shaykh is there
                        praying, sir.   110
[*M*: Oh.]

---

13. Apparently, a reference to the hanging wooden device mentioned previously, but the arrangement is unclear.

14. *moshtā-xor be golū mīzanom*, literally, "beat my throat with my fists." When the expression first appeared in the story it seemed to refer satirically to devotional activity in the Sufi gathering. Now that the group has dispersed, the reference seems misplaced. Auditors were unable to clarify the reference at this point. *Kūnī*: male or female passive partner in anal intercourse.

Her lover is somebody else.
[*M*: All right.]
She left, and all at once, that guy woke up.
And the woman is the gypsy woman.   115
That guy started talking, »
  "Fuck your father, if you weren't taking it up the ass, if you weren't
                    a slut,

  what's with so-and-so's son?"
and someone— this— uh— if this dame speaks, she'll be <u>recognized</u>—
[*M*: Yeah, yeah.]   120
And when you're cursing someone, sir, if they don't say anything, one's
                   anger increases.

[*M*: Yeah, yeah.]
No matter how he cursed her, the woman doesn't say anything. »
  —because she's the gypsy woman and her voice would show it.
  The one who's working for her.   125
[*M*: Yeah.]
So he got enraged, and he picked up a sharp knife and went and
        [*laughing*] grabbed the gypsy woman's nose
        and just <u>whacked</u> it off at the root! [*Laughs*]
[*M (in amused alarm)*: Ooh— ah! (*laughs*)]
[*Laughing*] The shoemaker!
[*M*: Yes.]   130
He cut off her nose, and the blood was spurting into the air!
He came back and laid down his head and went back to sleep. »
The woman—

his wife came back, [and said], "What happened?" »
She said, "Oh, you *kūnī*, your <u>husband</u> cut off my nose! Bastard!
              Let me loose!" »   135
  —she put her clothes, all full of blood, back on.
She tied her— back up on the hooks, »
and the gypsy woman picked up her nose and went running off to her
                own house.

After she went to her own house, sir,
and she was leaning against the wall, and she about passed out, »   140
  and she's getting up her strength to say to her husband, "They cut
              off my nose."

Let's let her be,
the gypsy woman. [*Mokhtār makes inaudible clarificatory comment/query*]
Yeah.
Then, the [other] woman says,   145
  —what was done was done, but her nose is all right and her
            clothes are full of blood—
  "Oh, Lord!
  If I'm adulterous,
  then tear off my head!
  If he's lying, heal my nose from the Treasuries of the Unseen!
              [*laughingly*]   150
  And shame this bastard, give him his comeuppance, the bastard,
             oh Lord!"
She's hollering, carrying on.
Her husband says, "Oh, you bastard, wha—
     will the Seat of the Lord accept adultery?"
"Oh, father-of-so-and-so!"[15]   155
If I'm an adulterer, let God tear off my head, and if not, from the
           Treasuries of the Unseen—
  straighten you out!
‹›
Yay! I turn to the Lord! There now, my nose is cured!" »
He lit a light, kind sir,
  and there's her nose, cured, well.   160
The guy threw himself at her feet, »
  "Ohhh, I've eaten shit! Oh, for the Lord's sake, forgive me!" »
—And her lower parts were <u>wet</u>, she'd just been giving cunt, the bastard!
[*Laughs. Audience laughs.*]
So in the end, since he threw himself at her feet and did this and that— 165
let's leave that.
‹›

Now about the gypsy.
In the middle of the night—those gypsy people are very quick—they're
              jat,[16] after all.

---

  15. The customary manner in which she addresses her husband incidentally asserts his legitimate fathering of children, presumably her own (since he has no other wife), against his accusations of infidelity.
  16. See note 6 in the second part of chapter 7. The *jat* (also called *kherrāt*, here translated

—So he
took up his bow and arrow—and he has a blade[17] in his hand »   170
   —that blade that they use for shaving.
He said to his wife, »
   "Give me that— that bow and arrow, I'm going to such-and-such
                                        place, I have work to do."
   —because he didn't <u>know</u> yet.
And he <u>hit</u> the blade against the wall,[18] and she said, »   175
   "Ohh! He's cut off my nose! <u>Yaa-aghhh</u>! On your granddaddy's
                                        corpse!"

They lit a lamp.
The woman's brothers all gathered there, and said— »
   "The poor thing," he said, "It must have been my blade that hit her
                                        nose—" [*laughs*]

[*Audience laughs*]

The next day first thing in the morning the poor shaykh picked up his
                                        coat, ha! »   180
   Run, if you're running!
He said, "The judge is a friend of mine, I'll go [to him]."
He went to the court, and from one direction they were bringing the gypsy,
   that same one, along with
   his wife with the cut-off nose.   185
From the other way they were bringing that guy with the corpse[19]
The judge gave the order, "Kill him in return for her, and cut off his nose in
                                        return for hers."
He got up, the shaykh, and went before the judge, and petitioned.
Said, "Oh, sir."

---

as "gypsy") are a primarily endogamous group of professional musicians, comic actors and
entertainers, blacksmiths and barbers (among other low-status trades), some itinerant for
their professions, but maintaining permanent residences in various cities of Afghanistan.
Their relationship to the European Rom gypsies, if any, is not established. Like the gypsies
in Europe, however, the *jat* were stereotyped by non-*jat* as sharp traders and morally loose.
Their language is a form of Persian. For detailed studies of different *jat* groups, their language, social organization, and professional activities, see Baghban (1977) and Rao (1982).
   17. *gazand*: from the context, a sharp tool, probably a razor, but the word was unfamiliar to Persian-speaking auditors of the tape. The Ākhond's phrasing makes it unclear who or
what is being shaved or scraped smooth with the implement, but barbering is a customary
job of *jat*, making it likely that the edged tool is a razor.
   18. Apparently, by accident.
   19. Literally, "That guy's corpse," a slip of the tongue.

He said, "What do you have to say?"   190
He said, "If I—
      hadn't made that thief my devotee,
          how would he have stolen my money and books?
      If that—
      fox   195
      had contented himself with the blood on the stones,
          how would he have gotten his head broken [*laughs*]
               between the two wild sheep?
      If <u>she</u> hadn't been blowing powdered poison, and if she hadn't
               sneezed, »
          how would it have gotten into her own throat?
      If <u>she'd</u> — hadn't been working for the shoemaker's wife,   200
          how would her nose have gotten cut off?" »
He explained all the circumstances to the judge.[20]
He acquitted them all and left.
It's told that a woman's tricks go to that extreme,
that we, sir—   205
that she could get herself to her lover
and her bastard husband, too— [*Mokhtār*: She took care of her husband,
               too—]
She put one over on her husband, too.
[*M (laughing)*: That's about women's tricks.]
[*Ā laughing*] —about women's tricks, yeah.   210
[*MM laughs*]
[*M to MM*: That's the end.]
[*MM*: Yeah, fine.]
Yeah.
[*Short break to check tape followed by discussion of this story and personal experience
               narrative*]

---

20. The highly elliptical narrative strategy of the shaykh up to this point could be simply the storyteller's "shorthand," saving his listeners a full recapitulation of the story's events which they have just heard, but it closely resembles the literary version of the story, which also uses an elliptical recapitulation at this point, for enigmatic and dramatic effect. See discussion following.

"It's a French schoolmaster!"

Continuing our conversation the next morning, while he was waiting for public transportation back to his village, the Ākhond offered a tale which he entitled "Women's Tricks," and identified its source as the famous fifteenth century C.E. (late ninth century A.H.) tale collection, Wā'iz Kāshifi's *Anwār-i Sohaylī* (see chapter 11). The relationship between the Ākhond's oral performance of a tale and a literary version or versions of it, explored as a possibility in the case of "Salīm the Jeweller" and a high probability with regard to "Mahmūd of Ghaznī and the Thieves," can here be examined as a certainty. Comparison of the way the story is framed and glossed by the Ākhond to its frame and gloss in the literary collection is particularly revealing with regard to the Ākhond's rhetorical techniques and processes of adaptation of literary tales to oral performance contexts. This tale also provides one view of stylistic adaptation of literary material by a traditional oral performer. The Ākhond was one of the most highly educated traditional storytellers I met, conversant with the intricately ornamented Persian literary style. Kāshifi's work (1983), from which he took this tale, is regarded as a model of the intricate style, yet little of that verbal elaboration appeared in the Ākhond's performance of this or other stories.

As in the discussions of "Salīm" and "Mahmūd of Ghaznī" (chapters 6 and 8), an examination of this tale's thematic development in the context of the joint performance of the Ākhond and Karīm will precede a comparison of the Ākhond's performance to its literary antecedent. Like stories preceding and following it, "Women's Tricks" rings changes on themes running throughout the two-part story session. Some of these associations are explicit, some implicit and more readily discerned in juxtaposition to the literary tale which the Ākhond took as his model.

At the most obvious level, this story, like the previous two, begins with acts of thievery and deceit. The main character is a shaykh, a mystic of the charismatic sort whose desire for disciples brings him to grief. This portrayal recalls the Ākhond's distinction between "Sufis of pure faith" and "deficient shaykhs" (chapter 5, ll. 74–76), the issue of legitimate and illegitimate spiritual authority, and the relationship of devotional consciousness to practical life. All these topics have manifested themselves in various ways previously, in "Mulla Mongol the Martyr," "Salīm the Jeweller," " 'Ādel Khān," "Mahmūd of Ghaznī and the Thieves," and in the figure of the old fraud who impersonated a religious man in "The Old Thief with Five Sons."

The female tricksters caught in their own tricks also recall the old man of the previous story, except with regard to gender. The title which the Ākhond chooses for this story, "Women's Tricks," connects its renderings of the female to the sexually demanding, disruptive, and deceptive women in Karīm's " 'Ādel Khān." But these women have no magic about them, only cleverness and, in the case of the shoemaker's wife, a borderline-sacrilegious willingness to risk divine censure (l. 156). Female sexuality and manipulations of female dress were also exploited as a trickster's resource by the disguised hero in "The Old Thief with Five Sons."

Finally, the relationship between public administrative authority and private perspectives on justice reemerges as a theme at the end of the story, when the shaykh explains matters to the *qāżī* (religious judge) who has misjudged the cases. In one way, this story continues a topical movement first evident with "The Old Thief," from public to private spheres of justice. The human problems presented have moved into the most private realm, having to do with the regulation of sexuality. The representative of public authority, the *qāżī*, though present, is only a minor character, not an initiator of major plot action like Mahmūd, 'Ādel Khān, or Hojāj. The person who sees injustice and has the power to correct it, the shaykh, acts as a private individual whose observation of these events is accidental, in the course of private hospitality and that most private of activities, meditative prayer. The shaykh's spatial movement within the story recapitulates a movement from outer to inner, from extrasocial to progressively more intimate spheres: the shaykh departs from his isolated retreat, encounters his first lesson, that of the fox in wild country, along the road to the city, and his second in the house of a stranger at the edge of the city. The third and longest episode takes place in the house of someone who knows him and wants intimate association with him, a disciple, and the final scene, at court, presents the judge as the shaykh's friend and peer, with whom he shares the insight gained from his whole previous experience.

Yet the most intimate personal connection is also a public and institutional one: the shaykh uses his personal friendship with the judge and his private information to insure that public justice is done. But, as in the Ākhond's two previous stories in which central authority figured ("Salīm the Jeweller" and "Mahmūd of Ghaznī and the Thieves"), he stresses restoration rather than retribution. The Ākhond concludes, "He acquitted them all" (l. 203). Private misbehavior reaps its own retribution in death and dismemberment. The state must seek to avoid misapplication of its powers, but ultimately, private and public order are mutually dependent, a configuration which will recur before the storytelling session concludes. All these recurrent themes of the story series—the question of religious consciousness in everyday life, the questions of sexuality and the control of women's disruptive powers, and the problem of right guidance in the sphere of public authority and its relationship to private acts—interact with each other in new ways in the structure of this story.

My own struggle to get the correct title of this particular story written down (ll. 1–9) memorialized on tape my incompetence in Herat dialect and also epitomized several inconsistencies in my own interaction with the storyteller. I was concerned to understand the story title properly because I was at pains to write it down correctly. The fact that I was writing notes in Persian and English while recording the stories was visible to the Āk-hond. The Ākhond valued literacy and schooling for both himself and his children, and the line of our questioning tended to reinforce the idea that stories are part of erudition more broadly defined. Schooling and literacy were central topics in our questioning of both storytellers, followed in the interview format by a question about literary story sources. I had expressed interest in the possible literary connections of the Ākhond's stories, an interest which led, in the conversation that followed this story (chapter 11), to a fuller discussion of his reading activities. I could not comprehend more than perhaps 20 percent of the conversational speech, yet I recognized and wrote down the title of *Anwār-i Sohaylī*, his source for this story (chapter 11, l. 8).

The title he gave the story, "Women's Tricks" (*makr-e zan*), is not its designation in Kāshifī, but a traditional topical designation or generic title, in extended application here. I subsequently found that storytellers attach it to a variety of stories of women who outwit their spouses, some of whom are found out and punished and some not.[1] The stereotype of the naive or stupid female presented in Karīm's "Rasūl's Mother" and the Ākhond's

---

1. The story I most frequently heard told under that title, which I recorded from several different performers, concerned three or four women, wives of the king, the vizier, the *qāżī* (religious judge), and sometimes one other, a merchant's wife or a nonelite woman, who enter into a wager as to who can most thoroughly fool her husband (cf. Marzolph Tale Type 1406 [1984:209] and associated notes). Tales of tricksterish women abound in Marzolph's entire category of Schwankmärchen, balanced by an equal number portraying female fools. Haag-Higuchi (1984:16) notes the recurrence of the topic of women tricksters in the collection she describes and cites a study of the *Tūtīnāmah* (*Book of the Parrot*) by Mahroo Hatemi (1977) which explores positive and negative roles of female tricksters.

"Ten *Qerān*" is complemented by this more negative image of the adult woman trickster, sexually experienced, who manipulates men on behalf of herself or others. By having such difficulty even comprehending the phrase, "women's tricks," I placed myself among the ignorant naïfs. Yet my skills and interest in writing and reading bespoke a degree of education virtually nonexistent among provincial Afghan women.

This story represented a departure for the Ākhond, in his portrayals of women. Up to this point, his female characters had been positive in "Salīm," or in the case of the sister in "Ten *Qerān*," no more foolish than her male counterparts. If clever women were the object of serious criticism by the Ākhond through this story, I was not looking particularly clever in the initial interaction over the story's topic, and when I finally understood it, I received it with embarrassed laughter (l. 8). The joke was on me, perhaps even more than the Ākhond intended. Later, he balanced this picture of disruptive female tricksters with the portrait of a clever and beautiful woman employing trickery in gleeful defense of her own chastity and her husband's honor (chapter 13, "Black and White").

With regard to spiritual matters, this tale presents a more skeptical view than either "Salīm" or "Mahmūd and the Thieves." If the shoemaker's wife were operating on the same spiritual plane as Salīm or the heroes of " 'Ādel Khān," one might expect her head to fly off immediately when she fraudulently petitions for healing (ll. 147–51). The shoemaker's response, "Will the Seat of the Lord accept adultery?" (l. 154) seems a good question, given the apparent lack of divine retribution for her action. But the shaykh has yet to play his role as the agent of both worldly and divine justice.

The shaykh himself has left his retreat for materialistic reasons, in pursuit of the false devotee who has stolen his offering money and books (l. 18). He does not catch the thief, but his observations of the fox and the various women serve as lessons for him concerning worldly desires and their pursuit. The shaykh's impulse is to flee, when he observes such vicious goings-on as his first hostess's sexual entanglements, her murderous scheme and accidental death, and the duplicity of the shoemaker's wife and her gypsy accomplice (ll. 67 and 181). He witnesses these events because he has kept himself awake to engage in the all-night prayer vigil which is a basic part of Sufi devotions. Supposedly so absorbed in prayer and meditation that the perpetrators take no notice of him, the shaykh receives not experiences of mystical union with the divine, but visions of human chicanery which, as he realizes, ultimately reflect on his own character failings (ll. 191–93). He himself has relished the charismatic role of a spiritual leader who attracts valuable offerings and devotees, a worldly attachment which the thief could exploit. Corruption of disciples by masters, or vice versa, is one humorous topic in a very extensive body of traditional Muslim anti-clerical humor (Baghban 1977, 2:407–8). Pretentiousness, hypocrisy, and gullibility are the three roots of Islamic religious humor. Faith itself is not maligned as delusional or ludicrous, only the attempts of foolish and corrupt people to approximate it.

In a tradition that abounds in humorous material critical of would-be religious authorities,[2] this story is as close as either the Ākhond or Karīm gets to anticlericalism. But even the Ākhond's portrait of a shaykh of flawed spirituality does not compromise the dignity of the clergy, of which he himself is a member, nor the "Sufis of pure faith" to whom he has referred. The Ākhond's humorous portrait of Sufi gatherings involving loudly vocal group devotions, such as group recitation and breast-beating (ll. 75–81), jibes with a Naqshbandī Sufi orientation, which he probably had. The Naqshbandī order favors silent devotions rather than the loud group goings-on of which less sober orders are sometimes accused, with music, chant, and uncontrolled ecstatic behavior such as might accommodate a woman trying to rendezvous with her lover.

Mokhtār, aware of the wide range of anticlerical material in the tradition, anticipates that the shaykh himself (whom he revealingly calls "the Ākhond," though shaykhs are not clergy and the two terms are not at all synonymous) will get mixed up with the lascivious doings he observes (l. 108). The real Ākhond is quick to correct him:

"—it's the shoemaker's wife, and the shaykh is there praying, sir.
  Her lover is somebody else." (ll. 110 and 112)

For some moments thereafter, Mokhtār, corrected in such a basic and slightly tactless misunderstanding, is more than usually emphatic with prompts (e.g., ll. 120 and 122, "Yeah, yeah") to assure the Ākhond that he does understand the story.

---

2. Marzolph (1984:27) offers a profile for Iranian Persian oral stories which is roughly accurate for Afghan Persian as well. Generally, he notes that the qāżī (religious judge) is a bribe-taker and the "worst of men," while the mulla, or ākhond, is "a blockhead or an idiot," with Mulla Nasr ud-Dīn as the prototype. (He does not mention lasciviousness and avarice, other failings of shaykhs and clerics in Afghan folk narrative.) Legitimate religious feeling is not represented by institutional persons but by private piety in the figure of the dervish, especially Kheyzr, the archetype of the dervish, and (in Iran) such venerated Shi'a figures as 'Ali, or the martyrs Husayn, Imam Reza or Abol Fazl. The dervish is a wandering, mendicant mystic. The shaykh in this story is a dervish figure facing the temptations of property and status.

In the Ākhond's telling of this story, the *qāżī* who misjudges the cases is the only really misguided religious authority, and his misapprehension is due to a lack of inside information, not to character weakness. The shaykh, whose religious status is a matter of personal devotion rather than institutional responsibility, is an example, like Salīm, of the private individual who bears witness to what he has experienced in order to bring authority figures around to more just action, and whose personal moral development is implicated in his acquisition of insight.

The pattern in which the ordinary man decisively corrects authority figures' opinions or information recurred throughout the evening and morning of stories. This populist view, whereby right judgment is invested in ordinary common sense (informed by Islam) and a worldview directed up from below, is one that has wide credibility among Afghans of different backgrounds, but it is not the only view of authority available in their oral tradition. Two other sources of personal legitimacy of heroes or their allies are noble birth (exemplified by a wide variety of kings, princes, and princesses in fictional folktales) and the distinctions based on faith and/or genealogical relationship to the Prophet, which figure in sacred legend. While the Ākhond does not lampoon clergy or private devotees like the shaykh, neither does he idealize them. He presents charismatic aspects of religious attachment in a persistently negative light, as in this story, or in his portrayal of the inarticulate *sayed* (descendant of the Prophet) from his village (see chapter 11). As his story of Sultan Mahmūd (chapter 8) illustrates, the justice of monarchs is often achieved through their ability to assume the roles and appearance of common men, and princes in folktale and romance more often than not disguise themselves as, or are reduced to the status of, poor nonentities as part of their romantic quests. The ideal of the king who descends to the common level to set himself straight also manifests itself in real life at times. In the waning days of the Pahlavi dynasty in Iran, the anthropologist Thomas Thompson recalled how elders in the village he was studying in northern Iran remarked that Iranian society was in bad shape because the Shah's advisors were keeping the truth from him, and that if the Shah could escape from the court and visit the countryside, he would quickly understand the problems and correct them (Thompson, personal communication, October 1978).

This distribution of ethical legitimacy between ordinary folk and the elite might be partly attributable to the genre, folktales being generally more populist than epics, for instance. But even Afghan interest in epic (which in my collecting experience in the Herat area was limited to some of Rostam's adventures and of the bandit hero Gūrgholī) does not seem to entail much interest in royal genealogical legitimacy, as does the neighboring Iranian tradition centered on the national epic *Shāhnāmah*, in which the royal descent of several heroes is revealed in various manifestations of the *farr*, or aegis of sovereignty. A closer look at the performative aspects of Iranian epic also reveals that the legitimacy and significance of legendary royal exploits is shored up by analogy to or association with Islamic formulations (Page 1977).

In the presence of the subgovernor, the Ākhond and Karīm both made repeated story choices which tended to demystify institutional authority and lodge legitimacy of judgment with common people or authority figures who temporarily assume the role of commoners. Stories bearing that theme are not far to seek in Afghan oral tradition, given the general currency of such populist views. The two storytellers' omission of any explicitly anticlerical matter seems less typical of the general run of popular narrative tradition, especially humorous narrative, wherein anticlerical material is plentiful. While neither storyteller offers any narrative harmful to the dignity of the Ākhond's office, the Ākhond's own stories and comments repeatedly call into question the trustworthiness of religiously based personal charisma. Together, these two thematic trends in the story series place rightly guided religious persons in the company of common men.

The Literary Text and the Oral Performance

When the Ākhond's story is placed alongside its avowed source in *Anwār-i Sohaylī* (*The Lights of Canopus*—the whole collection is described in chapter 11), certain differences immediately command attention. One is the title: this is the first tale for which the Ākhond had a ready topical title, "Women's Tricks," but Kāshifī did not so designate the story. It appears as the seventh story in the first of the collection's fourteen sections and in the table of contents is entitled "The story of the ascetic and the thief of [his] clothes, and the explanation of the danger of selfish desires,"[3] where "self" translates the word *nafs*, which in Muslim terminology designates the lower, or carnal, soul. Another pertinent topical summary of the tale, from Kāshifī's point of view, is to be found within the text. The tale is framed as a fable told by Kalīlah—a jackal who, though attached to the court of the

---

3. This title is the author's translation from a standard Persian edition of *Anwār-i Sohaylī* (Kāshifī 1983/1362). In Wollaston's English translation (1904:79–84), the story is the eighth in the section.

Lion who is King of the Beasts, has abstained from courtly intrigue—to Dimnah, a second jackal, whose self-destructive machinations form the frame tale of the collection. Dimnah has sought the favor of the Lion, by acting as go-between for the king and an ox who has wandered into the lion's domain, and in the process Dimnah exploits the mutual fear of the two potential adversaries. The Lion comes to admire and prefer the ox Shanzabah and ignore Dimnah, so that Dimnah resents the ox and wants to bring about his destruction. Kalīlah introduces the tale of the ascetic, as the shaykh is called, with proverbs in verse and in prose which he quotes to Dimnah with reference to Dimnah's political activities,

> "My beloved, you did it yourself.
>> There is no way to manage what one has oneself done.
> And you have struck your own foot with your own axe, and raised the dust of your own mischief on your own path, and to you has happened that which befell the Ascetic." (Kāshifī 1983:91)

Kāshifī's Dimnah repeats the same assessment of self-inflicted harm twice more in the story, with other proverbs and verse aphorisms, once after the death of the ascetic's first hostess and again at some length in the final scene when the ascetic explains matters to the judge.[4] He mentions the theme of women's tricks directly only once in a verse introducing the barber's wife who panders for the shoemaker's wife and has her nose cut off. She alone among the women is accused of engaging in mischievous magic to further her pandering activities (Kāshifī, p. 94). Thus, the stated moral of the tale in Kāshifī's collection is not primarily about women's tricks, but about the self-inflicted harm of reprehensible actions. Kalīlah concludes the tale with another prose aphorism.

> "Whoever does wrong must not expect good, and whoever seeks sugar cane should not plant the seeds of the wild gourd," (Kāshifī p. 97)

and more verses to the same effect.

The Ākhond, characteristically, omits from his oral performance almost all the overt moral glossing of events, either in prose or verse aphorisms, which are a particularly relentless feature of Kāshifī's text (Kāshifī's

---

4. Cf. Marzolph (1984:150–51), Tale Type 837, "Alles, was du tust, tust du dir selbst," the same moral theme apparently with different exempla, one of which concerns a female would-be poisoner who kills not herself but one of her loved ones in lieu of her intended victim. Marzolph also quotes other associated proverbs.

title, "*Wā'iż*," means "preacher"). The first such proverb attached to the literary tale, "You have struck your own foot with your own axe," recalls precisely how the "Mongol Martyr" achieved his dubious martyrdom, and that proverb may have served as an additional, unspoken mnemonic for the Ākhond in choosing this story. Self-inflicted harm was central to the Ākhond's brief concluding gloss to the last story told the night before (chapter 9, l. 183: "the treacheries that their father had done, [came down] on their heads to that degree"), and further back, in Karīm's portrayal of the barber's misfortune (when he was castrated, the barber called himself a "miserable *kosah*" [ll. 464–66 and footnote], the *kosah* being a stock folktale trickster who is generally caught by his own machinations). Nor does the Ākhond entirely neglect the topic of self-inflicted harm in favor of women's tricks in this tale: his shaykh, in the final law-court scene, connects his own misfortune in taking the thief as a disciple with the misfortunes of others who harm themselves through self-serving actions (ll. 191–203). But the Ākhond follows that observation by the shaykh, and concludes the story, with his own observation about the power of women's tricks (ll. 204–8).

In service of that emphasis, the Ākhond moves with uncharacteristic rapidity through the first incidents of the story, until the shaykh arrives at the first woman's house. Generally speaking, the Ākhond would begin a tale with single propositions in short phrases and frequent pauses, including some reiteration of basic points, during which the listeners by eye contact or prompts could indicate their comprehension and attention (e.g., chapter 5, ll. 93–132; chapter 6, ll. 15–29; and chapter 8, ll. 18–32). "Women's Tricks," by contrast, begins with a series of rapidly narrated compound sentences (ll. 11–12, 17–18, and 19–20), and moves quickly through the original theft which motivated the shaykh's departure and the incident of the fox (ll. 20–32).

Thus, in the Ākhond's telling, the main theme of the literary original, the self-destructiveness of bad actions, becomes a subtext secondary to the stated topic of "women's tricks." The literary version itself also has its main moral text, and a less directly stated, corollary subtext. The main text, repeated in direct statements, verses, and proverbs, is "You brought this on yourself." The subtext, illustrated by the shaykh's own experience with his false disciple and the destruction of the fox and the two women, is "Do not try to exploit the passions of others." The Ākhond's focus on women's tricks and sexual passions as themes tends to reduce the illustrative force of the shaykh's first experience, with the fox destroyed by the rams. The literary version of the demise of the would-be murderess makes her clearly exploitive of others' passions, a whoremonger who is planning to kill the lover of one of her girls in order to regain control of the girl's earning potential. Her motivation for trying to kill the young man (not the girl) is thus not personal but strictly financial because the two lovers refuse her attempts to introduce the girl to other clients. As a bawdyhouse-keeper, she invites the stranger in, in the way of business, not because of a lover's hopeful but mistaken recognition as in the Ākhond's story. In Kāshifi's version, the ascetic arrives at the town after the gates are shut for the night and, confused and tired, accepts hospitality at a house outside the gates without realizing the nature of the place. He apparently assumes that hospitality is offered in deference to his spiritual standing. The Ākhond transfers the confusion from the shaykh to the woman looking for her lover (ll. 46–48), then switches the victims and presents the woman's attempted murder of her servant girl as a crime of passion, undertaken in a rage when she discovers that her lover is unfaithful. These changes remove an element of calculating exploitation from her character and considerably increase the human drama of the episode. The literary version, by making her a panderer, lines her up more closely with the fox who licked the blood of the fighting rams, the barber's wife, and the ascetic himself, who was willing to exploit the devotional fervor of others for the self-gratification of having disciples. Not just any selfish desires, but the particularly bloodless selfishness of those who would exploit others' passions and affections, is Kāshifi's subtext.

The Ākhond makes another change in narrative detail which also has the effect of rendering a malefactor in this story more sympathetic. In the literary version, the ascetic has been given rich garments, a suit of clothes and a robe of honor, by a king who admires him. It is these badges of worldly status that the thief-disciple steals. In the Ākhond's version, the shaykh loses both a large sum of money given to him as alms and his books, but it is the books that he chiefly regrets losing and seeks to recover:

He served him for two or three months and one day the shaykh went to perform ablutions,
and he gathered up his books and the ten thousand *afghānī* and ran off,
left.
The shaykh came back and his heart really burned for those books, and
following his trail, he picked up his walking stick
and set off after him. (ll. 17–19)

In the conversation following this story (chapter 11), the Ākhond described his own passion for books and reading in a way that suggests a degree of sympathy with the shaykh for the loss of his library, and perhaps also a note of self-parody. For traditional Afghan Muslims, as for Jews, all books and writings partake of some degree of the respect and veneration due the Holy Writ. Of possible material possessions, the shaykh's books, presumably on religious subjects, are the least venal. My own interest in books, expressed in the interview and conversational remarks, may also have supported this portrayal of the shaykh.

The Ākhond's joking references to noisy group devotional practices of certain Sufi groups (ll. 75 and 80–81) are also his own and not found in Kāshifī's story. In Kāshifī, the shoemaker is simply invited to dine out with friends and the lover attempts to meet the wife at her home in the shoemaker's absence, but the shoemaker, returning early, sees him hanging around the gate and gives his suspicions free rein. The Ākhond uses the idea of a lovers' rendezvous during a Sufi gathering, apparently at or near the shoemaker's home, to take a sly dig at the potential for insincerity and the indulgence of venal passions in outwardly showy styles of religious expression that he does not greatly respect. In so doing, he makes the shoemaker's wife, like her pandering gypsy friend, somewhat of a manipulator of others' passions in pursuit of her own ("I'll go there too and beat my breast," ll. 81 and 106). But he does not develop his theme with the consistency that Kāshifī does throughout the tale's episodes, only in reference to matters of faith, themes touched on elsewhere in his stories and comments during this visit.

Afghans like other Muslims make a distinction between *nafs*, the earthly or carnal soul, and *rūh*, the immortal, spiritual soul. *Nafs*, which is mortal, is the seat of carnal passions and desires. *'Aql*, the wisdom that engenders thoughtfulness and self-control, must be cultivated over time and lived experience in order to master the *nafs* and to avoid precisely the sorts of errors perpetrated by the characters in this story. Women are thought to have a stronger *nafs* than men, and consequently, less capacity for *'aql*.[5] Tricksterish women such as these are clever (*zīrak*) in the service

---

5. The topic of the *'aql/nafs* dichotomy in Islamic moral discourse has cropped up widely in Middle Eastern anthropology, but so far, without a comprehensive overview. Relevant discussion can be found in Anderson (1985:203–11 and 1982:397–420), and Rosen (1978:561–84). Daisy Dwyer (1978) uses folktales as part of her primary data for examining traditional constructions of gender and character but neglects even the most obvious contextual information crucial to the interpretation of such materials, such as the age, gender, and social status

of *nafs*, their own or others', whereas one *should* strive to be wise (*'āqel*) in the service of *rūḥ*.

The emphasis the Ākhond placed on the character of women, in reframing this tale as "Women's Tricks," reflects interestingly on his original denial of any knowledge of the "disposition of women" (chapter 5, l. 81). Given time over night to recall Mokhtār's teasing about his knowledge of women and to think of other stories, he offered in his morning performance two which directly concerned the "disposition of woman," this one and "Black and White" (chapter 13). If the Ākhond's portrayals of rightly and wrongly guided authority figures can be interpreted to reflect his relationship with the Woləswāl, then perhaps this portrayal of women who are clever but not wise can also be taken as a veiled comment to present company, to a female whose peculiar mix of intellectual capacities and incapacities is being applied to unclear ends, namely myself. But even if my presence did inspire the choice of the two stories, "Women's Tricks" and "Black and White," each sustained other themes pertinent to the history of the Ākhond and Woləswāl and the question of public and private order and disorder. In any case, orderly sexuality is centrally implicated in the healthy operation of religiously based public and private ethics, the pervasive theme of his performance. Balancing the theme of disorderly women which dominates "Women's Tricks," "Black and White" offers a female hero, like the disguised male hero of "The Old Thief," acting in a private capacity on behalf of social order.

Another possible but implicit level of congruency among "Women's Tricks," other elements of the performance series, and the personal history of the Ākhond and Woləswāl, can be traced in the origin legend associated with the story collection called *Kalīlah and Dimnah* or *Anwār-i Sohaylī*. According to the legend (reported by De Sacy, in connection with his translation of the older, Arabic *Kalīlah wa Dimnah*, cf. Wollaston 1904:xi–xv), the story collection was written down in India by the wise Brahmin vizier Bīdpāī at the behest of the sometime tyrant Dābshelīm, who had wrested his throne from a governor appointed by Alexander the Great after his legendary conquest of India. Among Dābshelīm's initial tyrannical acts was the jailing of the wise man, who tried to steer him away from excesses of power. After Bīdpāī had been incarcerated for some time, the king was made sleepless by bad conscience, released the vizier, and commissioned

of the tellers of individual tales and her sources for generalizing statements used to corroborate her interpretations.

him to write a book which would both instruct kings in right behavior and guide and entertain ordinary people. The *Fables of Bīdpāī*, known in Arabic as *Kalīlah wa Dimnah*, and in Kāshifī's later Persian translation as *Anwār-i Sohaylī*, was the result.

This origin legend was connected with the Arabic version of the work, translated from a now-lost Middle Persian text in the mid-ninth century C.E. (third century A.H.). Kāshifī substituted a less contentious portrayal of Dābshelīm the King and Bīdpāī the Brahmin storyteller, within an outer frame concerning yet another king and *his* vizier, who repeats Bīdpāī's stories at the king's request. The older origin legend parallels both the story of Salīm and Hojāj, and the Ākhond's earlier experience of jail at the hands of the Woləswāl followed by his invitation to perform stories. Although the Ākhond did not retell the legend, it is part of a larger associative context for the story which he used to illustrate his knowledge of literature, and the aptness of the older origin legend to the Ākhond's circumstances leads one to suspect that he knew it. A surmise of this kind can only be tested by sensitive follow-up conversations with the storyteller, which circumstances did not permit, but the resonance of the origin legend with the larger context of the performance is too provocative to be ignored outright.

According to later auditors of the tapes, *Anwār-i Sohaylī*, though a well-known text in the traditional Muslim educational system,[6] was not much used in the government school systems; hence, the work and the legend of its origin were probably not familiar to the Woləswāl. Even were the particulars of the origin legend of the story collection not consciously on the Ākhond's mind, the work's overall stated purpose as a mirror for magistrates would be impossible to ignore. The legend of Bīdpāī's imprisonment and release is supplemented by the other "advisory" frame tale, which begins Kāshifī's text, in which another king, Homāyūn-e Fāl, asks his vizier to tell him the famous stories of Bīdpāī and Dābshelīm so that he can learn from them. The individual tales of the collection are thus nested into a three-layered frame (Homāyūn and his vizier, Dābshelīm and Bīdpāī, the two jackals conversing), each layer of which reinforces the didactic, cautionary import of the stories, their connection with principles of gov-

---

6. Rypka (1968:313) and Ghani (1988:431); Schimmel (1978:40–41) describes the attachment of Muslim scholars, mystics, and poets to the work. The Ākhond's comments in chapter 11 corroborate her assessment.

ernance, and the idea of a storyteller enlightening a sovereign at the sovereign's request.

The Ākhond omits most of the direct moral commentaries embedded in Kāshifī's text in the form of verses and proverbs. In particular, he quotes none of Kāshifī's many verses and couplets, whether morally interpretive or ornamental. Also omitted from the Ākhond's performance are the frequent and tendentious lists of types of people and varieties of human reactions to circumstances which Kāshifī puts into the mouths of various characters. Kāshifī's enumerations of, e.g., all the kinds of disappointed courtiers of whom a king must be wary, or in the case of this story, in Dimnah's response to his friend's narrative, a list of the five contingencies in which men of intelligence may be pardoned for taking action, serves in a way to keep the literary text interpretively open. Through such lists the reader is invited to consider a range of possible pertinencies. The narrative flow of the literary text is at times delayed for the listing of circumstances which do not apply directly to the events at hand.

The Ākhond and other oral performers of literary material whom I recorded (drawing from such works as Rūmī's *Mathnavī* or Naqshabī's *Tūtīnāmah*) tended to reduce or omit metanarrative material of this sort, leaving the narrative interpretively open at a more basic level. In their hands, a multiepisodic tale such as "Women's Tricks" became not a meditation on a repeated set of aphorisms but a kind of interpretive puzzle in the course of which the listener was left to infer the connecting theme in a series of complex and apparently diverse plot events. Analysis of the shared significance of the story's events, if such was offered, was usually contained in a brief concluding statement, as in ll. 204–10 of the present example. In general, interpretations were more likely to be left implicit in oral performances than in their literary prototypes, but interpretive openness is served in both oral and literary formulations, by different techniques located differently in the flow of each complex discourse. The statement and counterstatement built into literary frame-tale collections are generally silenced in oral performances which dislodge single elements from such complex written structures, but the oral performers then reframe these units in the living performance context at a different level of statement and counterstatement (some of which may be implicit, unspoken, or articulated in another context, see chapter 16).

The Ākhond omitted not only interpretation but most of the verbal ornamentation of his literary model, despite his stated admiration for its language (chapter 11, ll. 13–20). The book presents numerous extended metaphors (e.g., for the dawn rising) and detailed, stereotypic descriptions of the charms of various characters. Introductory sections are the most ornate, after which hyperbolic description and metaphor subside somewhat in favor of more straightforward narration. Both narration and reported speech are embellished with rhymed-prose sequences, parallel syntactic structures which give the text a rolling cadence and symmetry of detail as well as a level of redundancy which may be of practical use for readers and listeners unfamiliar with literary vocabularies. The Ākhond also omits the physical descriptions of various lovers on which Kāshifī lavishes such eloquence. Although the Ākhond was perhaps the most conversant with classical Persian literature of all the storytellers I recorded, he made less use of literary-style verbal ornamentation than some others whose literacy was more limited or even doubtful. The question of the educational status of narrators and the claims they made to various kinds of authority through their choice of words is a complex one (explored with respect to four narrators, including the Ākhond, in Mills 1984). Relative to other narrators' greater use both of literary-style verbal ornamentation and of oral formulas of opening, closure, and description, one might see the Ākhond's plainer style as an understatement of the craftedness of speech, part of a general strategy to downplay his narrations as performances, and integrate them more with general, conversational observations of the passing human scene for didactic and critical purposes which, for tactical reasons, he kept implicit. A comparison of his narrative style in this performance to that of other master narrators I recorded suggests that the performers' level of education does not correlate simply with speech styles: others, far less educated than he, were assiduous users of literary-style ornamentation, through which they assimilated their performances to the classical literary aesthetic and thus made claims to erudite verbal artistry and control.

In one obvious respect, the Ākhond's language is more colorful than Kāshifī's. Generally speaking, his reported speech is earthier and more vehement, while Kāshifī, though hyperbolic, remains decorous. For instance, Kāshifī's gypsy woman, returning home bleeding with her nose in her hand, does not know whether to laugh or to cry, and remarks philosophically, "What a strange affair! One has tasted the pleasure, another has experienced the pain!" (Kāshifī 1983:95). Whereas Kāshifī makes even the shoemaker in his rage address his wife chastely, "Oh, wicked, corrupt [woman]" (p. 96), the Ākhond gives lively and frequent renditions of Herati oral cursing styles (ll. 92–94, 103–4, 117–18, 135, 162–63, and 176). The freedom of language throughout this joint performance surprised Mokhtār and made him deem these tapes unsuitable for the ears of the Ministry of Culture. Other later auditors also remarked on the roughness of the language, considering the audience and setting (cf. Başgöz 1975). One listener educated in the modern urban school system judged the narrators incompetent on this basis. It seems to me that they both challenged listeners' sensibilities deliberately and collaboratively, each man modulating the effect differently so that Karīm functioned as something of a foil for the slightly more restrained Ākhond.

In a few places, the Ākhond appears not to control his own words, perhaps confused by Kāshifī's language, perhaps feeling a need to clarify matters. Both Kāshifī and the Ākhond call the "wild animals" whose blood the fox licks *nakhchīr* (Steingass: "beasts of prey; wild goats"), but the Ākhond and his listeners then negotiate the meaning of the word (ll. 20–24). The word is not common, nor are such wild sheep as the Ākhond has in mind. The two types of indigenous horned animal to which the term best applies are ibex and Marco Polo sheep, now found only at high altitudes in the eastern part of the country, far from Herat.

When the shoemaker ties up his wife, Kāshifī has him bind her hand and foot to a wooden pillar (*sotūn*) in the house, but Herati houses have no pillars. The hanging wooden object the Ākhond describes is somewhat indeterminate (ll. 90, 97, and 137). Kāshifī's word, *sotūn*, is the same one used in the chapbook *Salīm the Jeweller* for the iron club Salīm carried, an object which also seemed unclear in the Ākhond's description (chapter 4, ll. 340, 353–54, etc.). The word itself seems to be a source of uncertainty for him in both contexts, increasing the likelihood that the Ākhond had read or heard the chapbook version of *Salīm*, where that term was used, and remembered it without really knowing its meaning.

The Ākhond also seems uncertain what tools the gypsy woman's husband wanted her to give him or what his profession was. *Gazand* (l. 170 and footnote) is not a common word in Herat City dialect. I never was able to elicit a confident explanation of it from auditors of the tape, though the context would imply "razor" and the man's *jat* identity makes the profession of barber a likely inference for Herati listeners. Kāshifī makes it clear enough that the object is a razor (*ostarah*) and the man is a barber or cupper (*hajām*), but perhaps these terms were not common in Herat. The Ākhond's addition of a bow and arrows (l. 173) seems confused. These verbal confusions retained in his performance suggest the Ākhond's close dependence on the written text, even including some words of which he was not sure.

These few minor confusions are balanced by the Ākhond's eye for the human detail which he interpolates into his performance, such as his portrayal of Sufi activities, or his brief but vivid description of the blood-stained clothing of the shoemaker's wife and how she uses the blood on her clothes to convince her husband that she was really mutilated and then healed (l. 146). He also enhances the drama of the final court scene by adding to the scene the wrongly accused lover and the corpse of the would-be poisoner (l. 186), which Kāshifī did not include. While the Ākhond avoids the embellishments of rhyme and alliterative parallel constructions which are abundant in Kāshifī and used more by other storytellers more bent on pure entertainment, he has a lively eye for the human foibles that form the ethical backbone of the narrative. Kāshifī's ascetic observes the role-switching machinations of the shoemaker's wife and the gypsy woman with "astonishment mounting on astonishment" at "those wonders that appeared from behind the veil of the unseen." The Ākhond reserves his expression of astonishment for the bold hypocrisy of the shoemaker's wife (l. 163). The malefactors' actions and their outcomes are not just marvelous or surprising, but also, from the shaykh's point of view, reflections on his own moral weakness and activities. In the Ākhond's version of the story, it is the shaykh alone, not an omniscient interpretive voice from the outside (such as Kāshifī supplies) who infers a critique of his own actions from his observation of others. As in daily life, the interpretation of experience is left to the experiencing subject. The shaykh takes responsibility for seeing in events "a warning to whoso would be warned," as the oft-quoted Qur'anic verse has it. By the Ākhond's general de-emphasis of didactic commentary, the storytelling audience is left to decide whether to follow the shaykh's example.

11. "Fill a Pipe for the Ākhond!": The Ākhond and the Rabbi of Herat

Mokhtār: Uh— from where did you learn this— from— who told you
this story?

Ākhond: By God, sir, I read books a lot.

M: OK, this was from a book, the book of—?

Ā: Yes, yes. [*MM*: Ah, yeah—]

M: What's the name of the book? This one—   5

Ā: The *Lights of Canopus*,[1] sir.

M: Lights—?

Ā: *Lights of Canopus*, that's [also] known [*MM*: Oh, yes, *Lights of*
                                  Canopus—] as *Kalīlah and Dimnah*.

M: *Lights of Canopus*.

Ā: Yes. [*Mokhtār*: Yes. *MM*: Yes.]   10
It's known as the *Lights*— as *Kalīlah*— sir, it's just—
[*MM*: *Kalīlah and Dimnah*—]
It's the kind of book, sir, that if a person has the time to read it, totally,
he doesn't need any other, sir,
it's a schoolmaster,   15
it's a <u>French</u> schoolmaster [even],
this— <u>all</u> the works of the world are used in it, [*M*: Yeah.]
[*intensely*] they <u>didn't</u> leave a <u>thing</u> out, sir!
[*M*: Yeah.]
You could say it's all— like in the language of the animals, and verses of
                           the Qur'an, and sayings of the Prophet, and
                           His exemplary actions, for proof. [*coughs*]   20
[*M, looking at interview question list*: Good. *MM*: Good.]
‹›

---

1. One of the best known literary collections of moral tales in Persian, *Anwār-i Sohaylī* is the Timurid-period (late fifteenth or early sixteenth century C.E.; ninth to tenth century A.H.) version of a tale collection of Indian origin (see discussion below and in chapter 10).

M: Do you have that book now?

Ā: No, sir, it belonged to an Ākhond, I borrowed it. The Ākhond—

M (*interrupting, speaking rapidly*): How many years ago did you learn it?

Ā: I, sir— I read the *Lights of Canopus* over f—   25
  four times.

[*MM*: Uh-huh. *M*: Good.]

There's a <u>lot</u>— twelve—

um— thirteen sections, sir,

fourteen sections.   30

<u>Every</u> one of them, sir, about government,

about teaching,

about society, and the Sufis and— <u>every</u> kind,

sir, it's a very marvelous book.

And I, to the extent of my power, sir,   35
  when I'm at home,
   —I have a lot of children.
   And I do have two wives. [*M*: Yeah—God protect them.[2]]

When I eat my meals, I don't stay with them. »
  I go to my room.   40

"Where's the Ākhond?" — "He's <u>asleep</u>!"

<>

I say, "Fuck your thick pricks!" —I'm peacefully looking over books,
                by myself.

[*M laughs*]

I pray there, sir, and I'm lying down,
  looking at books.
  To the extent of my strength.   45

[*M*: Yeah.]

And then, it was a kindness from God, sir, that from the time of the
           Rooster King[3] I was studying, »
  and my friends didn't put me in the mill.

[*M*: Yeah.]

---

2. *Nām-e khodā*, literally "in the Name of God," a protective blessing intended to avert harm, especially the evil eye, from things or especially persons precious to another person, when they are mentioned in conversation.

3. Speculative translations here. *Be sannah ye Khorūs Pādshāh*: "from the time of the Rooster King"? cf. English, "From when Hector was a pup"? "The mill": understanding *kherrās* as an oil-seed mill or other mill turned by an animal, tended by one man (so by extension, working at some menial physical labor). The word is somewhat unclear on the tape, and may also be *khorras*, a Herati term for snoring, however, and if so: "My friends didn't allow any sleeping, either."(?)

By the Lord, sir, whether I'm in the city, in Bād Morghān,   50
    whether I go to the— the city itself,
    in Bād Morghān or in Jakkon, or Qeyzon,[4]
I have over a <u>hundred</u> households of relatives, fathers-in-law and
                                               suchlike.
As God is present and watching, sir, if I'm with relatives in the city for
                                      two months, »
    I won't be in one place (twice).   55

Right now these
    people who— in the city, now, people talk to each other, every-
                             one— [*inaudible phrase*]
[*M*: Yes.]
One time, sir— I'll tell you with my own tongue.
Back when the city was full of Jewish people,[5]   60
[*M*: Yeah—]
I was going to the Malek Gate.[6]
[*M*: Uh--huh.]
There's a descendant of the Prophet[7] from our village, by the name of
                'Abdullah Jān, and, now, the Jewish
                 clergy[8] are recognizable, sir,
    they have beards like this [*gestures to show a long beard*]   65
    and they have remarkable clergy—

---

4. All now sections of Herat City, located south and east of the congregational mosque and the central bazaar (*Chār Sū*), which the Ākhond refers to as "the city itself." See Map No. 3.

5. According to Herati informants, there was a substantial Jewish community in Herat, which was expelled by the young king, Zaher Shah, in connection with the financial difficulties of the mid-1930s, at the same time that there was a general expulsion of Hindu merchants from Afghanistan. Hindus and Jews are allowed to offer loans at interest, which is forbidden to Muslims, but their business activities make them easy scapegoats in times of fiscal crisis. There is a substantial community of Afghan origin in Israel, some of whose oral traditions have been recorded and archived by Israeli scholars (Galit Hasan-Rokem, personal communication 1988). The return of large numbers of Jewish émigrés to Afghanistan, noted by Dupree (1973:111), was not noticed in Herat. Muslims estimated that half a dozen households remained in the 1970s.

6. A major bazaar area on the west side of the city.

7. Called *āqā* in Herat, as well as *sayed* (the more general term), individuals who claim descent from the Prophet enjoy special prestige and are often professionally involved in religious activities.

8. *mojtahedā*: '*ajīb* "amazing, remarkable" in the next sentence implies well-developed, well-versed and powerful in scholarship. The *mojtahed* is an interpreter of doctrine and scholar of jurisprudence, particularly important in Shi'a Islam, and the Ākhond, although himself a Sunni, not a Shi'a Muslim, makes this apt analogy to the training and role of Jewish rabbis.

One time that *āqā* of ours said to me, "Come on, Ākhond, sir,
                                        to the shop."
[*M*: The Jews.]
No, that —village *āqā* of ours.   70
He was acquainted with them, the Jews.
You could tell he [another individual] was clergy for them, anyway.
[*M*: Oh, yeah—]
When I stepped in [to the shop], he said, "Fill a pipe for the Ākhond."
        —I'm so full of <u>talk</u>!⁹   75
[*M*: Yes.]
I said, "I don't smoke a pipe from the hands of a Jew."
[*M*: Oh, yeah—]
They pressured me [*claps once*]!
"Don't you accept the influence of your own Prophet?   80
        Your Prophet
        made marriage with us lawful for you,
        because we are people of the Book.¹⁰
[*M*: Yeah.]
        Meat slaughtered at our hands is lawful to you.   85
You say that, there —we—
        —you said—Don't you obey your own Prophet?" »
[I thought] "Oh, Lord, Blessed One, help [me] here!"
[*M laughs*]
I said, "Look, there's two terms.
        One is what is discouraged, according to one's inclination,¹¹
                                        one permitted—   90
        —completely forbidden.¹²
        What's discouraged according to one's inclination—if a fly falls in
                        one's tea, if one's own inclination demands,
                        he drinks the tea, and if not, he pours it out.

---

9. The host anticipates that they will talk for some time and wants to entertain his guest.
    10. Under Muslim law, Jews and Christians are afforded freedom of religion and certain other legal protections not afforded unbelievers, because they follow the same prophetic tradition as Muslims and have a revealed scripture, though they fail to recognize Muhammad's completion of the prophetic succession. The Torah and Gospels are regarded by Muslims as Divine Word, predecessors of the Qur'an which have been edited and distorted by misguided Jewish and Christian interpreters.
    11. *makruh-e tabʿai*.
    12. *harām*. In a slip of the tongue, the Ākhond first says *halāl* ("permitted, lawful").

It's true that meat slaughtered at your hands is [lawful but]
>   discouraged by the Prophet, it doesn't suit my inclination.
>   So meat slaughtered at your hands[13]
>   isn't completely unlawful for us, anyway.   95
>   When did I say it was unlawful?"
Then he said, "Look!
>   We people are
>   people of the Book.
[*M*: Yes.]   100
>   These Shī'a people
>   don't have a book.
>   You mix with their society.
>   You eat their food. [*Mokhtār*: Yeah.]
>   You marry with them, talk to them.   105
>   Well, they're not people of the Book, either.[14]
>   Well, we're people of the Book, as you—" »
I said, "Now look,
>   —I'll tell you one thing." »
He said, "Say it."   110
I said, "You say there are Shī'a people in this city of Herat. »
>   I could take your hand,
>   walk you around to all these households, »
>   and if they won't [all] say our statement of faith aloud,
[*M*: Yeah—]   115
>   And if they don't accept our brotherhood in religion,
[*M (more faintly)*: Yeah—]
>   as sure as I'm sitting here right now—aren't I?" »
—he said, "Yeah—" »
I said, "If you say 'There is no God but God and Mohammed is His
>   Prophet,' you can wash your testicles
>   I'll drink the water!"   120
[*Audience laughter. M*: Bābā—]

---

13. The logic used by the Ākhond extends the idea of *zeb'*, ritual slaughter, to include all consumables prepared by Jews, including tobacco for smoking. Smoking is considered to be ingestion and by that token, is forbidden along with food during the daylight hours in Ramazan, the month of fasting.
14. The rabbi cites an extreme anti-Shī'a position sometimes argued among Sunni Muslims. For details, see below, this chapter.

"All right, if some guy says the statement of faith,
   prays in our company, on what grounds would we call him
                                           an unbeliever?"
[*M*: He was trying to stir up divisiveness—]
Look!   125
I said, "You say right now, 'There is no God but God and Mohammed
                  is His Prophet,' and you can wash your testicles
                  and I'll drink the water!"
[*M (amid laughter)*: Use his penis for a hand-mill—]
[*Ā laughs*] —Let his penis be the pipestem!
Then he said, sir, the Āqā said, "Brother, why don't you become
                                           a Muslim?"
He said, "Oh, brother   130
      what are you saying, Āqā?"
            —our Āqā knew him.
[*M*: Yeah—]
He said, "There's adultery—you [Muslims] commit adultery.
      You steal.   135
      We have twenty or thirty thousand households,[15] »
            [though] we don't own a single *dāng* of lands,[16] »
      have you seen [even] one beggar among us? »
      And didn't your Prophet prohibit begging? »
      When do we [ever] have beggars? »   140
      What is it to you? Who are you? Now, why should we bother
                                           with such a religion?"
The Āqā shut up. [*Audience member laughs*]
"Ayy, Āqā, shut up," I said, [*in high, tight voice—perhaps as soliloquy*]
"Let him talk to me, ehh— bastard!"
I said to him "What are you saying?"
◇   145
I said, "Is the devil crazy that he would work among you for his credit, »
      like Pharaoh?

---

15. A considerable exaggeration of the size of the Herat Jewish community, though it
may have numbered several thousand individuals at the time of the events described. Even by
the mid-1970s, no thorough census had been undertaken for Afghanistan, and exact numbers
of ethnic groups were unavailable.

16. One *dāng* equals 1/6 of a *jerīb*, which is approximately 0.5 acre, according to Smith
et al. (1973:427).

[*M*: Yeah—]
> From the time that the Prophet of the Last Times[17] appeared,
>> you completely and totally lost[18] religion. 150

[*M*: Yeah—]
> All right. When you— it's written in the Torah, the Gospel, and
>>> the Qur'an, »
>> that when Mohammed appears, our other religions are ab-, ab-

[*M prompts*: —abolished.]
>> abolished. 155
> When you didn't accept [Islam], you became Jews.

All right, the devil works for his own credit, ja—
> if there aren't any grapes in the garden, »
>> where is the jackal that would come around howling?

[*M*: What use is it to him?] 160
> Where are the flies that would buzz around a jar with no honey in it?

[*M*: Mm-hmm.]
> All right, the devil has uses for <u>us</u>.
> In that mine of gold and silver that is our breast,

[*M*: Yeah—] 165
> those devils are in my body, I that am a mulla, »
> if even <u>one</u> remained in your place, by your beard, »
> if you wouldn't have fucked your own mother thirty times, you can
>> spit in my face!"

[*Audience laughter*]
> "Get up, Āqā, you couldn't even answer one foreigner!
> How are you going to rely on this kind of mediation on the
>> Judgment Day? » 170
> Get up, you *kūnī*!"

We got up and went out before he stopped us with <u>another</u> one, [*laughing*] »
> now that I'd gotten us out of that!

Every time I passed by there, sir, those rabbis would greet me with both
>> hands!

---

17. Mohammed is the "Seal of the Prophets" according to Muslim doctrine. Groups such as the Bahā'īs or the Yazīdī Kurds, who recognize a continuation of the prophetic tradition subsequent to Mohammed's message, are regarded as apostate, a far worse offense than remaining loyal to one's ancestral religion in the face of the Islamic prophecy, which Jews and Christians are regarded as doing.

18. *bāy dādī*: literally, "gambled away, lost (in a game or wager)" (from *bākhtan*).

[*Ā laughs*]
But seriously, the Lord intended [it], sir,   175
    and if not,
sir, the Noble Mathnavī—
[*The conversation was interrupted by the entrance of more guests, just as the Āk-
hond was about to launch into a discussion of Jalāl ud-Dīn Rūmī's* Mathnavī-e
Maʿanavī. *Mokhtār gestures to Mills, to turn off the tape recorder, Mills replies in
English,* "I wanted to record some conversation . . ."]

"They have remarkable clergy . . ."

The personal experience narrative which the Ākhond constructed after he finished the story he called "Women's Tricks" moves between two main topics. The first, concerning his reading habits and particularly the virtues of *Anwār-i Sohaylī*, the story collection from which he had taken the previous story, was prompted by our expressed interest in the use he made of written sources for storytelling. From the topic of his solitary home reading habits, he moved briskly to mention his many connections in Herat City and, thence, to retelling the personal narrative of his religious debate with a Jewish rabbi of Herat, which occupied most of this segment of conversation. Such debate is a basic part of mullas' training and professional activities (cf. Fischer 1982). At the end of that story, he reintroduced the topic of authoritative texts, in particular the *Mathnavī-e Maʿanavī* of Jalāl ud-Dīn Rūmī, the masterful verse collection of hundreds of tales, anecdotes, proverbs, and aphorisms all interwoven with the most intricate of mystical meditations, known as "the Qurʿan in Persian tongue." Unfortunately, we did not get to hear his views on this work, the probable source of his version of the story of Mahmūd and the Thieves (chapter 8), because his discussion was interrupted by the arrival of other guests (l. 177). We were not able to reintroduce the topic before his departure an hour or so later.

Having portrayed the shaykh of the previous story as a book lover and motivated his pursuit of the thief by the loss of his books (chapter 10, l. 19), when the Ākhond expresses his own admiration of certain books and his devotion to reading (ll. 13–45), he reveals a certain brotherhood of spirit with the shaykh as he has portrayed him. The ascetic of Kāshifi's literary narrative betrayed unsuitably worldly attachments in accepting robes of honor from a royal patron, in accepting the services of a supposedly admiring devotee, and in pursuing his false disciple when he stole the valuable clothes. The Ākhond's shaykh likewise succumbed to worldly feelings in accepting the supposed devotee's service, but it is less clear whether the Ākhond would interpret the shaykh's distress at the loss of his books as materialistic. In assigning his own enthusiasms to his less-than-perfect hero, he both rehabilitated the shaykh somewhat from Kāshifi's portrayal and gave his narrative a reflexive dimension which hints at self-parody (cf. Fischer 1982). This tendency to ironic self-portrayal is further developed in his memoir of the debate with the Jew which followed his discussion of the merits of *Anwār-i Sohaylī*. His humorous description of his strategic withdrawal from further argument with the Jew (ll. 172–73) recalls the rapid retreat of the Shaykh in "Women's Tricks" from the homes of the transgressors whose activities he has witnessed: flight is an appropriate tactic for protecting one's faith under such circumstances.

As for the source of the story of the shaykh, the Ākhond is by no means unusual in his admiration for *Anwār-i Sohaylī*. The book was a standard component of the traditional Muslim educational curriculum in the first decades of the twentieth century, when he received his education (Ghani 1988:431). Dating from the Timurid period (late fifteenth and early sixteenth century C.E., ninth and tenth centuries A.H.), when Herat was an imperial capital and a center of arts and letters, *Anwār-i Sohaylī* was composed in Herat, in prose and short verses, by Kamāl ud-Dīn Husayn Wā'iz Kāshifī (d. 910 A.H./1504–1505 C.E.), a prolific writer of moral philosophical works. Besides the *Lights of Canopus* (so named in honor of Kāshifī's patron, the poet Niẓām ud-Dīn Amir Shaykh Ahmad, whose *nom de plume* was Sohaylī, "the Canopeian"), Kāshifī is known especially for his *Rauẓat ul-Shuhadā*, or *Garden of the Martyrs*, which is still regarded in Iran as the premier work on the martyrology of the Imam Husayn, patron of Shī'a Muslims and grandson of the Prophet (Rypka 1968:313).

The Ākhond also knows *Anwār-i Sohaylī* by its earlier title, *Kalīlah wa Dimnah*. Western literary histories trace its origins to the Sanskrit *Panchatantra*. According to the origin legend mentioned in chapter 10 (Wollaston 1904:xi–xv), the story collection was originally composed in India in the years shortly after Alexander the Great's campaigns, by a wise Brahmin vizier, Bīdpāī, at the command of the King Dābshalīm, who had previously mistreated Bīdpāī but had come to recognize the error of his ways and desire instruction. Bīdpāī's story of the jackal-courtiers Kalīlah and Dimnah is additionally framed in Kāshifī's version by mention of a second king, with a Persian name, Homāyūn-e Fāl, who asks his own vizier to help him procure the stories of Bīdpāī for his own edification. The didactic dimension of storytelling is relentlessly emphasized by all these constructions. With or without the theme of tyranny corrected, both the origin legend and the frame stories within Kāshifī's text reiterate the pattern of stories conveying guidance, told to a ruler by a wise advisor. Kāshifī's introduction and numerous comments by both characters and author throughout the text reiterate the instructive purpose of the collection, and the comprehensiveness of its message, reflected in the Ākhond's own evaluation of it (ll. 13–20). Inheriting and valuing this tradition, the Ākhond clearly recognizes that stories, however informally told, may be something more than simply entertainment and that it is appropriate for those who rule to learn from the narratives of those who offer ethical instruction.

What is known of the collection's transmission from India to Persia reiterates its instructive role. According to tradition, the collection was translated from Bīdpāī's Sanskrit into Middle Persian (Pahlavī) in about 550 C.E. by the famous Sassanian physician Burzoë, who served Khosrau Noshīrvān "the Just," the last great Sassanian king, but no part of that translation survives. The earliest Arabic translation still exists, however, made from the Middle Persian by Ibn ul-Muqaffaʻ (a Persian convert to Islam who made many important translations of Sassanian literature into Arabic; he was executed ca. 759 C.E./141 A.H.). From Arabic, the collection was translated back into classical Persian several times by poets and writers attached to different courts. The two most important surviving versions are that of the sixth-century A.H./twelfth-century C.E. by Abu'l Maʻālī Naṣru'llah of Shiraz and, derived from it, the more ornate late ninth-century A.H. / fifteenth-century C.E. version of Kāshifī. Jan Rypka judges Naṣru'llah's version a masterpiece of stylistic simplicity. Kāshifī's version, which added Iranian material to the earlier translation and was cast in the more ornate style of the Timurid period, became the more widely known and was used as a school text and model for high literary style, leaving, says Rypka, "an ineffaceable and unfortunately calamitous mark on Persian literary style" (cf. Rypka 1968:222 ff., 313).

Though the book had been part of the traditional school curriculum for several centuries, both Mokhtār's lack of familiarity with the title (chapter 11, l. 7) and remarks by Kazim Alami, a relatively recent graduate of Herat's government school system, confirm that the work was not much used in the government schools of Afghanistan by the time of this performance. The dominance of the secular government schools by the 1970s was unquestionable. The numbers enrolled in the schools had increased from about 1600 in 1930 to 928,000 in the middle 1970s in a total population estimated between 16 and 19 million (Ghani 1988:439 and 442). Baghban's (1977) assessment of attitudes among actors' families during his research on folk drama suggested that any exposure to secular education in this low-status group increased individual self-esteem and tended to encourage the individual to leave the acting profession for something of higher status, but Baghban also reported ambivalence among the religious elite concerning the government education system and reluctance on the part of some such families to send their children to those schools (Baghban 1977, 1:134; cf. chapter 5).

The foundations of the foreign-modeled secular education system were laid in the first years of this century. Habībīya College, founded by Amir Habībullah in 1903, was modeled after Aligarh College in India. In the reign of his son, the reformist Amir Amānullah (ruled 1919–29), the first European language high schools were opened in cooperation with foreign governments. Istiqlāl Lycée was organized on the French model with French staff in Kabul in 1923. Nejāt College on a German plan with German staff followed in 1924, and Ghāzī College on a British model in 1928. Habībīya College had been reorganized as an English-language facility by Amānullah in 1923 (Dupree 1973:447).

The Ākhond's comparison of *Anwār-i Sohaylī* to a "French schoolmaster" for virtuosity and scope (l. 16) reflects the national reputation which these schools retained down to the 1970s. This remark also reaffirms the Ākhond's own eclectic acceptance of different educational modes, manifested in the different educational paths pursued by his sons (chapter 5, ll. 17–26). Given his attitude toward books and my obvious literacy, it may have helped his impression of me that I readily recognized the title of *Anwār-i Sohaylī* (l. 8) but not the cultural topos of "women's tricks" by which he introduced the story itself. He praises the book for its linguistic virtuosity (l. 20), which taken together with his reference to it as a "French schoolmaster" assimilates the work itself to a positively valued polyglot intellectual tradition, apparently including the West. His praise for the book's range of language reflects interestingly on both Rypka's (1968:313) assessment of it as a stylistic disaster and the unsigned introduction to the Tehran edition of Amir Kabir, wherein it is asserted that Kāshifī made the collection more accessible to a Persian-speaking audience by substituting Persian verses and aphorisms for the Arabic expressions retained by Naṣru'llah, and simplifying other obscure expressions (Kāshifī 1983:2).

Jiri Cejpek (1968:609) acknowledged the difficulty of erecting tight boundaries for "folk" and "polite" literature categories but distinguished them on the basis of folk literature's preference for a simpler style and less use of Arabic loanwords. Of Kāshifī's collection, Cejpek writes, it "turned out to be such an affected affair that it appealed only to the educated classes—its effect on true folk-literature was slight and of no consequence" (p. 661). Given the undeveloped state of research on living folk narrative traditions in Persian in the mid-1960s when Cejpek wrote this, it is hard to tell on what he grounded this observation, unless perhaps it was a preconception of "true folk literature" constructed to exclude material assigned to the "polite" category wherever it might occur. The Ākhond's admiration for the work and his integration of items from it into his oral performance, his use of it as a resource and authority without any attempt at close imitation of its verbal style, suggest that an understanding of the relationship between stylistic and content influences in the symbiotic world of Persian oral-literary tradition is not well served by generalizations like Cejpek's. By the same token, the authority granted certain texts in the estimation of different segments of the population bears an indeterminate relation to the forms used when those texts are adapted for oral performance in different contexts. The Ākhond venerates the *Mathnavī* of Rūmī, calling it "noble" (*sharīf*, l. 177) as one would the Qur'an, but his performance of "Mahmūd and the Thieves" retains none of its actual verse and few of its rhetorical strategies. Others may perform in verse, quoting the poet's individual lines verbatim but still editing significantly and thus selectively suppressing certain rhetorical features of their original (cf. Mills in press).

In the interview, we learned that the Ākhond no longer had physical possession of the book (l. 23) and his access to it at this time was thus memorial, like his access to stories he learned orally. Mokhtār tried to determine how long ago the book had been in his possession (l. 24), but the Ākhond misheard the question and gave us even more interesting information on his reading procedures, instead. He reported that he had read the book over completely, four times during the period he possessed it, and he remembered accurately the book's division into fourteen sections. Following his own topical inclinations, he then described the conditions for study in his home, with a vividly humorous picture of his strategy for fending off the attention of his large family in order to concentrate on his reading (ll. 35–45). Apparently, reading is an interruptible activity, whereas sleeping is not.

The large size of his extended family (l. 53), and the many contacts it produces, seem to be the immediate associative link for his entry into the topic of Herat City as a place for intellectual exchanges (l. 57), as illustrated by his conversation with the Jew. He introduces the story as a personal reminiscence: "One time, sir— I'll tell you with my own tongue," (l. 59) is as clear a marker of a type of narrative to follow as are the formulas he avoids using for fictional folktales. The narrative's topical relevance to the main themes of the immediate conversation (reading and books) or to the stories that have been told, remains unstated. A sayed (descendant of the Prophet) is introduced, recalling the Ākhond's exchange the night before with the other sayed, also addressed as "Āqā," whom he appeared to want to have present to hear the story of "Mahmūd and the Thieves" (chapter 8 ll. 75 and 81–84). The Ākhond again cites beards as a mark of male respectability and judiciousness (l. 65; cf. chapter 9 ll. 2–3 and 10), in this case real, not feigned, in introducing the "remarkable clergy" of Herat's Jewish community. The word he uses for "clergy" (l. 64 and note), *mojtahedā*, means "interpreters of jurisprudence," emphasizing their scholarly preoccupations. This observation on the quality of Jewish religious scholarship links the topic of his meeting with the Rabbi to the Ākhond's description of his own preoccupation with religious study, in the foregoing conversation about books and reading.

The Ākhond's sayed friend from the village who introduces him to the Rabbi and the Rabbi himself apparently anticipate engaging the Ākhond in religious discussion (ll. 74–75), which immediately ensues over the Ākhond's rather brusque refusal of the Jew's hospitality. To refuse refreshment as the Ākhond does is a strong statement of social separation and, as the Ākhond acknowledges, an optional one (ll. 90–95). Hospitality is a basic social value among all social groups in Afghanistan. Muslims in particular regard hospitality to strangers as a religious duty. The offering and acceptance of hospitality also enter host and guest into a reciprocity relation in which the guest, having "eaten the host's bread and salt" (*nān o namak khordah*), will, ideally, at some point be able to offer his erstwhile host sustenance or other services in return. In refusing the Rabbi's pipe, the Ākhond refuses a whole spectrum of potential reciprocity relations, an offer of ongoing social exchange. Although acknowledging the Rabbi's interpretive powers and religious scholarship, the Ākhond does not accept him as a member of his social exchange network.

In reaction to the Ākhond's refusal, the Jew taxes him with ideas and values drawn directly from Muslim ideology. Jews, Christians, and (in Iran) Zoroastrians are considered under Muslim law to be "people of the Book," people who have received revelation in the prophetic tradition which culminated in the Prophet Mohammed and who have retained that revelation, considered to be the revealed word of God, in written form. As such, they are entitled to certain legal protections and to noninterference in their religious practice. Asserting that Shī'a Muslims are not people of the Book (ll. 101–7), the Rabbi has recourse to an extreme anti-Shī'a position sometimes argued among Sunni Muslims. The charge is that Shī'a

Muslims are apostates because they venerate the Prophet's nephew and son-in-law 'Ali and the Imams (lineal descendants of the Prophet through his daughter Fatima and 'Ali), as though they too were prophets, even though these personages received no direct revelation from God in the form of a book, no prophecy as the revealed Word of God.

The Ākhond counters with a more moderate Sunni position that, since the Shī'a recite the same articles of faith as other Muslims (adding a statement venerating 'Ali) and consent to pray with Sunni Muslims, they are Muslims (l. 123). Mokhtār's collaborative comment, "He was trying to stir up divisiveness" (l. 124), supports the idea of Muslim solidarity. Shī'a and Sunni populations were both sizable in Herat, perhaps with a Sunni majority, although precise figures were not available on such a sensitive topic. I do not know if the Ākhond had determined that Mokhtār was Shī'a, but Mokhtār's voiced sympathy for the Ākhond's conciliatory position over Sunni-Shī'a matters (which were a source of intermittent tension and violence in Herat over the years) indicates his sensitivity to that topic and is the most positive engagement Mokhtār showed with the Ākhond's religious observations up to that point. Previous to this, he had greeted the Ākhond's more obviously proselytizing statements with a degree of vagueness (e.g., chapter 8, l. 151, where he responds to a similarly phrased rhetorical question concerning God's acceptance of the faithful, l. 150).

In his inimitable way, the Ākhond invites the Rabbi to repeat the Muslim statement of faith (l. 120), which if done with sincerity constitutes the act of conversion to Islam. Repeating twice for this audience, ". . . and you can wash your testicles and I'll drink the water" (ll. 120 and 126), the Ākhond emphasizes the ritual and sectarian rather than hygienic basis for his refusal of the Rabbi's offer of a pipe. The privates are washed with the whole body in the greater ablution, *ghosl*, which is required prior to prayer after ritually polluting acts such as sexual intercourse. This offer to drink the Rabbi's ablution water is an absurd statement of religious acceptance, even deference, received with laughter by the audience. It is typical of the self-satirizing tendency in the Ākhond's humorous style, and in its original context addressed to the Rabbi, it undercuts the sting of the Ākhond's initial refusal of his hospitality. Mokhtār picks up the absurdity and ribald imagery with an aggressively supportive statement, "Use his penis for a hand-mill" (l. 127; *dastāz*, a hand-operated grain mill), but is instantly bested at that rhetorical game by the Ākhond, who links the original topic of the offered pipe with the reference to his interlocutor's private parts ("His penis for the pipestem!" l. 128).

In the Ākhond's narrative, the sayed then takes a turn on the offensive, asking the Rabbi in a friendly tone why he does not convert. The Rabbi readily counters with an appeal to facts regarding the relative evidence of corruption in the two communities (ll. 134–40), facts which the Muslims do not contest.[1] The sayed fails to answer him at all, to the Ākhond's comically expressed disgust (ll. 143–44). The Ākhond moves to the defense of the faith with the argument that Jews, having rejected Mohammed's prophecy, have already lost their status as believers and thus are not appropriate quarry for Satan (ll. 146–68). He ornaments his argument with proverbs (ll. 158–59 and 161) as well as allusions to religious legend (Pharaoh, l. 147) and to *hadīth*, the sayings of the Prophet which constitute a body of Muslim wisdom and belief supplementary to the essential revelation of the Qur'an.[2] Line 164, "In that mine of gold and silver that is our breast," refers in passing to the well-known *hadīth al-nās ma'ādan*, "men are mines [of gold and silver]," in that they have different natures and capacities (Nicholson 1925–40, 7:313). He clinches his argument with another of his pungent sexual images (l. 168), which paradoxically inverts the common insult, to assert that the Jew has only *escaped* the status of mother-rapist because he is not subjected to the pressure the forces of evil inflict on believing Muslims to try to turn them from religion.

This close juxtaposition of sanctified images from *hadīth* and Qur'anic legend, of everyday proverbial wisdom, and daring play with the language of insult is not an anomalous combination of Herati speech styles, but the Ākhond displays a greater-than-average virtuosity in combining them, appreciated by his audience as their laughter reveals. He then portrays himself as using actual invective (*kūnī!*; passive partner in anal intercourse) on his sayed companion in comic rage (ll. 169–71). The Ākhond laughingly describes his strategic retreat from the Rabbi's shop, "before he stopped us with another [argument]" (l. 172), a left-handed compliment to the Jew's powers of religious debate. He also describes respectful greetings he hence-

---

1. This point about the relative virtue of the two communities may be a topos in the discourse between the two communities. Goldstein (1986:160) reports an anecdote from her Iranian Jewish informants, about a Jew who embezzled from the community and escaped punishment by a last-minute public conversion to Islam on a street in Yazd as he was being escorted by other Jews to an inquiry on his activities. The Muslim onlookers expressed their delight, to which the rabbi who was present replied, "What are you so happy for? You've got yourselves a thief."

2. Anderson (1985:207) remarks on similar use of multiple forms (folk quatrains, proverbs, the Qur'an and *hadīth*) to punctuate conversation in Pashtu-speaking Afghan communities.

forth received when passing the Rabbi's shop (l. 173), using the Jews' recognition as an indirect claim for his own eloquence but then disclaiming personal credit for his effectiveness in ll. 175–76, "But seriously, the Lord intended [it] sir, / and if not—". Even in the matter of eloquence in defense of the faith, one's success is only made possible by God's will. His success, like Salīm's eventual rescue, is a matter not only of faith but of grace.

Portraying himself as a religious teacher who narrowly bests a rabbi in argument, the Ākhond maintains both lightness and self-respect in constructing himself as hero of his own reminiscence. In the Persian-language fictional narratives of Muslims, Jews where they appear are often maligned (Marzolph 1984:29). They, in turn, have their own tales and legends portraying Jews as heroically resistant to the proselytizing efforts of Muslims (Goldstein 1986). No derogatory portrayals of Jews figure in this tale series but only this ruefully admiring reminiscence of the intelligent outsider (*khārejī*, "foreigner," l. 169) encountered on the Ākhond's home ground. Whether or not the Ākhond usually regarded these Jews, part of an ancient community, as "foreigners" in the sense of immigrants or visitors, this designation assimilates them to present company, in my own unequivocally foreign and non-Muslim presence. Talking about his debate with the Rabbi also allows him again to address indirectly the problem of unbelief and acceptance of Islam, which the Woləswāl's presence represented for him and the community as well. The previous stories did not deal much with outsiders to the religious community, and presented Muslims in a wide variety of unflattering views, including stupidity, chicanery, sexual compromise, and sexual excess. In this reminiscence, the inarticulateness of the sayed is held up for ridicule, continuing the Ākhond's theme of the unreliability of charismatic religious personages.

The Ākhond's storytelling was honed as a discourse of Muslims for Muslims, perhaps subject to misinterpretation by an outsider listener such as myself or the Woləswāl who had intentionally distanced himself from the community of believers. By presenting the Rabbi's argument, that more corruption is to be found among Muslims than among non-Muslims and countering it as he does, the Ākhond can implicitly fend off a stereotypification of Islam, and Muslims, according to the negative portrayals of the foregoing stories. The Ākhond's customary audience is fellow believers, good and bad. His rhetorical repertoire is thus tailored to an internal critique of his own community, but his personal experience narrative nicely averts the possibility that an outsider could interpret this internally generated critique to condemn the community and the faith as a whole. Yet he also avoids denying the moral defects of the community, protecting his role as a moral critic. He is able to use the image of the Jew, the traditional and long-standing resident outsider, to stand in for the newer and less familiar threats of Christian (and female!) visitor or homegrown Marxist apostate.

Thus, traditional didactic configurations can be juxtaposed creatively to address new intellectual challenges. That these juxtapositions tend to be implicit (he leaves it to us whether to see ourselves in the Jew's role or not) is also part of traditional oral rhetorical technique in this informal, conversational context. Michael Fischer (1984:230) describes modern Iranian intellectuals, writers, and filmmakers as trying, according to their lights, to "awaken [moral consciousness] from the slumber of convention." The Ākhond demonstrates in this personal experience narrative, juxtaposed to his traditional storytelling, how moral consciousness is, in some traditionally educated individuals at least, awake and alert in and through traditional images appropriately marshalled to meet new forms of threat to the social order.

It is easy for the nontraditionally educated to see only the repetitiveness of traditional forms and miss the creativity in the older modes of expression. In traditional expressions, such as stories or proverbs, critical power is largely lodged not in innovations in form or phrasing but in the placement of the utterances in a conversational matrix and especially in the juxtaposition of the received verbal form and a particular human action or attitude observed in the real world. The images are received wisdom, but their placement is highly creative, even innovative. This placement includes not only the lively combination of rhetorical levels (e.g., the Ākhond's balance of *hadīth*, proverbs, and sexual invective) but also an interpretive bite achieved by juxtaposition of statement to behavior. The English maxim, "If the shoe fits, wear it," governs the receiver's interpretive responsibilities within these speaker-receiver transactions. Fischer (1984:230), notes the demonstrated revolutionary potential of traditional themes of *ta'aziah* passion plays and religious mourning narratives in contemporary Iran. The Ākhond's discourse is more oblique, but just as pointed and just as energetically engaged with current real-life experience.

It is now fashionable for social scientists to emphasize that no individual, traditional or "modernizing," speaks for (or to) the whole society. This, the home truth of recent trends in so-called postmodern ethnographic interpretation, is for us the fruit of the study of cultural conflict in rapidly changing societies, which are generating increasingly articulate critiques of previously dominant western intellectual models, but this insight is equally applicable to the diversity of traditional voices and long-standing indigenous critical modes. The "other" toward whom a traditional expression is addressed may be an insider or an outsider. Traditional rhetorical resources can be adjusted accordingly by accomplished speakers like the Ākhond. The *jihād al-lisān*, the "struggle of the tongue" for peaceful persuasion to the faith (cf. Shahrani 1984:28), is as clear and original a Muslim duty as the more violent form of *jihād* we have recently seen in defense of faith and land in Afghanistan.

From his general choice of repertoire in this story session, one may infer that the Ākhond's usual audience *cum* target is Muslims whose behavior leaves something to be desired. With this short anecdote of his debate with the Rabbi, raising directly the questions of conversion and community morality, he reframes that self-criticism for the outsiders' gaze. The surface association of the anecdote of the religious debate to the proximate topics of conversation, *Anwār-i Sohaylī*, and his own study and reading seems tenuous, but its overall pertinence to the storytelling event and audience is far-reaching, if characteristically oblique.

The Ākhond talking about his own experience reveals a strongly developed sense of serious fun and of irony in the role he takes in defense of absolutes. His refusal of the Rabbi's hospitality asserts the priority of Islam's stand against unbelief, over the strong social obligations of guest and host. The Ākhond acknowledges that such a debate is both serious (serious enough to be rude over) and a game, as illustrated by his laughing portrayal of his strategic retreat from the Jew's argumentative powers. Absolutes *are* at stake, but given his human fallibility, what the Ākhond can demonstrate is not necessarily the essential rightness of his position but how effective a rhetoric he can mount in opposition to someone who is powerful (via an alternative education and training). Hence, his indictment of the sayed, "How are you going to rely on this kind of mediation on the Judgment Day?" when each Muslim will have to answer for himself. Though the Woləswāl, his host, is silent throughout this narration, he too represents an ideological challenge to the Ākhond's essential position. The Woləswāl's chosen rhetorical forum was his office and the execution of its duties, not his guestroom and the conversations we held there. The Woləswāl's pointed refusal to accept bribes, according to Mokhtār, had alienated the community but was intended to demonstrate that ethics were not dependent on religious affiliation and/or that Islam is relatively corrupt despite its claims, precisely the Rabbi's line of argument in comparing the behavior of his own and the Muslim community. The whole ground of the Ākhond's rejection of the Jew's claim to communal virtue, is a cryptic counterstatement to Marxists who intended to bring uncorrupted (e.g., non–bribe-taking) administration to the hinterlands: What good is virtue, the Ākhond asks, without God?

12. Ākhond Mulla Mahmūd, "That Little Donkey and That Little Door" and "If/But"

Ākhond to Mokhtār: Are you familiar with the origin of [the saying],
         "That little donkey and that little door," sir?

M. Mills: *Kharak o darak*—? [*repeats Persian phrase, writing it down*]

Ā: When they say, "That little donkey and that little door"?

M: "That little donkey and that little door" —yeah.

Ā: Yeah . . . it has an <u>origin</u>, like every saying.   5

M: Good.

Ā: For instance,

doesn't one person say to another,

that—

"He did 'if/but' "?   10

"He did 'if/but' " —now that— <u>that</u> has a story, now.

M: Yeah.

Ā: You see?

M: Yes.

Ā: Every— <u>every</u> saying that's used, sir, has an origin, now.   15

M: Yes, [*inaudible word*]—

Ā: "That little donkey and that little door."

M: Yes, right.

Karīm: If it didn't have one, people wouldn't say it, sir—

Ā: [*to MM, who is writing notes*]: Write it down right there, the story of
         'That Little Donkey and That Little Door,' and I'll tell it—?   20

MM: Yes, I wrote it down.

Ā: You wrote it?

MM: Yes.

$\bar{A}$: There was this fisherman, sir—
  He'd catch fish.   25
M: Yes.
$\bar{A}$:
He caught a very good fish and put it in a bucket and brought it to the
                                          king of that time.
He brought it to the king, and he gave him two thousand rupees as
                                          a reward.
There was another fisherman, sir, who was his neighbor, and his wife
                                          said to him,
  "Hey, since they didn't fuck you over,[1] you go catch a fish, too,
                                          and take it— 30
  If we could get our hands on a thousand rupees— we're [half
                                          dead] from hunger."
[M: Yeah.]
He went and got a fish, too, »
  and the king, sir, was going around among the people in dervish dress.
He's coming along with the fish in a bucket in front of him,   35
  mounted on a donkey, and just then the king met up with him.
[M: Yeah—]
He said, "Bābā, what's that?"
  He didn't recognize that it was the king. »
He said, "It's a fish, I'm taking it to the king."   40
He said, "Take it and sell it in the bazaar, it'll make ten *qerān* for your
                                          wife and kids, now.
      Are you crazy, what kind of profit will the king give you?"
‹›
He said, "No, I'll give it to him, he's a king, maybe he'll give me two,
                                          three thousand—" »
He said, "The king can't be that big a fool,
    to use up the wealth of the treasury,   45
    for ten *qerān*
    to give you two thousand rupees.
    ‹›
    Take it and sell it, it'll make ten *qerān*" —

---

1. *tor keh nagāīdam*: Perhaps in the sense of "What have you got to lose?" or "What have they done to harm you (that you should avoid them)?"

He said, "If he doesn't give anything to you, what will you do?"
   He said it to the old man.   50
He said, "Hope is in God, that he'll give, he's a king, he's generous."
He said, "Bābā, I tell you, —" He doesn't <u>recognize</u> that he's the king.
   "Take it and sell it, it'll make ten <u>qerān</u>."
He said, sir, he <u>really</u> pressured him, "If he doesn't give anything, what
                                      will you do?"
He said, "If he doesn't give anything, I'll stuff all four of this donkey's
            legs [*laughing as he speaks*] in his wife's cunt!"   55
[*laughs*]
[*M laughs*]
When he spoke like that, the king
   drew himself up like a snake, »
   and went right back to his court.
He was holding court when the old man came along with his bucket.
He said, "Bring that old man [forward]."   60
They brought the old man, and he said, "Bābā, what's that?" »
He said, "A fish." »
He said, "Why did you bring it?" »
He said, "I just brought it, sir, for you, perhaps, hope is in God,
       that you might give two or three thousand *qerān*." »   65
He said, "A king isn't <u>that</u> big a fool.
      That for a ten-*qerān* fish he would give away three thousand
                    qerān of the government's wealth.
      Take it and sell it, it'll make ten *qerān* for your wife and kids."
He said, "No, sir, I brought it, if perhaps— hope is in G—" »
He said, "If I <u>don't</u> give anything, what will you do?"   70
[*M*: Yeah—]
      "If I don't give anything, what will you do?"
He really pressured him, and when the old man really looked at him hard,
   he said [to himself],
   "By God, he's the same one!   75
     ‹›
   That same one that I talked to like that!" [*smiles*] [*M*: Yeah.]
He said, "If you don't give anything, —"
He said, "Sir, —" but now he couldn't do it openly—
He said, "If I [*sic*] don't give anything, sir,
   [there's] this little donkey and that little door."   80

That is, "These four legs [*laughing*] of my donkey's in your wife's
cunt, now!"
[*M (laughs loudly)*]
"This little donkey and that little door."
[*M, MM (laughing)*: Yeah— Uh-huh!]
Now, so to say, the origin of "this little donkey and that little door"—
   —the king gave him two thousand rupees, [*laughs*]   85
   —four thousand rupees reward! [*smiles*]
[*MM*: Very good— (*laughs*)]
[*M*: As a gift.²]
It's his gift! [*Laughter*]
That's the origin of "this little donkey and this little door."   90
[*M (laughing)*: Fine.]
Now there was this other king, sir,
   who used to go off with the viziers from his court,
   to the desert plains to hunt.
[*M*: What's the name of this?]   95
Ā: This— this, now what's the name of it, sir? — "If/But."
[*M*: "If/But."]
Ā: "If/But."
[*MM interrupts to ask permission to change tape. Tape change.*]
Ākhond to Mokhtār and/or the Woləswāl regarding M. Mills:
Sir, you must give permission for her to go to our place, to see the
     wives and daughters-in-law.
M: Fine, she'll go to see them.³   100
Ā: Yeah, she should see [*unintelligible word(s)*],
afterward she can take [this] to America. [*laughs*]
M: She can see that here, too.
Ā: Yeah! [*laughs*]
Woləswāl: Yes, she should see them.   105
M: She could say hello to them . . . [*MM*: Yeah—] . . . when it's
     time to say goodbye to you— [*MM*: Yes.]
Ā: Yeah—

---

   2. *bakhsheysh*: "charity, largess." Mokhtār's term makes a subtle change from the Ākhond's term, *en'ām*, which implies a reward or prize <u>earned</u>.
   3. This gracious invitation was never taken up because of my uneasiness around the Woləswāl and concern that I would be identified with his politics or with government authority if I continued under his sponsorship. Local people's views of central government representatives and the importance of these views to my field presence will be discussed at length in the next chapter. The Ākhond apparently assumed at this point that my itinerary was controlled by the government.

M: Good!
"If/But"!?
Ā: "If and But."   110
M: The story of "If and But."
Ā: Yes.

Shall I start now?
M and MM: Yeah, start. Yes, start.
Ā: A king, sir, along with two or three viziers from his court, went out
                                                                to wander around.   115
    From road to road, till they met a shepherd.
When he met the shepherd, the king <u>without</u> any conversation,
    immediately touched his riding crop to the top of the shepherd's head.
[*M*: Yeah.]
    Even when he placed his riding crop there, he doesn't say a thing.   120
And the shepherd [*demonstrating by extending his tongue*]
    stuck out his tongue.
[*M*: Yeah.]
The king said, "If."
He said, "But."   125
They went on by, after that.
[*M*: Yeah.]
After they'd gone a little way, he said to the viziers from court,
    "What was <u>that</u> all about, that I put my riding crop to that shepherd's
                                                                head, and he said—
    —stuck out his tongue? »   130
    I said, 'If,' »
    and he said, 'but.' "
They said, "What do we know [about that]?"
He said, "God's truth, if you can't tell me the meaning of it,
    if I don't give you the 'forties'⁴   135
    and extract from you whatever you've consumed in the way
                                                                of wages!"

They came back, brought the king back to his place, then they came
                                                                back to the shepherd, and said,

---

4. *chehlworĭ*, probably for literary, *chehlbārĭ*: "forty-times-a-thing." From context, a sustained series of beatings or other extreme punishments.

"Bad <u>luck</u> to you, you're going to get us <u>killed</u>, so tell the <u>meaning</u>
of this, anyway."
He said, "Sir, if you give me ten thousand rupees, I'll tell you.
If you don't, I won't."   140
They said, "We won't." »
He said, "Then my cock can tell you.
God arrange it, I'll fuck your wives."⁵ [*muffled audience laughter*]
They were forced to it, sir.
[*M*: Yeah.]   145
Sir, they gave him the ten thousand rupees.
He said, "The king's motive was this," sir.
"The wh— When he put the riding crop on my head, his
heart was [asking],
'What is it that can gamble away this green [flourishing]⁶
head?' »
I said, 'Eh—[*sticks out tongue*]   150
—this red tongue, here.' "
[*M*: —yeah—]
"He said, '<u>But</u> don't tell anyone.'
I said, '<u>If</u> they give me a lot of money, I'll tell.⁷
‹›
If they give a little, I won't.' "   155
[*M*: Goo-ood. (*laughs*) MM. (*laughs*)]
There, so to say, the story is—
it's just this, that
"if and but,"
the green head, it's this [*sticks out tongue*] [*M*: —tongue gambles
it away—]   160
—tongue that gambles it away.
[*M*: Yeah—]
Now the green head, it's the tongue gambles it away, that's the way it is.
[*Karīm*: —that's the way it is.]
[If] once,
in the presence of this governor,   165

---

5. More male-male verbal aggression, equivalent to American "fuck you."
6. *sar-e sabz*: "green" has the sense of flourishing, prospering, vigorously healthy (not naïve as in English).
7. The storyteller has reversed the order in which the words are given in the aphorism.

or maybe the leader of the republic[8] or somebody,

    a man talks with this <u>tongue</u>.

[*Karīm, speaking simultaneously*: With the tongue— (*inaudible word or words*)]

It's right then that a man gets caught, anyway. [*Karīm*: —is no little

                                         thing, anyway.]

[*M*: No, it's really bad.]   170

[*Another, elderly audience member*: Unbelief and Islam are in the tongue.]

Ā (*speaking with emphasis*): How<u>ever</u> much, <u>every</u>thing is in the tongue.

[*Several more off-mike affirmative comments from the audience*: Everything—

                                They say, if the tongue—[9]]

[*M*: Life and death—]

Ā: <u>Every</u>thing's in the tongue, anyway.   175

If not, [*sticking out tongue*]

    a man's tongue is just that big.

[*M*: Yes.]

You see that

    a hand is the size of ten tongues.   180

If the tongue were mute,

    what could the hand accomplish? He just has to make signs, "Anh-

                                   anh-anh-anh!"

    [*with a laugh, imitating a mute's attempts to speak*]

[*general audience laughter*]

Ā [*laughs*]

[*M to MM*: All right? *MM*: All right (*turns off tape recorder*)]

---

8. *rā'īs-e jamhūr*: "president of the republic." Mohammed Daud was both president and prime minister at the time.

9. This was the point of most active audience comment in the performance series so far. Several comments were simultaneous with the Ākhond's remarks. Some, originating further from the microphone, cannot be deciphered from the tape.

"*Every*thing is in the tongue!"

"Every saying has an origin." With that observation, the Ākhond began a run of three short proverb-based narratives with which he ended his story-telling. He offered them as a general illustration of narrative substrates in proverbs ("Every saying that's used, sir, has an origin, now," l. 15), but from the very large universe of Persian-language proverbs, he chose three with special resonance to elements, explicit and implicit, of the preceding story session and the relations of its participants. Not only does every proverbial saying of the type he discusses have an "origin," an implicit narrative sub-strate or context that it carries with it, but every saying properly used also has an immediate motivation in present conversational context. Alton Becker put this quality of the proverb succinctly: "Proverbs . . . are not really self-sufficient texts, but rather small texts used to evaluate (give value to) *new* situations . . ." (emphasis mine) (Becker 1984:137; cf. Barakat 1980 passim). Even as the Ākhond discusses the non-self-sufficiency of proverbs in the abstract, his examples carry out, without direct discussion, the function of oblique commentary on the present context, which proverbs share with didactically framed conversational narratives.

In his discussion of proverbs and their stories, the Ākhond has adopted and subsumed our preoccupation with naming stories and record-ing those names (cf. chapter 5, ll. 90–92). By this point in the proceedings, he is urging me to write down the phrase which epitomizes the story, "That little donkey and that little door" (ll. 20–22). He wants us to get them down correctly, not because the stories have names, by which they can be epitomized and indexed, but because these proverbs have stories, by reference to which their intricate and highly condensed meanings can be understood and appropriately applied.

Both "That little donkey and that little door" (*kharak o darak*) and "If/ but" (*agar magar*) are well-known expressions in Herati and other Afghan Persian dialects. Variants of two of the proverbs involved with these stories are to be found in recent major collections of Persian proverbs and prover-bial expressions. Said Bahā Borqaʿī (1985/1364:231–32) lists the saying, "The little black donkey is at the door" (*kharak-e sīāh bar dar ast*), in connection with a more decorous variant of the first story, described in detail below. Yūsof Jamshīdīpūr (1980:146) lists the saying "The red tongue casts the green head to the wind" (*zabān-e sorkh sar-e sabz mīdehad bar bād*), without a story but with a brief explanatory gloss, "Be careful that you don't give away your head with your tongue" (*behūsh bāsh keh sar dar sar-e zabān nakonī*).[1] The phrase, "if/but" (*agar magar*), is not indexed in these Iranian collections, perhaps because of differences in the dialect use of *magar*. In literary Persian, *magar* as a preposition means "except" and as a conjunction, "but" or "unless." It can function as an interjection prefacing statements contrary to fact (like "but" in English, as in "But I thought he had left already,"; cf. Haim, *Persian-English Dictionary*). In Herat dialect, however, one of the commonest usages of *magar* is as a particle indicating necessity, e.g., *magar majbūrom*, "But I *have* to (do something)," or with the enclitic copula, as an adjective, *magarom borom*, "I have (am obliged) to go."

The Ākhond expects Mokhtār to recognize the proverbial sayings, as he does, but perhaps not to know their narrative substrates. The first saying, "That little donkey and that little door" is the actual punch line of its story (ll. 80 and 82). The second story contains two proverbial expressions. One is the expression by which the Ākhond introduces it, "He did [an] 'if/but' " ("*Agar magar kard*," l. 10), which characterizes a particular kind of speaking in riddles, enigmatic conversation entailing a juxtaposition of possibility and necessity, option and obligation, power and weakness, as exemplified by the exchange between the king and the shepherd.[2] Vis-à-vis the viziers from whom an explication is demanded, the exchange takes the form of a neck-riddle, a puzzle on the solution of which their lives depend. The Ākhond uses a second expression, a more formally evaluative and

---

1. Marzolph (1984) lists as his Tale Type *921, the same basic plot, with different cryptic expressions, all of which are verbal, not gestural, and with no sociopolitical commentary implicit in the question-and-answer series between the king and the poor man. The viziers have to pay the poor man for the solution of the riddle he and the king have constructed, making him rich. The dependence of the Ākhond's version on gestures rather than words, making it hard to convey in writing, may have influenced its absence from written tale and proverb collections. Marzolph (170) cites examples of the nongestural variant he describes, from the Luristani tale collection of Friedl and an unpublished typescript catalogue of popular tales compiled by Boulvin. "*Agar magar*" and "*Kharak o darak*" were both familiar expressions to a Kabul native consulted in 1985 in the United States.

2. Another aspect of the formulation of the phrase *agar magar*, meaning speaking in riddles or double-talk, is the Persian manifestation of what Alan Dundes (1974) had called the "Henny Penny phenomenon," the practice of adding a rhyme word, with a different initial letter, to a base word to form a catchphrase. In Persian, the commonest initial letter used for such doublet constructions is *mīm* ("m"), as in *chīzī mīzī*, "something or other" (*chīzī* derives from *chīz*, "thing," plus the indefinite suffix *ī*). Sometimes the doublet is a nonsense word, but here, the doublet is derived from an actual word *agar*, by attachment of the negative prefix *m-*.

cautionary proverb, "The green head, it's this—tongue, that gambles it away " (ll. 160–61), to close the story. The kind of verbal strategy characterized by the expression, "he did [an] if/but," *agar magar kard*, is thus necessitated by the truth of the second statement, on the perils of inappropriate speech. The first proverb-narrative, "That little donkey and that little door," is another illustration of the same concept, the power of cryptic or elliptical speech in situations where direct speech would be dangerous.

Both sayings and stories are about saying the unsayable, getting a critical point across without explicit statement. As Alton Becker has observed, proverbs "are public and not private language and depend on recognition to work " (1984:139), but the proverbs chosen by the Ākhond are public statements *about* private language, particularly as pertaining between weak ordinary citizens and a powerful ruler, an interesting choice given the context of the performance. These particular proverb-based narratives illustrate the ability of an ordinary man to use constraints on free speech imposed by superior powers to his own advantage (in the case of the shepherd, who avers that he will be forced to tell the secret of his exchange with the king if the courtiers pressure him with enough money, ll. 140, 153–54), or (in the fisherman's case) the ability to make a statement critical of a supreme authority figure in his presence and still avoid punishment, perhaps even win a reward for cleverness and discretion (ll. 79–80, 85–86). The Ākhond and Karīm have been asked, as private citizens, to speak at length in the presence of the man who is, effectively, the central government for them, a performance context in which proverbs about the perils of injudicious speech before authorities have resonance, particularly in light of the risks they have been taking with rough speech in powerful company.

These two short narratives have explicit topical links to stories previously told, such as the motif of the king going around in disguise to learn about the condition of his subjects (l. 34; cf. "Mahmūd and the Thieves") or the concern that the king not exhaust the state exchequer in displays of royal largesse (ll. 44–47; cf. " 'Ādel Khān"). Common to all these stories is the ideal of the king and the commoner reaching a face-to-face understanding, obviating the role of royal courtier-advisors, even to the point of the king's taking instruction from his subject, as in the story of Salīm. They also all involve a flow of largess from ruler to subject, confirming the ruler's ideal function as a distributor of wealth, the reverse of the flow of tax revenues the Woləswāl tried for in jailing the Ākhond.

For the particular spirit of sovereign-subject relations conveyed by the two proverb-stories, it is interesting to compare the version of the "donkey and door" proverb and story which Borqaʿī (1985:231–32) anthologizes. In it, a poet by the name of Maʿarūfī has traveled by donkey across Central Asia from Balkh to Sistan to present to Amir Khalaf al-Sanjarī, the king of Sistan, a praise poem (*qaṣīdah*) which he has composed for him in hopes of a reward. The king is out hunting and meets the poet along the road. Unrecognized, he gets the poet to recite the poem for him, then questions whether the king will grant the 1000 dinars the poet hopes for as a reward. The poet says he will then ask for 500, or if that is refused, 100. The king says, "What if he refuses to give that much?" The poet replies, "Then I will put the poem in the name of my little black donkey." All poems in *qaṣīdah* form include, in their closing lines, mention of the name of the poet. Attributing the poem to a donkey implies that only a foolish donkey *would* praise such a king. The king, laughing (and *not* "drawing himself up like a snake" with offense, as the Ākhond sees him), goes his way, and in due time, meets the poet again at his court. Maʿarūfī recites his poem, and the king asks him what he expects for a reward, refusing each sum down to 100 dinars, at which the poet says, "Oh, Amir, the little black donkey is at the door" (*kharak-e sīāh bar dar ast*). Like the concluding statement in the Ākhond's variant of this story (ll. 80–86), the petitioner's elliptical comment could be heard in a variety of ways by uninformed listeners, either as a cryptic statement indicating some kind of prior understanding between the king and petitioner or, more likely, as a capitulatory statement by the petitioner announcing his intention to leave as he had come. Defiance masked as capitulation, subversive deference, amuses the king and earns a reward. Cryptic mutual recognition between the king and the petitioner also echoes the closing scene of "Mahmūd and the Thieves."

As in the Ākhond's version of the proverb and story, the private citizen who has come seeking a reward manages to express his defiance of the king discreetly, in a way that the king understands on the basis of their prior acquaintance, but the court cannot, and he thereby saves face for the king even while condemning him for lack of generosity. The king appreciates the subject's cleverness as well as his independence of spirit and rewards him handsomely. Hence, what the king gives him is *enʿām*, an earned reward or prize, according to the Ākhond not, as Mokhtār would have it, *bakhsheysh*, charity (ll. 86 and 88). The Ākhond's word choice upholds the dignity of the common man in the presence of authority; Mokhtār portrays him as a relatively passive recipient of charity.

In the Ākhond's story, though, the original defiant statement is so obscenely offensive (l. 55) that it causes the king to "draw himself up like a snake" (l. 57), an elaboration on the more severe forms of male-male invective, in which men express aggression toward each other by threatening sexual abuse of their female dependents. The overtly sexual content of this version of the story echoes the sexual explicitness of many of the preceding stories, either in the use of invective or in plot content or both (chapters 4 to 7, 10, and 11). The very use of this language threatens the decorum of the performance setting, the subgovernor's guestroom, with its high-status outsider guests, one of whom is female. Kazim Alami, who helped transcribe this tape, remarked at l. 30, where the fisherman's wife uses an obscenity to urge her husband to go to the king, "They must be very bad people—a woman wouldn't speak to her husband that way."

Not only does the petitioner's defiance of the king within the story challenge his authority, but the particular form of this first story-proverb which the Ākhond brought forward in this storytelling event challenges the decorum of the event and the dignity of its host, as had several previous stories in the session. Whether or not the Ākhond knew any nonobscene version of that story, he did know other pertinent proverbs which did not take such risks with decorum. For the second example of a proverb-narrative, the Ākhond chose one which is not obscene, backing off from that particular form of rhetorical challenge to remake his general point about the riskiness of words.

These two stories, especially the concluding proverb, "The green head, it's the red tongue that gambles it away," aroused the most vocal immediate audience response of any of the tales the two men had performed up to this point (ll. 168 ff.), a string of collaborative comments not only from Karīm and Mokhtār, but from other audience members as well. One elderly male listener's comment ("Unbelief and Islam are in the tongue," l. 171) went beyond the *realpolitik* dimensions of the stories to link the power of the tongue to the ultimate question of eternal salvation or death through the Muslim declaration of faith which is the index of one's conversion (recalling the Ākhond's personal experience narrative, in which he emphasized to the Rabbi the importance of the Muslim statement of faith in establishing one's status as a believer).

Meeting this enthusiastic corroborative response from his audience, the Ākhond replies with an interpretive encore, restating the key proposition linking the two stories, "Everything's in the tongue, anyway" (l. 175), then elaborating, with gestures, on the power of the tongue despite its small size (ll. 176–81), and clinching the performance with an amusingly dramatic imitation of a tongueless man's attempt to speak (l. 182). None of this restatement is needed for audience comprehension or to press his argument; it is more like a celebration of the interpretive consensus already achieved by performer and audience over these two stories and perhaps also of the rhetorical strategy of gesture itself, as used in the second story. The gestural phase of the main narrative of "*Agar magar*," virtually a silent proverb in which the king touches the shepherd's head with his riding crop and the shepherd puts out his tongue, is particularly apt to its topic, avoiding the use of dangerous words while pointing out their danger.

Just as the Ākhond could offer an overt discourse on the mechanisms of proverbs, which carried the possibility of covert discourse about the present situation *through* proverbs, the receivers of this message explicitly acknowledged the general import of the proverbs, but gave no clue as to whether they had received a covert message from them concerning themselves or our present setting. Thus, while Mokhtār readily agreed in principle with the Ākhond on the dangers of injudicious speech (ll. 170 and 174), it remains unclear whether Mokhtār or the Woləswāl applied this concept to the storytelling event at which they were present, whether they perceived the story choices of the Ākhond and Karīm as particularly judicious or saw the storyteller's language as covertly challenging to the power relations implicit in the event, or even whether they would recognize judiciousness on the part of performers as particularly necessary in such a setting. The Woləswāl offered no direct commentary on stories during the storytelling event or afterward. His response, an indirect one, can be read through his offstage comments to Mokhtār concerning his prior treatment of the Ākhond and his behavior on a visit to a small local shrine later that morning, described in chapter 16.

During a tape change that interrupted the Ākhond's performance, the Ākhond graciously extended an invitation to me to visit his home and family (ll. 99 ff.). He phrased this as a polite request to Mokhtār and/or the Woləswāl that I be allowed to visit in order to add to my information about local life, assuming (accurately at this point) that my movements were controlled by my government contacts. Mokhtār turns the invitation aside (l. 103: "She can see that here, too," "here" being the administrative center where we then were, an hour or more distant from the Ākhond's home). He does not seem quite to realize that the Ākhond is proposing a longer trip, but suggests that I pay a short visit "when it's time to say goodbye" (l. 106).[3] This invitation, never taken up because of my discomfort with local political conditions and government sponsorship, remains a frustrating reminder of the Ākhond's warmth and humanity, his good-humored generosity despite the complexity of his relations with our host.

---

3. I often made the acquaintance of the female relatives of my male hosts at the end of a first visit or recording session, when I would be ushered into the private part of the house to convey my greetings and thanks for the trouble they were taking behind the scenes to make my stay comfortable. Subsequent or longer visits enabled me to establish primary friendships among a household's female members, but for the most part, my initial contacts were male-mediated, since it was men, not women, I met outside their homes.

13. Ākhond Mulla Mahmūd, "Black and White"

Ākhond: This is a story that we—
—you may have heard told among the people, if she[1] hasn't heard it.
[They say], "Such-and-such a guy went to so-and-so and made
himself white."[2]

Mokhtār: Fine, yeah.

M. Mills: Pardon me?   5

Ā: You see—

M: "He made himself white with so-and-so."

Ā: Yeah.
The story of "Black and White."

M: Yeah— "Black and White."   10

Ā: He went and made himself white, sir.

Karīm: "Black and white."

Ā: Yeah.
[*to Mokhtār*] You must have <u>heard</u> it!

M: Yeah, uh-huh.   15

Ā: It's a very— bad thing to say, anyway. That someone—

M: Yeah— I've heard the story.

Ā: Huh?

Another listener: He's heard the story.

Ā: If you've heard it, then I won't tell it, after all.   20

M M: Why? <u>I</u> haven't heard it. Please go ahead.

---

1. Using the third-person plural/polite pronoun *ūnā*. It is polite in formal contexts to avoid many kinds of direct questions to a guest, instead inquiring, if possible, through a third party who is present.

2. "*Folūniak beraft pīsh-e folūnī xor safīd kard.*" The Ākhond begins this tale, like the previous two, with a proverbial expression which the story explicates. Black and white have connotations of blameworthiness and virtue, respectively, as well as general connotations of physical attractiveness, in Persian popular thought. Note, however, that Persian pronouns have no gender: gender is introduced as an artifact of translation into English.

Karīm: She hasn't heard it, go ahead.

Ā [to Mokhtār]: Have you heard the story behind it?

M: Yes, uh-huh.

Ā: You might not have heard it this way.   25

M: Fine, we'll hear it this way.

Ā: Huh? Who did you hear it from, yourself?

Karīm [louder, with some impatience]: Well, all right, <u>she</u> hasn't heard
                                                                it, anyway,

    even if he did. They wrote it down [*inaudible word*]—so tell it.

Ā: There was a man, sir, a miller.   30

He had a wife who was <u>so</u> white, and <u>so</u> beautiful,

    that there was none like her in the <u>world</u>, anyway.

[*M, M M*: Yeah. Uh-huh.]

There was a man, a merchant,

    who was his next-door neighbor, sir,   35

    and his wife was blacker than ebony.

The wife of the merchant.

This merchant fell in love

    with that woman. [*M*: Yeah—]

    With the miller's wife.   40

[*M*: Yeah, uh-huh.]

Although he fell in love with her, the woman was very virtuous and pure.

No matter how he trailed around after her,

    ‹›

    she didn't give him her hand.

This merchant.   45

One night she said, "Come on, [then], I'll put him into my husband's
                                                                hands."

She said, "Come this evening and hide in the hayrick,³ and I'll come
                                                                to you," »

    she said that to the merchant. [*M*: Yeah.]

That midnight, the guy went and got in the hayrick, this merchant.

[*M*: Yeah.]

---

3. This would be a mud-walled hay-storage enclosure or room, located inside the walls of a traditional house, which is a complex of rooms built against a surrounding wall, often on two levels with animals, supplies and tools housed below, and family rooms above.

She said to her husband, "I think somebody just went into the hayrick,
                pick up a light and go see."   50

When he got inside the hayrick, sir;
    he saw that the 'khān'[4] was there, and he said, "Khān, sir, it's you!"
                    —that miller. »
He said, "Yes."
"But where have you been?"
He said, "By God, my servants weren't there, »   55
    guests arrived late, »
    and I came to take a little hay
    for their horses,
    my guests."
He took the nose-bag,   60
    gathered the hay and helped the khān carry it over to his house.
[*M*: He even helped him—]
Yeah.

So that night passed.
[*Karīm*: What did he know, poor guy!?]   65
Yeah, and the next night, too, she said, "Come tonight, to the cookshed."[5]
       ◇
    To the— pantry.
And when he came, she came and woke up her husband, »
    "Somebody or other
    is stealing our copper pots!" »   70
Yeah, he went, "Who are you?
              It's you, Khān? Where were you?"
He said, "By God, a guest arrived late, and the door
      to our storeroom is locked,
        I came after your rice-rinser."   75
[*M*: The rice-rinsing sieve—[6]]
Yeah, he gave it to him, sir, and he left.

---

4. In this context, a wealthy local landowner.
   5. The kitchen in a traditional house is a separate room, also in the compound but detached from the eating and sleeping areas, so as to keep the heat and smoke of cooking, done with wood on a small open hearth that vents through a smokehole in the roof, away from the living rooms.
   6. The Ākhond uses a more obscure dialect term, *torūsh-palau*, for which Mokhtār supplies, probably for my benefit, a commoner synonym, *chelau-sāf*.

The next evening she said, "It'll never work that way.

        I'll sleep in the back room,

            and I'll tie a thread around my foot,   80

            and tie it to the door of the room.

        So you come and pick up that thread,

            and when you get to me, you can pick

                    up my legs."

[*M*: Yeah—]

When she was about to fall asleep, she took the thread and tied it

               around her husband's ankle.   85

This dame. [*M*: Yeah—]

When he came along like that, he picked up her husband's legs and put

               them around his own neck.

As soon as he picked them up,

    he jumped up out of his bed,[7] and said, "Khān, sir?" »

He said, "Peace to you."[8] [*M*: yeah— (*Some audience snickering*)]   90

"Where have you been?"

He said, "By God— don't get up." —the khān said. »

He said—"How do you mean?"

He said, "A guest arrived at our place, and I made a bet with him.

        He said, 'That miller has only one testicle,'   95

        and I said, 'No, he has two,' »

        so then I said, 'If I can get my hands on them, I could lift

                 them separately,'[9] "

[*Ā and audience laughing*]

    "—We bet two thousand rupees!"

He lifted up his legs and said, "There, now, be careful you don't lose

                 your bet."

He had a look, and went on his way.   100

[*M laughs*]

---

    7. Bedding, consisting of a cotton-batting mattress and quilts, is placed directly on the floor at night, and made into bundles and placed against the wall during the day, when it is used as backrests for sitting. Family members roll out their beds as convenient, near one another in one or more sleeping rooms depending on the size and composition of the family and, in winter, the number of rooms which have heat sources.

    8. The standard form of greeting.

    9. To prove that there are two.

He got himself away by this trick. »
The wife said, "That's the third time I've set him up, and this dolt
doesn't catch him."
[*Audience: Laughing comments off microphone.*]
So they went, sir, as it happened, to the baths.[10]
‹›
[*M*: Yeah.]
And the khān's wife went, too.   105
She said, "Dear sister, what happened to you, that you got so white,
so beautiful?"
She said that to the miller's wife. [*coughs*]
This dame said, "I used to be blacker than you are.
My husband went to such-and-such a Sufi order, and
became a devotee.
In his whole life he only coupled with me once, and I
turned white like this.   110
If he had done it twice, I would have become a houri
of Paradise."
This— this dame said that to her— to the merchant's wife.
She said, "Couldn't you countenance it just once, for him to couple
with me, too?"
[*M*: Yeah—]
—the merchant's wife. »   115
<u>She</u> said, "Ooo— he gave it up, in any case, what to do?
He doesn't even approach me,
from night to morning he's praying and mourning.[11]
He's only coupled with me <u>once</u> in his life.
And I was uglier than you." [*M M giggles.*]   120
She gave all kinds of reasons and promised her money and did this and that,
and she said, "All right, whenever
I can get my husband to agree, I'll send for you.
Maybe he'll make you
white, too."   125

---

10. The sense is that the miller's wife and other women went to the public baths, not that she and her husband went together. Men's and women's baths are separate establishments. In small communities with only one bath, men's and women's days alternate.

11. *raużah*: Literally, "garden," the common term for the Shi'a narratives repeated in remembrance of the martyrdom of the family of the Prophet's grandson, Husayn, at the battle of Karbalā. The word also means "religious fasting" in common parlance in Herat and Kabul.

She came to her husband and said, "Oh, you dolt.

Three, four times now, I've set

you up. Bastard!

It's four years he's been trailing after me.

You go get a couple of *man* of charcoal,

willow charcoal,   130

and a *man* of oil

of mustard."[12] »

She pounded them up in a big bowl, sir, let them soak.

If she was to rub that on someone's body,

no one could clean it off, [*laughs*] except with hellfire!   135

Now she explained, "I'll send for the merchant, and he'll come.

I'll summon his wife tonight, too.

Right when we're about to eat, the merchant and I,

you come and knock on the door.

Now I'll make him into a lamp stand, strip him, do

thus-and-so-" 140

—didn't there used to be those lamps with

four wicks?

[*M*: Yeah— yes.]

She said, "I'll rub him from head to foot,[13]

and put the lamp on top of his head."

[*Audience member shouts "Yes?" to someone outside the room and goes to*

open the door.] 145

"I'll light the wicks, too—" —sir— [*M*: Yeah—]

"—that will put him out of business, »

and then I'll send for his wife, and say, 'Make her white.'

Then I'll go out and stand right in front of her husband, with

the lamp on his head,

and you fuck his wife standing up." 150

---

12. *roghan-e mandau*, an acrid oil pressed from the seeds of a type of rocket plant, or mustard, used for lamp oil before petroleum products were available and for some medicinal uses.

13. That is, with the charcoal and oil mixture she has prepared.

She taught her husband what to do.
[*M*: Yeah . . . fine . . .]

She carried out all these plans, and said to the— merchant, "T—
      My husband went to do his milling, so you come."
He gathered up all sorts of gear, sir, tents and pavilions, »   155
      saying "I'm going hunting,"
      brought it all to this dame's house.

[*M*: Yeah.]
The— this other dame is relieved, because her husband's gone hunting,
                                                                anyway.
She said to her, "Come tonight, and my husband will make you white."   160
And <u>she</u> [made] a nice bundle of supplies and things¹⁴ and
      at bedtime, all of a sudden this guy, her husband, came back, the miller.
And this guy said, "I'll run for it," »
but she said, "I'll <u>feed</u> him, I'll get <u>rid</u> of him."
She took him, sir, and made him into a lampstand.   165
[*Interruption: door opens*]
She made him into a lampstand, sir,
      stripped him naked as a lip,
      rubbed him head to foot.
She put the lamp on top of his head, and he cast a shadow clear over
                                                                to here.

All at once his wife came in with her bundle.   170
[The miller's wife] said, "Father of so-and-so, for the sake of the Lord,
                  she's after me, saying, 'Make me white just once.'
                  You made me this [white], when you coupled
                                          with me just once,
                        and I got so beautiful, »
                        [do it] with this poor thing too,   175
                        just once—" »

------

14. As becomes clear from later context, she made up a bundle of gifts for the miller's wife, according to her promise in the bath.

He said, "Oh!
        After all, I gave it up, I— to— to you— you're my wife, and I
                                        don't go to you!"
She said, "Well, the doorway to the Lord is charity.
            You can go afterward and become a devotee again, let it go!" »   180
He said, "All right."

This dame came out and stood right in front of the lamp, where the
                                        husband is sitting,
        with the lamp on top of his head, »
and he fucked this dame standing up.
<>
The merchant's wife. [*M*: Yeah.]   185
After he fucked her, she got up— at night people look very good in
                                        mirrors—¹⁵
        she said, "By God, you made me nice and white, blessings on you!"
And she gave the other dame the bundle and
        she set out, and left, that dame.

After she left,   190
he came, that guy, and he's running his hands all over the "lamp."
He— and his testicles and prick are hanging down,— he said, »
        "Give me the razor,
        because this lamp's burning badly [*laughing*]— »
        I'm going to cut off these bits and pieces around its [*laughing*] feet."   195
[*Audience laughter. M*: Clean it up—]
She said, "Me— not me, I'm afraid, the razor is in that room, go yourself." »
Her husband left, and—
she said to the merchant, "Get up, bastard, he's going to cut off your
                                        testicles!"

Just <u>naked</u> [*claps once*] like that, all <u>black</u>, he ran out of their house.   200
He left, and the dame said, "He's gone!" [*brushing hands together briskly*]

He knocked on the door, and his wife rushed out,
        and said, "May I be sacrificed for you!
                Who made you all black?"
He said, "You *kūnī*, the same one that made you white!"

---

    15. Because lamplight is flattering.

[*Laughs. Audience laughter.*]   205
[*M*: "The same person that made you white!"]
Yeah. She said, "May I be your sacrifice, <u>who</u> made you black like this?" »
He said, "You *kūnī*, the same one that made you white!"
[*Laughs again. More audience laughter.*]

That's the story of "Black and White," sir. [*Laughs.*]
[*MM*: Very good—]   210

"He went to so-and-so and made himself white": The Ākhond's Last Word

The Ākhond introduces a third proverb-based narrative, as he has the first two, with the expression which the story supports. On the surface, one obvious association between this proverb and the one just before it is their metaphorical juxtaposition of pairs of colors. In the proverb concluding *"Agar magar,"* the colors are the red of the tongue and the green ("flourishing, living") head. The redness of the tongue which endangers it is perhaps also associated with the shedding of blood. Green is the color of life and of sanctity throughout the Muslim Middle East. The black and white of the second proverb are equally complex and pervasive in their metaphorical associations. As in the West, black in Afghanistan is associated with sinister and inauspicious forces and conditions (thus, the thieves tell Mahmūd, "God made our faces black (with shame)," chapter 6, l. 127; cf. Qur'an 3:106–7 and Pickthall n.d., pp. 60–61). Additionally, there is a strong aesthetic preference for lightness of complexion in both men and women. This pair of attitudes marginalizing darkness does not, however, yield a simple color prejudice associating darkness of complexion with sinister or dangerous character. The banner of the Abbasid caliphate was black. The "blackness" the thieves describe is metaphorical, referring to the Qur'anic promise that God will darken the faces of transgressors (and whiten those of the virtuous) on Judgment Day, as well as to the ethical implications of their deeds. Orthodox Islam strongly asserts the spiritual equality of all sincere believers, regardless of skin color. Additionally, in the iconography of Sufi mystical poetry, which infuses the imagery of secular poetics and cultural aesthetic as well, there is an established contrast pair, the fair, beautiful, but cruel Turk, who is the epitome of the elusive, proud, and punishing mystical love object, and the small, dark, enslaved, lowly, but loving Hindu, who is a type for the soul in servitude to the mystical beloved (Schimmel 1975b). Radiant beauty is thus associated with power; darkness with weakness. The character of the merchant's dark wife, helpless, deferential to her husband (the only deferential female the Ākhond has portrayed), and pathetically eager to win his admiration even to the point of compromising her chastity, conforms to some of these associations of dark skin operating in classical poetic symbology. The blackness of soot and mustard oil applied to her husband for his bad deeds, which can only be removed by "hellfire" (l. 135), mimics the blackening of the faces of such transgressors in the next world (Qur'an 3:105), in ironic contrast to the unlucky but loving wife's natural coloring.

If color contrasts were a possible mnemonic cue linking two of the Ākhond's proverb-narratives in their adjacent positions in his performance, there are also deeper and more complex patterns to the story of "Black and White" which echo patterns in other narratives told by the Ākhond in the series. Like the women in the Ākhond's "Salīm the Jeweller" (see chapter 6), the main character in this story is a loyal wife who is visibly stronger than her husband (ll. 102 and 126). But like the male hero of "The Old Thief with Five Sons" (see chapter 9), she uses female allure as bait to trap her would-be exploiter. Also like the "Old Thief" story, this is a tale of private revenge confronting a private abuse of prestige and power. While the old fraud of the earlier story merely posed as a pious elder, the Khān, the would-be seducer, is a member of the elite and a wealthy man relative to his miller neighbor, whose simplicity and generosity he repeatedly exploits.

With respect to the theme of righting wrongs, the array of three proverb-narratives, taken together, repeats a sequence which has already occurred twice before in the Ākhond's storytelling in this session, moving from portrayals of a confrontation between the individual and central authority, in which the central authority's problematical dedication to justice must be resecured through interaction with common people, to a confrontation between private individuals in which fairness and justice are also at stake but only secured through private measures of trickery and revenge. The previous two proverb narratives portrayed little men dealing cleverly and successfully with the potentially abusive power of a king and moving the king to act generously. The hero of the third story is in a weaker position yet, a woman, the wife of a poor man, who must defend her own virtue discreetly, by cleverness, on behalf of a husband who lacks the boldness and intelligence to defend his interests himself. A similar pattern developed in the transition among the three thief stories, from "Mahmūd of Ghaznī and the Thieves" to the young boy's private revenge on the old thief and, finally, to the privately acquired insights on domestic sexual violence provided by the shaykh in "Women's Tricks." The public justice system can achieve proper redress of these private wrongs only with the addition of private information. We have also seen this sequence from public to private before in the internal structure of "Salīm the Jeweller," in which the public problem of Hojāj's tyranny, and the narration of Salīm's adventures and trials in the public world of work, pilgrimage, and holy war were succeeded by adventures and trials in the private realms of sexuality and matrimony, finally coming full circle in his interview with Hojāj, in which the tyrant's commitment to more just behavior was achieved through insight into a private citizen's trials, personal and institutional.

The third sequence, that of the proverb-narratives, does not seem to come full circle as did the previous two, bringing private forces to bear in the perfection of public justice, unless one takes into account that the point of this last story, which is enacted entirely in the private domestic space, is the construction of a proverb which becomes, as Becker has pointed out, "public language" (1984:139). In a shift from the narrative to its pragmatic application in proverb form, this tale of very private revenge and social control is thus made available for actual use in the public evaluation of other people's deeds. It is, as the Ākhond points out, strong stuff: "It's a very—bad thing to say, anyway. That someone—[went to someone else and made himself white.]" (l. 16). With use of the saying, "He went to so-and-so and made himself white," the world of the story, its radical terms of attempted harm and clear retribution, are inserted into the events of real-life experience and serve to judge, unambiguously for communal use, the wrong actions of others and, in so doing, to have a corrective effect. The corrective effect of narrative which is kept internal to the story of Salīm, is launched into the real world of the storyteller's speech pragmatics by a proverb-narrative. By moving from tales which are optionally didactic to tales which are proverb-substrates, the Ākhond makes the didactic and in-terpretive dimension of his tales increasingly unambiguous. Narrative in didactic use effects a real-world movement from public (the performance setting) to private experience (what is reported in the tale) back to public evaluation, a pattern which the Ākhond's overall arrangement of tale topics also traces.

The plainest idiom of male-male aggression, wrong and retribution, is sexual tampering, real or threatened, with a man's female relatives (or with a male self in a female role), as we have seen repeatedly in this story series (in both invective and plot content). In the Ākhond's final story, that aggressive pattern is deftly ironized, making a woman, the potential tam-peree, into the architect of the sexual revenge of her husband on his would-be abuser through the other man's wife. She even gives her husband an opportunity to threaten the man himself with castration, permanent sexual disaster, after they have jointly humiliated and cuckolded him.

This woman, as a female hero who is both a trickster and a force for social order, contradicts generalizations about the roles of female charac-ters in Persian folktales which Marzolph (1984:28) offers on the basis of his comparative work on existing oral tale collections and studies such as Friedl's (1978). Female characters in general are described as passive or, if they are active, destructive. In my own collecting experience, women story-tellers seemed to cast female characters in a wider variety of active roles than did men, and when men told stories with female heroes, the women tended to be operating in male disguise, in public spheres of male endeavor such as quests and battles (Mills 1985). To this extent, the Ākhond's por-trayal of a woman's domestic heroism is unusual, though a story type to which this tale is related (Marzolph Tale Type *1730) is widely performed by men.[1] The Ākhond's portrait of the clever female hero, manipulator of sexual roles, is in any case balanced by the figure of the Khān's wife, a foolish sexual victim who recalls the images of women in "Rasūl's Mother" and "Ten Qerān." The image of the woman trickster as a force for order, in this story, also balances the mayhem perpetrated on social order by the gypsy woman, the shoemaker's wife, and the murderously jealous lover in "Women's Tricks."[2]

Strikingly, the Ākhond's last word in each of three tripartite story clusters ("Salīm" as a multiepisodic structure, the three "thief" stories, the three proverb stories) is that female understandings are central to the achievement of justice. In the private sphere, the mediators of justice either *are* female (in "Salīm," the vizier's daughter and her *parī* foster mother; the miller's wife) or are *acting* as females (the young boy who avenges himself on the old thief) or are men with privileged access to the world of women (the shaykh, supposedly lost in prayer while he occupies intimate domestic space and observes the women of the house). Privatization of moral in-sight, necessary to the achievement of justice, entails possession of or access to female perspectives and roles for both male and female heroes, in five out of nine of the Ākhond's narratives, a striking pattern for the man who declared at the outset of his performance that he had little familiarity with "the disposition of women" (chapter 5, l. 81). Even the foolish woman in "Ten Qerān" has the last word concerning the justice of her case ("Can you

---

1. The type, which Marzolph calls "Die betrogene Freier," usually involves multiple would-be seducers who are humiliated in turn by the woman, with her husband's complicity, in a badger game in which she actually lures them into compromising positions. There is no subplot concerning the sexual violation of a would-be seducer's wife, nor is it so clear that the men are totally to blame for their predicament, a key element in this narrative's status as a proverb substrate, as told by the Ākhond.

2. Haag-Higuchi notes a similar balancing of themes, portraying women as tricky for good or ill, in the collection she describes (1984:16), and in Mahroo Hatami's 1977 study of the *Tūtīnāmah*. Fischer (1978) points out the importance of female saints.

wall off half of it?" chapter 5, l. 151). The relative prominence of female perspectives at the ends of all three story runs (the complex tale of Salīm, the three-story "thief" series, and the three-story "proverb" series), especially in the last story of his whole performance, with its female hero, establishes the conclusive force of the theme within the total performance. Given the Ākhond's declared ability to "speak to each according to his disposition" (chapter 5, l. 78), one might count this persistent turning toward portrayals of the female, and finally to female heroism, as a resourceful endeavor to construct a performance appropriate to his female listener. In any case, the presence of this array of stories in the Ākhond's active repertoire bespeaks a closer study of the female than he was willing to own up to in the initial interview. While the Ākhond's narrative fluency in utilizing images of the feminine has to be a constituent of his general worldview, one cannot discount the effect of this performance setting's exigencies, especially my own presence, in bringing these themes so richly to the fore.

If an overall thematic unity can be detected, beginning with "Salīm the Jeweller" in the Ākhond's story sequence, centering around issues of justice and social order and the importance of private individuals' insights and active intervention in securing that order, one can similarly trace a repeated movement from public to domestic spheres and relationships, in which that order is contested. At a minimum, such general and repeated patterns may be said to convey a sense of the connectedness of public and private morality, insight, and order and a repeated focusing down on the domestic sphere.[3]

Having traced a repetitive movement in the Ākhond's storytelling from public to domestic spheres, and having asserted a connection between the Ākhond's repeated presentation of themes of justice and his previous jailing by the Woləswāl, one might wish to ask, what connection

---

3. Indeed, an outsider, coming from the impersonal urban West, is struck by the configurations of defended domestic privacy and publicly discussed morality that pertain in Afghan Muslim society. For example, I was visiting a woman friend in her home compound during a day when her own children and a stream of neighbor children were running in and out of her yard, making a great deal of noise. She complained loudly, and I asked her why she did not simply shut her gate. She explained that as long as the neighbor children were free to come and go, her neighbors would know that she had nothing to hide, whereas if she shut them out, neighbors might infer that she was engaged in improper activities. Foreign visitors like myself were enough to arouse their curiosity about her activities; using available privacy mechanisms to shut out the scrutiny provided to adults through their children would be downright suspicious behavior. The walls that protected her from the gaze of male nonrelatives did not shut out the scrutiny and licensed judgment of her neighbors, mediated by children, who are culturally defined as ignorant and asocial, "innocent."

might exist between the idea of the privatization of justice, mediated by the Ākhond's arrangement of stories, and the history of his relations with the Wolǝswāl? Does his repeated movement from explicit representations of the private citizen in confrontation with a government authority figure, to the portrayal of private confrontations, constitute a flirtation with the theme of public justice, a series of approaches to a sensitive topic followed by strategic retreats? One might better infer that the Ākhond sees the problems of public and private justice as so enmeshed that he is asserting, consciously or not, the essentially private nature of his struggle with the Wolǝswāl, by returning repeatedly to meditations on private revenge, especially sexually mediated revenge.

If one takes the stories together, they all assert the primacy of private visions of justice, whether their effects are felt in private or in public institutional transactions. A closer look at the relations and character of the men in this last story enriches the possibilities with regard to the Ākhond's interpretive intentions for this theme of private moral authority vis-à-vis institutional power. The Khān, the abuser of private power, is represented as having fallen in love with another man's wife because of her appearance (ll. 38–40). His essential failure is to let the *nafs*, the earthly side of his character, overcome *'aql*, his adult wisdom and discretion. *Nafs*, though not the repository of wisdom, has a kind of cleverness and resourcefulness associated with it, manifested in the ingenious excuses the Khān gives each time he is discovered by the gullible miller (ll. 55–59, 73–75, and 94–97). Each time, he imposes on the miller's simplicity and eagerness to please, much to the exasperation of the miller's wife (l. 102). With each of her first three attempts to trap him, she lures the Khān closer to the intimate center of her home, which she is trying to protect: first the stable, then the cookshed, and finally, the sleeping chamber itself. His impositions on her husband are correspondingly more and more intimate: first for the loan of animal fodder, then of equipment for preparing human food, then for an inspection of the man's own private parts.

The husband, a generous simpleton and deferential to his wealthy neighbor even in the most outrageous circumstances ("Khān, sir?" l. 89), has to be informed by his wife before he perceives the threat to his home (ll. 126–28). She knows exactly what her husband is, but in loyal fashion, and strategically, she represents him as a great deal more than that to outsiders. To the merchant's gullible wife, she presents her husband as a spiritually advanced ascetic whose inattention to domestic sexual matters is the fruit of mystical discipline, not stupidity (ll. 109–20). This ironic play on forms of unworldliness allows the Ākhond another joke at the expense of charismatic Sufis and the idea of miracles brought about by religious discipline, which he has already cast in a dubious light in "Women's Tricks" and in his interview comments (see chapter 5), following the humorous lead of Karīm's "Mongol Martyr."

In the final encounter, though, the miller, having followed his wife's instructions to the letter, takes an initiative which casts in doubt the whole portrayal of him as a fool. After the Khān, in the guise of a lampstand, has been forced to witness his own cuckolding and the happy departure of his simple-minded wife, the miller on his own initiative then goes over to examine the "lampstand," running his hands all over "it," and finally announcing "This lamp burns badly" (l. 194). Pretending to believe that the Khān's exposed testicles and penis are part of a badly trimmed wick, he tells his wife to go fetch a razor with which to trim them. This little razor scene, with the husband's request and the wife's refusal, circumstantially reminiscent of the dramatic scene between the gypsy woman and her barber husband in "Women's Tricks" (chapter 10, ll. 173ff.)—and indeed, perhaps a mnemonic link between the two stories in the Ākhond's construction of the story sequence—has a very different outcome. The clever wife picks up her husband's cue immediately and, in the few moments of his absence abets the drama by telling the Khān his testicles are in jeopardy. Her husband makes an important transition in this scene, taking the initiative in the perfection of their joint revenge on the Khān, moving from being a fool to playing the fool. He terrifies his would-be abuser and induces him to flee, naked, soot-covered, and publically disgraced, specifically by playing on the Khān's conviction that he *is* a fool who might really take a man covered with soot for a lampstand and his testicles for wicks, even on close inspection.

In the Khān's final, exasperated exchange with his solicitous wife (ll. 203–8), the clever woman and her formerly simple husband are consolidated into one personage, "the same one that made you white." But as the title-proverb, "He went to so-and-so and made *himself* white," makes plain, the real perpetrator of the deed is the original offender himself, the Khān who tried to take advantage of his neighbor's simplicity to seduce his neighbor's wife. "He did it to himself," the shaykh's message in "Women's Tricks" (chapter 10, ll. 191–201), is also a core element of this proverb-narrative. The person who sets out to manipulate or damage someone else receives instead the damage he intended to do to the other.

This message, twice repeated in the Ākhond's performance, can be brought to bear on the performance situation. The Ākhond in his interview portrayed himself as a consummate entertainer, who could turn even a funeral into a wedding with his stories (chapter 5, ll. 64–65). The Woləswāl summoned him precisely for this ability to entertain, for which the Ākhond was locally renowned. On closer examination, turning a funeral into a wedding is not necessarily a socially appropriate thing to do nor is it likely that a man of the Ākhond's age, position, and dedication to traditional educational matters would ignore or violate the decorum of an event of that kind. Rather, he uses hyperbole to describe the transformative and inversionary power of narrative, a power which he has mastered. He announces the power of narrative skill to effect the total reinterpretation of social events and relationships. Having been cast as an entertainer, perhaps a buffoon (given the low social status of professional entertainers), and this by a man who has previously compromised his personal autonomy by locking him up, the Ākhond good-humoredly accepts the role of entertainer. But he never relinquishes the instructive potential of his performance, and its didactic dimension becomes structurally more overt as he brings it to a close with proverb-narratives. Like the miller, he uses the role of social and intellectual inferior into which he has been cast, to gain a rhetorical advantage over his oppressor and to redefine the situation for his own purposes. If the Woləswāl ever realized that the Ākhond, though traditional in education and attitudes, was no fool, that the whole story sequence was open to an interpretation highly and humorously critical of himself, he did not acknowledge it, just as it remains unclear whether the Khān ever fully realized that his humble miller neighbor was, in the last analysis, no fool. The Ākhond leaves the interpretation of this last story open, as he has left others open. By way of conclusion, he simply repeats the climactic realization of the Khān, "Who made you all black?" — ". . . the same one that made you white!" (ll. 204–205) for our contemplation. It is not told whether the Khān ever realized that he set himself up for this outcome, that *he* "made himself white" with the help of the miller and his wife. Nor will the Ākhond tell us how closely he connects the performance context with the situations represented in his stories. But he is at least relishing, if not directly applying, the notion of the manipulator manipulated, the fucker fucked.

It must be acknowledged that the responsibility for such an extended interpretation of the Ākhond's narrative strategy ultimately rests with the interpreter, not with the performer. If the Ākhond intended such a send-up of his host, it might be desirable, though not strictly necessary, for the host himself to see that this was intended and in fact perpetrated. The perpetration of an act of social criticism by the mediation of a story or a proverb requires only that some listeners, not necessarily the object of the criticism, get the message. In taking any particular message from the performance, one can only hope to have understood correctly things which by their nature will not be said directly. Perceptive listening is as much an act of virtuosity as is pointed speaking, and one less easy to observe or test against the norms for social competence prevailing in the environment of the performance. Ultimately, one can only hope the Ākhond would be pleased with the particular ways one has found power in his words.

14. Khalīfah Karīm, "The Corrupt and the Good"

Karīm: This story that we're going to tell now?
　　—I don't know what to tell, anyway, sir.
　　The story . . . I'm . . . going . . . to tell—

[*M. Mills interrupts to move microphone closer to Karīm*: It's a little faint . . .]　　5
Mokhtār: Like prov—stories should have [*inaudible word*]—[1] stories like—
‹›
K: The Story of Evildoers and Good.—Good.[2]
M: The Corrupt and the Good.[3]
[*while M M writes title*]—Good. Good.

Karīm: Yeah.　　　　　　　　　　　　　　　　　　　　　　　　　　10
There was a man, sir, he had a son.
His son had become a youth, newly so,
　　　ah—one day he said to his mother, "Ma?" »
She said, "What is it?"
[*Inaudible audience comment*: Put this— *second audience member*:
　　　　　　　　　　　　　　　　　　　　That's OK.]　　15
He said, "Ma?" »
She said, "What is it?"
He said, "What's this— difference between corrupt women
　　　　　and virtuous ones?
[*M*: Yeah.]　　　　　　　　　　　　　　　　　　　　　　　　　　20

---

1. Mokhtār seems to stutter over using the ordinary term for proverb, *żarb ol-masal*, nor was it used previously by the Ākhond in describing the stories attached to proverbial expressions which he has just told. The term was readily understood by other people in the area when I used it myself in later conversations.
　　2. *Qessah-ye Badkārah o Nīk.*
　　3. *Badkār o Nīkkār.*

That one could test them?
If there isn't any well-known— any obvious test,
    a person could get fooled.
You could go and stretch your hand— in her direction, so to say,
    approach her,   25
      look to see that she isn't corrupt.

[*M*: Yeah.]

    How do you do that?
    If one can't be recognized— how can one be recognized?"
She said, "Now that's not a very difficult job.   30
    They're easily recognized." »
He said, "How?"
She said, "Any woman that you see on the way,
      get close to her,
      and say something sort of suggestive,   35
    if she's like this,
      that she denies and speaks to you in anger,
      tells you to get lost,
      acts angry, she's corrupt.

[*M*: Yeah.]   40

    If she just says to you calmly, 'Have you no shame?' and passes by,

‹›

[*M*: That one's pure.]

    —she's pure.
    Be careful that you don't bother her."
He said, "Fine."   45

‹›

Well, sir.
Two days passed after that and
ah— his father said to him,
    he— he had a sister, his father, »
    who would be this boy's aunt.   50
And she's a bit farther down the road, in another village, and
uh— he said to him, "Bābā—"⁴ »
He said, "What is it?" »

---

4. The father uses the term *bābā*, "old man, papa," in affectionate address to his son. This reverse use of kin terms for affectionate address is normal.

He said, "Take a donkey and go,
    bring that aunt of yours.   55
    Because we're going to kill the sheep for jerked meat,⁵ »
        and she can eat the 'skin-meat' with us. »
    The old lady will have gotten sad, »
        it's been a while since you went to her."
He said, "That's good."   60
He got out a donkey—if you'll pardon me—⁶ and put a pad on it »
    and brought it from there and
    came to his aunt's house.
His aunt kissed him and made a big fuss over him and said, »
    "Well, where have you been?!" »   65
He said, "Um— yeah—
    well, m— my father sent me, your brother,
    that you should go there for a night or two, »
        it would pass the time for you, »
    we're killing our sheep for dried meat,   70
    so you have to be there."
This poor old woman said, "Fine."

She got on the donkey and came down the road.
As they came down the road, a thought crossed his mind.
That "My mother said, 'You   75
        can tell the difference between corrupt and
                uncorrupted women,
      if you get close to her, »
        and if she denies you,
        if she speaks angrily,
      she's corrupt.   80

---

5. *gūsfand-e land*: a family which could afford it would often fatten one or more sheep over the summer to slaughter in autumn and dry the meat with salt for winter consumption. *Gosht-e land*, mutton jerky, is especially tasty and figures in a number of favorite winter recipes. "Skin-meat" here refers to portions of the meat not suitable for drying, which are eaten fresh at slaughtering time.

6. *Golāb be surat*, literally, "Rosewater on [your] face", a phrase used, like the similar *gol be rū*, "flowers for [your] face," to apologize in advance for the use of language or subject matter which the listener(s) might deem offensive. Cf. *barādar gol*, "flower brother," the more intimate term of address which the storytellers substitute for *sayb*, "sir," when about to narrate a rowdy sexual or other potentially indecorous scene.

If she puts you off calmly and goes on by,

—uh—she's not corrupt, so watch out, be discreet.'

Well, come on, let's see how this aunt of mine is."[7]

‹›

The old woman was mounted on a donkey, sir, »

he came alongside of her,   85

got close to her like that and reached out a—

and touched her thigh.

[*M*: Yeah— uh— huh.]

When he touched her thigh, squeezed her,

she said, "Get out, curse your father and mother!   90

Eh, you motherless, sisterless *kūnī*![8]

Don't you have any shame, you!!?

‹›

After all, I'm your aunt, now!!"

‹›

He said [to himself], »

"It's clear she's corrupt."   95

[*M*: "I found (one)." *M M laughs softly.*]

Yeah.

"See how she tries to deny me, talking to me?"

He said, "It just happened, my hand just touched you, I didn't intend

anything!"

They came down the road a way.   100

Again the devil pricked him, "Touch her again, see how she is this time—

or isn't she?"

Well.

---

7. The potentially offensive topic which the storyteller anticipated is now revealed as incest.

8. Appeals to feelings for mother and sister are a standard way for a woman to shame a man who is being sexually aggressive. Cf. "Rasūl's Mother," chapter 4, ll. 108 and 114. When a man must speak to a woman who is not his relative and not of higher status than himself, he indicates respectful intentions by addressing her as "mother" or "milk-sister, foster sister" (*hamshīrah*). Two people who have been nursed by the same woman are considered foster brother and sister, not sexually available to each other. The storyteller leaves exceptionally long pauses between the next three sentences. Similar pauses in previous stories provided openings for brief audience comments, but here the audience is quite silent, perhaps ill at ease with the developing incest theme. The audience by now was only three or four people besides ourselves, reduced from the night before.

This time again, sir, his hand reached out—it was a more protected place—
and this time again, he squeezed her thigh harder   105
    and uh— more painfully,
    really pinched her thigh and
she yelled.
This old woman [whacked] him on the head, »
said, "Now!!"   110
    "Hey! In your mother's daddy's mouth!⁹
    You made [mother's] milk a sin,
        you shameless one, you—!
        Motherfucker! »
        you, lawless! »   115
        you heathen! You! » [*speaking ever more rapidly*]
Have you gotten so rusty-headed that out of the whole world,
                           you're starting on <u>my</u> body,
    curses on the father of your nature, you *kūnī*!!"¹⁰

He said, "Where could you find anyone corrupter than this, anyway?"
[*Audience laughs. M*: "There— she really puts up a fuss."]   120
    "Look, from one minute to the next she's getting darker and
                                more shameful!
    So be it,
    in a more secluded spot I'll get my hands on her—!"
They went a little way, and right on the way there was a deep pit
    where there wasn't very much water. »   125
Arriving there, he said, "Here's just the spot, this is the chance, anyway!
            Enough with touching and pinching and
                        poking, anyway.
          Now I'm going to start the real stuff, the big
                    thing with her."
He grabbed the old woman off the donkey.

---

    9. A contraction of a full-scale female curse, "I piss in the mouth of [your ancestors, your father, etc.]!" the scatological, female equivalent of male curses which emphasize sexual aggression. The reference to mother's milk invokes the standards of classificatory parenthood and incest rules which the boy is violating.

    10. This complex clause is approximately translated. The original (spoken in one breath up to the final curse), is "*keh to az hameh jā degeh donyā be sar-e to zan(g) shodah keh be jon-e meh deslāf kardī be pefar-e zāt-e to kūnī nālat!*" The phrase "rusty-headed" compresses the Persian, for which there is no real English equivalent.

[*In response to inaudible audience murmer*]
Yeah.   130
He took her down off the donkey, and
she said, "What's this?" »
He said, "It's matters for repentance,"[11]
     because I'm certain according to my own mother's tests,
     the <u>science</u> of knowing how to tell, —you're corrupt.   135
     If I get my hands on a corrupt one like you, and let you
              get away, »
      where <u>would</u> I go bury myself?"[12]

‹›

[*Audience laughs, after a pause.*]
Kind sir, he fucked this poor little old bent-over, seventy-year-old
      woman.
[*M*: Yeah. *M M laughs quietly*]
Then he put her back on the donkey, and the old woman couldn't say
              a thing,   140
she said [to herself], "What can I do now, anyway?
         Now that that happened—"
Well, the old woman came along on the donkey and
the news went ahead, "There now—" to—to his father,
"There, now, he's brought that milk-sister of yours."   145
He came out to meet his milk-sister on the road and
    told her, "Peace be on you,"
saw that she was upset and angry and
    well, to such an extent.
He got her down off the donkey and they came along to a [secluded]
              corner,   150
     and she covered her face with her hand and just sat there, all upset.
He said, "Sister, you're very welcome, step on my eyes.[13]" »
She said, "Ey, curses on my father
     and on my ever coming here,
     curses on your father, too, that there's shared milk between us, »   155
     and on your sending any messenger!

---

    11. *taubahhā yē.*
    12. That is, for missing such a sexual opportunity.
    13. A courteous hyperbole, more common in Iranian than in Afghan Persian, to say that the speaker is entirely at the service of the addressee.

[*with rising pitch and delivery speed over muted audience giggling*]
>   Were people in short supply? »
>   If this is how this boy delivers things, may God make
>   you childless!
>   May his sapling fall over!¹⁴ »
>   What is it that he delivers for you? »   160
>   What perfections have you taught him!!?" [*Audience laughter*]
◇
He said, "Maybe, Go— Sister, God forbid,
>   if he spoke to you rudely or lightly, God forfend!"
She said, "If <u>only</u> he <u>had</u> just spoken rudely or lightly, that one!"
He said, "Maybe he beat your donkey—   165
>   along the way?" »
She said, "If only he'd hit my donkey and gotten my neck broken!"
◇
[*M: Yeah.*]
He said, "What did he <u>do</u>, hit you with a stick?" »
She said, "If only he had hit me, and broken my head!"   170
He said, "What did he <u>do</u>?" »
She said, "Me, in my condition, »
>   at my age, »
>   with my years, »
>   this death-and-sin <u>fucked</u> me!"   175
[*Audience laughs. Karīm laughs.*]
The guy was really enraged, sir,
right away he landed on his son's head.

[*M: Yeah.*]
Yeah.
He started to beat him good with a stick, and the kid was crying and
>   squalling and sir,   180
>   his mother came out like that
She said, "What happened, what <u>is</u> this?
>   What's all this beating and hitting?
>   ◇

———————

14. *Nehol az i beghaltah*!: apparently a curse, but the sound on tape is not entirely clear and the expression as deciphered is not a common one.

After he went of his own accord,
    got your sister all ready there and put her on a donkey
    and brought her here,   185
is it fitting that you hit him like that?"

<>

He said, "Oh, bastard, you put her on a donkey, »
    if only it had been just putting her on a donkey! »
    after all, do you <u>know</u> what he did?!"

She said, "What <u>did</u> he do?"   190
He said [*very intensely*], »
    "He <u>fucked</u> my poor, helpless, old sister, that *kūnī* son of yours!!"
[*M and MM laugh. M*: Yeah . . .]

<>

She said, "Strange news on your head!
    It's clear enough that your brain is rotted!   195
    He can't fuck <u>her</u>, she's his aunt, »
    [just like] he can't fuck me, his si— his mother, »
    he can't fuck his sister, »
    he can't fuck his neighbor,
    All right, now, he's gone blind for lack of cunt, so who's he
                    supposed to fuck?! 200

<>

    I—"
[*Storytelling interrupted by new arrivals, another elderly man, with friendly
    greetings*:
    "Peace to you!"
    "How are you?"
    "Are you well?" *etc., etc. Brief break in taping till audience settles.*]

    "Well, the sky hasn't fallen on you and hit you,   205
    so get your sister a new overdress."

<>

[*M*: Uh-huh . . .]
    "Get her a new *chāderī*, make it up to her, and let her go her way, »
    if he did it, he did it, it'll be all right, anyway."

<>

[*Audience laughs. M*: Good!]   210
[*Laughing*] Yeah, sir!

He made it up to his sister, anyway, gave her some comforting words.
  Gave her a little bribe,
and said, "Forgive my son's fault, because he did it out of compulsion, »
      anyway, there was no one else there."   215
[*M, laughing*: He's right.]
[*Karīm laughs*]
[*Greeting of new arrivals, interrupted to finish the story, resumes.*]

"What can you do about it?": Khalīfah Karīm Regains the Floor

Shortly after completing "Black and White," the Ākhond departed to take the truck-transport back to his village, about one hour distant on the main district road. With a little urging from us, Karīm was persuaded to take the narrative floor again, with Mokhtār steering his attention back to the topic of proverb-narratives, which the Ākhond had addressed (ll. 4 and 6). A proverb-narrative did not readily occur to him. Karīm's designation for his story, "The Corrupt and the Good," lacks the metaphorical dimension of proverb and thus is more like a topical title than a tag-proverb. With its explicit reference to virtue and vice, it could be the gloss for the metaphorical contrast pair in the Ākhond's tag-proverb for his last story, "Black and White" (*Sīāh o Safīd*).

The premise of the story, a sexually naïve youngster asking an older female for advice, recalls his earlier offering, "Rasūl's Mother," except that the young questioner is himself the protagonist, is male, and having received explicit advice from his mother (ll. 33–43), proceeds to wreak sexual havoc rather than have it inflicted on him. Karīm's return to sexual foolishness and sexual excess in general, as topics, may have been immediately motivated by a desire to match those themes in "Black and White," but more specifically, this story of Karīm's rings changes on themes of all three of his own previous stories ("Mongol Martyr," "Rasūl's Mother," and " 'Ādel Khān"), especially foolishness (of the male variety) and the helplessness of women in the face of sexual victimization and humiliation. There is no ethnic distancing to this tale of foolishness and rape, however, and the element of incest gives a new twist to the humor of disorderly sex. The only distancing of the protagonist from the listeners is by age, he is "a youth, newly so," (l. 12), just old enough to be curious about sex without the protection of adult male wisdom. The fact that it is his father's sister that he violates, the woman for whom his father should have the closest and most affectionate lifelong loyalty (demonstrated by his sending for her to share in the family's special food, ll. 56–59), makes this error of judgment a most conspicuous failure to follow in his father's footsteps toward male maturity and judiciousness.

Hafizullah Baghban in his comprehensive study of the humor of Herati folk plays (177:368) found that incest was the least used of heterosexual humor themes and ascribed its low frequency to "the serious nature of the taboo involved." The theme of incest was first raised, in a hyperbolic statement, by the Ākhond describing the hypersexuality of the old thief (chapter 9, l. 104). The ambivalence of incest humor which Baghban identified on content grounds is reflected in Karīm's apology for what he is about to relate (l. 61), and the hesitant audience response to Karīm's comic portrayal of the incest rape scene (ll. 128–39). It is probably the incest, not the forced nature of the sex, which makes the audience uneasy. Our current western notions of rape and voluntary sex cannot be directly imposed on this scene. Indeed, Afghan women are expected by their men to be at least putatively reluctant sexual partners; those who take sexual initiative may be considered dangerously depraved like the barber's seducer in " 'Ādel Khān."

Karīm portrays good women as humiliated into speechlessness by coitus, whether licit or illicit. The violated old lady at first "couldn't say a thing," recalling the bride's repeated complaint in the face of sexual indignity in "Rasūl's Mother," "Who can you tell it to?" (chapter 4, ll. 111, 163, 170). The old lady regains her voice only in response to her brother's solicitous inquiries (ll. 153–61). The audience greets this foray of female recrimination with more ready laughter than they did her rape. It is precisely the vociferousness of old women which has gotten the old lady into trouble. The young boy has been told by his mother that women who answer back in vehement denial are actually corrupt (ll. 37–39, 78–80), while those who reject an overture with few words are good. What she fails to point out to him is that these rules of circumspection and silence apply to young, sexually available women, not to elderly women, and especially not to those female elders who fall within the category of sexually unavailable relatives. Such persons have the right to act in loco parentis to young males and to speak frankly to them. To her brother, she has the most right to speak frankly, as Karīm's spirited rendering of her heated complaint (ll. 153–75) demonstrates. The silence of women is a function of age, sexual status, and relationship, not an absolute.

The boy's mother, whose accurate but incomplete advice was the basis for his misbehavior, also readily speaks out, in his defense. She remarks rather sarcastically to her husband, "Strange news on your head!" (*'Ajab awāl be sar-e to*, l. 194) and calls her husband soft in the head for not realizing that the boy has been carried away by sexual frustration (ll. 195–200). It is normal and expected for fathers to be the disciplinarians and mothers to be indulgent and protective of their children, especially of their sons. Whereas parents are expected to marry their children off early enough to avert sexual frustration, it is also expected that parents would be very reticent with their children on sexual matters so that young people pick up most of their instruction from slightly older peers or indirectly through stories or overhearing adult conversation about the behavior of others. The ellipsis in the mother's advice to her son partly reflects shyness on sexual matters and partly the stupidity of the boy in not having already assimilated an understanding of incest taboos. That he could inquire directly of his mother on such a matter, bespeaks his simplicity, perhaps his incipient deviance, and her indulgence. The mother also minimizes the outrage to her husband's sister ("Well, the sky hasn't fallen on you and hit you," l. 205) and tells him offhandedly to smooth the matter over with a gift (l. 208). The potential for competitiveness between a man's sister and his wife, over his loyalty, is an unspoken dimension in the mother's defense of her son.

The story ends with a questionable material redress offered to the elderly lady for her rape (in the form of a new *chaderī*—a veil to protect her modesty) and assertions that no permanent harm was done, if only because there were no witnesses (ll. 209 and 215), which the male listeners laughingly accept. The devaluation of elderly women common to many folktales is evident here. As in other stories Karīm told in this series, the resolution of this story does not entirely restore the wronged parties to their former condition. The Mongol leaves his meeting with the mulla under the mistaken impression that the written document given to him establishes his brother's status as a martyr (chapter 3, ll. 94–99). "Rasūl's Mother" emerges from her wedding night with the realization that the actualities of "housekeeping" (i.e., sex, chapter 4, l. 12) are such as to "bring people's houses down in ruins" (l. 179). The barber in " 'Ādel Khān" receives a princely reward only because he has suffered irreversible physical harm at the hands of a destructive female (chapter 7, ll. 611–20).

The picture presented by all four stories is of ordinary people making do in the face of comic disaster and loss. Compensation, when available, does not fully restore them to their prior dignity or well-being nor does the perspective of the less powerful reliably sway those powerful persons who are in a position to help or harm them. Karīm's worldview in this performance series, thus, seems more pessimistic, less uncompromisingly convinced of the power of the common man, than the Ākhond's. With his final offering, Karīm proceeded to broach the question of sexual disorder and social recompense in a more serious vein, one that reveals further systematic differences between his portrayals of order and disorder and those of the Ākhond.

15. Khalīfah Karīm, "The Ill Fortune of the City of Rūm"[1]

[Karīm is speaking about the Ākhond, who has departed to meet the truck which carries passengers and freight in the direction of his own village.]

He hasn't left— <u>has</u> he left? *[Break in taping.]*

Karīm: Yeah— *[laughs]*

M Mills: What's the name of this story?

Mokhtār: What is the name of the story you're going to tell?

K: The name of the story?   5

<>

The name of the story, sir,

it's the story that, the one that,

that ill fortune— it's— it's [about] an ill fortune, an ill fate.

M: Yeah— the burning of the city of Rūm.[2]

K: That burning of the city of Rūm.   10

M: Wah— ahh, yeah— very good.

     [to M M, dictating] "The Burning of the City of Rūm."

M M (writing): "The Burning of the City of Rūm."

M: "About the Ill Fortune— of the City of Rūm."

M M: Ah— Yeah— "the Burning of the City of Rūm."   15

M: "The burning of the City of Rūm."

     Goo—od, that's a very good story.[3]

Karīm: Sir, it was like this, the point is, at that one time, —

[Pauses while audience settles down to listen and the microphone is repositioned]

---

1. *Shūmīyat-e Shahr-e Rūm: Rūm* in Persian generally designates greater Byzantium, especially present-day Anatolia, and/or the city of Constantinople before its conquest by the Muslim Turks. The scene is thus set in a Christian city of imperial size and power.

2. *Sokht-e Shahr-e Rūm. Sokht* refers here not to a literal burning, but to devastation more generally conceived.

3. Mokhtār gives the impression he has heard the story before.

[*Young male audience member to M M on restarting the tape*:
They said, "Tell it, we've heard this story, [but] I said . . .]
[*M M*: Good, good—]   20
Another audience member: Write that down.
K: In the city of Rūm, sir,
there was a king, and the point is, that he
        saw in a dream one night, [that said]
        "You, on such-and-such a night—   25
        —a day—must come to such-and-such a mountain valley, tomorrow."

He laid his head down [to sleep] again and
he said, when he woke up [*whispered*], "What's in the mountain valley,
                                    and what's this about—?"
Again, the second time his head—
        his heart was carried off by sleep,   30
again he saw in a dream that they said, »
        "You must <u>come</u> to such-and-such a mountain valley."
Well,
he passed the night and
the point is, the next morning came and he came out of there and   35
went to that valley and
he saw there was a very beautiful gathering there, »
        a number of beautiful people, »
        sitting there so fine.
When he came close like that,   40
he stood
and gave his greetings.
They said, "You go,
                because in that city,
                a great ill fortune has come about,   45
                you must <u>oppress</u>
                the people,
                so that they
                will be humbled,
                will be impotent,   50
                so that God will pass over their offenses."
[*inaudible audience comment*]
He said, "Very well."

He came back.
He set conditions picked out of the air on these people's heads,
    with administrative rules   55
    and taxes and this and that, »
    and set lots of rules over their heads, and
well,
this one night he saw a dream again that
he should increase the tyranny on them.   60
He increased it.
In the end, it finally reached a place
    where they ordered him, "Kill people."
‹›
Yeah.
Innocent and guilty.   65
Anyway, sir, he—
[*Young male enters talking and is hushed by other audience members, point-*
                                          ing out the tape recorder.]
He said, "Good."
He came back, kind sir, and he took and
did things to the population and
took them like for a draft,   70
every day he would call for ten people,
    and have them brought and say, "Take these ten and hang them on
                                        the gallows."

For some time he carried on like this and the vizier and the people
                                      became very
    troubled, »
the people were being tortured, [saying] "Oh, what <u>is</u> the situation,
                                    that he,   75
                          he, he— that he kills people
                                like this, and— ?"
This vizier said [to himself], "Bābā, he's going to finish off the whole
                              <u>country</u>'s population, »
                    he takes them all of a sudden and doesn't
                                    <u>say</u> what <u>for</u>.
                He doesn't tell the purpose, either,
                    and kills people.   80
                Come on, I'll petition him," »

his wife said to him, "You make him <u>understand</u>, »
        he's put people to the <u>gun</u>!
          In the end the good of his kingship lies in his subjects,
             and his subjects will be wiped out,   85
                <u>why</u> is he <u>doing</u> like this?"
He came and, sir, he petitioned before him, "Sir, I have a petition." »
He said, "Speak."
He said, "From the time that I have been in this service,
        I— you haven't seen even one piece of treachery from me—" »   90
He said, "No."
He said, "I have a petition, whether you accept it or not—" »
He said, "Speak."
He said, "My petition is that you
        tell me   95
        the wisdom of this killing of the people.
        That you bring ten people a day and kill them
            without proof,
            without documentation,
            without an offense,   100
        on what authority?"
He kept saying, "Don't try to go into this," »
and when he again pressed him very much, he said,
        "I am not acting of my own choice,
        there is an <u>order</u> upon me.   105
[*M*: Yeah.]
        That I should execute this action."
[*M, very quietly*: Yeah.]
Yeah.
He said, "What kind of an order?" »   110
He said, "[We'll make] an appointment, now, you and I,
        for tonight."
He said, "Good."

When that night came, sir, at bedtime prayer, when they'd eaten
                          and drunk,
        after that he came out and   115
        said to him "Come on, let's go."
He went in front, and the vizier behind him. »

They went to that mountain valley, it was nearby,
    and there were the lights there and the illumination and
he came there.   120
He said, "Stay here."
He stopped right there.
And <u>he</u> went a few steps farther forward, toward a few people,
    and he stopped farther in front, »
    and the vizier was standing there,   125
he didn't have the courage to go closer to this gathering,
    because there were a number of people,
    very radiant and beautiful,
they have a gathering there and are sitting [around].
He came and stood there, and gave his greetings. »   130
When he gave his greetings,
they turned to him, [saying] "Go.
        Carry out the duty that you have, »
          until the face of impotence is revealed
             to these people.
[*M*: Huh! *M M*: Hmm—]   135
        That they be [totally] impotent."
He came back to the vizier and said, "You see?
      ‹›
        That I don't do this on my own
           authority?
      ‹›
        There is an order upon me, I am
           obliged to do it."
[The vizier said] "If you speak the truth,   140
      <u>think</u> about this business, that is, »
        what has happened to the people »
        and what fault the nation has,
      that this sort of thing should befall them.
      [*inaudible word*] of God."   145
He said, "Good."
[The vizier said,] "Give me three days, and I will go,
      but for those three days,
        stay your hand from this killing,
        bring all those to be killed and keep them
           in one place.   150

After three days, after I've come back, »
  if the reason for this has been discovered, good; »
  if not, if it hasn't,
  kill them all, all at once." »
He said, "That's good."   155

He let him leave and kind sir, he mounted his horse and
  set out and came along.
He came to this village and that village, and the point is, »
  all at once he came to this one particular place,
  cut off from the villages and the watered places,   160
there was a fortified house+ there with great, tall walls
  and doors and all, well set up,
and outside the fortress there's a mosque,
  right by the fortress door.
<>

He came and dismounted at the door of the mosque.   165
When he dismounted there,
  he saw that people were coming out of this fortress
  and going and coming and— yeah.
Some have a piece of bread in their hands, »
some have a bit of meat in their hands,   170
  and they were eating. »
He said, "What's going on, here, brothers?" »
They said, "There's a public charity distribution, they've been giving it
                                    out for several days.
    We go and eat the charity food— if you're hungry, too,
                                    go and eat."
<>
He said [*whispering*], "That's better."   175
He tethered his horse there and
  kind sir, went into the fortress.

When he went in, he saw that people were eating here, »
  and over there they were cutting up more meat, »

---

4. *qal'ah*, the fortified extended-family residential complex of rural Afghanistan.

and they have big pots,   180
   and they're starting to slaughter more cows.[5]
A very beautiful youth was sitting on a high seat right there,
   not saying aye or nay to anyone, the people eat and go and he's
                                         sitting right there.
Well.
He came and   185
   greeted him well,
   stood before him and said, "Bābā, where are you from?" »
He said, "I'm just a traveler."
He said, "Did you eat?" »
He said, "No."   190
He said, "Bring him food." »
They brought food,
   he ate it and
   after that
   he went out.   195
He didn't say anything,
   he came and
   it was noontime,
   he came to the mosque.
He prayed there.   200
   Made ablutions,
   prayed.
He saw that nooo-body came inside that mosque. NOT a soul.
‹›
The people who were traveling left, and the people right there,
   so to say, those who were staying,   205
   they didn't come either.
Well, afternoon came, and he saw that of all these people no one made
                                    a move in that direction.
[*Older male audience member*: They didn't come to pray. *M, speaking simul-*
                taneously: He was the only one in the mosque, all alone.]
And only he was there. [*M M*: Ohh.]

---

   5. Preparations for more charity for the following day.

Dinnertime came.   210
When dinnertime came, kind sir,
    none of these people made one step toward the mosque.
    He went alone and said prayers.
One person came to see if it was the same traveler who had come [earlier],
    whether he had left or was still there.   215
He came and said, "He's sitting right there,"
said to him, "Would you like something to eat or drink?" »
He said, "No.
       I don't want food."
He went back, and [the youth] said, "What did he say?" »   220
He said, "He says he's not eating."
He came there and said,
uh— "Go, tell him 'Come and eat,
        then go back to the mosque. »
        If you don't come, we'll send it to you there.' "   225
He came and said that to him, and he said, "No.
                I'm not eating anything and I
                    won't go there."
He came back and told him that.
The second time,
he got up himself and went, [saying]   230
    "What is this?
    If you're a traveler and, the point is, you're sitting in this mosque and
    you won't eat and you won't come to talk, and you won't do any of
                      that?"
He said, "I—
    I took an— oath,   235
    that as long as you won't tell me
    the reason for this charity distribution that you give out
                   every day,
    uh— I don't want any more of your food.
    ◇
    What is this about? »
    They announce a charity distribution for one day, two days,
                   ten days,   240
    and you've got all this livestock that you're slaughtering like this,
    what are you doing it for?"

When he really pressed him,
he said to him, "If I tell,
   that is,   245

   can <u>you</u>

   drive <u>away</u> my sin?"
◇
[*whispering*] "—This is my business—" —the vizier said, "—Yeah.
   I'll petition God, sitting in the mosque,
     weeping,   250
   perhaps the Great God will take away your fault on
              my behalf, »
   so you won't use up more of your livestock, that
           would be better.
   A charity distribution should be two days, anyway— »
     how long can this [go on]?
   ◇
   The way you've arranged it,   255
     your whole livelihood will go and be used up, this way is
     better." »
He said, "Fine."

Well, he came and
he said,   260
   "M— You, too, make supplications,
   see if God will forgive me
   or not."

He said, "That's good." »
That night passed, and morning came, »   265
   and he said, "What happened?"
He said, "I
   petitioned before God,
   may God protect you,
   the sin of a servant [of God], as long as the servant does not
         confess his sin in the presence of God, 270
   the Great God does not forgive him, either.
   So you tell me your sin, so I can tell it and petition God, »
     saying 'Lord <u>this</u> is his sin,
       please forgive <u>this</u> sin.' "

[*Older male audience member*: Repentance on him— (*Inaudible phrase*)]
[*M*: Uh-huh.]   275
Yeah. [*Other inaudible audience comments*]
He was very upset, and said [to himself], "What is he saying?"
Well.
He said,
  "I <u>have</u> a sin," »   280
and he said, "No, tell it."
When he really pressed him, after that
  he said, "Come on, let's go."
He brought him into his own house.

When he brought him, brought him into his own house, sir,   285
  when he put him in his sitting room,
  a very beautiful lady
  came there, like that.
She sat down too, and
he said, "Do you understand?" »   290
He said, "No."
He said, "Do you see her?" »
He said, "Yeah."
He said, "This
  is my sister.   295
<>
[*Inaudible comment from older male audience member*]
  She was very lovely and beautiful,
   and after that, as it happened, my fate, so to say, fell on her shoulders,
    my life and living depended on her,
   however much I thought, 'If I give her [to be married] somewhere, »

      the guy will take her <u>away</u>.   300
[*M*: Uh-huh . . .]

     I'll be left alone.
     No, on account of that necessity »
      that I would have to accept from him
      brideprices[6] or property or do
       something like that—' 305

---

  6. *pīshkash*, in Herat refers specifically to the payment gives to the bride's father or guardian by the groom's family as compensation for the expense of raising her.

I couldn't bring myself [to do it].
I engaged her to my<u>self</u>, on my own.
◇
[*M (faintly)*: Yeah.]
        'There's someone—' »
    I said, at the time when I went to ask the guy, the mulla for the
                                                        engagement—   310
        'he's giving his daughter to me, here, to be engaged,' »
    and the mulla didn't stick his neck out [to see] if this is my sister or
                                            some other woman.[7]
    Yeah, he engaged her to me.
    Now, it's been some time that she's been in my house.
    She has had children, too.   315
        ◇

[*Inaudible audience comment*: Repentance . . .]
    <u>Now</u> as I think about it,
◇
[*Audience member*: Huh!]
    that is,
    unless God Himself forgives this sin, I have no recourse.   320
    So my thinking came to this,
        that life doesn't want me,
        this living that I have,
        this wealthy life that I have, to take all of it
        and spend it for God,   325
    so that God will forgive this fault of mine for me."

[*Faint, inaudible audience comment.*]
He said, "Now, you
    be at ease, don't grieve.
    Till now   330
        the point is, you didn't tell me properly.
    Tonight I will petition God,
        'Lord, this incestuous adultery that this person has
                                    engaged in for some time,
        oh, pardon <u>it</u>.' "

---

7. The woman would have been veiled.

[*Audience murmur.*]   335
Yeah.

> "Wh— when your sin is made plain to God,
> He will forgive it," he said, "People have many sins, anyway,
> > which shall I say?"

‹›
[*M*: Yeah.]
He said, "Good."   340
Well.
He came and
> kind sir,
in expectation of this, anticipation of this, that this guy will come,
> he mounted his horse and   345
> "Oh, God!"⁸ got himself back to the king.

When he got there,
he said, "Where were you and what did you do?" »
He said, "Don't pursue that."
Yeah.   350

> "Don't kill anyone, don't tyrannize anyone, don't do anything.
> God willing, I have found
> the source of this sin."

He said, "Where is it?"
He said, "It's just this, send someone right away,   355
> > as I'll describe it to him,
> > in such-and-such a place,
> > there's this particular person.
> He must bring him to [your] presence."
He said, "If he acknowledges this to you yourself,   360
> > you will be informed and understand that it's he,
> > after that we can see what will happen.
> If it was <u>he</u>,
> > God willing,
> > it will be a solution, »   365

---

8. *yāllah!*: interjection used throughout Persian- and Arabic-speaking areas to initiate rapid or forceful physical activity. It can mean anything from "Hurry up!" to "Heave-ho!"

good, and if not, and it was another, then we'll see what we
will see, anyway." »
He said, "That's good."

Well, from there, sir,
yeah—
he   370
sent guards, "By God, take yourself to the gate of such-and-such a
fortress,"
he described it and
they brought him out there. »
They said, "Come out," and he came out, »
they just dropped the food distribution and all—   375
Along with his wife,
they brought him out to the outside. »
When they brought him into the king's presence,
he said, "What is this?" »
He answered humbly, said "There, now, sir, this is the youth and this is
the other person, too."   380
He put him in a special corner and said, "Tell me the reason for this."
He began to weep, "Sir, there is no [other] reason for this, anyway.
The truth is that this—
this is my milk-sister.[9]
[*M*: Ah— yeah.]   385
I, as I failed to follow the law out of compulsion,
the devil pricked me,
it's been some time that I have performed this act
with her, »
I took her in marriage."

[*M*: Akhkh, ohh! (*makes disgusted noises*)]
Well,   390
so anyway, right there, the king said, "It's clear that the ill fortune is
from this."
He said, "Take them and burn them both."

---

9. Speaking to the vizier, the man had called her *khowār*, "sister by blood," but now he
uses *hamshīrah*, "foster-sister, milk-sister." The incest rule applies in either case.

The woman also revealed in his presence, "Yes, right, I am his sister.
‹›
[*M (murmurs)*: Yeah.]
It's been some time that I've performed this act with him, and I have several
                                                children." »   395
They took them, sir,
        delivered them to their punishment.
After that, when evening came, he said, "Come on, let's go."
‹›
The two of them went, kind sir, back to that same gathering that they had
                                        gone to the other night.
They came there.   400
When they got close there,
        they said, with great satisfaction,
        "From now forward you must treat all the people of your nation with all
                                        compassion and regard,
            and give them the greatest ease of life, »
            give them all commiseration,   405
—for they were afflicted by you—that they may pardon you."

Yeah.
So there, anyway, kind sir, he ca—
        he came back,
after that, anyway, he released those who were to be killed,   410
        gave the people assistance,
        performed compassionate acts for the people.
The Great God,
        the point is, from the ill fortune of this one bad omen,
            that burned the city of Rūm,   415
        it was these people that he was compelled to kill
            and tyrannize
            and do things to them,
        it was from the ill fortune of one person.
His bad fortune, when this bad omen was set aside, the Great God gave the
                                        people assistance.   420

[*M, M M, and others*: Yeah. Uh-huh. Hmnn. Very good.]
[*M M*: Good. That was very interesting.]
[*Short break in taping.*]

M: "The Burning of the City of Rūm."

M M: Uh-huh, yeah.

K: Uh-huh.   425

M: On account of one ill fate—

M M: —The burning of the city of Rūm.

M: The burning of the city of Rūm.

M M: From . . . where did you get this story?

K: This one, sir—there's a book, that it—   430
    uh—they call it the "Histories of Shah 'Abbās,"[10]
    it's from that history.

M M (writing): Uh-huh. "The Histories of Shah 'Abbās."

K: Yeah.

◇

M M: Good—it must be a good one.   435

M: Can this book be found now?

K: God knows, sir, it's possible, one might get one's hands on it
                                   somewhere.

M: Did you learn it
    from the book itself, or did someone else [tell] it for you?

K: It was from someone else's telling.   440

M M: Uh-huh.

---

10. *Tawārīkh-e Shāh 'Abbās.*

Sex and Civic Disaster: Khalīfah Karīm's Last Word

In contrast to the previous story, presenting incest as a humorous topic, Karīm's next story placed incest at the center of a serious, even sinister presentation of the problem of righteous and unrighteous government. In so doing, he returned to several themes which had been prominent earlier in the storytelling session. As with other tales earlier in the series, Karīm did not have a title ready to hand for this tale but was induced to construct one by our desire to write something down (ll. 5–17). He had identified the story by subject matter before we turned the tape recorder on, and the title he offered (in two forms, alternating the terms *shūmīyat* "ill fortune," and *sokht* "burning, consumption by fire," ll. 8, 10) is a brief capsule of the story's subject. It sets the story on the border of the non-Muslim West, in "the City of Rūm." "Rūm" designates Constantinople, the imperial city of Christianity best known in the eastern Islamic world, and by extension, Anatolia. In this story as in some others, the area is conceptually a Muslim-Christian borderland.

The story begins with a king who receives visionary dreams, like Hojāj, and, like him, is unable to interpret them fully. He does not receive his revelation directly from one of the Islamic saints or prophets who usually bear such messages to the heroes of Afghan story (e.g., ʿAlī, in the case of Salīm, or Khoja Kheyzr). The apparent irrationality of his divine instructions (corresponding to the garbled condition of the scriptures of the non-Muslim "People of the Book," Christians, Jews, and Zoroastrians) is another indication of the fact that this king is not the hero of his story nor even, probably, a Muslim. This king is not, however, being chastised for his tyranny like Hojāj, but receives what appear to be divine orders to *become* a tyrant, and so he does, unquestioningly (ll. 37–74). The king acts as an unenlightened instrument of divine displeasure. It is his vizier (and the vizier's wife, ll. 82–86), concerned like Hojāj's vizier for the decimated population, who urges (ll. 140–54) that there must be some discoverable grounds for the angelic orders, some way to discover and expunge the "offenses" (l. 51) to which the angels have alluded.

The logic of a general plague descending on a population on account of an individual sin is very ancient and widespread, one of its most powerful articulations for westerners being the Oedipus story. The idea in Islamic context is succinctly articulated by Jalāl ud-Dīn Rūmī (*Mathnavī* I:88–89):

Abr bar nāyad pay-i manʿ -e zakāt,
   vaz zenā oftād vabā andar jahāt.
Har chih bar to āmad az zolmāt o gham
   an zih bī bākī o gostākhīst ham.

Rain clouds fail when the poor tax is unpaid,
   and from fornication pestilence spreads to the [four] directions.
All that befalls you of oppression and grief
   comes alike from [overweening] boldness and impudence.

Boldness and impudence—pernicious pride—are the logical opposite of Islam, submission to the power and will of God, which is the basis of faith. Not only are those without religion considered to be without social rules (Afghan popular belief holds that the Soviets in particular, lacking religion, do not recognize incest taboos and have sexual relations indiscriminately with their mothers and sisters), but apostasy breeds tyranny, and a breakdown in rule-keeping at the individual level brings on physical and social chaos. Thus, the Russian invasion was attributed by some Afghans to a failure of religious duty within their own population.

Although individual sin can have global consequences in Muslim thinking, the idea of confession and atonement for particular sins (ll. 270–72), one fairly accurately rendered Christian element in this story, is alien to Islam. To single out one particular sin for atonement would be to imply that a person is otherwise sinless, an impossibility given the generally weak nature of humankind. Thus, the incestuous young man is in the wrong, not only because he has apparently not desisted from his sin and still expects to atone for it with charity (ll. 321–26), but because he sees his problem as a matter of one specific act rather than the general failure of faith which is a precondition to any such action, the act being merely a symptom. When the vizier questions the young man, he presses him to confess his particular sin with a promise of specific intervention, a tactic which arouses a murmur of dissatisfaction from the listening audience (ll. 275 and 333). At line 275, the audience member enjoins "repentance" on the vizier, not the young man, for suggesting the possibility of an exclusive petition for forgiveness.

The vizier poses as a religious traveler like the shaykh in "Women's Tricks," who spends his time in prayer and meditation in the deserted mosque (ll. 199–216). The disused mosque, set apart from the community, adjacent to the young man's isolated fortress-dwelling (ll. 159–64), is suggestive of the marginal religious status of this society, associated with the young man's sin. The vizier plays along with the young man's misguided notion of saintly intervention (ll. 244–51) in order to identify and expunge from society the sinful source of disorder which has brought on the king's oppressive behavior. As in "Mongol Martyr," "Black and White," and several of the Ākhond's offhand remarks, votive practice itself (in this case food offerings distributed to the general public in hopes of a divine boon) is not admired in this tale of Karīm's. It is here represented as having replaced the more orthodox, less self-seeking practices of communal worship (the disused mosque). Unlike the practice of particular confession, votive food offerings are a very widespread practice in popular Islam, as the vizier's remarks about their normal form indicate (ll. 240–42 and 253–54). Though very popular, votive activities meet with disapproval from some orthodox clergy, who regard them as bargaining for blessings, whereas thank offerings are acceptable and general acts of pious charity (including the zakāt poor tax mentioned in the verse of Rūmī, above) are among the duties of Islam (cf. Betteridge 1980, Jamzadeh and Mills 1986).

The young man's incestuous attachment to his sister and unwillingness to release her into a normal marriage (ll. 296–307) are a pathological extreme of the affectionate loyalty expected to exist between brothers and sisters, as illustrated by the brother and his elderly sister in the previous story. A family is expected to be reluctant to exchange a daughter for goods, just as a girl is expected to resist leaving home, but Afghans hold as part of religion the injunction that all physically and mentally capable adults should marry. Ideally, a brother remains in touch with his sister and concerned for her welfare all through life. If she marries and her situation is intolerable, it is to her brother's house, or her father's, that she goes for refuge, and among her male relatives it is especially her brother who tries to negotiate for her better treatment. If she is widowed, she may return to her natal household, presided over by her father or, if he is deceased, her brother, until she remarries. If she violates her marriage bond, it is her male blood relatives, not her husband, who are responsible for punishing her.

The audience greeted the section of the story in which the young man described his incestuous affection, with quiet attention, with murmers of "Repentance!" (l. 316), the usual response when one hears of some major breach of behavioral norms, and disgusted noises ("Huh!" l. 318; Mokhtār's "Akhkh, ohh!" at l. 389) when the young man described his actions and his belated remorse.

Having begun the story session the night before with raucous parodies of the religious and sexual dealings of ordinary folk ("Mongol Martyr" and "Rasūl's Mother"), Karīm drew his visit to its close with a more serious and integrated vision of the interrelations of religious faith, sexual behavior, and social order, especially righteous government. In so doing, he wove together themes which the Ākhond had also integrated in the flow of his story performances but with a discernibly different emphasis. Not only can rehabilitated private malefactors, such as Salīm or the shaykh in "Women's Tricks," bring about reform in the authority figures with whom they interact, as the Ākhond's choice of plots demonstrates, but Karīm's story, like Jalāl ud-Dīn Rūmī's verse (above), reciprocally asserts that private vice can confound legitimate authority and cause it to malfunction also. The two propositions are corollaries, with Karīm characteristically presenting the negative, the Ākhond the positive side.

In Karīm's stories told on this occasion, the things and actions of the world are ultimately in somewhat less control or balance than in the Ākhond's stories, a pattern which, if it extends beyond the context of this particular storytelling event, may reflect the difference in personal power and prestige between the two men. In Karīm's stories, disorder erupts and is counteracted but only partially compensated. At the end of "The Burning of the City of Rūm," the king has been instructed to recompense his people for their suffering with wise and generous rule (ll. 401–12), but the randomly executed dead are still dead, and the sinners have been expunged, not rehabilitated. In virtually every one of the Ākhond's stories—"Salīm," "Mahmūd and the Thieves," "The Old Thief," "This Little Donkey," "If/ But," and "Black and White"—the little people whose well-being is jeopardized emerge from their trials with their fortunes fully restored, even improved, and the rehabilitation of would-be malefactors or potential tyrants is a recurrent, if not quite constant, theme. In the case of "Women's Tricks," those who suffer permanent harm are those who set out to take advantage of others, and the shaykh's intervention insures that the innocent do not suffer. The problematical resolutions of Karīm's earlier stories—"Mongol Martyr," "Rasūl's Mother," and " 'Ādel Khān"—have already been reviewed in the context of the resolution of "The Corrupt and the Good" (chapter 14). "The Burning of the City of Rūm" continues that compromised vision into a strictly noncomical sphere.

"The Burning of the City of Rūm," in its seriousness, presents a thoroughly Islamic vision of the problem of evil. The word *shūm* or *shūmīyat*, which Karīm uses for one of his alternative titles (l. 8) and which he uses repeatedly at the end to gloss the story (ll. 414, 419 and 420), has a dictionary meaning of "ill fortune" or "ill omen." The involuntary aspect of the term chosen to describe this misfortune, a curse, really, and the apparent injustice which the king involuntarily inflicted on his whole population as the result of the *shūmīyat* of one individual (l. 419), create a moral puzzle which looks slightly different to Afghan Muslims than it does from a secular western viewpoint. Like the excuse offered by the thieves to Mahmūd, "God made our faces black, and we did it" (chapter 8, l. 127), the assumption of personal responsibility appropriately includes an acknowledgment of God's superior power. Fate (the order and direction of divine creation) plays a role in an individual's fall from grace, just as grace plays a role in one's achieving repentance and faith (compare the Ākhond's disclaimer at the end of his account of his debate with the rabbi, "But seriously, sir, the Lord intended it— / and if not . . ." chapter 11, ll. 175–76). Hence, in "The Burning of the City of Rūm," the young man's incestuous obsession with his sister, "out of compulsion," as he puts it (l. 386), can be conceived as *shūmīyat*, bad fortune or ill omen, but he is still responsible and punishable for his wrong behavior. Recognizing the superior power of God is the necessary first step to repentance, but it is not sufficient, one must also take responsibility for and desist from one's errors.

Nor are the central authorities, kings or governors, autonomously moral or immoral. The quality of their governance also depends on a combination of submission to God and grace. In this case, the king was submissive to divine decree, but lacked the inward guidance to act out that submission wisely. This story, though set in a country of uncertain religious loyalties, is not irrelevant to the Muslim predicament, for leaders of Muslim background can also lose their guidance, as in the case of the legendary Hojāj in the story of Salīm, or perhaps that of the Woləswāl.

Karīm's selection of stories in this context assigns intercessory power to wise viziers to correct their misguided masters (such as 'Ādel Khān and the king of Rūm), whereas the Ākhond's stories tend to lodge the corrective moral force not with those who hold institutional advisory roles but with ordinary folk, some of them female. As with the discernible distinction between the Ākhond's optimism and Karīm's more guarded view of the possibility of restoring social order, discussed above, it may be inappropriate to extend this generalization about the two men's worldviews beyond the context of the present performance series, shaped for its audience. Both views of the corrective forces acting on central authorities and of the need for such correction, are abundantly represented in traditional stories, of which both men knew many more than they told here. At a minimum, it seems logical that the Ākhond's prior experience as a private citizen on the receiving end of the Woləswāl's administrative power would supply a motive for a strong counterstatement *in present context* about the need for authorities to heed the insights of ordinary citizens. The Ākhond's positive portrayal of the possibilities for redress, compared to Karīm's more guarded view, is less easy to link directly to the present context of his dealings with the Woləswāl, but functions as a component of his strong statement in favor of moral authority emanating from nonbureaucratic levels of society.

Coda: Karīm's Lost Story

Having begun this analysis with the observation that certain kinds of communicative incompetence can become resources under the paradoxical conditions of fieldwork, one must also acknowledge that inexperience exacts a price. In this case, through a taping error I accidentally lost Karīm's last story, one more brief tale we cajoled him to perform just before he departed for his home in a nearby village. I did not discover the loss until after I had returned to Herat City to edit the tapes. What was lost was a tale Karīm entitled, "On the Faithfulness of Dogs and the Faithlessness of Women" (*az wafā-ye sag o bīwafā-ye zan*), taken, as he said, from the same book, *The Histories of Shah ʿAbbās*, from which "The Burning of the City of Rūm" was taken. The book has proved to be untraceable under that title. Karīm acknowledged that he had not read the stories himself but had them told to him (l. 439) at some time in the past. The few words remaining on the accidentally over-recorded tape reveal only that the story begins with Shah ʿAbbās, another legendary righteous king like Mahmūd of Ghaznī, going out in disguise to check on the condition of his citizens. The contrast pair of loyal but unclean dogs and disloyal women is a commonplace that recurred in two or three other stories performed for me later by others. The pattern recalls the fate of the vizier's disloyal wife, changed to a dog, in Karīm's " ʿĀdel Khān." It is regrettable not to be able to examine Karīm's story in detail because of its apparent conformity to a general pattern in Karīm's performances, on this occasion, associating women and female sexuality with themes of social disorder. He ended his performance series on a note which portrayed women as primary agents in the disruption of social order as they were in " ʿĀdel Khān," rather than as passive victims as in "Rasūl's Mother" (or for that matter, the transformed king in " 'Ādel Khān"), or junior partners in male error as in "The Burning of the City of Rūm." Karīm's rich portrayal of the female role in social disorder contrasted with a relatively positive view of female roles in the totality of the Ākhond's performances. Perhaps Karīm, less affected by old scores with the Wolǝswāl than was the Ākhond, focused more on my presence as a disturbing feature in the social event, while the Ākhond concentrated more on developing the theme of private critiques of misguided governmental authority, even when the putative topic was "women's tricks."

16. "I speak with each according to his understanding . . ."

THIS STUDY has been concerned with language and power, specifically narrative language and interpretive power. Prior to the interpretive project constituted by a study such as this, acts of narration themselves, like other speech acts, are acts of interpretation, assigning causal and other relationships and relative emphasis to clusters of propositions (e.g., actions, objects and persons, and qualities) (White 1980). This study has sought to demonstrate how traditional Afghan oral narrators can fashion complex, oblique, and implicit commentaries about actors and actions in the social world around them out of narratives drawn from a large body of communally familiar material. They craft a particular statement out of a series of configurations (in this case, primarily stories but also proverbs, poems, and quotations from scripture and prophetic traditions) which, like the words of a sentence, have a consensually recognized range of possible meanings, but realize particular meanings only in juxtaposition to other similar configurations and in relation to referents conceived to be independent of and different from themselves. Especially under conditions of political repression (in this case, nonconsultative government represented by an outsider whose ideology is radically and explicitly opposed to the storytellers') but also in any circumstance where the narrator has substantially less power than the listener, obliqueness becomes a particularly characteristic aspect of traditional meaning-making, and didacticism merges with protest.

From a phenomenological point of view, in our efforts to understand other people's idea systems, it may well be appropriate for us to take "ideas to be first about other ideas, rather than about something extra-ideational" (Anderson 1986: 172, paraphrasing Frederic Jameson). But a postmodern desire to give the "other" a more independent voice in our portrayals of them would caution against making *them* into purely abstract logicians, or situation-obsessed phenomenologists. An Afghan Muslim view of the relationship between experience and speech is rather grounded in the conviction that the universe is intentionally designed and created by an absolute and perfect power, which acts directly upon but is beyond the normal comprehension of the perceiving and interpreting self.

Within this ideology of an absolute, immanent, *and* transcendent reality, Afghan storytelling (like human experience in general) is inevitably particularized and rendered interpretable by its performance context, understood as several sets of connections (Becker 1984). Audience participation entails interpretation; thus, each listener has a direct role in meaning-making. The storyteller, whatever the power wielded in the formulative role, does not control the meanings made of the performance by audience members. If a storyteller like the Ākhond can "make a funeral into a wedding" with stories, that transformation can only be accomplished with audience complicity in his project, by his success in "speaking to each according to his understanding."

It is important, but not always easy, to distinguish our own meaning-making projects from those of our interlocutors. A written examination of a set of complex recorded utterances such as this, provides leisure for what must almost inevitably be overinterpretation, from the oral/aural viewpoint. Such an analysis, forced to present observations sequentially, rather than simultaneously as the effects are experienced, artificially isolates narrative content from narrative mode or technique, separates intracommunal relations existing prior to the observer's arrival on the scene from new versions of those relations emerging in (and partly due to) his or her presence, which are the only relations which the observer actually observes. Complex, richly revealing interactions do not always wait to occur when the observer is best equipped to comprehend them, as witnessed by my almost totally inarticulate presence at this storytelling event. In fact, had I been more articulate, I would probably have been more interactive in the storytellers' performances, which might in turn have become less suggestive of preexisting relationships and more distracted and redirected by my anomalous presence and research agenda.

We have certain preoccupations about representation, which shape our own articulations, while our interlocutors may have related ones which look quite different from their point of view. We are presently concerned with finding ways to represent the openness and polysemy of "texts" (whatever we count as texts). We may view the traditional rhetorical technique of obliqueness in the social use of oral narrative as an Afghan-style realization of our desire to create open texts. Stories may be interpreted as analogies to event configurations in the social context (broadly construed) of the narrative acts. "Others" from within the community have license and, to an extent, responsibility to interpret the storyteller's intentions where such analogies are concerned, on the basis of their prior experience within the group, including their familiarity with a large body of conventional (but not necessarily mutually consistent) narrative and other propositions about the ways the world and society should or do work. While adult perspicacity may entail the ability and willingness to "read into" narrative acts analogies to local events, these interpretations vary (the texts are open and multiple). But this openness of the performed "text" may be seen not as a free-association exercise but instead as a kind of microcultural test of the listener's interpretive competencies.

Additionally, what the listener gets from the performance may in part determine what the speaker has intended. In the case of the Ākhond and the Woləswāl, if the Ākhond intends his stories to set up a critical interpretive context for the Woləswāl's governmental activities (something I strongly suspect but cannot know for sure), the Woləswāl has some options. He may recognize (probably tacitly) the implied criticism and use it to fine-tune his interaction with the community and improve his effectiveness as a local authority. If he does so, what the Ākhond has provided is guidance of a very traditional sort, part of his long-practiced professional role as teacher and preacher. If the Woləswāl elects to construe the storytelling event as mere entertainment, without more particular situational significance, and sees the Ākhond's cooperation in the event as tribute to his superior power and authority (Betteridge 1985), *and* if the Ākhond does not so construe the event, then another possibility emerges: the storytelling may become an act of entrapment and revenge in which the Woləswāl by refusing to take up the responsibility of analogical interpretation demonstrates himself incompetent in an important form of traditional adult moral discourse, and the Ākhond demonstrates the other man's incompetence by lodging criticisms of him in forms he cannot or will not understand. In either case, the Woləswāl's response is tacit, unspoken, leaving the rest of the audience to guess what has actually happened between himself and his storyteller guest.

One bit of evidence that suggests he did infer critical intent on the part of the Ākhond, is the fact that he privately told Mokhtār the story of his prior jailing of the older man, after the storytelling was over. The obscenity of the storyteller's language and the sexually explicit content of several stories caused Mokhtār to remark to me on the unexpected social tenor of the event. The Woləswāl's story of his prior relationship with the Ākhond provides for an interpretation of the storytellers' less-than-decorous choice of material and language. The fact that it was Karīm, not the Āk-hond, who committed the first major breach of decorum, with "Rasūl's Mother" (chapter 4), and that the Ākhond's subsequent pursuit of sexual topics differed in emphasis from Karīm's, invite consideration of the questions of complicity and competition in the relations of the two storytellers' performances (of which, more below).

The general and particular openness of story texts provides for complicitous and/or adversarial relations between teller and hearer. Textual openness is manifested in social transactions over stories, and the options taken for interpretation are not without social consequences for speaker and receiver. The teller may not gain greater practical autonomy through such tests of a more powerful listener, but he can make certain claims to moral authority thereby. One point of the Ākhond's story, "That Little Donkey and That Little Door" (chapter 12) is precisely this: "I offer you something of value. You may or may not value it or reward me, but if unrewarded, my relationship to you becomes one of covert defiance and contempt, nonetheless real and mutually understood, even if covertly expressed. The ultimate responsibility for establishing the meaning of this transaction rests with you, the receiver." In this total interaction, the institutional power of the Woləswāl as government official is juxtaposed to the moral authority of the two elders (especially the mulla) by virtue of their age, religious consciousness, and experience. Karīm in particular played on the theme of elders and wisdom in both the interviews and tales.

Certain ironies and tensions recurred persistently in this night's entertainment and the next morning's storytelling, partly manifest in story content and the topical flow within the array of stories and partly implicit in the interactions between performers as well as performer and audience. One such issue was that of power relations and alternative powers and authorities in Muslim society. Mundane power, wielded by temporal rulers, has traditionally been subject to critique and opposition by clergy and/ or the populace who make claims to moral authority on religious grounds. Asad (1973:110, citing Cahen and Hodgson) discussed the persistence of popular opposition to the state in the Middle East, at least since medieval times, and serves to remind us that the recent state of affairs in Afghanistan is part of a long-standing, regional ethicopolitical dynamic:

> But what we do know a little about is the populist tradition in Muslim societies as expressed in the repeated popular revolts deriving their legitimation from Islamic ideology, as well as the popular distrust of aristocratic insti-

tutions . . . Most orientalists have tended to see these revolts as evidence of disorder and decay rather than as a reaffirmation of a populist tradition in Islamic politics. Why, instead of emphasizing disorder and repression and explaining this by reference to an intrinsic flaw in Islamic political theory (usually invidiously contrasted with Greek and Christian political theory) did orientalists not attempt to account for the continuing vitality of a populist tradition with changing socio-economic circumstances?

It does not require the offices of a folklorist to point out the pervasive, historical Afghan skepticism of central authority, but a close look at traditional narrative can support the realization that this resistance to centralized leadership is not a matter of a stunted or underdeveloped notion of human interaction. The stories are a window onto a complex vision of noninstitutional moral authority and autonomy, intensely egalitarian and tending to extreme demystification of state power. In peacetime, the articulation of populist critiques of a state which cannot fully realize the Islamic ideal of social order can take form in a rich body of oral tradition—folk farce, self-declared imaginative fiction (*afsānah*), jokes and anecdotes, sacred and secular legend and oral history, and proverbs, aphorisms, and other nonnarrative critical forms. The bulk of this material, like the majority of the stories Karīm and the Ākhond performed on the occasion under discussion, is saturated with overt and implicit Islamic ideology. Whether in war or peace, as David Edwards (1987 a,b) has pointed out, explicitly Islamic themes emerge differently in shifting portrayals of an ongoing historical event (in his case, the Afghan-Soviet war). Michael Meeker concurs: "Values and ideals are interpreted in terms of their function in a particular form of discourse rather than as timeless truths which stand beyond a speaker or writer" (1979:30; cf. Bauman 1986:75, Briggs 1988:180–81). This particular run of stories exhaustively explores, among other things, the role of the private individual in observing, interpreting, and bringing to the attention of the institutionally powerful the effects of private and institutional actions, and thus securing redress or averting further injustice.

The adventures of these private individuals (and authority figures like 'Ādel Khān or Mahmūd, temporarily in the status of private individuals) are amusing, often outrageously so. Entertainment is integral to such performances. Didactic interpretation in this case (and in my experience, in oral performance in general) is somewhat muted and generalized (e.g., the Ākhond's observation on foolish people lacking " *'orfān*" at the end of "Ten Qerān," or his excursus on divine mercy at the end of "Mahmūd and the Thieves"). The particular, possible links between the topical content of these stories and the shared personal histories of performers and audience remain implicit throughout. If moral authority and perspicacity by definition lodge with those who do not wield formal temporal power, then the didactic role intersects that of protest. For practical reasons as well as reasons of decorum in the guest-host relationship, such protest may be indirect.

One aspect of this indirection is buffoonery. Humorous exaggeration and presentations of the absurd can act as a screen for pointed criticism. Particularly in this tale series, body humor and themes of sexual disorder (perhaps partly inspired by my own anomalous, female presence) provide vehicles for more general communications about social order and disorder ("Ten Qerān," "Salīm the Jeweller," " 'Ādel Khān," "The Old Thief with Five Sons," "Women's Tricks," "That Little Donkey and That Little Door," "Black and White," "The Corrupt and the Good," and "The Ill Fortune of the City of Rūm"). By performing indecorous humorous material, the storyteller casts himself in a less-than-dignified role, but may assume the role of buffoon to construct a social criticism up from under. Buffoonery and righteousness meet in social critiques using media such as these tales, or folk farces with similar humorous content (Baghban 1977), and also in Sufi discourse, where an absurd view of worldly affairs, including sexual affairs, can be a tool to spiritual enlightenment. Both the Ākhond and Karīm were familiar with Sufi discourse, the Ākhond more directly with Sufi writings, including those of Jalāl ud-Dīn Rūmī, a master among other things of the ironic interpretation of everyday experience and the didactic and meditative use of earthy humor. The role of the buffoon, while highly entertaining, traditionally mediates mystical and mundane skepticism about temporal power and dignity. Introducing rowdiness and buffoonery into a private, but somewhat formal, performance setting such as this either invites a more informal, hence egalitarian, relationship between performer and audience or, if the host refuses the invitation to intimacy, compromises his control over the more distanced decorum which he might prefer to maintain.

This performance sequence illustrates the general multidimensionality and interpretive indeterminacy characteristic of socially situated narrative performances and also manifests specific fields of reference and rhetorical techniques (levels of speech, manipulation of decorum rules, physical rhythms) shared by both performers. At the same time, close inspection of the tales in their sequence uncovers more subtle but systematic differences in the ways the two performers developed their shared themes, which in turn affected their relationships to the audience. These patterns, visible over the performance sequence, are constitutive of the respective performance personas of each storyteller. The emphasis in this study has been on the aspects of meaning-making which reflect the social situatedness of the performance and the intertextual relations of its elements. By the same token, my consideration of individual differences between the performers does not aim to trace general psychological profiles for two individuals but rather their distinct, constructed personas manifested in this particular performance set (cf. Wehse 1986 and Chock and Wyman 1986:17 for the history and problematics of general repertoire-and-personality studies). These personas most likely do bear systematic relations to longer-term patterns in these two men's performance histories and their modes of self-presentation in nonperformance contexts, but my short visit with them did not yield the kind of information that could establish what those more enduring patterns are. In any case, recent work on the social construction of the self (e.g., Anderson and Eickelman 1985, especially Betteridge and Caton in that volume) cautions against simple application of a western notion of the self and personhood to Middle Eastern societies. In general, recent work on ideas of the self has stressed the emergent quality of individual identities in the variety of social settings in which individuals act. The storytelling session offers a rich example of one such setting. Not only the storyteller's own persona, but his or her understanding of the audience is also emergent. Hence, the Ākhond began with an outspoken (though foolish) female character (in "Ten Qerān") but went on to explore examples of loyal and perspicacious women and ultimately "signed on" to my project, directing me to take my notes properly and inviting me home to meet his womenfolk.

Karīm for his part began the evening's performance with a sequence of two rather risky stylistic ventures, perhaps meant to test his audience's comprehension or tolerance of local preoccupations, perhaps just meant as a tour de force but, because of a limited perspective, a highly localized one. His first venture, "The Mongol Martyr," was an extended dialect joke, playing on local stereotypes of manners of speech and living habits with which the outsiders in his audience were not familiar. Thus, the humor of the piece lacked the piquancy of recognition for the outsiders (the Woləswāl, Mokhtār, and certainly my totally puzzled self) which such ethnic humor requires to be fully effective. Such a performance raises the question, when is a tour de force (which the story certainly was, with its layers of reported speech and intricate use of dialect) not an effective performance? Are we to assume that solidarity with the audience and mutual comprehension are the aims of a performance? Or could it be that this insiders' joke was meant in part either to demonstrate that outsiders were present or to test their (our) willingness to collude, our good sportsmanship in encouraging a performance whose fine points were lost on us? This question of Karīm's intentions vis-à-vis the outsiders in his audience recalls his observation during his interview, that his preferred audience was "learned people" and "Sufis in the villages," and that throughout his life his interlocutors had mainly been people like himself in age and interests (chapter 3, 19–20 and 28–34).

Karīm's second venture, "Rasūl's Mother," was if anything, riskier than the first, and more explicitly challenging to the dignity of the elite (and foreign) members of his audience. It tested (in Mokhtār's opinion, violated) the limits of decorum of the social setting. Couched like the first story as an ethnic joke, it broached the topic of sexual relations (not normally a topic for mixed company, certainly not for mixed official company) in a most explicit way, while at a more subtle level it questioned the adequacy of words in general to represent experienced reality.

The Ākhond, beginning his turn on the floor with "Ten *Qerān*" (chapter 5) collaborated with Karīm both in the choice of fools as a topic and in completing the transition Karīm initiated in the course of "Rasūl's Mother," away from ethnic and dialect to a more generalized sexual humor of foolishness. The Ākhond generalized, metaphorized, and moralized the tale of fools by his interpretive remarks regarding people who lack " '*orfān*" at the end of that story ("that they buy for ten *qerān* but give seventy. / And they don't even know how to milk the cow," ll. 164–65). In his interview, he had already touted his ability to converse with "Sufis of pure faith" as well as "deficient shaykhs" (chapter 5, ll. 74–76). For his second offering, he launched into the long, complex, and probably premeditated "Salīm the Jeweller," almost a folk novel of moral development, both for Salīm the adventurer and sometime religious backslider, and for the tyrannical Hojāj whose own healing hinges on his hearing and being moved by Salīm's story and correcting his injustices to that man. The story integrates a single element of sexual humor (the Monkey Bride episode) into its more general discourse on faith and faithlessness. Salīm's task is to make Hojāj both laugh and cry; the absurdities of bestial sex provide the laughter, while the tears are provoked by hardships along Salīm's path to religious faith and reunion with his family. The sublime and the ridiculous, religious education and the sexual adventures which cause Salīm to appreciate the home and family he has lost, must ultimately conjoin to restore Hojāj's humanity and Salīm's freedom.

This complex tale introduced the topic of just and unjust rulers and the educative role of the little man, which dominated much of the succeeding performance series. Karīm, taking the performance floor again with the equally complex and multilayered " 'Ādel Khān," managed to move graphically humorous portrayals of rape and sexual mayhem back to center stage even as he carried along the topic of justice and *noblesse oblige* as a problem presented to a ruler through an ordinary man's personal narrative. Mahmūd's contribution following " 'Ādel Khān 'the Just' " was the mystically informed tale of Mahmūd of Ghaznī, that legendary ideal of the just monarch, in which the Ākhond found space, following Rūmī, his probable source, for a short interpretive disquisition on divine forebearance and the intercessory powers of the Prophet (chapter 8, ll. 146–54). In his final tale of the evening, the Ākhond pursued the topic of urban criminal gang activities out of the courtly and into the private sphere, in the story of "The Old Thief with Five Sons" (chapter 9). Now the little man, wronged by another private individual, pursues his own vengeance, without any redress or aid from higher authorities. Sexual vulnerability assumed by the disguised hero in this tale of the Ākhond's becomes a force for redress and the restoration of social balances, rather than for their destabilization as in Karīm's two stories.

Reassuming the performance floor the next morning, the Ākhond replicated the previous evening's thematic movement from public to private administration of justice ("Women's Tricks," "That Little Donkey," "If/But," and "Black and White") but, as before, always with the ordinary person, the private observer, as the key moral interpreter and instigator of accurate retributive justice. Sexual disorder, sometimes of acts ("Women's Tricks," "Black and White"), sometimes of words ("That Little Donkey"), remained for the Ākhond a key element in the portrayal of potential social imbalance, but as on the night before, his final statement portrays someone (first a young male, now an adult female) using feminine powers to entrap a would-be oppressor and thus secure revenge, redress, and a restored social order. Given general Afghan Muslim acceptance of the appropriateness of male dominance, this role for the feminine constitutes perhaps the most radical statement of the moral authority of the underdog in the whole performance sequence. The Ākhond's choice of *these* three particular narrative-based proverbs as examples of the narrative substrate underlying proverbs

("Every saying has its story"), the overt organizing topic for the last sequence of his performance ("That Little Donkey," "If/But," and "Black and White") also supplied a strong concluding subtext on the power of words, spoken and unspoken, the social use of cryptic statements, and the need for narrative knowledge to elucidate them and to understand the more general relationship of words to acts.

Unlike the Ākhond, Karīm never presented women as sensible actors for social order, with the exception of the vizier's mother in " 'Ādel Khān" and, fleetingly, the vizier's wife in "The Ill Fortune of the City of Rūm" (chapter 15, ll. 82–86). In the morning, Karīm's thoughts turned to incest and the roles of tempting female sex objects, one an elderly (and thus, in this tradition, comical) rape victim, the other apparently an acquiescent partner, in man's fall from grace. "The Ill Fortune of the City of Rūm" and his last, lost story, "On the Faithfulness of Dogs and the Faithlessness of Women," both departed from his humorous mood up to that point, to present more serious views of the disruptive influence of women in men's lives. In the "City of Rūm" in particular, he combined the chilling portrayal of sibling affection gone wrong with yet another reflection on the potential tyranny of rulers and their need for guidance by those with direct access to the world outside the court. In this case, the mediating figure is the vizier who, like Mahmūd the Just King, rides out on his own investigative errands, posing as an ordinary man. Overall, Karīm's choice of stories shows more of a tendency than the Ākhond's to assign the role of moral and social arbiter not to private individuals acting in private capacities, but to those who have some institutional responsibility for guidance (the ākhond in "The Mongul Martyr" and the viziers in " 'Ādel Khān" and "The City of Rūm"). Generally, the resolutions of Karīm's narratives also present a more compromised view of redress and the restoration of order, while the Ākhond's tales appear to hold out more hope of complete and permanent restitution.

This schematic rendition of the narrative flow of the whole evening and morning rather travesties the thematic complexities both of individual tales and of their relations to one another. It illustrates, minimally, how two recurrent themes, sexual disorder and the achievement of public justice through private insight, are intertwined throughout the story session. But though the Ākhond and Karīm both avail themselves of these two themes repeatedly, their use is differently nuanced. The Ākhond gives women and the female principle more positive possibilities and sexual mayhem a lower profile than does Karīm, whereas Karīm, in " 'Ādel Khān" and "The City of Rūm," has more actively positive roles for viziers, adjuncts to the ruler who use their powers of persuasion to keep him in touch with the right guidance that emanates from the practical world outside the court. Karīm's more daring choices of material at the beginning of his performance challenged the decorum and the collaborative relationship between himself and us more directly than did the Ākhond's muted didacticism. Overall, Karīm's portrayal of the female as a more uniformly disruptive force also suggests a more adversarial response to my anomalous presence in this otherwise strictly male social setting. The joint narrator-audience relationship established by the two men's storytelling can be construed as alternatively challenging or collaborative. Different aspects of the performance can be seen to have different effects, to shock, to surprise (as when the Ākhond says, "This isn't a common story, now" [chapter 5, l. 92], or when he resists telling a story Mokhtār already knows [chapter 13, l. 20]), to entertain and amuse, to admonish. Of the two, Karīm took the more overtly challenging role, the Ākhond a more decorously oblique, admonitory line. This interpretation of these two storytellers' personas recalls a configuration common in Persian-language adventure literature, in which the hero, the dignified exponent of social order and romantic loyalty, is accompanied by a trickster-companion, the *'ayyār*, who is responsible for reconnaissance, testing the adversary's defenses, and in the process perpetrating various tricks that compromise the enemy's dignity.

Karīm's riskier narrative choices gave the Ākhond room for some risk-taking of his own within a generally more decorous and gently didactic total performance. When the Ākhond wanted to prepare the audience for the rowdy sexual episode in "Salīm," he did so by brief allusion to the tone Karīm had already set with "Rasūl's Mother" (chapter 6, l. 425). He also eschewed the use of opening and closing formulas which would unequivocally label his performances as entertainment fictions, located in a separate and illusory fictional world. Not to avail himself of such a rhetorical framing device kept the didactic dimension of his performance more open; not to avail oneself of such devices in a whole storytelling career (the Ākhond professed that he did not know the formulas, and when pressed to use them, misquoted them) suggests that he routinely protects his performances from a pure entertainment interpretation.

Both encouraged by us to perform material from literary sources if they knew any, the two storytellers made choices characteristic of their respective educational backgrounds and roles, the Ākhond drawing from the highly prestigious *Mathnavī* of Rūmī and *Anwār-i Sohaylī* of Kāshifī, while

Karīm, after several performances from oral sources, offered only at the end of our visit, two stories he attributed to a so-far untraceable story collection, the *Tawārīkh-e Shāh ʿAbbās*. The study of the relationship between written and oral traditions in Persian is still in its infancy, but a close examination of both these storytellers' use of words suggests that poetic forms such as the couplet and quatrain, which are prominent in the literary tradition, have syntactic analogues in the prose speech of more and less literate oral performers. Whether the spoken forms are the product of exposure to literary language, or the literary forms are overdetermined versions of organizational principles also operating in what both we and they would call oral prose, would be worthy of investigation with a larger sample of oral performers. The prestige of literature tends to encourage the imitation of literary-style embellishments in oral narrative performance, but some of the most literate performers (the Ākhond included) do not use the more obvious of those sorts of ornamentation in speech. Prestige and authority can be claimed for one's words, both by attributions to authoritative sources and by the arrangement of those words themselves. The storyteller's preferences in the matter of teller-audience relations (in the Ākhond's terms, "to speak with everyone in a way they will understand") will figure in, and partly be revealed by, the differential use of such speech effects.

Wit and artfulness are not by their nature exclusively literary skills (Polanyi 1982), certainly not in a predominantly oral culture such as Afghanistan's. The assessment of verbal skills must take into account the much more elusive question of the performer's intended effects, as in Karīm's choice of potentially obscure and/or offensive material. Nor need aptness always imply premeditation: the question of the relationship between coherency and consciousness and the matter of degrees and kinds of consciousness are still open, where narrative improvisation is concerned. In the foregoing chapters, I have traced organizational, stylistic, and topical resemblances among the stories in series and have argued that surface similarities (e.g., of incidents or "motifs"), while they may function as mnemonic cues from story to story, are generally accompanied by another set of resemblances of more abstract configurations (e.g., of ascribed causalities or the ethicoreligious status of actors and actions portrayed). The exact roles of these concrete and abstract echoings and reiterations in story and performance construction remain unclear. Given the structure of the basic research on which this study depends, it is unsafe to assert categorically that the storytellers intended any or all of the possible associations traced here. Extended follow-up discussions of the storytelling session, with each of the two, might have helped to uncover kinds and degrees of intentionality and premeditation in the framing of this performance set, but would doubtless also have resulted in new aspects of consciousness emergent from the interview. But even this worthy desire assumes that they would somehow be willing or able in such a discussion to ignore canons of indirection which apply in approaching authority figures or others, such as myself, whose goals and motives are less than clear.

Not only does the researcher/audience member need a greater, temporally deeper knowledge of his or her performers than this one event could supply, but the performers too must come to know their interlocutor better before effective joint interpretation can occur. Still, the interaction of these two individuals on this single occasion gives some sense of alternative strategies and the possibility of personas constructed both in anticipation of and in the course of a performance.

As befit their respective statuses as craftsman and clergyman in the world beyond the Woləswāl's guestroom, Karīm's choice of the more outrageous material and language made him more buffoon-like, and the Ākhond, by comparison, more dignified, as each coped with the essentially problematic role of entertainer into which the Woləswāl's invitation (or summons) had cast them. Taken as a whole, their respective performances to me seem contrapuntal, not at crossed purposes, collaborative with one another in the parallels and contrasts they develop in a complex web of shared images, themes, and stylistic alternatives. That the Ākhond was no less acutely aware than Karīm of the presence of the religiously and ethnically "other" in his audience is suggested by his detailed personal experience narrative concerning his religious debate with the Rabbi of Herat, but his very presentation of that topic portrays encounters with "others" outside one's own ethicoreligious circle as familiar and manageable, though interesting and challenging, events. His attitude toward a female presence (mine) seems more dynamic and certainly more positive than Karīm's. His invitation to me to visit his home, extended toward the end of our visit, established him in the controlling role of willing and generous host and teacher, rather than exploited subject, in our transactions over his stories.

Postlude: The Woləswāl's Counterstatement

Counterstatement is perhaps a misleading term for the Woləswāl's manner of acquainting me with the local culture of Pashtūn Zarghūn. He was an attentive host, feeding us and the storyteller guests an ample meal (in separate rooms), arranging well for our comfort overnight, and attending both the night and morning storytelling. He was not a very vocal participant in the storytelling. Only one or two of the audible comments on the tape are his. In dress and demeanor, both he and Mokhtār presented themselves as western-educated city folk, hatless, in western-style suits and laced shoes (awkward to remove when entering a room as is customary), and stockings. Two men who attended the Woləswāl much of the time and seemed to be serving him as aides (one as his driver), official or unofficial, were similarly though less fashionably dressed, while the rest of the audience like the storytellers wore conventional male Afghan dress, loose trousers and long shirts, weskits, slip-on sandals, and skullcaps with or without turban cloths wrapped around them.

In conversation with Mokhtār and the Woləswāl, I had mentioned my desire to visit a certain shrine near Herat City in a few days' time and my interest in shrines in general. The Woləswāl offered to take us by car to visit a local shrine to get a wider look at the area. Next morning, after the storytellers departed, the three of us and the Woləswāl's two aides departed by jeep over a dirt track to a small local shrine, located at the base of the hills bordering this section of the Herat River valley, a typical site for shrines because of their association with natural springs which frequently well up where lines of hills join a valley floor. This particular shrine was small, an open-air grave precinct with a small gnarled tree, with some rags and small banners tied to poles and to the tree. Half a dozen marble gravestones marked the graves of the saint and some of his relatives, surrounded by a low wooden fence, broken in places, and the graves of others. A few houses made a small settlement next to the cemetery, but no one came out to greet us when we drove up, only a few children and a woman or two peeked out of their gates and then retreated. No one attended the grave area, nor did I learn who was buried there. The Woləswāl explained that the place was losing its water supply (the water table was dropping throughout the Herat River valley) and the shrine was generally going into decline. When we arrived at the grave area, the Woləswāl and his aides strode into the grave precinct and over the graves without removing their shoes, a major expression of disrespect. I took one or two photographs and, disheartened by their behavior, did not press them to seek out any of the people who lived there to try to learn more about the shrine. After a few minutes, we left.

The Woləswāl's disrespect for this particular site was manifest; it seemed to me that his choice of a shrine in such decline, when there were more active pilgrimage sites all over the area, was also intentional. His Parchamī Marxist ideology, which included in an intensified form a common urban-elite disdain for traditional culture, may have determined his choice of a moribund site to represent local religion for my informational purposes. It seemed to me that he was using the occasion of a foreigner's visit to present local religious practice as passé, a harmless and faintly boring curiosity. This declining local shrine was a safe place to act out a disdain for Islam. It is hard to imagine that one could have led such a tour of the local mosque or of a major shrine precinct such as the nearby Gazūr Gāh, with equally innocuous results. Yet it is ironically true that in their stories, Karīm and the Ākhond also expressed little respect for the charismatic side of religious practice, and repeatedly displayed their own skepticism concerning shrines and saint-veneration. Canfield (1977, 1986), Roy (1983, 1984), Shahrani (1984, 1985), and others have pointed out how multifarious Afghan Islam itself is, a comprehensive system within which various claims and counterclaims of solidarity and difference are mounted.

If the Woləswāl intended this visit as a counterstatement to the religious consciousness and assertions of the two storytellers, it was thus a bit off the mark. As a performance, however, it was consistent in the frame of his more official activities. He did not, to all appearances, engage readily in ideological debate with local people (the Ākhond would likely have engaged with him, as with the Jew, had he chosen to do so over the storytelling). One weakness of the Afghan Marxist parties, all too obvious from the present perspective, was their failure to engage indigenous Afghan historical consciousness, except negatively, the homegrown Marxists being perceived by many people as a continuation of ethnic Russian, later Soviet, foreign expansionism. The Woləswāl apparently preferred a rhetoric of action, refusing to take bribes and, as in the case of his temporary jailing of the Ākhond for tax evasion, acting decisively against at least some prominent members of the community when they got on the wrong side of the law. This tactic, it seems to me, bespoke an assumption that deeds would speak louder than words to the local nonelite whom the Marxists hoped to win over, but that assumption may have been erroneous, part of the consistent tendency of modernizing urban elite culture-bearers to discount the verbal sophistication of the nonliterate rural population and their interpretive activities (Fischer, 1984; Ghani, 1988).

As the Ākhond's reminiscence about his debate with the Jew illustrates, words, preeminently the Muslim declaration of faith, are vitally important to establish the meaning and value of deeds from a traditional point of view. Without Muslim faith, the virtue of the Jewish community,

356 "I speak with each according to his understanding"

for instance, is of no significance, in the Ākhond's formulation. The Ākhond, of course, spoke as a member of a highly educated, word-oriented, and ideologically self-aware subgroup of the population, but the corresponding relationship of actions and words in the minds of the nonliterate nonelite is an area now in need of serious investigation on account of its central relevance to Afghanistan's immediate future, especially to the complex task of reestablishing a credible national government with effective lines of communication to the general population.

As Fischer (1986:175) points out, "Competition between rhetorics often provide[s] powerful indexes of social and class competition." Whether statements and counterstatements in different rhetorics are accurately decoded by the respective parties is a matter of considerable complexity, as Fischer's ensuing discussion illustrates. In recent close studies of performer-audience relations (Caton [1985], Abu-Lughod [1986], Slyomovics [1987], Narayan [1989]), the basic interaction has been taken to be between a competent performer and a potentially competent audience such that the emergent relationship(s) would be recognized as possible or appropriate by both parties. In the present case, not only the ethnographer, but the event sponsor was largely unfamiliar with the rhetorical techniques of traditional storytelling, didactic and playful. New kinds of tensions over competence and decoding come to the fore in periods of acute social change, when members of the indigenous audience are by their status expected to be competent but by their experience not so. In such an unstable situation, one is encouraged not to romanticize the powers of traditional expression and interpretation. Afghan Islam does not *make* people ingenious and flexible interpreters of experience, any more than Afghan Marxism does. But some individuals, equipped with broad and deep experience of the uses of narrative ideological debate and social criticism, develop a flexibility and ironic reflexivity which may infuse even the most idealizing belief system. In this regard, the Ākhond shows more intellectual scope than either Karīm or the Woləswāl. Yet the notion of verbal and action exchanges as "games," which Caton (1985) and others have usefully borrowed from George Herbert Mead, breaks down in a situation like this performance event. For one thing, there is no longer a mutually agreed-upon concept of "the 'generalized other' which entails not merely the person's awareness of particular individuals' or groups' attitudes toward him, but also their attitudes towards the social activity in which they are engaged as a whole" (Caton 1985:147).

The two "sides" of this "game" are now playing with different rules and equipment, with differences in assumptions which may reciprocally enable each "side" to interpret itself as the rhetorical "winner" in an eccentric exchange. Thus, the Woləswāl might attribute the crudities of Karīm and the Ākhond to rustic stupidity and literal-mindedness (as did one of my "modern," urban-educated Herati editor-advisors) and thus dismiss their performance, while the performers were, for their own respective purposes, using what they themselves deemed risky words (risky to their own status among other things) to challenge the Woləswāl to a meaningful engagement. In such circumstances, the "me" (in Mead's sense) no longer "knows what particular individuals, groups and the generalized Other expect or anticipate of the self's responses to conventional situations" (Caton, 1985:147). The Woləswāl's silence at the storytelling event was susceptible to conventional decipherment (e.g., "He probably knows what we're saying but can't acknowledge it is aimed at him, without losing face") or unconventional decipherment (e.g., "These old men are being stupid, crude, superstitious and fanciful, manifesting all the things that are wrong with Afghan traditional culture, but fortunately my foreign guest's Persian is so limited that she doesn't understand their crudities, and anyway she is from the West where women are sexually liberated and socialize with men and thus is probably not embarrassed by such stuff, so I won't make an issue of it"). Many other understandings and misunderstandings are of course possible; these two phrasings are meant only to be illustrative. The latter paraphrases the actual response of an urban-educated Afghan friend when I asked him what he would guess to have been the Woləswāl's attitude, as host, toward the men's performance of obscene material.

Such a mismatch of interpretations, on a single occasion such as this, can achieve a superficial (but deceptive) stability so that each side can declare itself the winner and go home (as with certain recent wars). Continuing negotiations between groups with such mismatched rhetorics are likely, however, to uncover essential disagreements over both the authority of communicated substance and the authority of communicative medium or mode. In the last analysis, my visit with the Woləswāl, the Ākhond, and Karīm doubtless remained something quite distinct for each of us. For me, it was one of the first great puzzles of my stay, an invitation to a journey of interpretation which is by no means over.

Appendix 1: Transliteration Sample[1]

Ākhond Mulla Mahmūd: "Kharak o Darak"
("That Little Donkey and That Little Door," Chapter 12)

Ākhond to Mokhtār: 'Kharak o darak' monshara shomā baladīm, sayb?
M. Mills: 'Kharak o darak' —? [*Repeats in Persian, writing it down*]
Ākhond: Keh mīgam, 'kharak o darak'—?
Mokhtār: 'Kharak o darak'—Ā.
Ākhond: Hā. Ī mansha' dārah ko har gappī.   5
Mokhtār: Kho.
Ākhond: Masal,
      yakī nemīgah be yakī,
      keh amī
      'Agar magar kard'—?   10
      'Agar magar kard'—ī ko qe—ī qessah dārah.
Mokhtār: Khau.
Ākhond: Sāy konīm?
Mokhtār: Balī.
Ākhond: <u>Har</u> ga—<u>HAR</u> gapī keh estemāl mīshah, sayb, yak mansha'
                              dārah ko-o.   15
Mokhtār: Balī [*inaudible word*]—
Ākhond: 'Kharak o darak.'
Mokhtār: Balī, sahīh—
Karīm: Tā nabāshah goftah nemīshah, sayb—
Ākhond: [*to M. Mills, who is writing notes*] Qesseh-ye 'kharak o darak'
                      hamunje neveshteh konīm keh mah bogom.   20
M. Mills: Hā, neveshteh kardam.
Ākhond: Neveshteh kardīm?
M. Mills: Balī.

---

1. Vocalization in this transcription, especially of short vowels *a, e, i*, preserves some nonphonemic variations: e.g., *qessah*, "story" (l. 11) becomes *qesseh-ye* (l. 19) as a result of vowel euphony when the *ezāfeh(ye)* is attached to it. Distortions of speech (e.g., l. 84, *m(o)ansha(r)* for literary *mansha'*, accurately pronounced elsewhere) are also preserved. The acute accent over *é/yé* and *í* distinguishes the enclitic copula ("it is," "you [sing.] are" respectively) from *ezāfeh*.

Ākhond: Yak shaks-e sayyādī būd, sāeyb—
      ī māhī mīgīreft.   25

Mokhtār: Balī.

Ākhond:

Yak māhī besyār khobī gīreyft o mābayn-e satl kard o (ā)word be
                                      pādshāh-e ū wakht.

Be pādshāh āword, b-azū hazār rūpīeh en'ām dād.

Sayyād dīgeh sāyeb hamsāyeh az ū būd, zan-eū goft,
      "Ā, tor keh nagāīdam, t-am boro yak māhīn begīr, bobor—   30
      yak hazār rūpīeh ko be gīr-e mā mīāyah—az gūshnegay [hizan
                                      shodīm]."
         [last two words mostly inaudible]

[*M*: Ā.]

I ham ra(ft) māhīnī gīrīf, »
      pādshāh-sāeyb be lebās-e darvīshī mābayn-e mardom (mīg)-asht.

I mābayn-e satl be jelau-rū-ye ū am mā'īno   35
      kharī am sawār é, yak martabeh pādshāh b-az ī tasadof kard.

[*M*: Ā.]

Go, "Bābeh, ī chīst?"
      Nemishnas(eh) keh ī pādshāh yé, »
go, "Māīn é, mībarom be pādshāh."   40

Go, "Bobor m— be-bāzār bofrūsh, yak dah qerānī mishah b-om chūch
                                  o pūch-kho.
      Dīwāneh í? Pādshāh we to chī fāīdeh mīresūneh?"
‹›

Go, "Nah, mītom, pādshāh yé, balkom mah yak dū seh hazār [mīdeh]," »
go, "Pādshāh ītau a(h)maq nakhā būd
      keh māl-e bayt ol-māl   45
      be dah qerān,
      be to dū hazār rūpīeh bedeh.
      ‹›
      Bobor bofrūsh, dah qerānī mishah."

Gof, "Ageh nadād chī mīkonī?"
      B-am pīr mard gof.   50

Go, "Omīd be khodā yé keh bedeh, pādshāh yé, amī jawānmard é."

Go, "Bābā, (m)be to mīgom, bābā—" I nemishnaseh keh ī pādshāh yé.
      "Bobor, bofrūsh, dah qerānī mīshah."

—Goft—Sāyeb, īr besyār sakht kard keh "Agar nadād, chekār mīkonī?"

Go, [*laughing as he speaks*] "Agar nadādam, hamū har chār dast o pā-ye
                          khar-e khor b-am, kos-e zan-eū mīkonom."   55
[*laughs*]
[*M laughs*]
I keh ītau gof, pādshāh
    mārwarī khor lokkeh kard o »
    beraf darbār.
I darbār kard pīrmard am khod-satl-e kho biāmād.
Go, "Biārīm am pīrmardar."   60
Pīrmardar biāwordam, go "Bābā, ī chīst?" »
Go "Māhīnī." »
Go, "Cherī āwordī?" »
Go, "Biāwordom, sāyeb, be shomā, balkeh omīd-e khodā yé,
    dū seh hazār qerānī bedīm." »   65
Go, "Pādshāh ighzar a(h) maqī nakhā būd.
    Keh be dah qerān māīnī seh hazār qerān māl-e daulatar bedeh.
    Bobor bofrūsh, dah qerānī mishah be chūch o pūch-e kho."
Go, "Nah, sāeyb, biāwordom balkom omīd be kho—" »
Go, "Agar nadādom chī mīkonī?"   70
[*M*: Au—]
    "Agar nadādom chī mīkonī?"
Īr besyār sakht kard, nazar-e khor, ī pīr mard keh khob sayl kard,
    go [*sotto voce, to himself*]
    "Wellah, hamūn é!   75
    ‹›
    Hamū keh ītau(r) goftom."
Goft, "Agar nadādī," goft, "Sāeb—" —āleh am āshkārā kho nemītonah
                                        kardah—
Go, "Agar nadādom [*sic*], sāyeb,
    hamī kharak o hamū darak."   80
Yanī, "Hamī chār dast o pā-ye khar-e meh be kos-e zan-e to, ko, āleh—"
    [*laughs*]
[*M laughs loudly.*]
"Hamī kharak o hamū darak."
[*M, MM, laughing*: Ā— au!]
Ena, gūyā, m(o)ansha(r)-e "Kharak o darak"—
    —b-azī pādshāh dū hazār rūpīeh [*laughs*]   85
    chār hazār rūpīeh en'ām dād. [*smiles*]

[*MM*: Besyār khob. (*laughs*)]
[*M*: Bakhshīsh dād.]
Bakhsheysh-īn é! [*Laughter*]
'Kharak o darak' mansha'-yū hamīn é.   90
[*M, laughing*: Kho!]
Bāz pādshāh-ye dīgeh sāyeb,
      bā wazīrā-darbār-e kho mīraf
      b-am sahrā be shekār zadeh.
[*M*: I nām-e ū chī é?]   95
Ī p— I sāyeb, hamī nām-eū chī é? —"Agar-magar."
[*M*: "Agar-magar."]
"Agar-magar."
[*MM interrupts to ask permission to change tape. Tape change.*]

Appendix 2: Glossary

This glossary includes words of general importance which appear more than once in texts or discussion. They are also defined in notes or discussion on their first appearance. Words which appear only once and are discussed at that point are for the most part not included.

afghānī, the main unit of currency in Afghanistan, divided into 100 *paisa*. One afghānī is equivalent to two *qerān* (the previous major currency unit).

ākhond, a *mulla* or Muslim cleric with teaching duties in the traditional religious schools, often at an elementary level. Used as a respectful title or mode of address.

ausānah (literary Persian, *afsānah*), fictional folktale, wonder-tale.

bābā, "old man," "papa," "grandfather." As a term of affectionate address, often also used by adult men and women to address youngsters, or between two speakers of the same age.

bū-ye māron, a traditional pain medicine prepared by infusion (chapter 7, note 33).

chāderī, the form of veil worn by adult married women in Afghan cities and larger towns, an enveloping full-length garment set in tiny pleats, with an embroidered grid over the eyes to allow for vision (see chapter 9, note 12).

deyb (literary Persian *dīv*), a malevolent and usually monstrous supernatural, of humanlike or animal form (see chapter 6, note 35).

farsakh (literary Persian, *farsang*), an ancient Persian unit of distance equivalent to 6.24 kilometers or 3.75 miles.

gerau, the normal Afghan form of lending arrangement in which a lender of capital receives the usufruct of a piece of real property (usually land) for seven years in lieu of interest on the loan. If the principal is not repaid at the end of the loan's term, the property belongs to the lender.

hajj, the pilgrimage to Mecca, one of the religious duties of Muslims, enjoined upon those with sufficient means.

hājjī, masculine title for someone who has made the *hajj* pilgrimage to Mecca.

jat, a low-status group conceived to be ethnic but also occupational, including such professions as barber, blacksmith, musician, bath-keeper, folk theater actors, and stereotyped by others as dishonorable, tricky, and avaricious (see chapter 7, note 6 and chapter 10, note 16).

khalīfah, "representative," used in Afghan Persian (Darī) as a title for hired craftspersons.

khān, masculine title, used in address as rough equivalent of "mister," also used descriptively to designate local landlords or heads of nomad groups.

khāndan (literary Persian, *khwāndan*), to read, recite, sing, or call (as in call by name).

kharwār (literary Persian, *kharbār*), a unit of weight, literally "a donkey-load," calculated at 100 *man* (650 lbs.) in Herat.

Kheyzr (literary Persian, *Khizr*), a legendary figure, revered as a Prophet, who is mentioned obliquely in the Qur'an in connection with the legend of the waters of immortality located in the darkness at the farthest limit of the world and other legends. He is an old, white-bearded man, perpetually wandering, whose role in stories is usually to meet and advise the hero who is on a quest (see chapter 9, note 2).

Khoja, title for an elder or respected man.

kosah (Persian from the Turkish), the "thinbeard," a stock folktale figure, a self-serving trickster who is usually outdone by a trickster hero.

kūnī, passive partner in anal intercourse; a common insult for men or women.

maktab khānegī, "household school," the traditional elementary-level religious school for boys and girls, taught by a local *ākhond*.

man, a unit of weight equivalent to approximately 3 kg (or 6.6 lbs.) in Herat.

mathnavī (colloquially, *masnawī*), the Persian rhymed couplet form used for classical narrative poetry.

mulla (English spelling for Persian *mollā*), general term for a Muslim clergyman.

Naqshbandī, one of the two most popular Sufi orders in the Herat area, distinguished for its restrained, silent meditative style and avoidance of charismatic extremes (the other major order was the Qādiri, likewise characterized as "sober").

'orfān (literary Persian, *'erfān*), esoteric religious knowledge, gnosis; the Ākhond extends it to imply other forms of wisdom and perspicacity, including common sense.

parī, nonsacred supernatural, generally benevolent in Afghan stories. Cognate to English "fairy."

qalah (literary Persian, *qal'ah*), a fortified residence, surrounded by walls often 15 feet high or more, often situated by itself in the countryside.

qāzī, a Muslim religious law judge.

qerān, a former unit of currency equivalent to a half afghani (about one cent U.S.) at the time of the performance, but formerly of significant value.

qessah, "story, narrative."

rubā'ī, the classical lyric quatrain poetic form, rhymed *aaxa*.

sā'eb (also variously pronounced *sayb, sāyeb,* or *sā'eyb*, classical Persian, *ṣāḥib*), polite title for masculine address, "sir."

sarhadī, "borderer," resident of the foothill area east and south of the Herat valley.

sayed, a descendant of the Prophet Muhammad, given special respect in Afghan and other Muslim communities.

shaykh, a charismatic religious leader. Some are reputed to have special powers to divine, heal, or resolve others' difficulties through prayer.

sūfī, a follower of one of several mystical/meditative disciplines in Islam.

wazīfah, profession, calling, duty, or function; in some village usages, a private religious vocation.

woləswāl (from Pashto), a subgovernor in charge of the subprovincial unit called *woləswālī* (district or county).

Appendix 3: Motif and Tale Type Index

Resemblances and relations between the tales translated here and the cited types and motifs vary in proximity but are worthy of attention for comparative morphology purposes. References are to Antti A. Aarne, *Types of the Folktale*; Stith Thompson, *Motif-Index of Folk-Literature*; and Ulrich Marzolph, *Typologie des Persischen Volksmärchens*. This list is not meant to be exhaustive but only to indicate the more prominent resemblances, as the type- and motif-comparative method is not implicated in the methodology of the study.

Mulla Mongol the Martyr (chapter 3)
    Motifs J1705.1, J1738, J1263.1
Rasūl's Mother (chapter 4)
    Motifs J1744, J1745, X700, X760
Ten Qerān *(chapter 5)*
    Motifs J935, J1820, J2080, J1905
    Type Aarne-Thompson 1266V
Salīm the Jeweller (chapter 6)
    Motifs D672, D1813.1.2, D1819.7, J1675.6, T511.3, F610, F610.4, F610.9, F614.10, C700, C942, B100, B103.7, B103.0.7, B103.4.2, T465, B601.7, B221.1, B535, F300, F302.3.1.3, F302.4.2, F302.4.2.1
    Types Marzolph *832A, Aarne-Thompson G511.
ʿĀdel Khān (chapter 7)
    Motifs D10.2, D1174, D10, D10.2, D12, T471, D141, D2062.4.2
    Types Marzolph 449
Mahmūd and the Thieves (chapter 8)
    Motifs K1812, K1812.2, D1815.2, B216
    Types Aarne-Thompson 951A*, 951C
The Old Thief with Five Sons (chapter 9)
    Motifs K300, K419.2
    Types Marzolph 1539, *1525S
Women's Tricks (chapter 10)
    Motifs B264, D1812.5.0, K1512, J2315.2, K1843.4, Q451.5.1, K1501.2
    Types Marzolph 837, Aarne-Thompson 1417

Ākhond and the Rabbi of Herat (chapter 11)
　　Motifs V350, C240, C780
"That Little Donkey and that Little Door" (chapter 12)
　　Motifs J1280, J1289, Z64
"If/But" (chapter 12)
　　Motifs J1280, J1675, Z604
　　Types Marzolph *921
Black and White (chapter 13)
　　Motifs K1558, Z10.2, Z65, T320, T323
　　Types Aarne-Thompson 1359C, Marzolph *1730
The Corrupt and the Good (chapter 14)
　　Motifs T410, T421, T423
The Ill Fortune of the City of Rūm (chapter 15)
　　Motifs D1814.2, D1810.8.2, J157, J157.0.1, R9.6, C114, K1377, K2121.1, T415, J1675

Bibliography

Aarne, Antti A.
  1961 *The Types of the Folktale: A Classification and Bibliography*. 2nd rev. ed.,
         trans. and enlarged by Stith Thompson. Folklore Fellows Communi-
         cation No. 184. Helsinki: Suomalainen Tiedeakatemia. (Originally
         published as *Verzeichnis der Märchentypen*, FFC no. 3, 1910.)
Abrahams, Roger
  1985 "Storytelling and Achieving Meaning: A West Indian Case." In Rei-
         mund Kvideland and Torunn Selberg, eds., *Papers III: The 8th Congress
         for the International Society for Folk Narrative Research, Bergen, June 12–
         17, 1984*. Bergen: International Society for Folk Narrative Research.
Abu-Lughod, Lila
  1986 *Veiled Sentiments*. Berkeley: University of California Press.
Anderson, Jon W.
  1982 "Social Structure and the Veil: Comportment and the Composition of
         Interaction in Afghanistan." *Anthropos* 77:397–420.
  1985 "Sentimental Ambivalence and the Exegesis of 'Self' in Afghanistan."
         In Anderson and Eickelman, eds., pp. 203–11.
  1986 "Popular Mythologies and Subtle Theologies: The Phenomenology of
         Muslim Identity in Afghanistan." In Chock and Wyman, eds., pp. 169–
         84.
Anderson, Jon W., and Dale F. Eickelman, eds.
  1985 *Self and Society in the Middle East. Anthropological Quarterly* (Special Is-
         sue) 58:4. Washington, DC: Catholic University of America.
Anjavī Shīrāzī, Said Abul Ghāssem
  1973 C.E./1352 A.H. *Jashnhā o Ādāb o Motaghadʿāt-e Zemestān (Feasts, Customs
         and Beliefs of Winter)*. Tehran: Amir Kabir.
Arberry, Arthur J.
  1955 *The Koran Interpreted*. New York: Macmillan.
Asad, Talal, ed.
  1973 *Anthropology and the Colonial Encounter*. London: Ithaca Press.
Asadowskij, Mark
  1926 *Eine Siberische Märchenerzählerin*. Folklore Fellows Communication
         No. 68. Helsinki: Suomalainen Tiedeakatemia.
Azoy, G. Whitney
  1982 *Buzkashi: Game and Power in Afghanistan*. Philadelphia: University of
         Pennsylvania Press.
Babcock, Barbara
  1987 "Taking Liberties: Writing from the Margins, and Doing It with a
         Difference." *Journal of American Folklore* 100:390–411.

Baghban, Hafizullah
  1977   *The Context and Concept of Humor in Magadi Theater*, 4 vols. Ph.D.
          Dissertation, Indiana University.
  1980   "The Functions of Metafolklore in Farce and in Life." Delivered paper,
          American Folklore Society Annual Meeting. Pittsburgh, October 17,
          1980.
Bakhtin, Mikhail M.
  1981   *The Dialogic Imagination: Four Essays*. Michael Holquist, ed., Caryl
          Emerson and Michael Holquist, trans. Austin: University of Texas
          Press.
Banuazizi, Ali, and Myron Weiner, eds.
  1986   *The State, Religion, and Ethnic Politics; Afghanistan, Iran, and Pakistan*.
          Syracuse, NY: Syracuse University Press.
Barakat, Robert
  1980   *A Contextual Study of Arabic Proverbs*. Folklore Fellows Communica-
          tion No. 226. Helsinki: Suomalainen Tiedeakatemia.
Başgöz, Ilhan
  1975   "The Tale Singer and His Audience." In Dan Ben-Amos and Kenneth
          Goldstein, eds., *Folklore: Performance and Communication*. The Hague:
          Mouton, pp. 143–205.
Basso, Ellen
  1985   *A Musical View of the Universe: Kalapalo Myth and Ritual Performance*.
          Philadelphia: University of Pennsylvania Press.
Basso, Keith
  1984   " 'Stalking with Stories': Names, Places, and Moral Narratives among
          the Western Apache." In Bruner, ed., pp. 19–55.
Bauman, Richard
  1977   *Verbal Art as Performance*. Rowley, MA: Newbury House
Beck, Lois, and Nikki Keddie, eds.
  1978   *Women in the Muslim World*. Cambridge, MA: Harvard University
          Press.
Becker, Alton
  1984   "Biography of a Sentence: A Burmese Proverb." In Bruner, ed., pp.
          135–55.
Beeman, William O.
  1986   *Language, Status and Power in Iran*. Bloomington: Indiana University
          Press.
Betteridge, Ann
  1980   "The Controversial Vows of Iranian Women." In N. A. Falk and R. M.
          Gross, eds., *Unspoken Worlds: Women's Religious Lives in Non-Western
          Cultures*. New York: Harper & Row, pp. 141–55.
  1985   "Gift Exchange in Iran: The Locus of Self-Identity in Interaction." In
          Anderson and Eickelman, eds., pp. 182–202.
Blackburn, Stuart, and A. K. Ramanujan, eds.
  1986   *Another Harmony: New Essays on the Folklore of India*. Berkeley: Univer-
          sity of California Press.

Borqa'i, Said Bahā
  1985 C.E./1364 A.H.   *Kāveshī dar Imsāl o Hokm-e Fārsī (Investigation into Persian Proverbs and Precepts)*. Qum: Qum Namāyashgāh o Nashr-e Ketāb/ Hekmat.
Bottigheimer, Ruth, ed.
  1986 *Fairytales and Society: Illusion, Allusion, and Paradigm*. Philadelphia: University of Pennsylvania Press.
Boulvin, Adrienne
  1975 *Contes populaires Persans du Khorassan*. 2 vols. Paris: Klincksieck.
Bourdieu, Pierre
  1977 *Outline of a Theory of Practice*. Richard Nice, trans. Studies in Social Anthropology No. 16. Cambridge: Cambridge University Press.
Briggs, Charles L.
  1986 *Learning How to Ask: A Sociolinguistic Appraisal of the Role of the Interview in Social Science Research*. Cambridge: Cambridge University Press.
  1988 *Competence in Performance: The Creativity of Tradition in Mexicano Verbal Art*. Philadelphia: University of Pennsylvania Press.
Bright, William
  1982 "Poetic Structure in Oral Narrative." In Tannen, ed., pp. 171–84.
Bruner, Edward M.
  1986 "Ethnography as Narrative." In Turner and Bruner, eds., pp. 139–55.
Bruner, Edward M., ed.
  1984 *Text, Play and Story: The Construction and Reconstruction of Self and Society*. Washington, DC: American Ethnological Society.
Bruner, Edward M., and Phyllis Gorfain
  1984 "Dialogic Narration and the Paradoxes of Masada." In Bruner, ed., pp. 56–79.
Burton, Richard F., ed. and trans.
  n.d. [1885–88] *The Book of the Thousand Nights and a Night*. 17 vols. London: The Burton Club.
Canfield, Robert L.
  1977 "What They Do When the Lights Are Out: Ethnic and Sectarian Boundary Myths in Afghanistan." Delivered paper, Middle East Studies Association Annual meeting, New York, Nov. 10, 1977.
  1986 "Ethnic, Regional and Sectarian Alignments in Afghanistan." In Banuazizi and Weiner, eds., 1986:75–103.
Caton, Steven C.
  1985 "The Poetic Construction of Self." In Anderson and Eickelman, eds., pp. 141–51.
Cejpek, Jiri
  1968 "Iranian Folk-Literature." In Rypka, pp. 608–709.
Chafe, Wallace
  1980 "The Deployment of Consciousness in the Production of a Narrative." In W. Chafe, ed., *The Pear Stories: Cognitive, Cultural and Linguistic Aspects of Narrative Production*. Norwood, NJ: Ablex, pp. 9–50.

372   Bibliography

Chock, Phyllis Pease
    1986 "The Outsider Wife and The Divided Self: The Genesis of Ethnic Identities." In Chock and Wyman, eds., pp. 185–204.
Chock, Phyllis Pease, and June R. Wyman, eds.
    1986 *Discourse and the Social Life of Meaning*. Washington, DC: Smithsonian Institution Press.
Chodzko, Alexander
    1842 *Specimens of the Popular Poetry of Persia*. New York: Burt Franklin Reprints facsimile, 1971.
Clifford, James
    1986 "Introduction: Partial Truths." In Clifford and Marcus, eds., pp. 1–26.
    1988 *The Predicament of Culture*. Cambridge, MA: Harvard University Press.
Clifford, James, and George E. Marcus, eds.
    1986 *Writing Culture: The Poetics and Politics of Ethnography*. Berkeley: University of California Press.
Clinton, Jerome
    1986 "Madness and Cure in the *Thousand and One Nights*." In Bottigheimer, ed., pp. 35–51.
Crapanzano, Vincent
    1986 "Hermes' Dilemma: The Masking of Subversion in Ethnographic Description." In Clifford and Marcus, eds., pp. 51–76.
Doubleday, Veronica
    1988 *Three Women of Herat*. London: Jonathan Cape.
Dundes, Alan
    1974 "The Henny Penny Phenomenon." *Southern Folklore Quarterly* 38:1–9.
Dupree, Louis
    1973 *Afghanistan*. Princeton, NJ: Princeton University Press.
    1984 "The Marxist Regimes and the Soviet Presence in Afghanistan: An Ages-Old Culture Responds to Late Twentieth-Century Aggression." In Shahrani and Canfield, eds., pp. 58–73.
Dwyer, Daisy
    1978 *Images and Self-Images: Male and Female in Morocco*. New York: Columbia University Press.
Edwards, David
    1987a "Poetics of Order in the Afghan Resistance." Delivered paper, American Anthropological Association Annual Meeting, Chicago.
    1987b "Words in the Balance: Honor and Sacrifice in the Poetry of the Afghan Jihad." Delivered paper, American Ethnological Society Annual Meeting.
Eickelman, Dale F.
    1978 "The Art of Memory: Islamic Education and Its Social Reproduction." *Comparative Studies in Society and History* 20:485–515.
Elisséeff, Nikita
    1949 *Thèmes et motifs des mille et une nuits: essai de classification*. Beirut: Institut Français de Damas.

Encyclopedia of Islam
　　1924　Original Edition, Leyden: Brill.
　　1978　New Edition, Leyden: Brill.
English, Paul
　　1973　"The Traditional City of Herat, Afghanistan." In L. Carl Brown, ed.,
　　　　　From Medina to Metropolis: Heritage and Change in the Near Eastern
　　　　　City. Princeton, NJ: Darwin Press, pp. 73–90.
Farr, Grant, and John G. Merriam, eds.
　　1987　*Afghan Resistance: The Politics of Survival*. Boulder, CO: Westview.
Fischer, Michael M. J.
　　1978　"On Changing the Concept and Position of Iranian Women." In Beck
　　　　　and Keddie, eds., pp. 189–215.
　　1982　"Portrait of a Mullah: The Autobiography and Bildungsroman of Aga
　　　　　Najafi-Quchani." *Persica* 10:223–57.
　　1984　"Towards a Third World Poetics: Seeing through Short Stories and
　　　　　Films in the Iranian Culture Area." In H. Kucklik and E. Long, eds.,
　　　　　Knowledge and Society 5, pp. 171–241.
　　1986　"Ethnicity and the Post-Modern Arts of Memory." In Clifford and
　　　　　Marcus, eds., pp 194–233.
Friedl, Erika
　　1975　"The Folktale as Cultural Comment." *Asian Folklore Studies* 34:127–44.
　　1978　"Women in Contemporary Persian Folktales." In Beck and Keddie,
　　　　　eds., pp. 629–50.
Frye, Richard N.
　　1954　"Harāt," In *Encyclopedia of Islam*, 2nd ed., vol. 3, pp. 177–78.
Geertz, Clifford
　　1983　*Local Knowledge: Further Essays in Interpretive Anthropology*. New York:
　　　　　Basic Books.
Genette, Gérard
　　1980　*Narrative Discourse*. Ithaca, NY: Cornell University Press.
Ghani, Ashraf
　　1988　"The Persian Literature of Afghanistan, 1911–78, in the Context of Its
　　　　　Political and Intellectual History." In Ehsan Yarshater, ed., *Persian Lit-*
　　　　　erature. New York: Bibliotheca Persica/SUNY Press, pp. 428–53.
Goldstein, Judith
　　1986　"Iranian Jewish Women's Magical Narratives." In Chock and Wyman,
　　　　　eds., pp. 147–68.
Goody, Jack
　　1968　"The Consequences of Literacy." In J. Goody and A. Watt, eds., *Lit-*
　　　　　eracy in Traditional Societies. Cambridge: Cambridge University Press,
　　　　　pp. 27–68.
　　1978　*The Domestication of the Savage Mind*. Cambridge: Cambridge Univer-
　　　　　sity Press.
Government of Afghanistan, Ministry of Planning Department of Statistics
　　1972 C.E./1350 A.H.　*Statistical Pocketbook of Afghanistan, 1350 (1972)*. Kabul:
　　　　　　　　　　　　Government Printing Office.

Graham, William
  1987   *Beyond the Printed Word.* Cambridge: Cambridge University Press.
Haag-Higuchi, Roxanne
  1984   *Untersuchungen zu einer Sammlung Persischer Erzählungen.* Berlin: Klaus Schwarz.
  ms   Selections from ms., "Chihl o shish ḥikāyat yā jāmi' al-ḥikāyat." Photocopy.
Haïm, S.
  1961   *Persian-English Dictionary.* Tehran: Beroukhim.
Harris, Roy
  1986   *The Origin of Writing.* Peru, IL: Open Court Press.
Hatemi, Mahroo
  1977   *Untersuchungen zum Persischen Papageienbuch des Nahsabis.* Freiburg im Bresgau: Klaus Schwarz.
Havelock, Eric
  1982   *The Literate Revolution in Greece and Its Cultural Consequences.* Princeton, NJ: Princeton University Press.
Hernadi, Paul
  1981   "On the How, What and Why of Narrative." In Mitchell, ed., pp. 197–99.
Herzfeld, Michael
  1986   "The Status of Culture and the Culture of the State." In Chock and Wyman, eds., pp. 75–93.
Heston, Wilma
  1991   "Footpath Poets of Peshawar." In A. Appadurai, F. Korom, and M. Mills, eds., *Gender, Genre and Power in South Asian Expressive Traditions.* Philadelphia: University of Pennsylvania Press.
Hoppál, Mihály
  1980   "Genre and Context in Narrative Event." In Lauri Honko and Vilmos Voigt, eds., *Genre, Structure and Reproduction in Oral Literature.* Budapest: Akadémiai Kiadó, pp. 107–28.
Hymes, Dell H.
  1981   *"In Vain I Tried to Tell You": Essays in Native American Ethnopoetics.* Philadelphia: University of Pennsylvania Press.
  1985   "Language, Memory and Selective Performance: Cultee's 'Salmon's Myth' as Twice Told to Boas." *Journal of American Folklore* 98:393–434.
Jamshīdīpūr, Yūsof
  1980   *Farhang-e Imsāl-e Fārsī (Dictionary of Persian Proverbs).* Tehran: Forughi.
Jamzadeh, Laal, and Margaret Mills
  1986   "Iranian *Sofreh*: From Collective to Female Ritual." In C.W. Bynum, S. Harrell, and P. Richman, eds., *Gender and Religion: On the Complexity of Symbols.* Boston: Beacon, pp. 23–65.
Johnson, Robbie Davis
  1973   "Folklore and Women: A Social Interactional Analysis of the Folklore of a Texas Madam." *Journal of American Folklore* 86:341, pp. 211–24.

Josipovici, Gabriel
    1988   "Interpretation versus Reading: From Meaning to Trust." *Salmagundi*
            78–79:228–54.
Kāshifī, Baihaqī Wā'iz̤
    1983 C.E./1362 A.H.   *Anvār-i Suhailī yā Kalīla va Dimna*. Tehran: Amir Kabir.
Keiser, R. Lincoln
    1984   "The Rebellion in Darra-i Nur." In Shahrani and Canfield, eds., pp.
            199–35.
Kermode, Frank
    1979   *The Genesis of Secrecy: On the Interpretation of Narrative*. Cambridge,
            MA: Harvard University Press.
    1981   "Secrets and Narrative Sequence." In Mitchell, ed., pp. 79–97.
Kerr, Graham B.
    1977   *Demographic Research in Afghanistan: A National Survey of the Settled
            Population*. Asia Society Afghanistan Council Occasional Paper No. 13.
            New York: The Asia Society.
Kirshenblatt-Gimblett, Barbara
    1972   "A Parable in Context: A Social Interactional Analysis of a Storytelling
            Performance." In Dan Ben-Amos and Kenneth S. Goldstein, eds.,
            Folklore: Performance and Communication. The Hague: Mouton, pp.
            105–30.
Knabe, Erika
    1977   *Frauenemanzipation in Afghanistan*. Meisenheim am Glan: Hain.
Krupat, Arnold
    1987   "Post-Structuralism and Oral Literature." In Swann and Krupat, eds.,
            pp. 113–28.
Lane, Edward, ed. and trans.
    1927   *The Arabian Nights' Entertainments—or The Thousand and One Nights*.
            New York: Tudor.
Lord, Albert B.
    1960   *The Singer of Tales*. Cambridge, MA: Harvard University Press; re-
            printed New York: Atheneum, 1965.
Marcus, George, and Michael M. J. Fischer
    1986   *Anthropology as Cultural Critique: An Experimental Moment in the Hu-
            man Sciences*. Chicago: University of Chicago Press.
Marzolph, Ulrich
    1984   *Typologie des Persischen Volksmärchens*. Beirut and Weisbaden: Franz
            Steiner.
Meeker, Michael E.
    1979   *Literature and Violence in North Arabia*. Cambridge: Cambridge Uni-
            versity Press.
Mills, Margaret A.
    1978   *Oral Narrative in Afghanistan: The Individual in Tradition*. Ph.D. dis-
            sertation, Harvard University. [New York: Garland Press, 1990.]
    1983a   "Afghan Folktale: The Prosody of Oral Performance." *The Harvard
            Advocate* 117:3A (Special Issue on Folklore, Myth and Oral History),
            pp. 58–66.

1983b   "The Lion and the Leopard: The Composition of a New Fable in Traditional Style Articulates a Family Dispute." *ARV Scandinavian Yearbook of Folklore* 1981 (1983), pp. 53–60.

1984   "Orality, Literacy and Identity: Afghan Popular Narratives." Delivered paper, American Folklore Society Annual Meeting, San Diego.

1985   "Sex Role Reversals, Sex Changes, and Transvestite Disguise in the Oral Tradition of a Conservative Muslim Community in Afghanistan." In R. Jordan and S. Kalčik, eds., *Women's Folklore, Women's Culture*. Philadelphia: University of Pennsylvania Press, pp. 187–213.

in press   "Folk Tradition in the *Mathnavi* and the *Mathnavi* in Folk Tradition." In Amin Banani, ed., *The Heritage of Rumi*. Cambridge: Cambridge University Press.

Mitchell, W.J.T., ed.

1981   *On Narrative*. Chicago: University of Chicago Press.

Musil, Alois

1928   *The Manners and Customs of the Rwala Bedouin*. American Geographical Society Oriental Explorations and Studies No. 6. New York: Crane.

Naby, Eden

1986   "The Changing Role of Islam as a Unifying Force in Afghanistan." In Banuazizi and Weiner, eds., pp. 124–54.

Narayan, Kirin

1989   *Storytellers, Saints and Scoundrels: Folk Narrative in Hindu Religious Teaching*. Philadelphia: University of Pennsylvania Press.

Nicholson, Reynold A.

1969   *A Literary History of the Arabs*. Cambridge: Cambridge University Press.

Nicholson, Reynold A., ed. and trans.

1927–40   *The Mathnawí of Jalál u'ddín Rúmí*. 8 vols. London: Gibb Memorial Trust.

Ong, Walter

1982   *Orality and Literacy: The Technologizing of the Word*. London: Methuen.

Page, Mary Ellen

1977   *Naqqālī and Ferdowsi: Creativity in the Iranian National Tradition*. Ph.D. dissertation, University of Pennsylvania.

Pentikäinen, Juha

1978   *Oral Repertoire and World View*. Folklore Fellows Communication No. 219. Helsinki: Suomalainen Tiedeakatemia.

Pickthall, Mohammed M.

n.d.   *The Meaning of the Glorious Qu'ran*. Text and Explanatory Translation. Karachi: Taj Co. (originally published 1938).

Polanyi, Livia

1982   "Literary Complexity in Everyday Storytelling." In Tannen, ed., pp. 155–70.

Price, Richard
    1983   *First-Time: The Historical Vision of an Afro-American People.* Baltimore: Johns Hopkins University Press.
Propp, Vladimir
    1968   *Morphology of the Folktale.* Laurence Scott, trans. Austin: University of Texas Press.
Radner, Joan N., and Susan S. Lanser
    1987   "The Feminist Voice: Strategies of Coding in Folklore and Literature." *Journal of American Folklore* 100:412–25.
Rao, Aparna
    1982   *Les Gorbat d'Afghanistan: aspects économiques d'un group itinérant "Jat."* Paris: Institut Français d'Iranologie de Téhéran Bibliothèque Iranienne No. 27, Éditions Recherche sur les Civilisations.
Rosen, Lawrence
    1978   "The Negotiation of Reality: Male-Female Relations in Sefrou, Morocco." In Beck and Keddie, eds.
Roy, Olivier
    1983   "Sufism in the Afghan Resistance." *Central Asian Studies* 3(4):61–79.
    1984   "The Origins of the Islamist Movement in Afghanistan." *Central Asian Survey* 3(2):117–27.
    1985   "The Islamist Movement in Afghanistan." Ms.
Rūmī, Jalāl ud-Dīn
    n.d.   *Mathnavī-e Maʿanavī,* ʿAlā ud-Daula, ed. Tehran.
    1927–40   See Nicholson 1927–40.
Rypka, Jan
    1968   *History of Iranian Literature.* Dordrecht: Reidel.
Sakata, Hiromi Lorraine
    1983   *Music in the Mind: The Concepts of Music and Musician in Afghanistan.* Kent, OH: Kent State University Press.
Schimmel, Annemarie
    1975a   *Mystical Dimensions of Islam.* Chapel Hill: University of North Carolina Press.
    1975b   "Turk and Hindu: A Poetical Image and Its Application to Historical Fact." In Spiros Vryonis, ed., *Islam and Culture Change in the Middle Ages.* Wiesbaden: Harrassowitz, pp. 107–26.
    1978   *The Triumphal Sun: A Study of the Works of Jalaloddin Rumi.* London: Fine Books / The Hague: East-West Publications.
    1982   *As Through a Veil: Mystical Poetry in Islam.* New York: Columbia University Press.
Schurmann, H. F.
    1962   *The Mongols of Afghanistan.* The Hague: Mouton.
Shahrani, M. Nazif
    1979   *The Kirghiz and Wakhi of Afghanistan.* Seattle: University of Washington Press.
    1984   "Introduction: Marxist 'Revolution' and Islamic Resistance in Afghanistan." In Shahrani and Canfield, eds., pp. 3–93.

1985　"Tradition and Social Discourse in the Cultures of Afghanistan and Turkistan in the Modern Period." Paper prepared for the School of American Research Seminar on "Greater Central Asia as a Cultural Area," April 14–19, 1985, Santa Fe, NM.

1986　"State Building and Social Fragmentation in Afghanistan: A Historical Perspective." In Banuazizi and Weiner, eds., pp. 23–74.

Shahrani, M. Nazif, and Robert L. Canfield, eds.

1984　*Revolutions and Rebellions in Afghanistan: Anthropological Perspectives.* Berkeley: University of California Institute of International Studies.

Shalinsky, Audrey

1979a　*Central Asian Emigres in Afghanistan: Social Dynamics of Identity Creation.* Ph.D. dissertation, Harvard University.

1979b　"History as Self-Image: The Case of Central Asian Emigres in Afghanistan." *South Asian Middle Eastern Studies* 3(2):7–19.

1983　"Islam and Ethnicity: The Northern Afghanistan Perspective." *Central Asian Survey* 1(2/3):71–83.

1984　"Ethnic Reactions to the Current Regime in Afghanistan—A Case Study." *Central Asian Survey* 3(4):49–60.

Sharkat-e Nasabī Kānūn-e Ketāb (publisher)

n.d.　*Sargozasht-e Salīm Jawāharī, Behtarīn Hikāyathā-ye Khwāndanī o Khāndan-Āwār (The Experiences of Salīm the Jeweller: The Best Stories for Reading and Amusement).* Tehran.

Shukūrzādah, Ibrāhīm

1967/C.E./1346 A.H.　*'Aqāyid va Rusūm-i 'Āmmah-i Mardum-i Khurāssān (Popular Beliefs and Customs of the People of Khurāssān).* Tehran: Intishārāt-i Bunyād-i Farhang-i Īrān (Reissued Tehran: Surush, 1984 C.E./1363 A.H.)

Slyomovics, Susan

1987　*The Merchant of Art.* Berkeley: University of California Press.

Smith, H., et al.

1973　*Area Handbook for Afghanistan,* 4th ed. Washington, DC: United States Government Printing Office.

Sprachman, Paul

1988　"Persian Satire, Parody and Burlesque." In Yarshater, ed., pp. 226–48.

Steingass, F.

1892　*A Comprehensive Persian-English Dictionary.* London: Routledge and Kegan Paul.

Stoller, Paul

1986　"The Reconstruction of Ethnography." In Chock and Wyman, eds., pp. 51–74. Reprinted in revised form in Stoller, *The Taste of Ethnographic Things: The Senses in Anthropology.* Philadelphia: University of Pennsylvania Press, 1989, pp. 125–41.

Street, Brian

1984　*Literacy in Theory and Practice.* Cambridge: Cambridge University Press.

Swann, Brian, and Arnold Krupat
    1987 *Recovering the Word: Essays on Native American Literature.* Berkeley:
          University of California Press.
Tannen, Deborah, ed.
    1982 *Spoken and Written Language: Exploring Orality and Literacy.* Advances
          in Discourse Processes, vol. IX. Norwood, NJ: Ablex.
    1984 *Coherence in Spoken and Written Discourse.* Norwood, NJ: Ablex.
Tedlock, Dennis
    1972a *Finding the Center: Narrative Poetry of the Zuni Indians.* Translated
          from performances in the Zuni by Andrew Peynetsa and Walter San-
          chez. New York: Dial; reprinted Lincoln: University of Nebraska
          Press, 1978.
    1972b "On the Translation of Style in Oral Narrative." In Américo Paredes
          and Richard Bauman, eds., *Toward New Perspectives in Folklore.* Austin:
          University of Texas Press, pp. 114–33.
    1983 *The Spoken Word and the Work of Interpretation.* Philadelphia: Univer-
          sity of Pennsylvania Press.
Thompson, Stith
    1955–58 *Motif-Index of Folk-Literature.* 6 vols. Bloomington: Indiana Univer-
          sity Press.
Toelken, Barre
    1976 "The 'Pretty Languages' of Yellowman: Genre, Mode and Texture in
          Navaho Coyote Narratives." In Dan Ben-Amos, ed., *Folklore Genres.*
          Austin: University of Texas Press.
Toelken, Barre, and Tacheeni Scott
    1981 "Poetic Retranslation and the 'Pretty Languages' of Yellowman." In
          Karl Kroeber, ed., *Traditional Literatures of the American Indian: Texts
          and Interpretations.* Lincoln: University of Nebraska Press, pp. 65–116.
Turner, Victor, and Edward Bruner
    1986 *The Anthropology of Experience.* Urbana: University of Illinois Press.
Tyler, Steven
    1978 *The Said and the Unsaid.* New York: Academic Press.
    1986 "Post-modern Anthropology." In Chock and Wyman, eds., pp. 28–51.
Wagner, Daniel, and Abdelhamid Lotfi
    1980 "Traditional Islamic Education in Morocco: Sociohistorical and Psy-
          chological Perspectives." *Comparative Education Review* 24(2):238–51.
Waldman, Marilyn
    1980 *Toward a Theory of Historical Narrative: A Case Study in Perso-Islamicate
          Historiography.* Columbus: Ohio State University Press.
Wehse, Rainer
    1986 "Past and Present Folkloristic Narrator Research." In Bottigheimer,
          ed., pp. 245–58.
White, Hayden
    1980 "The Value of Narrativity." In Mitchell, ed., pp. 1–23.

Wiget, Andrew
    1987   "Telling the Tale: A Performance Analysis of a Hopi Coyote Story."
          In Swann and Krupat, eds., pp. 297–336.
Wilber, Donald N., et al.
    1962   *Afghanistan*. New Haven, CT: Human Relations Area Files Press.
Wollaston, Arthur N., ed. and trans.
    1904   *The Anwár-i-Suhailí or Lights of Canopus, Commonly Known as Kalílah*
          and Damnah. London: John Murray.
Yarshater, Ehsan, ed.
    1988   *Persian Literature*. New York: Bibliotheca Persica/SUNY Press.
Zwettler, Michael
    1978   *The Oral Tradition of Classical Arabic Poetry*. Columbus: Ohio State
          University Press.

Index

This book has been set in Linotron Galliard. Galliard was designed for Mergenthaler in 1978 by Matthew Carter. Galliard retains many of the features of a sixteenth century typeface cut by Robert Granjon but has some modifications that give it a more contemporary look.

Printed on acid-free paper.